ALL ABOUT TORTS

Constantinos E. Scaros

Prentice Hall
Upper Saddle River, NJ 07458

Acquisitions Editor: Elizabeth Sugg
Editorial Assistant: Delia Uherec
Director of Production and Manufacturing: Bruce Johnson
Managing Editor: Mary Carnis
Editorial/Production Supervision and
  Interior Design: Inkwell Publishing Services
Cover Director: Jayne Conte
Manufacturing Buyer: Edward O'Dougherty

Printed in the United States of America

10 9 8 7 6 5 4 3 2 1

ISBN 0-13-081161-0

PRENTICE-HALL INTERNATIONAL (UK) LIMITED, *London*
PRENTICE-HALL OF AUSTRALIA PTY. LIMITED, *Sydney*
PRENTICE-HALL CANADA INC., *Toronto*
PRENTICE-HALL HISPANOAMERICANA, S.A., *Mexico*
PRENTICE-HALL OF INDIA PRIVATE LIMITED, *New Delhi*
PRENTICE-HALL OF JAPAN, INC., *Tokyo*
PEARSON EDUCATION ASIA PTE. LTD., *Singapore*
EDITORA PRENTICE-HALL DO BRASIL, LTDA., *Rio de Janeiro*

CONTENTS

PREFACE

As a lawyer and a legal educator, I have long believed that tort law is at the core of a good legal education, and is the cornerstone of the legal profession. Inevitably then, a great deal of the teaching and practicing of law involves torts. This book is primarily designed for college students, but is valuable to attorneys, paralegals, law school students, and anyone else interested in learning all about torts.

ACKNOWLEDGMENTS

All those who have made a positive impact on my life, and who were directly or indirectly instrumental in the creation of this book, are too numerous to list. In any event, I would like to thank the following:

Melissa Blum and Elizabeth Sugg of Prentice Hall, both of whom helped to make this project a pleasant experience.

Everyone at the Interboro Institute, for their continued support. Particular thanks to my students, who continue to make teaching enjoyable for me.

The following reviewers, for their helpful comments:

Melinda Hess, JD, College of Saint Mary

Kent D. Kaufman, JD, Ulvy Tech State College

Robert D. Loomis, JD, Spokane Community College

Lucy Michaud, JD, Branford Hall

Last, but certainly not least, to all of my loved ones.

INTRODUCTION

Some people think that the subject of torts only deals with personal injury, and is thus valuable to learn only by those who want to work in that field. But tort law actually involves so much more than that. Although personal injury lawyers and paralegals make up a great portion of torts legal professionals, many other types of torts have nothing to do with personal injury. Besides, the importance of learning torts goes beyond applying it to a specific legal task.

When you learn all about torts, you will be able to better understand other important areas of law, such as contracts and criminal law. You will learn how torts can affect people from various walks of life: doctors, accountants, musicians, athletes, movie stars, politicians, even astronauts.

In the world-famous O.J. Simpson case, many people were confused about why there were two trials: "O.J. was found not guilty, so why is he back on trial? Isn't that double jeopardy?" Long before you're through reading this book, you will know the answer to that question—because the answer has a great deal to do with torts.

If this is beginning to sound complicated, don't worry; it's really very easy. Through simple language, common sense, and plenty of examples, this book will help you learn all about torts quickly and easily.

We begin in Chapter 1 with an introduction to law, followed by an introduction to torts in Chapter 2. Chapters 3, 4, and 5 deal with torts to the person, to property, and to reputation. Chapter 6 is about malpractice.

Chapter 7 covers torts to other civil rights, and Chapter 8 is about defenses, remedies, and damages involving torts. Finally, in Chapter 9 we talk about careers in torts for attorneys and paralegals.

By the time you are finished reading this book, you will have a very good understanding of the basics of torts. That knowledge will help increase your understanding about other areas of the law. And you'll probably be amazed at how easy the whole experience is.

1 INTRODUCTION TO LAW

Before we begin learning about torts, let us examine the American legal system as a whole. If you are a law student, you have probably already been exposed to an introductory law course. Even if you're not a law student, you will need a basic introduction to law to better understand torts. Accordingly, this introduction will cover the fundamentals, and you will see how the law of torts fits into the big picture.

To begin understanding the law, we will start by talking about American history. The United States today is a vast military and economic superpower, but it wasn't always that way. Over two hundred years ago, when our nation was formed, it was comprised of thirteen small colonies, which became states.

These colonies were not particularly eager to unite into one nation. After all, the colonists came to this land to enjoy more freedom than was available to them in their native countries. They were suspicious of government, and wanted as little government in their lives as possible.

But each colony, taken alone, was small and potentially vulnerable to military attack or other hostile treatment from other nations. For this reason, the colonies decided to join together and become the United States.

Notice those two words, *United* and *States*. They imply two different things. On one hand, *United* means that there are some who come together as one. But *States* indicates that there is some individualism in each.

This is precisely what the United States is—a compromise. The compromise is that each state in many ways retains its own individuality, while in other matters agreeing to be united with other states.

THE UNITED STATES CONSTITUTION

This compromise is specifically addressed in the **United States Constitution**, the document on which our government was founded. Essentially, the Constitution created our **two-tier, three-branch system of government.**

TWO-TIER SYSTEM OF GOVERNMENT

Our two tiers of government are **federal** and **state.** Generally, any power not specifically granted to the federal government is reserved for the states. For example, suppose that the state of Minnesota requires anyone who applies for a driver's license to have completed at least six hours of formal driver's education. The authority to determine driving standards is not specifically provided for in the Constitution; it is a power reserved to the states. Therefore, such a requirement is a state law, not a federal law.

SUPREMACY CLAUSE

At times, a state law may conflict with a federal law. In those instances, the federal law prevails. The Constitution recognizes that it is "the Supreme Law of the Land ... Laws of any State to the Contrary notwithstanding." This is known as the **Supremacy Clause,** which means that the Constitution is supreme over any state law.

For example, suppose that the state of Kentucky requires all of its citizens to declare what religion they belong to before they can register to vote. This requirement is contradictory to the Constitution, which states that religion is not a condition of the right to vote. In that instance, the Kentucky law would be in direct conflict with the Constitution, under the Supremacy Clause. Accordingly, it would be struck down as **unconstitutional.**

THREE-BRANCH SYSTEM OF GOVERNMENT

In each tier (federal and state) of government, there are three parts, or **branches: legislative, executive,** and **judicial.** Generally, the legislative branch creates the law, the executive branch carries out (executes) the law, and the judicial branch enforces the law.

Legislative Branch

The legislative branch of the federal (U.S.) government is **Congress.** Congress is made up of two **houses:** the **Senate** and the **House of Representatives.** The Senate is made up of senators elected from each state.

In each state, no matter how big or small, two senators are elected. Because there are 50 states, there are 100 senators in all. Senators are elected for a term of six years, and may be reelected an unlimited number of times.

The House of Representatives is made up of 435 representatives from the 50 states. Unlike the Senate, each state does not send the same number of representatives to the House. Rather, the number depends on each state's population.

For example, states with large populations, such as California or New York, send more representatives to Congress than less-populated states, like Alaska or Wyoming. Representatives are elected for a two-year term and, like Senators, may be reelected an unlimited number of times.

On the state level, each state has a "congress" of its own, typically referred to as a **state legislature.** Some of the laws governing these legislatures vary from state to state. In any event, legislatures' purpose and authority are similar to those of the United States Congress.

Executive Branch

In the federal government, the executive branch is headed by the **president of the United States,** also known as the **Chief Executive.** The president is elected to a term of four years and may be reelected only once. Thus, the president may serve no more than two elected terms (a total of eight years).

Note: Interestingly, a person may serve as president for up to ten years, if that person serves another president's term for two years or less (if, say, a president dies in office), then serves two elected terms. A person who serves another president's term for *more* than two years is permitted to serve only one elected term.

Various federal **agencies** that you may recognize, such as the Federal Bureau of Investigation (FBI), the Environmental Protection Agency (EPA), and the Immigration and Naturalization Service (INS), are part of the executive branch.

Each state has an executive branch, too. The Chief Executive of each state is that state's **governor.** Every governor is elected to a term of four years, and how many times a governor may be reelected varies from state to state.

Judicial Branch

The federal judicial branch consists of three levels of courts. The courts at the lowest level are generally known as the **district courts,** and are courts of original jurisdiction. In other words, a federal case typically begins in these courts.

If the case is **appealed** (we will discuss this process later), it moves to the federal **courts of appeals.** The highest court of appeals is the highest court of our country, the **United States Supreme Court.**

The Supreme Court is made up of nine judges, known as **justices.** Unlike legislative and executive leaders, Supreme Court justices are appointed, not elected. They are appointed by the president and the appointment must be approved by Congress.

State courts also have multiple levels of courts. In some states there are two levels; in others, three. Typically, each state's Supreme Court is that state's highest court, but there are exceptions. In New York, for instance, the Supreme Court is the state's *lowest* court.

CHECKS AND BALANCES

This, then, is our two-tier, three-branch system of government. Unlike in other countries, where there may only be one branch of government, the American government was designed with a system of **checks and balances** between the three branches, in order to prevent one branch from becoming too powerful.

Let's think about this for a moment: What would be the advantage or disadvantage of a very powerful government or leader? If you agree with the leader, things could be really good, but if you disagree, things could be awful. Rather than take such a high-risk, all-or-nothing gamble, the Framers of the Constitution decided to play it safe. They created a government in which each branch would "check" on the other two, thus "balancing" the power of government.

Take a look at some examples of checks and balances. As we discussed earlier, Congress has the power to make laws, but it is the president of the United States who signs a **bill** (proposed law) into law. Also, the United States Supreme Court may decide whether a law that Congress creates is consistent with the Constitution, and strike down the law if it is **unconstitutional.** The legislative branch, then, is checked by the executive and judicial branches.

Next, the president of the United States, while holding the single most identifiable American political office, nonetheless has limited powers. For example, it is Congress—not the president—that has the power to declare war on another country. Also, if the president **vetoes** (rejects) a Congressional bill, Congress may **override** the president's veto by a two-thirds majority vote. If the president commits an act that Congress believes to be unconstitutional, the House of Representatives may **impeach** the president. Then, if convicted by the Senate, the president may be removed from office.

Moreover, in impeachment proceedings, the judicial branch may determine whether the president's conduct is privileged. The executive branch, then, is checked by the legislative and judicial branches.

The judicial branch consists of courts and the judges who serve on the courts' **benches.** In the case of the United States Supreme Court, we mentioned that a justice is appointed by the president, and that appointment must be approved by Congress. Therefore, the judicial branch is checked by the legislative and executive branches.

THE ROLE OF LAW IN OUR SOCIETY

The United States is a free nation, and its citizens have the right to do virtually anything except as prohibited by law. The Framers did not believe that the Constitution *creates* such rights. Rather, they believed that these rights are *inherent* in all human beings and are *guaranteed* by the Constitution.

The law is created by the people and for the people. Of course, not every single American is involved in creating every law. That would take years and years because there are over 250 million people in the United States. But it is the people who elect the legislators who, in turn, make the laws. The president of the United States, state governors, city mayors, judges, and all other government employees are either directly elected by the people or appointed by other public officials who have been elected by the people. Accordingly, it is we, the people, who drive the engine that is the law.

Our judicial system is designed to be a vehicle for obtaining justice. If two or more people (parties) are in dispute, their matter may be settled in court. Many people do not realize this, but most disputes are actually settled out of court.

Consider this analogy. Think about instances in which people disagree with one another. Most times, people either talk things out calmly, or become tense and annoyed. Sometimes, that tension may cause them be rude, or to lose their tempers and argue. Taken to the extreme, these disagreeing parties may get into fistfights or otherwise commit violence upon one another.

But most disagreements are settled long before they result in violence. Either the parties have reconciled, or they walk away from the conflict. It is rare that a typical, everyday disagreement results in a physical battle.

Similarly, it is rare that a typical, everyday disagreement results in a legal battle. Courtroom battles are the extreme. Most people who begin that process settle their differences before the court has to decide their fate. Heavy investments of time and money and the risk of completely losing are reasons why many people prefer the compromise of settling out of court.

In any event, for those disputes that do go to court, the person bringing the lawsuit is generally known as the **plaintiff** and the person against whom the lawsuit is brought is the **defendant.** The case is typically referred to as the **trial.**

The person (party) who loses the case often wants to **appeal** the case to a higher court. The party bringing an appeal is called an **appellant** or **petitioner,** and the party against whom the appeal is brought is called the **appellee** or **respondent.**

In order to be granted an appeal, the appealing party must convince the court that there was some type of error at trial, either in the court's decision or in some other aspect of the process. In theory, then, a case may be appealed all the way to the United States Supreme Court. However, because appeals are not granted easily, very few cases actually reach the highest court of our country.

Consider this example to illustrate the point. Jack is driving his car one day and approaches an intersection. Suzy, a pedestrian, also approaches the intersection. As Suzy proceeds to cross the street, Jack hits her and knocks her down. Suzy is injured in the accident and wants to sue Jack for her medical expenses, financial loss from not being able to work, and compensation for pain and suffering. In that case, Suzy would be the plaintiff and Jack would be the defendant. Suppose Suzy wins at trial and Jack wants to appeal the decision. If Jack is granted an appeal, he will be the appellant/petitioner and Suzy will be the appellee/respondent.

Now let's consider how you, as a legal professional, would prepare to help your clients achieve their legal goals.

SOURCES OF THE LAW

Continuing with our example, suppose Jack claims that it was very difficult for him to see the road because there was heavy rainfall on the day of the accident. Suzy tells you that there was not a cloud in the sky. Rather than rely on Suzy's word against Jack's, you obtain the official weather report for the date and location of the accident. The report confirms that it was indeed a sunny day. The weather report is a **source** of the fact about the weather at the scene of the accident.

Similarly, when a court case involves questions of law, several sources of law are valuable tools for legal professionals.

A primary source is direct information from the source. A secondary source is information about the primary source. For example, if Diana tells you that she is going to have a baby, then you know about Diana's pregnancy through a primary source—Diana. However, if Barbara tells you that Diana is pregnant, Barbara is a secondary source.

Let's look at some of the main sources of the law.

Case Law

Case decisions, known as **opinions,** are a primary source of law. Suppose a court decides that a baseball bat is considered a "dangerous weapon." Five years later, the same question arises again in another matter. That court may refer to the decision of the original court as a source of law.

Reading Case Law

Throughout this book there are various cases for you to read. At first, it may seem difficult to understand some of the legal terms, loosely referred to as "legalese." As with everything else, practice makes perfect. Continue reading the cases, over and over, and try to **brief** them, whenever possible.

A case brief is a summary of the case, outlining:

1. the **facts** (what happened in the case);
2. the **issue** (the question that the court must decide);
3. the **holding** (what the court did in fact decide about the issue); and
4. the **reasoning** (why the court decided the holding as it did).

Note: At times, various judges on a court's *bench* may provide multiple points of view within a single case. Along with the *judgment*, which is the prevailing reasoning, there may be *concurring* opinions (when one or more judges agree with the holding, but for a different reason) and *dissenting* opinions (when one or more judges disagree with the holding).

A good rule of thumb is to not become overly affected by a single case *opinion,* nor to be frustrated when there are conflicting opinions among various cases. Rather, you should look at the cases as a guideline to help shape your legal analysis.

With a positive attitude, you will find that these cases are helpful, interesting complements to your study of tort law.

Statutes

Statutes are the laws made by national, state, or local legislatures. Like cases, statutes are primary sources of law. Administrative laws are created by administrative agencies (which are part of the executive branch); they are similar to statutes and are also primary sources of law.

Restatements, Hornbooks, Legal Encyclopedias and Case Digests

These are various types of texts that explain the law created by statutes or judicial opinions. Since they are not the direct sources whereby the law was created, these texts are secondary sources.

Law Review Articles

Law review articles are reports about a particular case or statute or broader analyses of a particular area of the law. They are formal versions of term papers. Quite often, they are helpful as a starting point in doing legal research. For instance, if you were looking for cases about laws banning smoking in public buildings, how would you begin?

One way would be to search for a law review article on that topic, which would, in turn, lead you to relevant cases and statutes.

Shepardizing: Updating the Law

Do you know who the leader is in every country throughout the world? If you do, that's very impressive, but also very rare; most people don't. But you *do* know who the president of the United States is.

Well, imagine that Alexa, who is from a foreign country, visits the United States and doesn't know who the president is. Next, imagine that Alexa reads English, and finds an old newspaper article that was written many years ago. That article talks about President Reagan's State of the Union speech. Now suppose that as a result of reading that article, Alexa believes that the president of the United States today is Ronald Reagan. If she really believed that, she would indeed be very misinformed. This illustration can be applied to presenting outdated sources of the law as current.

For instance, suppose that Angelo is on trial for murder in New York, and Douglas, his lawyer, assures him that the death penalty does not exist in that state. Douglas relies on a case decided in 1974, which proclaims that New York does not include the death penalty as a method of punishment. However, since 1974, the death penalty has been reinstated in New York. Accordingly, Douglas' advice to Angelo is wrong, because the information on which Douglas relied is outdated.

A service called Shepard's regularly updates the sources of the law, thus alerting the researcher about the law's current status. The process of updating the law is called **Shepardizing.** A good legal professional should always Shepardize, so as not to give incorrect advice based on outdated laws.

SUBSTANTIVE LAW AND PROCEDURAL LAW

Generally, a law is either **substantive** or **procedural.** Substantive law is the law itself, whereas procedural law is the legal process. If you don't quite understand what that means, you're not alone. Unfortunately, many law books and law instructors leave their students with that one-sentence definition and then move on to another topic. But this is an important point about which you should not be confused. The following examples will help you better understand the difference between substantive and procedural law.

Suppose Brian intentionally sets fire to Alan's house. Alan is not harmed, but his house burns completely. Brian will probably be charged with arson. The **elements** of the law of arson will be compared to Brian's actions. If they match, then Brian will most likely be found guilty of arson. This examination of the elements of a particular law is a **substantive** law analysis.

Now, let's suppose that Brian is arrested after setting the fire. There are certain rights that he has, such as the right to remain silent when questioned, the right to have an attorney, and the right to a jury trial. These rights are secured by laws that govern the legal **process,** and are known as **procedural** laws.

Do you see the difference? A substantive law deals with the elements, or ingredients. For example, something must be burned for there to be arson, or someone must be killed for there to be murder. A procedural law deals with what steps must be taken in the legal system to obtain justice. For instance, a person who is arrested must be told why.

CIVIL AND CRIMINAL LAW

Another way to categorize law is according to whether it is civil or criminal. Generally, the goal of civil law is *compensation,* whereas the goal of criminal law is *punishment.*

In civil law, a person (or group) who has somehow been harmed or wronged brings a lawsuit in order to receive **damages** in the form of money or some other compensation.

Criminal law involves certain acts that are considered to be so wrong that they do not merely affect the direct victims, but also harm society as a whole. A criminal case, then, is brought by all of the people (of a particular state or, for federal crimes, of the United States as a whole) against the accused. The people are usually represented by the attorney for the state or federal government. The goal in a criminal case is punishment.

Compensation versus Punishment

Suppose you are on your way to an important conference, dressed in your best business suit. As you are walking along, you pass a building where Evan is painting his window, three stories above the ground. Evan accidentally tips over the can of paint and it spills all over your clothes. You have been harmed. Your suit is probably ruined, and by the time you change clothes, it may too late for you to attend the conference at all. In any event, you realize that it was an accident, and you don't want Evan to go to jail, or otherwise be *punished*. Rather, you want to be *compensated*.

For instance, if Evan immediately offered to go with you across the street to a large department store and buy a brand new suit for you, and bought you a couple of extra shirts and ties to make up for the inconvenience, and then gave you money for a taxi to get to your conference, you would probably be satisfied. But if Evan refused to acknowledge his fault in the matter, you would probably want to take him to court and sue him for damages. Such a case would be a *civil* lawsuit.

Suppose, instead, that Evan did not spill paint on you. Instead, he jumped you from behind, knocked you to the ground, and stole your wallet. You would probably want the police to catch Evan and you would like to see him punished for what he did. In that case, Evan committed a **crime.** The act was so wrong that it was deemed to have affected not only you, but society as a whole.

Therefore, Evan's criminal trial would be brought against him by all of the people.

What if you were injured as a result of Evan knocking you to the ground? And what if you had a lot of money in the wallet? Maybe then your concerns would also be financial. In other words, you would want damages to recover the loss of the money in the wallet, your medical expenses, and other related expenses. In that case, Evan's *criminal* conviction would mean that he would be punished, but it would not bring you one penny in damages. Accordingly, you would have to sue Evan in a *civil* trial to receive damages. You may also want to bring a lawsuit against anyone else who may have been responsible for the attack. Suppose that Evan had jumped you in a dark parking lot of a shopping mall, and the lot was dark because the outdoor lights had been broken for weeks. In that case, you may want to sue the owners of the mall, because if they were more diligent in fixing the lights, the parking lot would have been better lit, and Evan might not have attempted to attack you.

Standard of Proof

If a person is found **liable** for a civil offense, he or she will most likely have to pay money as damages. While paying damages may be a heavy burden in some cases, civil penalties taken as a whole are usually not as serious as criminal penalties. Compare, for instance, having to pay $10,000 in damages with being sent to prison for ten years, or being sentenced to death.

Because the consequences that a defendant faces in a criminal case are usually more severe than those in a civil case, the standard of proof is greater in criminal law than in civil law.

In civil law, a plaintiff must prove a case by a **preponderance of the evidence.** This means that the plaintiff's argument must be somewhat more believable to the fact finder (judge or jury) than the defendant's. Whether the difference is large or small, the argument with the most credibility wins the case.

In criminal law, however, the standard is higher. The people (plaintiffs) must prove their case **beyond a reasonable doubt.** Mathematically, there is no exact measure of when a case reaches that point. However, though the plaintiff's case may be more believable than the defendant's, the defendant may nonetheless be found not guilty. Using the example in which Evan stole your wallet, suppose that you sued him in civil court, but the people brought a criminal case against him as well. If the evidence was such that the jury in both cases found your case slightly more believable, say, 60 percent to 40 percent, you would win the civil case. However, in the criminal case it would not matter that your case was *more* credible. Rather, the fact that the jury could find a 40 percent likelihood that Evan was not guilty amounts to a reasonable doubt. As a result of that reasonable doubt, Evan would probably be found not guilty, and **acquitted.**

A perfect example of this is the world-famous case of O.J. Simpson. In 1994, O.J. Simpson, the legendary football player, movie star, and sports analyst, was arrested and charged with the double murder of his ex-wife, Nicole, and Ronald Goldman. After a lengthy *criminal* trial that was covered by the media throughout the world, the jury found Simpson not guilty of the crimes.

However, the Goldman family sought damages for the wrongful death of their son, and sued Simpson in civil court. They won the lawsuit and were awarded damages. Many people outside the legal community were confused as to why Simpson was subjected to a second trial, wondering whether this was **double jeopardy.** It wasn't.

Double jeopardy is a Constitutional protection against being tried twice for the same offense. Here, Simpson was not tried twice for the same offense, although he was tried twice for the same act. In other words, the first trial was for the *criminal* offense of the double murder; the second trial was for the *civil* offense.

The next question that arose was why Simpson won the first trial but lost the second. There are many theories about this, too many to discuss here. One theory, however, is that civil liability is easier to prove than criminal liability; accordingly, there may have been enough evidence to find Simpson liable by a preponderance of the evidence, but not guilty beyond a reasonable doubt.

CIVIL LAW—CONTRACTS AND TORTS

We have discussed the breakdown of the law into the categories of civil or criminal. We now turn to a division within civil law.

Generally, civil law can be broken down into contracts and torts. Other types of civil laws flow from these two general areas. In Chapter 2 we discuss some of the differences between contracts and torts and begin our adventure in learning all about torts.

REVIEW QUESTIONS

1. What are the two tiers of our government?
2. What is the Supremacy Clause of the Constitution?
3. What are the three branches of our government, and what is the function of each?
4. What is the system of checks and balances? Give an example.
5. Which branch of government has the power to declare war?
6. What is a person who brings a lawsuit called, and what is a person against whom a lawsuit is brought called?
7. What is a person who appeals a case to a higher court called, and what is a person against whom an appeal is brought called?
8. What is the difference between primary and secondary sources of law, and what are the four main sources of the law?
9. What is the difference between substantive and procedural law?
10. What is the difference between civil and criminal law?

A TORT TALE

At the end of each chapter, you will find A Tort Tale. If you've read the chapter and answered the review questions, you should challenge yourself to see if you can solve the tale. In many cases, you will be given a set of facts and an unlikely conclusion. You must supply your own additional facts to justify the conclusion. Here's the first tale. Remember, there is one at the end of every chapter. Good luck.

In August 1974, Richard Nixon resigned as president of the United States, and, under the law, Vice President Gerald Ford became president. Ford finished Nixon's term, which ended in 1976. Ford ran against Jimmy Carter in the November 1976 election. Carter won the election and was officially inaugurated (sworn in) in January 1977.

If Gerald Ford wanted to run for president at a future date, could he? If so, for how many terms?

2 Introduction to Torts: Intent, Negligence, and Liability Without Fault

As we discussed in Chapter 1, civil law can be broken down into two general categories: contracts and torts. The word *contract* is one that we often hear or use, because it is a common word both in and out of the legal community. Specifically, a contract is an agreement enforceable by law. Quite often, people may not know *exactly* what a contract is, but they have a general idea. For instance, people think of a contract as a long, detailed written document (which is often the case) and so they assume that contracts must always be in writing. In any event, people from all walks of life have a general idea about what a contract is.

But what is a **tort**? When was the last time you heard someone outside of the legal community use that word? In order to reach our definition of a tort, let's review some of what we have learned about the law so far:

1. The law can be broken down into two categories—civil and criminal.
2. Civil law can further be broken down into two categories—contracts and torts.

We discussed that the goal in civil law is compensation, whereas in criminal law the goal is punishment. Therefore, someone who wants to sue another person for money has to file a civil lawsuit.

We also defined *contract* as an agreement that is enforceable by law. In other words, when two or more parties enter into a contract, they agree to conditions that are legally binding. If one party breaks the agreement, the other party can sue for **breach** of contract. For example, John and David entered into a contract whereby John would paint David's barn for $300. If John paints the barn but David refuses to pay him, John can sue David for breach of contract.

This, then, is an example of one person suing another person, when both parties had already entered into a transaction. What if, instead, John was driving his car and David threw a rock and broke John's windshield? For one thing, this act is a *crime,* and David may even wind up in jail for it. But what if John is not too interested in whether David goes to jail? Instead, John wants money to fix his windshield, and believes that David is the logical person to pay for it.

In that case, John would have to bring a *civil* lawsuit against David. But if the only types of civil lawsuits were based on contracts, John would be out of luck, because he and David never entered into a contract. David never *promised* John that he wouldn't throw a rock at his car. In fact, John and David never even knew each other until that incident occurred. May John, nonetheless, sue David in civil court for money damages for his broken windshield? Yes. Although David may not have breached a contract, he has committed a **tort.**

A tort is a civil wrong not based on a contract. It is a *civil* wrong, which means that a legal remedy is compensation rather than punishment. It is not based on a contract, which means the parties involved need not have entered into any agreement, or even know each other. Therefore, a wide range of incidents and situations fall under the category of tort law. In this book, we examine the main concepts and general principles.

A TORT IS NOT A CRIME

Stop and think for a moment about what type of law, more than any other, dominates the news. What type of law governs the stories that make the front page of the daily newspaper or become the lead story on the evening news? The answer is criminal law.

Unfortunately, crime is not something found only in movie plots or television dramas. It is a very real part of our society. However, as much as people hate the thought of crime, many are drawn to its juicy facts, investigations, trials, and other details. As a result, a serial killer's rampage makes headlines much more often than a story about a breach of contract or a tort. Accordingly, people are exposed to criminal law more than any other law, and tend to think of law in those terms.

When you are learning about torts, you should clear your mind momentarily of your exposure to criminal law, and remember that a tort is not a crime. Certainly, one particular act may be a tort, a crime, a breach of contract, and a violation of some other law, all at once. But when we are discussing torts, do not think *crime.* Do not think *jail,* or *beyond a reasonable doubt,* or any information you may have about a particular act being a *crime* while we are referring to it as a tort.

For example, suppose that we are discussing the torts involved when a **tortfeasor** (a person who commits a tort) steals another person's car. Someone may ask: "What if the person who stole the car returns it? Will that person still go to jail?" Now, in a torts discussion, what's wrong with that question? The word *jail*. The question is focusing on the act of stealing the car, and thinking about it as a *crime*. It certainly is a crime, but the answer to that question belongs in a *criminal* law discussion. Here, we are learning about *torts*.

If the focus was to punish the car thief, that's a criminal issue. If the goal is to require the car thief to pay damages to the car owner, the law involved deals with torts.

This concept is a little difficult to get used to at first. But if you make an effort to think about what the goal is, you will be able to figure out what type of law should apply.

TYPES OF TORTS

Generally, there are three main types of torts: intentional torts, torts involving negligence, and torts that involve liability without fault. In this chapter, we will learn about each type. Throughout the book, as we examine different torts, keep these three concepts in mind. Let's begin by learning about intentional torts.

INTENTIONAL TORTS

An intentional tort is a tort that is committed on purpose. In other words, the tortfeasor must have intended to cause the result. Intent to take a particular action does not necessarily mean intent to produce a particular result.

Suppose, for example, that you are playing baseball in the park. The batter hits the ball to you, and you attempt to throw it to your teammate. However, your aim is off-target, and the ball actually sails over your teammate's reach, into the parking lot next to the baseball field, and breaks a car window. Your act of breaking the windshield is *not* an intentional tort. Why? Because, although you intended to commit the act of throwing the ball, you did not intend to cause the result of breaking the window. You wanted your teammate to catch the ball. You had no desire to break the window. However, if you had intended to break the car window, then you would have committed an intentional tort.

Transferred Intent

Suppose that Jim and Brenda work together in a large company. They are both invited to the annual company dinner, which is a formal event. Jim is very angry at Brenda, and plans to ruin her beautiful gown by spilling red wine on it. Jim sees Brenda standing next to Julie, talking to her. Jim doesn't know Julie, and has nothing against her. He approaches Brenda and Julie and flings his glass of red wine in Brenda's direction. The wine, however, lands on Julie's gown instead. Although Jim never intended to spill wine on Julie, his intent to spill it on Brenda is *transferred* to Julie. Therefore, Julie can sue Jim for whatever tort he would have committed by spilling the wine on Brenda. This is the theory of transferred intent.

NEGLIGENCE

Thus far, we have learned that a tort is a civil wrong not based on a contract. Therefore, if Scott is injured by a rock that Kevin intentionally threw at him, Scott may generally sue Kevin in tort law. It does not matter if Kevin and Scott do not know one another. The fact that Kevin's act may also be a crime is a different issue altogether. If Scott wants to collect damages for his injury from Kevin, then Kevin's act must be looked at as a tort in that lawsuit.

But what if Kevin *accidentally* hit Scott with the rock? Suppose Kevin was merely trying to test how far into the woods he could throw a rock, and had no desire to harm anyone.

But Kevin's aim was off, and the rock hit Scott, who was sitting on a bench several feet away from where Scott had intended for the rock to land. In that case, would Kevin be liable for Scott's injury? Well, that depends on several factors. One factor that may render Kevin liable for the injury is whether or not Kevin was **negligent**.

Negligence is harm resulting from failure to use reasonable care, when such duty of care is owed, and when the act is both the actual and proximate cause of the resulting harm.

Hint: Whenever you encounter a new legal term with a somewhat complicated definition, it is a good idea to actually *write* the definition on a piece of paper. Quite often, rewriting something helps you learn it faster than if you merely read it.

Let's take a look at the definition, part by part.

Harm

First of all, notice that for there to be an **action** (lawsuit) in negligence, there must be some type of harm. When we think of harm, we often think of a sprained ankle or a broken arm. But harm is not entirely physical. In this book, the word harm typically refers to three types: physical, psychological, and financial. A particular act may cause none of these, or may cause one, two, or all three types of harm.

Physical Harm

Physical harm simply means harm done to a person's body. A punch to the stomach, a cut on the hand, and a sprained wrist are all examples of physical harm. In more extreme matters, loss of a body part, paralysis, and death are also types of physical harm. But a tap on the shoulder is, generally, not an example of physical harm.

Psychological Harm

Surely you have heard the phrase, "Sticks and stones may break my bones, but names will never hurt me." Well, that's not entirely true. Some people *are* hurt by names, or by threats, lies, or other behavior.

For example, a person who receives threatening phone calls in the middle of the night may have nightmares as a result. The person may become afraid and may be very nervous most of the time. Even though no physical harm has been inflicted, the distress resulting from the threatening phone calls is a prime example of psychological harm.

Psychological harm need not be intentional. For instance, suppose that Martin Stewart and Martin Stuart both went to Dr. Evans for a checkup. (Notice that their names *sound* the same, but the last names are spelled differently). Both were given blood tests, and both were told to call the doctor's office five days later for the results. The blood tests revealed that Martin Stewart was perfectly healthy, but Martin Stuart had hepatitis. But when Martin Stewart (the healthy one) called the office, Dr. Evans mistakenly told him that he had hepatitis. This caused Mr. Stewart needless worrying for ten days, until Dr. Evans realized the mistake and called him back to explain. In that case, Mr. Stewart's worrying may be psychological harm caused by Dr. Evans' error.

Financial Harm

Financial harm is harm that costs you money or causes you to lose something of value. Suppose you went to eat dinner in a fancy restaurant where formal attire was required. The hostess took your overcoat and you were seated at your table. The owner of the restaurant kept a pet dog in the basement of the restaurant, but forgot to lock the basement door.

The dog found its way up to the coat room and tugged, pulled, scratched, and bit your coat. By the time you finished your dinner and were ready to leave, your coat was destroyed. This is an example of financial harm. If you went outside to your car and discovered that someone had accidentally crashed into it, denting your rear fender, that would be another example of financial harm.

Financial harm involves more than property damage. It may involve damage to reputation. For instance, what if Drake told a lot of people that Paul was a bad lawyer? Drake may have spread this rumor to intentionally harm Paul, or may have mistaken Paul with another attorney. In any event, Paul's reputation may be harmed. He may lose a great number of clients, and thus lose a lot of potential earnings. This, then, is a classic example of financial harm.

As we have stated, there must be some type of harm for there to be an action in negligence. For instance, suppose that Larry the litterbug is sitting in his office, three stories up from ground level. Larry is relaxing, his feet up on the desk, and he takes out a piece of chewing gum, puts it in his mouth, and casually throws the gum wrapper out of his office window. You happen to be walking by, and the wrapper softly lands on your shoulder. When you notice it, you simply pick it off your shoulder and toss it into a nearby wastebasket.

Is it likely that you were harmed by Larry's act? Probably not. The gum wrapper is certainly too light in weight to cause you any physical harm. It probably did not frighten you, so it did not cause you any psychological harm. Your clothing was not damaged in any way, nor were you otherwise financially harmed. Therefore, you did not suffer any harm. For this reason, you probably do not have a cause of action for negligence against Larry.

Suppose instead, that Larry carelessly dropped a radio from his balcony and it hit Dexter, who was walking by. The radio fractured Dexter's collarbone. That is physical harm. If Dexter was also very frightened and distressed by the act, causing him to have flashbacks or nightmares, that would amount to psychological harm. If Dexter's injury was so serious that it forced him to remain in the hospital for a few days, or otherwise miss work, that would constitute financial harm.

Harm is a necessary element for a successful cause of action in negligence.

Reasonable Care

One of the most important words in torts—in fact, in all areas of law—is the word *reasonable*. It is a standard by which many legal matters are measured, so pay careful attention as we discuss it.

Actually, in torts, the word *reasonable* generally means anything from sensible, to appropriate, to typical. A **reasonable person,** then, usually means either an average person or a person of ordinary sense.

Reasonable care is the type of care undertaken by a reasonable person. Take a look at the following examples.

Suppose that you are sitting in class and the instructor, Professor Powell, begins to lecture. As Powell is lecturing he removes a pen from his pocket, holds it in his hand, and begins using it as a pointer in his discussion. Another student, Nancy, suddenly screams out loud. She then faints, falls out of her seat, and collapses to the ground. As a result of the fall, Nancy breaks her wrist.

Unknown to you, the instructor, or anyone else in the class, Nancy has a very strong fear of pens. A few months earlier, Nancy was almost stabbed to death with a pen by a maniac in her apartment building elevator.

Do you think that Powell will be liable for Nancy's broken wrist? First, let's assume that Powell had no intention of causing any harm to Nancy by removing the pen from his pocket. In fact, he had no idea that Nancy would have even the slightest negative reaction to it. Accordingly, Powell is not likely to be liable for an intentional tort.

Was Powell negligent in displaying the pen in front of Nancy? Let's determine whether Powell's action was a failure to use reasonable care. Would the reasonable person have been afraid of the pen? In other words, would the average person of ordinary sense be afraid of a pen?

If you were talking in a room full of people, and you removed a pen from your pocket, would you think that someone would scream and faint as a frightened reaction to seeing the pen? No, not very likely at all. We can determine that the reasonable person would not be afraid of a pen. Also, the reasonable person would not expect anyone to be afraid of a pen.

For this reason, it does not appear that Powell's action was a failure to use reasonable care. Accordingly, it is not very likely that he would be found negligent.

Suppose, instead, that Professor Powell had brought a machine gun into class and suddenly removed it from his briefcase. Tom, a student, had the same reaction to the gun that Nancy had to the pen. In that case, is it likely that Powell failed to use reasonable care? Yes, because while the reasonable person would not be afraid of pens, the same cannot be said for guns. A gun, unlike a pen, is generally considered to be an inherently dangerous weapon. Accordingly, the reasonable person would be expected to be frightened at the sight of a gun. Likewise, the reasonable person would not abruptly reveal a gun without warning, knowing that would alarm others in the area.

Of course, it is possible that there is a person out there who really *is* afraid of pens, just as there are many people who are *not* afraid of guns. In determining negligence, it does not matter whether such reactions are *possible*. What matters most is whether such reactions are reasonably likely to occur.

Note: Reasonable care does not necessarily mean perfect care. Therefore, in the example, Professor Powell's decision to display a pen was not unreasonable, even though it actually led to Nancy becoming very frightened. Powell was not expected to be able to read Nancy's mind and determine that she had an unusual fear of pens.

Duty of Care

To this point, we have determined that for there to be negligence, there must be harm, and that harm must result from a failure to use reasonable care. The next portion of the definition is **when such duty of care is owed.** Therefore, our next question is, When is such duty of care owed?

Each of us owes a duty of care not to cause harm to one another. Therefore, if you place some flowerpots on your outside window sill, be careful. You owe a duty of care to the world: a duty not to allow those flowerpots to fall on people and hurt them, or to fall on people's cars and damage them, or to fall two inches away from someone and cause a bad scare.

If you drive a car, you owe a duty of care to the world to make sure your brakes are in good working order, so that you do not accidentally crash into another car, a pedestrian, or even somebody's house. If you are smoking a cigarette, you owe a duty of care to everyone to properly extinguish it so that you do not start a fire. These are examples of the duty of reasonable care that we owe the world—both to strangers and to people we know.

Suppose that Brenda is walking along the beach. She sees Anna struggling in the water, apparently trying to stay afloat. Brenda is a good swimmer, but instead of saving Anna, she simply walks away. Anna manages to save herself, but gets hurt in the process and needs to be hospitalized. Did Brenda owe Anna a duty of care to save her, thereby rendering Brenda liable for Anna's injuries? No.

Certainly it can be argued that Brenda had a moral responsibility to try to save Anna's life. Although morality is often reflected in the law, the two are not always intertwined. In other words, something that we find to be *immoral* is not necessarily *illegal.* In this case, Brenda does not owe Anna a legal duty of care, because Brenda did not cause Anna to be drowning.

However, if Brenda had pushed Anna off a pier into the water, whether intentionally or accidentally, then Brenda would generally owe Anna a duty of care to save her. Or, if Brenda were a lifeguard at the beach, she would probably owe Anna a duty of care even if she had nothing to due with Anna's predicament.

A duty of care is owed to not place a person in a position of harm. A duty of care can also be based on a person's obligation to another person. For example, a parent has the duty to feed her minor child; a bus driver has the duty to transport his passengers safely; and a police officer has the duty to protect everyone in her area of patrol.

A person is obligated not to **breach** his or her duty of reasonable care, when such duty of care is owed.

Actual and Proximate Cause

Next, the breach of duty of reasonable care, or the negligent act, must be the **actual or proximate cause** of the harm suffered by the victim. In other words, for an act to be negligent, it must be both the actual and proximate cause of the resulting harm. Let's take a look at the difference between actual cause and proximate cause.

Actual cause—also known as **cause in fact** or **but for cause**—is a reason why something happened. "But for" that act, the result would not have occurred. For instance, suppose that Fran shows her new pet kitten to George. Unknown to Fran, George is deathly afraid of cats, no matter how small. As soon as George sees the kitten, he faints and falls to the ground, breaking his jaw. In that example, Fran's act of showing the kitten to George was an actual cause of George's injury. Does this mean Fran was negligent? Probably not. Remember, the act must be *both* the *actual* and the *proximate* cause of the resulting harm.

Proximate cause is *reasonably foreseeable cause.* In other words, the harm must be a reasonably foreseeable consequence of the act. The harm need not be definite or even likely, but it must be *reasonably foreseeable.* Would you think that showing a young kitten to someone would cause him to become so afraid that he would faint? Probably not. In that case, it would not be reasonably foreseeable, and thereby not a proximate cause.

For this reason, Fran's act of showing the kitten to George may have been an *actual* cause of George's injury, but it was not a *proximate cause.* Consequently, Fran will probably not be found to be negligent.

Consider another example. Andy spills some orange juice on a hardwood floor but does not clean it up. Keith enters the room, slips on the wet floor, and falls down, injuring himself. Two other people help Keith get to a doctor. A few minutes later, Steven enters the room. He has spent many years working as a custodian in a large high school. Steven becomes enraged at people who create a mess and do not bother to clean it up. He became so angry when he saw the spilt orange juice that he picked up a chair and hurled it across the room. Accidentally, the chair hit Walter. Now consider these questions:

1. Is Andy liable for negligently causing Keith's injury?
2. Is Andy liable for negligently causing Walter's injury?

The answer is that Andy will probably be found liable for negligently causing Keith's injury, but not Walter's. Although Andy's spilling the orange juice was an *actual* cause of both injuries, it was a *proximate* cause only for Keith's injury. That's because while it is reasonable to expect that someone will slip and fall on a wet floor, it is not likely that someone will become violently angry about a spill and hurl a chair across the room.

Note: Remember, the question is whether *Andy* would be found liable for *Steven's* act of throwing the chair at *Walter.* You may also be wondering whether *Steven* (who threw the chair) would be liable for Walter's injury. He probably would be, but that is not the issue. Just because one person is found liable for a certain act, that doesn't mean another person cannot be liable for the same act.

Gross Negligence

Gross negligence is not a separate mental state. Rather, it is a more extensive form of negligence. There are instances when a person's conduct, though not intended to produce a particular result, exceeds the usual bounds of failure to use reasonable care.

Consider this example. While driving her car, Samantha purposely hits Molly, who is crossing the street. That is intent. Instead, suppose Samantha accidentally hits Molly because Samantha's car brakes are faulty. If Samantha knows that the brakes are faulty but continues driving her car anyway, that is a classic example of negligence.

Finally, suppose that Samantha wanted to challenge herself by driving blindfolded. Though she did not mean to, Samantha hit Molly as a result. That is gross negligence.

NEGLIGENCE PER SE

In some instances, acts of negligence are predetermined by statute. **Negligence per se is harm resulting from violation of a negligence statute, when the vic-**

tim is a member of the statute's protected class and the harm resulted from violation of the statute.

Let's take a look at these elements, one by one.

Violation of a Negligence Statute

There are various laws designed to protect society against people's failure to use reasonable care. Setting speed limits is a prime example. Rather than requiring a jury to determine whether a certain driving speed is reasonable, driving speeds are typically set forth by statute. Therefore, exceeding the speed limit is a violation of a negligence statute.

Note: The words *negligence* or *reasonable care* need not be part of the statute in order for the statute to be a negligence statute. Generally, negligence statutes are those designed to protect people against negligence.

Victim a Member of the Statute's Protected Class

The victim of the harm must be the type of person the statute was created to protect. Suppose, for instance, that Ralph is driving his car on the highway at 90 miles per hour. The speed limit is 55. Christina is trying to film a documentary about the hatching of eggs belonging to a rare species of eagle. This type of eagle is very fearful of people, and so Christina has set up her filming equipment from quite a distance.

She has to film across a highway, but she is sure that she can capture the hatching and edit the film later. There is just one catch: This special film is useless if there is an object filmed that is moving faster than 75 miles per hour. At the precise moment of hatching, Ralph's car speeds by at 90 miles per hour, completely ruining the filming. Is Ralph negligent per se? No, because the speed limit statute was intended to protect motorists and pedestrians. It was not designed to protect photographers and filmmakers whose filming may be harmed by fast-moving objects. Therefore, Christina is not a member of the speed limit statute's protected class.

Harm Resulting from Violation of the Statute

Let's return to Ralph, driving on the highway. This time, suppose that he is not speeding, and that he has his headlights turned off. A statute in the state where Ralph is driving requires all motorists to turn on their headlights after 5 P.M. every night of the year. Though it is 6 P.M., it is the middle of July and the sun is still shining brightly. For this reason, Ralph is driving with his headlights off. He is involved in an accident with Penny. Penny's car is damaged. Is Ralph negligent per se, thereby liable to Penny as a result? Probably not. In this case, the fact that Ralph violated the headlight statute probably did not have anything to do with why the accident happened. Accordingly, in order to recover damages from Ralph, Penny will probably have to prove that Ralph was negligent through the steps of determining basic negligence.

However, if it had been a cloudy or rainy day, or if the sun was setting or had set, then Penny might have a good case against Ralph for negligence per se, without the need to prove whether or not Ralph used reasonable care in driving.

Note: The definition of negligence per se includes "resulting harm," but does not mention "actual and proximate cause." This is because "proximate cause," which is reasonably foreseeable cause, is generally presumed, because the statute was created to protect against such "reasonably foreseeable harm" in the first place. The resulting harm, then, *is* the actual cause.

These are the basic aspects of negligence. Now that we have examined intentional torts and negligence, let's take a look at liability without fault.

LIABILITY WITHOUT FAULT

Until now, we have talked about a person being liable who intended to cause a particular act, or who was negligent in doing so. But suppose a person causes harm neither intentionally nor negligently. May that person still be liable for a tort? Sometimes, yes. There are some types of torts whereby the tortfeasor is held liable even if he or she was not at fault (i.e., did not intentionally or negligently commit the act). Examples of this type of liability include **vicarious liability, strict liability,** and **products liability.**

Vicarious Liability

Vicarious liability means that one person is held liable for the acts of another person. This legal principle is grounded in the theory of **respondeat superior,** a Latin phrase that means "Let the master answer."

Note: Whenever you see a word or phrase that looks foreign to you, as if it is not written in English, there is a good chance that it is a Latin term. Many legal words are derived from Latin.

Respondeat superior basically means that one person is held liable for the acts of another person, based on their relationship. For instance, suppose Diana owns a limousine service and hires Patrick as a driver. Patrick has an excellent driving record and has always been a model citizen.

One day, Patrick decided to stop in a bar before beginning his evening duty, which was to drive Braxton to the airport. Patrick drank several beers before picking up Braxton. On the way to the airport, the beers slowly took their toll on Patrick. His coordination was impaired and he got into an accident, which injured Braxton. As you already know, Braxton probably has a good cause of action against Patrick. This is not an intentional tort, because Patrick surely did not *intend* to get into a car accident or to injure Braxton. Instead, Patrick will likely be found *negligent* for his actions. (Recall the elements of negligence and apply them to this example to determine why Patrick will likely be found negligent).

However, suppose Braxton's medical bills are very expensive, but Patrick hardly has a penny to his name. Diana, on the other hand, has plenty of money. Braxton cannot successfully sue her simply because she has enough money to pay his medical bills. He can prevail against her only if she is *liable.*

The question, then, is whether *Diana* is liable for Braxton's injuries, which were caused by Patrick. Based on the types of tort liability we have already covered—intentional torts and negligence—the answer is no. First, Diana certainly did not intend for Braxton to be injured. Next, Diana was not negligent because she had no reason to believe that Patrick would get drunk before driving the limousine. However, Diana probably *will* be held *vicariously* liable under the theory of *respondeat superior.*

Strict Liability

Like vicarious liability, **strict liability** is liability without fault. However, unlike strict liability, the liability is not based on the relationship between the person who is liable and the person who causes the harm. Rather, the focus is on the act itself. Typically, strict liability involves harm caused by certain types of animals and by conducting abnormally dangerous activities.

Owners of Wild Animals or Domestic Animals with Known Dangerous Propensities

A person who owns a wild animal, or a domestic animal known to be dangerous, will generally be held strictly liable for harm caused by that animal.

For example, suppose that John keeps a pet lion on his property. During the day, John keeps the lion chained to a solid oak tree. The chain is very strong, and the tree is quite sturdy, making it almost impossible for the lion to escape—*almost.*

One day, while John is at work, an earthquake strikes his town and knocks the oak tree from its roots. The tree trunk breaks in two, causing the lion to break free. The lion becomes quite excitable and runs loose, destroying large amounts of property in neighboring homes, injuring some people, and severely frightening others.

In this case, John certainly did not intend for his pet lion to cause any harm, nor was John negligent (the strong chain and the sturdy tree that secured the lion were reasonable precautions, and that an earthquake would strike and cause the lion to be released was not reasonably foreseeable). In any event, John will probably be found to be *strictly liable* for the harm, because his pet lion is a **wild animal.**

Let's change the example a bit. Suppose instead that John kept a pet dog on a leash chained to a tree. The dog was a very friendly dog and had never bitten anyone nor destroyed any property.

But suppose that the earthquake hit and the dog was freed from the tree. Alarmed by the earthquake, the dog caused similar harm as the lion did in the earlier example. In this case, John was again not negligent, nor did he intend for his dog to cause the harm. Accordingly, John will probably not be found liable for the harm.

However, if John's dog was known to have violent outbursts, then John *would* probably be liable for the harm. Although not liable for an intentional tort or for negligence, John would be *strictly liable,* as the owner of a **domestic animal with known dangerous propensities.**

Note: You can see from the three examples that a lion is considered a wild animal whereas a dog is considered a domestic animal. You can also probably imagine that an elephant would be a wild animal, whereas a parakeet would be a domestic animal. But what about a horse or a pig? Not sure? Read some case law about harm caused by horses and pigs, in order to get a sense of whether the courts consider those animals to be wild or domestic. Often, determinations in the law are consistent. Other times, they may vary from court to court. That's why reading as many cases as possible gives you a better understanding of the law in general.

Abnormally Dangerous Activities

Persons who engage in **abnormally dangerous activities** are generally held to be strictly liable for resulting harm. Examples of abnormally dangerous activities, sometimes called **ultrahazardous activities,** include transporting explosives, launching rocket missiles, or storing poisonous gases and fluids.

For example, suppose Omar is a scientist designing a new rocketship at his plant in Colorado. Omar has used a special fuel in all of his rockets for many years. Omar is careful to use the fuel only during the fall and winter months, because the fuel can become flammable in temperatures over 100 degrees.

One morning in December, the temperature at Omar's plant rises to 110 degrees—the warmest December day in the history of Colorado! Despite the massive flooding caused by rapidly melting snow, the fuel ignites Omar's rocket, which is launched and crashes into a nearby factory, destroying it.

In that case, though Omar did not *intend* for the rocket to cause the harm, and though Omar was not *negligent* (he could not possibly have been expected to predict that the temperature would be over 100 degrees in December), he will probably be held *strictly liable,* because the harm resulted from an *abnormally dangerous activity.*

Note: Strict liability for abnormally dangerous activities applies when the harm resulted from the characteristic that makes an activity abnormally dangerous. For instance, suppose Mike was driving a truck filled with sticks of dynamite. Through no fault of Mike's the truck overturned and the dynamite spilled onto the sidewalk. If the truck caught fire, igniting the dynamite, and Pamela was injured, Mike would be strictly liable.

However, if Pamela simply slipped on an unlit dynamite stick and injured herself, Mike would probably not be held strictly liable, because Pamela's injury would not have resulted from the dynamite's abnormally dangerous characteristic. In the latter case, the stick of dynamite may as well have been a candlestick.

Products Liability

Generally, a person who manufactures or sells a particular product may be held strictly liable for harm resulting from that product.

Suppose that Theresa produces a soft drink called Ice Cola. The secret ingredient in Ice Cola is a special syrup that gives the soda its delicious flavor. Theresa had the syrup tested by an independent team of technicians called Diet Wizards, who are nationally known experts in determining the safety of food and beverage ingredients.

The Diet Wizards confirmed that the syrup was completely safe. Accordingly, Theresa used the syrup in her formula, and Ice Cola was put on the market. Jennifer sold Ice Cola in her grocery store. One day, Donna went to Jennifer's store and bought a six-pack of Ice Cola. After drinking the first can, Donna became so sick, she had to be hospitalized. She had a severe reaction to the drink, and her stomach had to be pumped. Until the doctors made her well, Donna was in a great deal of pain.

As it turns out, the syrup used in Ice Cola becomes poisonous if it is out of the refrigerator for more than one hour. It reacts with the rising temperature, creating a noxious chemical combination. The Diet Wizards failed to notice this. In any event, Theresa, the owner of Ice Cola, will probably be found liable as a result, even though she neither *intentionally* nor *negligently* caused the harm to Donna.

Of course, it is possible that Diet Wizards were negligent, and they could be liable as well. In that case, Donna could sue them directly, and so can Theresa and Jennifer. In any event, Theresa will probably be liable, as the owner of a defective product (Ice Cola). Whether or not Jennifer, the seller, is strictly liable, or perhaps a distributor who bought the soda from Theresa and sold it to Donna, depends on the situation. If any other party caused the defect, that party may be strictly liable, depending on that person's role anywhere in the process from the creation of the product until the product caused the harm.

Again, if any of these parties is also *negligent,* that certainly helps the injured party's case; but negligence is not necessary to prove *products liability.* On the other hand, although it is not *necessary* for a tortfeasor to be negligent in order to be liable for a defective product, a person may recover for products liability based on negligence as well.

Generally, product defects are in the design or manufacture, and may cause harm if maintained or used improperly. A design defect occurs when the product was poorly designed, such as a heavy chair with weak, thin legs. A manufacturing defect occurs when, although the design may have been fine, there was an error in assembly. For example, a chair was made with strong legs but one of the legs was not fastened properly.

Faulty warnings or instructions may result in the liability of the person who should have provided this information (manufacturer, seller, etc.).

Note: Liability without fault is not the same as negligence per se, although many people often confuse the two. A person may be liable without fault without being negligent. However, a person who is negligent per se *is* negligent; his or her negligence is predetermined by statute, and the reasonable care standard does not necessarily have to be proven in court and determined by a jury.

These, then are the three main areas of tort law: intentional torts, negligence, and liability without fault. Think about them as we learn about different types of torts throughout the book. You will begin to realize how everything fits together, and you will be well on your way to learning all about torts. In Chapter 3, we discuss torts to the person.

REVIEW QUESTIONS

1. What are the two main types of civil law?
2. What is transferred intent?
3. What are the main types of harm?
4. How is reasonable care measured?
5. What is the difference between actual cause and proximate cause?
6. What is vicarious liability?
7. What is strict liability?
8. Owners of what type of domestic animals may be held strictly liable for their animals' acts?
9. What is products liability?
10. What is the difference between a design defect and a manufacturing defect? Give an example.

A TORT TALE

Louie is an auto mechanic who has recently opened his own business fixing cars. Although he means well, he is not a very good mechanic. One morning, he was working on Stella's Cadillac. Later that afternoon, he returned the car to Stella, apparently "fixed." In fact, he had done a poor job trying to repair Stella's brakes. He certainly did not use reasonable care.

By the evening, Stella had a car accident when she could not stop in time and smashed the Cadillac into another car. Fortunately, Stella was not hurt, but her car was damaged. However, Louie was not liable for the accident. **Why?**

3 Torts against the Person: Intentional, Negligent, and Without Fault

In this chapter we focus on torts against the actual person, rather than torts against property, reputation, or other civil rights. As we discuss each particular tort, keep in mind that we should consider whether the tort is intentional, based on negligence, or based on liability without fault. Remember, we are learning about the general principles of tort law, which may have exceptions and may vary throughout different states and **jurisdictions.**

ASSAULT

Stop: Before we even define assault, ask yourself if you've ever heard that word. Now, in the context in which you heard it, was it a *tort,* or a *crime?* Some acts are both torts and crimes, and the elements of each may vary depending on its classification. We deal with acts in this book as torts, not crimes. Keep that in mind for every tort that we discuss throughout the book.

Assault is intentionally placing another person in apprehension of an unlawful, unprivileged, imminent, offensive touching. Let's take a closer look at the definition.

First, assault is *intentional.* That means that a person will be held liable for assault only if the act was committed on purpose. There is no such thing as an accidental assault. Accordingly, there is no assault by negligence. Also, a person cannot be held strictly or vicariously liable for assault.

Note: While a person may not be held strictly or vicariously liable for assault, an employer may, for instance, be liable for assault committed by an employee, even though the employer did not personally commit the assault.

Let's test our knowledge.

Suppose that Brenda is riding her bicycle and she accidentally hits Jordan, who is crossing the street. Is Brenda liable for assault?

- **A.** Brenda is liable for assault.
- **B.** Brenda is not liable for assault.
- **C.** More information is needed about the definition of assault in order to answer the question.

How did you answer? You may have been skeptical about choice A, and even choice B. Choice C may have looked like the best choice to you. But even though you certainly need to learn more about the definition of assault (which we will shortly address), you don't need to know any more to answer the question: The best answer is B. Because Brenda *accidentally* crashed into Jordan, she did *not* do it *intentionally*. Where there is no intent, there is no assault. You need not look any further.

Note: Is Brenda liable for *something*? After all, she did crash into a pedestrian. Brenda probably is liable for something, but that wasn't the question. The question was, whether Brenda is liable for assault, and the answer is no.

Next, the intentional act of assault involves placing someone in **apprehension.** That means making the person aware of the intent to act. If the person is not aware, an assault has not been committed.

Let's try another question: Cynthia is walking home from school one day. Justine is jealous because her boyfriend took Cynthia to lunch earlier in the day. While standing about 20 feet behind Cynthia, Justine yells: "Cynthia, if I ever see you near my boyfriend again, I'll kill you!" Justine did not realize that Cynthia was wearing headphones, listening to music, and did not hear a word Justine said. Did Justine commit assault?

- **A.** Justine committed assault.
- **B.** Justine did not commit assault.
- **C.** More information is needed about the definition of assault in order to answer this question.

Again, the answer is B, because there must be *apprehension* (awareness) for there to be assault. Cynthia was wearing headphones and was not aware of Justine's threat. We need not look any further. Because Cynthia was not aware, no matter what else did or did not happen, Justine did not commit an assault.

Suppose one of the answer choices was: "Justine did not commit assault, because she never touched Cynthia." Would that also be correct? No. In fact, you would not even have to read the facts, because that sentence alone is incorrect. If you read the definition of assault carefully, you will notice that there does not have to be an actual touching. The tortfeasor must simply make the victim aware that there is about to be a touching. Accordingly, swinging a baseball bat at someone, as if to hit them, can be an assault even though there is no actual contact.

Imagine that you saw an old friend that you haven't seen in years, and you approached him, smiled, and stuck out your hand as if to shake his. He saw your gesture. Have you committed assault? Well, you probably know that the answer is no, but do you know *why* that's the right answer? After all, your gesture was intentional, and you did make the person aware that you were about to touch him. However, the potential touching would not be an *offensive* touching. Shaking someone's hand is an accepted custom in our society and is not considered to be offensive. Accordingly, a gesture implying that a particular nonoffensive touching is about to occur is not an assault.

Now let's reconsider the earlier example about Cynthia and Justine. Suppose Cynthia had not been wearing headphones, and she *did* hear Justine threaten to kill her. Would Justine have committed assault? Let's look at all of the steps again.

First, Justine's threat was certainly intentional; she didn't blurt the words out by accident. Second, if Cynthia was not wearing the headphones, she heard the threat and thus became aware of it. Third, the threat dealt with Justine killing her, which is certainly an offensive touching, to say the least. Would Justine's threat, then, amount to an assault? No, because the proposed offensive touching would not be **imminent,** which means immediate. In other words, Justine said: "If I ever see you near my boyfriend again, I'll kill you!" This is certainly not an imminent threat.

To begin with, if Cynthia simply complies and never talks to Justine's boyfriend again, Justine will apparently not try to harm her. Next, Cynthia has a number of options available to her. She can:

1. Call the police and have Justine arrested and possibly jailed.
2. Confront Justine with words or physical force as a counter to Justine's threat.
3. Move to another country where Justine can never find her, or choose from among numerous other options.

Whatever the case, the threat to Cynthia is not immediate. Therefore, while Justine certainly does not have a legal right to make threats like the one she made, her conduct does not constitute an assault.

What if Marvin works as a security guard in a sporting goods store where Jason tries to steal a baseball glove? If Jason heads for the exit and Marvin blocks the exit, yells "Stop!" and lunges to grab Jason, has Marvin committed an assault? Marvin's actions are certainly an intent to make Jason aware of an imminent, offensive touching (that Marvin will grab him). But remember, such touching must be **unlawful.** As a security guard responsible for the merchandise, Marvin would be within his lawful right to attempt to recover the glove. Accordingly, Marvin would not have committed assault.

Finally, consider this example: One of the most famous moments in professional boxing history was when Evander Holyfield defeated the seemingly invincible Mike Tyson. During the fight, both boxers hit each other with plenty of punches. At other times, they would throw punches at each other but miss. Given all of those punches, can one fighter sue the other one for assault? No, because both Holyfield and Tyson are adults who legally consented to fight each other, thus giving each other the **privilege** to attempt to punch the other. Privileged touching does not amount to an assault.

These are the elements of an assault: **Intentionally** placing another person in **apprehension** of an **unlawful, unprivileged, imminent, offensive touching.** Remember, awareness of the touching is essential, but the actual touching is not. What if there is an actual touching? Read ahead. That's the next tort we discuss.

BATTERY

Battery is a completed intentional, unlawful, unprivileged, offensive touching. This definition is shorter than the one for assault. You've already learned how to read and analyze each part of a legal definition, so understanding battery should be even easier now. Once again, remember that the phrase "assault and battery," as commonly used, may refer to *crimes* rather than *torts.*

First, keep in mind that as with assault, a battery must be **intentional.** There is no such thing as an accidental battery. Next, the battery must be **unlawful** and **unprivileged.** But here is where the similarities end between battery and assault.

For example, suppose that Chris throws a rock at Nelson. Nelson sees the rock, jumps out of the way, and avoids being hit. Has Chris committed assault? Yes. Battery? No. Unlike assault, a battery requires that an actual touching take place. This is the first difference between assault and battery.

Suppose Kyle hits Roland from behind. Roland never saw the attack coming. Has Kyle committed battery? Yes. Assault? No. Unlike assault, battery does not require the victim to be *aware* that he or she was about to be offensively touched. That is the second major difference between assault and battery.

Accordingly, for assault there must be *apprehension* (awareness) but there need not be a touching. For battery, there must be a *touching*, but there need not be apprehension.

Contact, Not Harm

Suppose that someone who does not like you rolls a piece of paper into a ball, throws it at you, and hits you. The paper ball bounces off of your chest. It did not harm you physically, psychologically, or financially. Did that person commit battery? Yes, because there need not be harm in a battery, as long as there is *contact*. The paper ball did not harm you, but was an intentional, unlawful, unprivileged, offensive touching.

Note: You probably would not bother to take the person to court for hitting you with a piece of paper. Nonetheless, the person committed battery against you.

Imagine that Bo is taking a walk one day and he sees Ashley walking by. Bo doesn't know Ashley, but he is attracted to her. Very boldly, he walks up to her, introduces himself, and gives her a kiss. If Ashley does not mind this advance, then everyone is happy. However, if Ashley *does* mind, Bo could be in a lot of trouble. Besides being liable for one or several crimes (which we will not discuss because we are learning about torts) and other torts (which we will discuss later), Bo is liable for battery: an intentional, unlawful, unprivileged, offensive touching.

If a romantically involved couple customarily kiss one another, such kisses are presumably consensual. However, if one of the parties is an adult and the other is a minor, the kissing (or other acts of affection) by the adult toward the minor may be unlawful. If that is the case, then the act would be a battery.

Usually, when such an act is considered unlawful, it is because the law deems the minor to be incapable of legally consenting. Accordingly, the act is really not privileged, even if the minor has consented. Later in the book, we will talk more about minors and their capacity to consent. Now, let's put what we have just learned to the test:

ASSAULT AND BATTERY REVIEW

For each of these acts, answer: Assault only, Battery only, Both assault and battery, or Neither assault nor battery

1. Jeff throws a snowball at Edna. She sees it coming, moves out of the way, and avoids being hit.
2. Bill throws a water balloon at Frank. Frank sees it coming, but cannot move out of the way in time, and is hit.
3. Brenda sneaks up behind Julia and dumps a bucket of water over Julia's head. Julia never saw it coming.
4. Nick sees James waiting for a bus. He stands behind James and shoots a gun at him. The bullet misses James and lands in a soft patch of snow nearby. James, who is listening to music on his headphones, neither sees nor hears the shot. A few seconds later, James boards a bus and leaves the area.

The answers are:

1. Assault only.
2. Assault and battery.
3. Battery only.
4. Neither assault nor battery.

In all of the examples, there was intent to cause unlawful, unprivileged, imminent, offensive touching. In the first example, there was apprehension but no contact. In the second example, there were both apprehension and contact. In the third, there was contact, but no apprehension, and in the fourth, there was neither contact nor apprehension. Note that the most harm would potentially have been caused in the fourth example. Again, harm is not the issue. The element required is apprehension for assault, contact for battery. In that example, Nick is certainly breaking both criminal and tort law, but he is not specifically liable for tortious assault or battery.

TRANSFERRED INTENT

We talked a little about **transferred intent** in Chapter 2. Now let's see how it applies to some intentional torts against the person, like assault or battery. **Under transferred intent, a person who intends to commit a tort against one person, but accidentally commits it against a second person, is held liable for an intentional tort as if he or she had intended to commit it against that person.**

Also, **a person who intends to commit one tort against a person but accidentally commits another tort against that person is held liable as if he or she committed that tort intentionally.**

For example, suppose Al found out that Barbara just cashed her paycheck. Wanting to rob Barbara, Al's plan is to point a gun at her, hoping that she will be frightened into giving her purse to him. He hides behind an alley, hoping to jump out and surprise her. Instead, Rachel walks by, sees Al with the gun, and becomes very frightened. Even though Al had no intention of frightening Rachel, he will probably be liable for assault under the theory of **transferred intent.** Because he intended to commit assault against Barbara, the intent will be transferred to Rachel and Al will thereby be liable for assault.

Suppose instead that Al saw Barbara walking in front of him. He planned to jump out in front of her and point the gun at her. Al had absolutely no intention of shooting her. He was clearly interested in taking Barbara's purse, but really wanted to avoid any violence.

However, as Al was about to surprise Barbara, his gun accidentally went off and shot her. Again, though he did not *intend* to commit battery, Al will probably be liable under the theory of transferred intent: He had intended to commit one intentional tort (assault), but accidentally committed another act, which will be deemed as an intentional tort (battery) under the theory of transferred intent.

The next tort we discuss is false imprisonment.

FALSE IMPRISONMENT

If we asked people to define "false imprisonment," they might say that it involves putting someone in jail for no good reason, or putting the wrong person in jail. By now, you already realize that in tort law, that cannot be the answer. You have already learned that *jail* is a form of *punishment*, which is an aspect of criminal law, not tort law.

In tort law, **false imprisonment is intentionally confining a person to a certain area, with no reasonable means of escape, by actual confinement or threat of force, when the victim is aware of the confinement.**

Let's take a look at each of the elements of false imprisonment, one by one, through some examples.

Martha is a college student who is studying for an upcoming exam. She goes to her college library late in the evening. It is a Friday night, and the library is almost empty. Martha finds a small study room on the third floor of the library and begins to read. The librarian, Anna, gets ready to close the library, but does not check all the upstairs rooms. Thinking the library is empty, Anna shuts off all the first floor lights and locks the door. The college closes its entrances, too. Martha has been so wrapped up in studying, she does not realize that she is locked inside the library. The phone system is automatically turned off for the evening, and Martha is trapped in the library overnight.

Has Anna falsely imprisoned Martha?

A. Yes, because Martha could not get out.

B. No, because Anna did not intentionally lock Martha inside.

C. More information is needed about false imprisonment in order to answer this question.

What is the answer? B, because Anna *accidentally* locked Martha inside the library, and the first element of false imprisonment is **intent.** Because Anna did not intend to lock Martha inside the library, Anna did not commit false imprisonment. There is no need to look any further.

Next, consider this scenario: Jeff and Louise are sitting in a class that is held on the ground floor of the school building.

There are two ground-level windows in the classroom, each of which lead directly to the schoolyard. Adam walks by and says to Jeff and Louise: "Ha, ha, I'm going to lock you in this room and you can't escape!" Adam then locks the door from the outside. Has Adam falsely imprisoned Jeff and Louise? No. Although Adam has made Jeff and Louise aware that the door is locked, they are not confined to the classroom. Because the windows are at ground level, simply climbing out of the window is a **reasonable means of escape.** Maybe it would be a bit inconvenient, but it is certainly not dangerous. Accordingly Adam's act would **generally** not be considered false imprisonment.

Note: Of course, the standard is whether there is a *reasonable* means of escape. Many courts would probably consider a ground-level window a reasonable means of escape, but others may not. Accordingly, as we discussed earlier, it is always a good idea to read many cases in order to get a better sense of what the courts determine to be reasonable.

Suppose instead that the classroom was on the tenth floor. In that case, the window would not serve as a reasonable means of escape, and Adam would be liable for false imprisonment. But suppose Adam did not actually lock Jeff and Louise in the room. Instead, what if he threatened to shoot them if they tried to leave the room? That would be false imprisonment, too.

Remember, the imprisonment may be established by either an **actual confinement** or **confinement by threat of force.** Therefore, by threatening to shoot Jeff and Louise if they try to escape, Adam used threat of force to falsely imprison them.

Finally, take a look at this example: Cassie, Dana, and Laurie go to Miami on vacation together. The three share a large hotel room on the twentieth floor, overlooking the beach. Cassie and Dana enjoy shopping and sightseeing, whereas Laurie likes to go to the beach, nap in the afternoon, and go to the hotel's "happy hour" festivities in the early evening.

Because they are upset with Laurie's lethargic attitude, Cassie and Dana decide to teach her a lesson. At 1 o'clock, as Laurie is enjoying her afternoon nap, Cassie and Dana set out on their shopping spree. However, they intentionally lock Laurie inside the hotel room, and even remove the telephone wire.

Cassie and Dana hope that Laurie will be trapped inside the room long enough to miss happy hour, which begins at 6 o'clock. At around 4 o'clock, the chambermaid uses a key to enter the room. She sees that Laurie is asleep, empties a couple of wastebaskets, and exits the room, leaving the door unlocked. An hour later, Laurie wakes up, showers, gets dressed, and goes to happy hour.

Did Cassie and Dana commit false imprisonment? No. Although they intentionally confined Laurie to the room, Laurie was asleep during the entire time she was confined. By the time she woke up, she was no longer confined.

In fact, she never even realized that she had been confined. Because she was not **aware,** the act of false imprisonment never materialized. Cassie and Dana's attempt to falsely imprison Laurie failed.

These are the elements of false imprisonment. Now let's take a look at the next tort: infliction of emotional distress.

INFLICTION OF EMOTIONAL DISTRESS

Emotional distress, also referred to as mental distress, is a classic example of psychological harm. Often, this tort is the result of another tort. Nonetheless, it can be a tort by itself.

Think back to our discussion about assault and battery. There is no assault if there is no awareness, and there is no battery if there is no contact. Therefore, if Bob stands 100 yards behind Aldo and throws a rock at him, but the rock doesn't hit Aldo nor does Aldo become aware of it, then Bob is not liable either for assault or battery. But suppose the rock was fairly large and, had it hit Aldo, could have killed him or seriously injured him. Aldo may be distressed if, say, Carolyn, a witness, told him what happened. If Aldo knew that he was very close to losing his life, or being hospitalized with a serious injury, this could have caused him **psychological harm.**

Of course, if the rock had hit Aldo as well, Bob would be liable for battery, or if Aldo had seen the rock coming, Bob would be liable for assault. If Aldo had seen the rock coming but could not get out of the way in time and was hit, Bob would be liable for both assault and battery.

If Aldo lived through the injury, and was lying in the hospital thinking about what happened, still very shaken up, and often woke in the middle of the night with nightmares of the incident, this would be psychological harm as a result of physical harm.

Psychological harm, then, can occur with or without physical harm.

Note: Some courts refuse to award damages for psychological harm when there is no actual physical harm. For example, in our example, some courts may award Aldo damages for psychological harm if he had also been hit by the rock, but not if he was physically unharmed. Other courts differ. Reading many cases can often help you determine how the courts in a particular *jurisdiction* tend to rule.

The Aldo example is an example of psychological harm. But is it emotional distress? Let's divide that tort into three types:

1. Intentional infliction of emotional distress;
2. Negligent infliction of emotional distress; and
3. Reckless infliction of emotional distress.

Intentional Infliction of Emotional Distress

This tort involves **intentionally causing, by extreme or outrageous conduct, emotional distress to another person.**

This particular emotional distress tort requires **intent.** Simply put, a person cannot accidentally cause intentional infliction of emotional distress. In fact, like the other intentional torts we have discussed, it has the word *intentional* built right into its name.

Extreme or outrageous conduct generally means the type of conduct that would be considered *intolerable* in a civilized society. What exactly do the words *extreme, outrageous,* and *intolerable* mean?

We can probably guess that threatening to kidnap someone's child would be considered extreme, outrageous, and intolerable; but threatening to squirt someone with a water gun would not. What about threatening to quit a job, or to expel someone from school? Is that extreme, outrageous, or intolerable? The answer may well depend on the circumstances, and on the *jurisdiction*. Accordingly, it is wise to read as many cases as you can about this tort in order to get a sense of how the courts tend to decide about these issues.

However, there is another aspect to this tort: If the tortfeasor knows of the victim's particular sensitivity to certain conduct, then the tortfeasor may be held liable for this tort even if the conduct is not considered intolerable by society.

For instance, if Jeff wants to cause Oscar to experience emotional distress by bringing a kitten into Oscar's house, because Jeff knows that Oscar is deathly afraid of cats, then Jeff will probably be liable for this intentional tort. Even though exposing someone to a kitten is generally not considered extreme and outrageous conduct, because Jeff knew what an awful effect it would have on Oscar, it was extreme and outrageous in that particular instance.

However, if a person were to bring a mountain lion into someone's house, that would generally be considered extreme and outrageous, because the average person would probably become very distressed at that, not only the oversensitive person.

Next, consider this example: Damian was a tenant in Luke's apartment building. Because Damian was often late with his rent, Luke terminated Damian's lease and evicted him. Damian called Luke on occasion, threatening to kill Luke in revenge. Luke never took these charges seriously, and laughed whenever he heard them. Is Damian liable for intentional infliction of severe emotional distress? No. Although Damian attempted to cause such distress, Luke was never fazed by Damian's conduct. As the saying goes, the threats fell on deaf ears. Therefore, Damian failed to inflict emotional distress upon Luke.

Suppose that Damian never intended for Luke to be distressed. Instead, he wanted Luke to pay him some money so that Damian could find another apartment elsewhere. In that case, even if Luke *did* experience emotional distress, it would not have been *intentionally* inflicted.

For the tort of intentional infliction of emotional distress to actually have been committed, the tortfeasor must intend to cause the distress, the victim must actually experience the distress, and the type of conduct must be extreme and outrageous—considered intolerable in civilized society. Again, when the tortfeasor knows of the plaintiff's particular sensitivity, the act does not have to be considered extreme and outrageous by society's standard.

Note: The "civilized society standard" is essentially the *reasonable* standard that we have already discussed. Therefore, whether or not the act was considered extreme or outrageous would depend on the reasonable person's point of view.

No Transferred Intent

Unlike other intentional torts, the theory of transferred intent does not apply to intentional infliction of emotional distress. Suppose Dennis owes a lot of money to Shawn. Shawn sends his friend Charlie to threaten Dennis at Dennis' favorite hangout. Charlie mistakenly approaches David, thinking that David is Dennis.

Charlie tells David: "If you don't give me ten thousand dollars right now, my boss will order me to kill you." David suffers emotional distress as a result. Charlie, however, will probably not be liable for intentional infliction of severe emotional distress, because this was a case of mistaken identity. He had intended to frighten Dennis, not David. But Charlie may be liable for another type of emotional distress. Read on.

Negligent Infliction of Emotional Distress

There are some differences between this tort and its intentional counterpart, which we have just dealt with. First, this tort is not intentional; it is based on **negligence.** Second, an ever larger number of courts usually require that there be actual **physical** harm as the result of the emotional distress.

For example, suppose that Angela invites her friend Monica to stay at Angela's house for the weekend. Angela loves keeping exotic animals as pets. As Monica sits in the living room, Angela's pet leopard jumps up on the couch next to Monica. Monica becomes deathly afraid and screams out loud. Angela hears the scream, enters the room, and says: "Oh, that's Pookie, my little kitty-kat." Angela then directs the leopard out of the room.

In this case, Angela did not **intend** for Monica to suffer emotional distress. If Monica wakes in the middle of the night with nightmares, the stress is still emotional.

Typically, because Angela's failure to warn Monica about the leopard was not intentional, Angela will be liable for Monica's mental distress only if Monica has physical side effects, for example, if Monica had suffered a mild heart attack during the scare.

On the other hand, had Angela *intended* to frighten Monica with the leopard, Angela would probably be liable for Monica's emotional distress even without additional physical harm.

In the example involving Charlie and David, Charlie would probably be liable for negligent infliction of emotional distress on David. Again, David would be more likely to recover damages if, say, Charlie punched him a couple of times. In that case, he could recover for both the physical harm and the ensuing emotional distress.

Reckless Infliction of Emotional Distress

In Chapter 2, we discussed *gross negligence* as a higher, more extreme type of negligence. *Recklessness* is a term used more often in criminal law than in torts; it is based on the elements that we have defined as gross negligence.

The applicable mental state is not intent, although there is a higher degree of probability of the outcome than with negligence. In the case of emotional distress, a separate tort occurs when the conduct that led to the distress was reckless. For instance, suppose Stacey is a babysitter who was hired to watch Michael while his parents, the Smiths, went out to dinner. Mrs. Smith gave Stacey her cellular phone number in case of an emergency. The Smiths told Stacey they would be home by 10 P.M.

At 10:30 P.M., the Smiths had not returned home. Stacey, who had a late date that evening, was getting restless. In order to get the Smiths to return home immediately, she telephoned Mrs. Smith on the cellular phone and said, "I don't know what's wrong with Michael; he stopped breathing. I think he's still alive, but I'm not sure." The Smiths rushed home frantically, and suffered severe emotional distress as a result of the false alarm. Stacey's conduct is a perfect example of reckless infliction of emotional distress. She did not actually intend for the Smiths to suffer emotional distress. Rather, she wanted them to rush home. However, her actions went beyond mere negligence.

OTHER NEGLIGENT TORTS AGAINST THE PERSON

Let us take a look at some acts that we covered earlier when the tortfeasor committed them intentionally. We already know that if Terry intentionally throws a rock at Victor, and Victor sees the rock coming and ducks out of the way, this is not a battery. If Terry intended to make Victor aware of the rock, it would be an assault. Moreover, if Terry wanted to severely frighten Victor, the act could be intentional infliction of emotional distress, depending on whether throwing the rock would be construed as extreme and outrageous conduct. But what if Terry did not mean to throw the rock at Victor?

Suppose instead that Terry wanted to harmlessly throw the rock on the roof of a building, just for fun. Wanting only to test his throwing arm, Terry had no intention of frightening or harming anyone. However, the rock did not actually land on the roof. Instead, it bounced off the building's brick side wall and hit Victor in the eye. Now even if the rock was small, about the size of a pebble, it could still cause damage to Victor's eye. Terry would probably be liable for the harm because he was **negligent.** Of course, if the pebble simply landed on Victor's shoulder and harmlessly bounced off, Terry would probably not be negligent, because there was no harm.

Now suppose that the rock *did* land in Victor's eye, and Victor was momentarily blinded and in a lot of pain. He started thinking the worst—that he would become permanently blind in that eye.

In that case, in addition to being liable for the physical harm, Terry would be liable for Victor's emotional distress, which was caused by Terry's negligence. However, had the pebble simply bounced off Victor's shoulder, not causing any physical harm but leaving Victor emotionally distressed nonetheless, Victor would have a much tougher time suing Terry for negligent infliction of emotional distress without the accompanying *physical* harm. Victor would have the same problem with an emotional distress claim if, say, the pebble missed Victor by six inches, but he was harmed in being shaken up by the experience.

If we look again at the tort of **false imprisonment,** we recall that it is an *intentional* tort. In other words, if Joyce accidentally locks Mark in a storage room, there is no false imprisonment. However, if the stockroom is very cold, and Mark becomes ill as a result, he can probably sue Joyce if Joyce was negligent in locking him in. Moreover, if Mark is claustrophobic (afraid of closed spaces), he can probably sue for the resulting emotional harm, too. In any event, the actual tort of *false imprisonment* would not apply, because Joyce's act was not intentional.

Torts Against the Person When There Is Liability Without Fault

Recall that liability without fault generally falls into three categories: vicarious liability, strict liability, and products liability. Let's take a look at each category, one by one, to see how such liability can be applied regarding torts against the person.

Vicarious Liability

Vicarious liability—when one person is held liable for another person's act—applies to various types of torts, including torts against the person. For example, suppose Kevin owns a bowling alley and Lou works there. Gary is bowling one evening and gets into an argument with Lou. Lou picks up a bowling pin and throws it at Gary. If Gary is hit, this is battery.

Depending on the jurisdiction and on the extent of Gary's injuries, Kevin may also be found liable for Gary's injuries, even though Kevin may not even have been in the bowling alley when the act took place.

A more likely scenario that could render Kevin liable is if Lou failed to clean up some beer that a previous bowler had spilled, and Gary slips on the wet spot and is injured. In that case, Lou may be negligent, and Kevin may be vicariously liable.

Strict Liability

Strict liability involves acts committed by certain animals or harm resulting from certain ultrahazardous activities. Suppose Morris orders his pit bull terrier, Spike, to attack Dawson. Depending on whether Dawson is aware of the attack or is actually attacked, Morris could be liable for assault or battery, respectively.

However, if Morris carelessly leaves Spike unleashed on a public street and Spike attacks Dawson, Morris will probably be liable for negligence (because he did not intend for the dog to attack Dawson). But if Spike attacks Dawson and Morris was neither negligent nor intended for Spike to attack, Morris may still be liable under the theory of strict liability.

Had Spike been a lion instead of a dog, Morris would be strictly liable for the harm caused by a *wild animal*. Because Spike is a dog, thereby a *domestic animal*, Morris can only be strictly liable if Spike had known dangerous propensities, in other words, if Spike had attacked other people before and Morris knew about it.

Similarly, Morris could be strictly liable to Dawson if an electrical storm caused an explosion in Morris's laboratory, and radioactive waste spread onto Dawson's property. Recall that handling radioactive waste is a prime example of conducting an *ultrahazardous activity*.

Toxic Torts

As America becomes more environmentally conscious, much attention is paid not only to pollution of land, but of people as well. While various federal and state laws protected against hazardous environmental conditions in the workplace, near the end of the twentieth century increasing concerns arose about hazardous toxic waste dumping in bodies of water, and the dangers of breathing secondhand smoke.

Accordingly, many states have created laws specifically dealing with harm done to persons by some toxic substance. Certainly, such actions may be intentional. Most of the time, however, they are negligent or otherwise accidental. In fact, damages are usually awarded when the tortfeasor is strictly liable, based on the toxic substance being considered ultrahazardous.

Toxic torts involve injury to persons and property. We will revisit toxic torts when we discuss torts against property.

Products Liability

A tort against a person may not necessarily be caused by another person or an animal. It can be caused by a defective car, chair, or shoe. Suppose Renee is an ice-skater and she buys ice skates made by the Superskate Ice Skate Company. Superskate is thrilled that Renee is using its product, because Renee is destined to become a national ice-skating superstar. However, one ice skate is defective and causes Renee to experience various foot problems. As a result, Renee's career is delayed until her foot properly heals. Superskate certainly did not intend for the skates to harm Renee. Supposing that Superskate did not fail to use reasonable care in creating the product, the company would not be negligent for the harm, either. Nonetheless, Superskate may be strictly liable to Renee because the company's defective skates caused the harm to Renee's feet.

DEFENSES

For any of the most common types of torts against the person, there are times when all the elements are present, but the prospective tortfeasor may not be held liable because of a **defense**. Keep in mind that general rules of law often allow for exceptions, such as defenses. In Chapter 8 we will learn a lot more about defenses.

REVIEW QUESTIONS

1. What are the common elements of assault and battery?
2. What are the different elements of assault and battery?
3. Give an example of the difference between contact and harm.
4. Give an example in which intent is transferred from one tort to another.
5. Is false imprisonment a negligent tort? Explain.
6. Give an example in which there is infliction of emotional distress, but there is no physical harm.
7. What is recklessness?
8. Explain why a business owner may be liable for intentional harm done to a customer by one of the employees.
9. Give an example of a toxic tort.
10. Give an example in which a product manufacturer may be negligent for harm done to a person because of a defective product.

A TORT TALE

Some people refer to assault as "an attempted battery." Can you prove why this is not necessarily true? Suppose that George attempted to commit battery upon Carter. George did not succeed in his attempt, but Carter was made aware that George was about to commit an offensive touching upon him.

How can George, who attempted a battery, not have committed assault? Even if he did not commit assault, why can George be liable for assault in such a case?

CASE LAW

Before we move on to Chapter 4, take a look at some interesting cases regarding torts to the person. Keep in mind what we discussed about case law in Chapter 2. Read the cases slowly and carefully. Before you know it, you will get the hang of it.

3. NEGLIGENCE ☞ 136(18)—LIABILITY OF MANU-
FACTURERS—QUESTIONS FOR JURY.

Whether the character of an article manufactured is such that injury would probably result
from its use may be a question for the court or for
the jury.

[Ed. Note.—For other cases, see Negligence,
Cent. Dig. §§ 307, 308, 310, 312; Dec. Dig. ☞
136 (18).]

4. NEGLIGENCE ☞ 24—LIABILITY OF MANUFACTUR-
ERS—KNOWLEDGE OF DANGER.

In order to make the manufacturer liable for
defects in goods sold, he must have knowledge that
in the usual course of events the danger will be
shred by others than the buyer, although mere
knowledge alone is insufficient to create his liability.

Ed. Note.—For other cases, see Negligence,
Cent. Dig. § 24; Dec. Dig. ☞ 24.]

5. NEGLIGENCE ☞ 27—LIABILITY OF MANUFACTUR-
ERS—DUTY TO INSPECT.

The duty of a manufacturer to inspect his
goods so as to guard against injuries to persons
therefrom is independent of contract, and the
obligation arises at law.

[Ed. Note.—For other cases, see Negligence,
Cent. Dig. § 25; Dec. Dig. ☞ 27.]

6. NEGLIGENCE ☞ 27—LIABILITY OF MANUFACTUR-
ERS—DUTY TO INSPECT—DANGEROUS ARTICLES.

An automobile is such a dangerous article that
a manufacturer thereof is under duty carefully to
inspect in order to prevent injuries to persons arising from defects therein.

[Ed. Note.—For other cases, see Negligence,
Cent. Dig. § 25; Dec. Dig. ☞ 27.]

7. NEGLIGENCE ☞ 27—LIABILITY OF MANUFACTUR-
ERS—KOWLEDGE OF USE.

Where an automobile manufacturer knew that
the car which he sold would be used by persons
other than the buyer, and the ultimate buyer of the
car was injured when a wheel, made of defective
wood and defectively constructed, collapsed, the
manufacturer was liable for the injuries.

[Ed. Note.—For other cases, see Negligence,
Cent. Dig. § 25; Dec. Dig. ☞ 27.]

8. NEGLIGENCE ☞ 27—LIABILITY OF MANUFACTUR-
ERS—IMMINENCE OF DANGER.

The liability of a manufacturer for injuries
caused by a defectively constructed automobile, if
danger was to be reasonably expected therefrom,
attached regardless of whether the danger was inherent or only imminent, so that it was not error to
instruct that the automobile was not an inherently
dangerous machine.

[Ed. Note.—For other cases, see Negligence,
Cent. Dig. § 25; Dec. Dig. ☞ 27.]

9. NEGLIGENCE ☞ 27—LIABILITY OF MANUFACTUR-
ERS—DUTY TO INSPECT.

A manufacturer of automobiles is not absolved
from the duty of inspection because he bought the
wheels from a reputable manufacturer, but he is responsible for the finished product.

[Ed. Note.—:For other cases, see Negligence,
Cent. Dig. § 25; Dec. Dig. ☞ 27.]

10. NEGLIGENCE ☞ 27—LIABILITY OF MANUFACTUR-

ERS—CHARACTER OF DANGER—DUTY OF INSPEC-
TION.

The duty of a manufacturer to inspect goods
produced by him varies with the nature of the
thing to be inspected, and is higher where the article itself is dangerous and greater degree of caution is required.

[Ed. Note.—For other cases, see Negligence,
Cent. Dig. § 25; Dec. Dig. ☞ 27.]

Willard Bartlett, C. J., dissenting.

Appeal from Supreme Court, Appellate Division, Third Department.

Action by Donald C. MacPherson against the
Buick Motor Company. From a judgment of the
Appellate Division (160 App. Div. 55, 145 N. Y.
Supp. 462), affirming a judgment of the Supreme
Court for plaintiff, defendant appeals. Affirmed.

William Van Dyke, of Detroit, Mich., for appellant. Edgar T. Brackett, of Saratoga Springs, for respondent.

CARDOZO, J. The defendant is a manufacturer of automobiles. It sold an automobile to a retail
dealer. The retail dealer resold to the plaintiff.
While the Plaintiff was in the car it suddenly collapsed. He was thrown out and injured. One of the
wheels was made of defective wood, and its spokes
crumbled into fragments. The wheel was not made
by the defendant; it was bought from another manufacturer. There is evidence, however, that the defects could have been discovered by reasonable inspection, and that inspection was omitted. There is
no claim that the defendant knew of the defect
and willfully concealed it. The case, in other words,
is not brought within the rule of Kuelling v. Lean
Mfg. Co., 183 N. Y. 78, 75 N. E. 1098, 2 L. R. A. (N.
S.) 303, 111, Am. St. Rep. 691, 5 Ann. Cas. 124.
The charge is one, not of fraud, but of negligence.
The question to be determined is whether the defendant owed a duty of care and vigilance to any
one but the immediate purchaser.

The foundations of this branch of the law, at
least in this state, were laid in Thomas v. Winchester, 6 N. Y. 397, 57, Am. Dec. 455. A poison
was falsely labeled. The sale was made to a druggist, who is turn sold to a customer. The customer
recovered damages from the seller who affixed
the label. "The defendant's negligence," it was
said, "put human life in imminent danger." A poison, falsely labeled, is likely to injure any one who
gets it. Because the danger is to be foreseen,
there is a duty to avoid the injury. Cases were
cited by way of illustration in which manufactur-
ers were not subject to any duty irrespective of
contract. The distinction was said to be that their
conduct, though negligent, was not likely to result in injury to any one except the purchaser. We
are not required to say whether the chance of injury was always as remote as the distinction
assumes. Some of the illustrations might be rejected today. The principle of the distinction is,
for present purposes, the important thing.
Thomas v. Winchester became quickly a land-
mark of the law. In the application of its principle
there may, at times, have been uncertainty
or even error. There has never in this state been
doubt or disavowal of the principle itself. The
chief cases are well known, yet to recall some
of them will be helpful. Loop v. Litchfield, 42

☞ For other cases see same topic and KEY-NUMBER in all Key-Numbered Digests and Indexes

N. Y. 351, 1 Am. Rep. 513, is the earliest. It was the case of a defect in a small balance wheel used on a circular saw. The manufacturer pointed out the defect to the buyer, who wished a cheap article and was ready to assume the risk. The risk can hardly have been an imminent one, for the wheel lasted five years before it broke. In the meanwhile the buyer had made a lease of the machinery. It was held that the manufacturer was not answerable to the lessee. Loop v. Litchfield was followed in Losee v. Clute, 51 N. Y. 494, 10 Am. Rep. 638, the case of the explosion of a steam boiler. That decision has been criticized (Thompson on Negligence, 233; Shearman & Redfield on Negligence [6th Ed.] § 117); but it must be confined to its special facts. It was put upon the ground that the risk of injury was too remote. The buyer in that case had not only accepted the boiler, but had tested it. The manufacturer knew that his own test was not the final one. The finality of the test has a bearing on the measure of diligence owing to persons other than the purchaser. Beven, Negligence (3d Ed.) pp. 50, 51, 54; Wharton, Negligence (2d Ed.) § 134.

These early cases suggest a narrow construction of the rule. Later cases, however, evince a more liberal spirit. First in importance is Devlin v. Smith, 89 N. Y. 470, 42 Am. Rep. 311. The defendant, a contractor, built a scaffold for a painter. The painter's servants were injured. The contractor was held liable. He knew that the scaffold, if improperly constructed, was a most dangerous trap. He knew that it was to be used by the workmen. He was building it for that very purpose. Building it for their use, he owed them a duty, irrespective of his contract with their master, to build it with care.

From Devlin v. Smith we pass over intermediate cases and turn to the latest case in this court in which Thomas v. Winchester was followed. That case is Statler v. Ray Mfg. Co., 195 N. Y. 478, 480, SS N. E. 1063. The defendant manufactured a large coffee urn. It was installed in a restaurant. When heated, the urn exploded and injured the plaintiff. We held that the manufacturer was liable. We said that the urn "was of such a character inherently that, when applied to the purposes for which it was designed, it was liable to become a source of great danger to many people if not carefully and properly constructed."

It may be that Devlin v. Smith and Statler v. Ray Mfg. Co. have extended the rule of Thomas v. Winchester. If so, this court is committed to the extension. The defendant argues that things imminently dangerous to life are poisons, explosives, deadly weapons—things whose normal function it is to injure or destroy. But whatever the rule in Thomas v. Winchester may once have been, it has no longer that restricted meaning. A scaffold (Devlin v. Smith, supra) is not inherently a destructive instrument. It become destructive only if imperfectly construct-

ed. A large coffee urn (Statler v. Ray Mfg. Co., supra) may have within itself, if negligently made, the potency of danger, yet no one thinks of it as an implement whose normal function is destruction. What is true of the coffee urn is equally true of bottles of aerated water. Torgesen v. Schultz, 192 N. Y. 156, S4 N. E. 956, 18 L. R. A. (N. S.) 726, 127 Am. St. Rep. 894. We have mentioned only cases in this court. But the rule has received a like extension in our courts of intermediate appeal. In Burke v. Ireland, 26 App. Div. 487, 50 N. Y. Supp. 369, in an opinion by Cullen, J., it was applied to a builder who constructed a defective building; in Kahner v. Otis Elevator Co., 96 App. Div. 169, 89 N. Y. Supp 185, to the manufacturer of an elevator; in Davies v. Pelham Hod Elevating Co., 65 Hun, 573, 20 N. Y. Supp. 523, affirmed in this court without opinion, 146 N. Y. 363, 41 N. E. 88, to a contractor who furnished a defective rope with knowledge of the purpose for which the rope was to be used. We are not required at this time either to approve or to disapprove the application of the rule that was made in these cases. It is enough that they help to characterize the trend of judicial thought.

Devlin v. Smith was decided in 1882. A year later a very similar case came before the Court of Appeal in England (Heaven v. Pender, 11 Q. B. D. 503). We find in the opinion of Brett, M. R., afterwards Lord Esher, the same conception of a duty, irrespective of contract, imposed upon the manufacturer by the law itself:

"Whenever one person supplies goods or machinery, or the like, for the purpose of their being used by another person under such circumstances that every one of ordinary sense would, if he thought, recognize at once that unless he used ordinary care and skill with regard to the condition of the thing supplied, or the mode of supplying it, there will be danger of injury to the person or property of him for whose use the thing is supplied, and who is to use it, a duty arises to use ordinary care and skill as to the condition of manner of supplying such thing."

He then points out that for a neglect of such ordinary care or skill whereby injury happens, the appropriate remedy is an action for negligence. The right to enforce this liability is not to be confined to the immediate buyer. The right, he says, extends to the person or class of persons for whose use the thing is supplied. It is enough that the goods "would in all probability be used at once * * * before a reasonable opportunity for discovering any defect which might exist," and that the thing supplied is of such a nature "that a neglect of ordinary care or skill as to its condition or the manner of supplying it would probably cause danger to the person or property of the person for whose use it was supplied, and who was about to use it." On the other hand, he would exclude a case "in which the goods are supplied under circumstances in which it would be a chance by whom they would be used or whether they would be used or not, or whether they would be used before there would probably be means of observing any defect," or where the goods are of such a nature that "a want of care or skill as to their condition or the manner of supplying them would not probably produce danger of injury to person or property." What was said by Lord Esher in that case did not command the full assent of his associates. His opinion has been criticized "as requiring every man to take affirmative precautions to protect his neighbors as well as to refrain from injuring them." Bohlen, Affirmative Obligations in the Law of Torts, 44 Am. Law Reg. (N. S.) 341. It may not be an accurate exposition of the law of England. Perhaps it may need some qualification even in our own state. Like most attempts at comprehensive definition, it may involve errors of inclusion and of exclusion. But its tests and standards, at least in their underlying principles, with whatever qualification may be called for as they are applied to varying conditions, are the tests and standards of our law.

[1–4] We hold, then, that the principle of Thomas v. Winchester is not limited to poisons, explosives, and things of like nature, to things which in their normal operation are implements of destruction. If the nature of a thing is such that it is reasonably certain to place life and limb in peril when negligently made, it is then a thing of danger. Its nature gives warning of the consequences to be expected. If to the element of danger there is added knowledge that the thing will be used by persons other than the purchaser, and used without new tests, then, irrespective of contract, the manufacturer of this thing of danger is under a duty to make it carefully. That is as far as we are required to go for the decision of this case. There must be knowledge of a danger, not merely possible, but probable. It is possible to use almost anything in a way that will make it dangerous if defective. That is not enough to charge the manufacturer with a duty independent of his contract. Whether a given thing is dangerous may be sometimes a question for the jury. There must also be knowledge that in the usual course of events the danger will be shared by others than the buyer. Such knowledge may often be inferred from the nature of the transaction. But is possible that even knowledge of the danger and of the use will not always be enough. The proximity or remoteness of the relation is a factor to be considered. We are dealing now with the liability of the manufacturer of the finished product, who puts it on the market to be used without inspection by his customers. If he is negligent, where danger is to be foreseen, a liability will follow.

[5] We are not required, at this time, to say that it is legitimate to go back of the manufacturer of the finished product and hold the manufac-

turer of the component parts. To make their negligence a cause of imminent danger, as independent cause must often intervene; the manufacturer of the finished product must also fail in his duty of inspection. It may be that in those circumstances the negligence of the earlier members of the series is too remote to constitute, as to the ultimate user, an actionable wrong. Beven on Negligence (3d Ed.) 50, 51, 54; Wharton on Negligence (2d Ed.) § 134; Leeds v. N.Y. Tel. Co., 178 N. Y. 118, 70 N. E. 219; Sweet v. Perkins, 196 N. Y. 482, 90 N. E. 50; Hayes v. Hyde Park, 152 Mass. 514, 516, 27 N. E. 522, 12 L. R. A. 249. We leave that question open. We shall have to deal with it when it arises. The difficulty which it suggests is not present in this case. There is here no break in the chain of cause and effect. In such circumstances, the presence of a known danger, attendant upon a known use, makes vigilance a duty. We have put aside the notion that the duty to safeguard life and limb, when the consequences of negligence may be foreseen, grows out of contract and nothing else. We have put the source of the obligation where it ought to be. We have put its source in the law.

[6, 7] From this survey of the decisions, there thus emerges a definition of the duty of a manufacturer which enables us to measure this defendant's liability. Beyond all question, the nature of an automobile gives warning of probable danger if its construction is defective. This automobile was designed to go 50 miles an hour. Unless its wheels were sound and strong, injury was almost certain. It was as much a thing of danger as a defective engine for a railroad. The defendant knew the danger. It knew also that the car would be used by persons other than the buyer. This was apparent from its size; there were seats for three persons. It was apparent also from the fact that the buyer was a dealer in cars, who bought to resell. The maker of this car supplied it for the use of purchasers from the dealer just as plainly as the contractor in Devlin v. Smith supplied the scaffold for use by the servants of the owner. The dealer was indeed the one person of whom it might be said with some approach to certainty that by him the car would not be used. Yet the defendant would have us say that he was the one person whom it was under a legal duty to protect. The law does not lead us to so inconsequent a conclusion. Precedents drawn from the days of travel by stagecoach do not fit the conditions of travel today. The principle that the danger must be imminent does not change, but the things subject to the principle do change. They are whatever the needs of life in a developing civilization require them to be.

In reaching this conclusion, we do not ignore the decisions to the contrary in other jurisdictions. It was held in Cadillac Co. v. Johnson, 224 Fed. 804, 137 C. C. A. 279,

L. R. A. 1915E, 287, that an automobile is not within the rule of Thomas v. Winchester. There was, however, a vigorous dissent. Opposed to that decision is one of the Court of Appeals of Kentucky. Olds Motor Works v. Shaffer, 145 Ky. 616, 140 S. W. 1047, 37 L. R. A. (N. S.) 560, Ann. Cas. 1913B, 689. The earlier cases are summarized by Judge Sanborn in Huset v. J. I. Case Threshing Machine Co., 120 Fed. 865, 57 C. C. A. 237, 61 L. R. A. 303. Some of them, at first sight inconsistent with our conclusion, may be reconciled upon the ground that the negligence was too remote, and that another cause had intervened. But even when they cannot be reconciled; the difference is rather in the application of the principle than in the principle itself. Judge Sanborn says, for example, that the contractor who builds a bridge, or the manufacturer who builds a car, cannot ordinarily foresee injury to other persons than the owner as the probable result. 120 Fed. 865, at page 867, 57 C. C. A. 237, at page 239, 61 L. R. A. 303. We take a different view. We think that injury to others is to be foreseen not merely as a possible, but as an almost inevitable, result. See the trenchant criticism in Bohlen, supra, at page 351. Indeed, Judge Sanborn concedes that his view is not to be reconciled with our decision in Devlin v. Smith, supra. The doctrine of that decision has now become the settled law of this state, and we have no desire to depart from it.

In England the limits of the rule are still unsettled. Winterbottom v. Wright, 10 M. & W. 109, is often cited. The defendant undertook to provide a mail coach to carry the mail bags. The coach broke down from intent defects in its construction. The defendant, however, was not the manufacturer. The court held that he was not liable for injuries to a passenger. The case was decided on a demurrer to the declaration. Lord Esher points out in Heaven v. Pender, supra, at page 513, that the form of the declaration was subject to criticism. It did not fairly suggest the existence of a duty aside from the special contract which was the plaintiff's main reliance. See the criticism of Winterbottom v. Wright, in Bohlen, supra, at pages 281, 283. At all events, in Heaven v. Pender, supra, the defendant, a dock owner, who put up a staging outside a ship, was held liable to the servants of the shipowner. In Eliot v. Hall, 15 Q. B. D. 315, the defendant sent out a defective truck laden with goods which he had sold. The buyer's servants unloaded it, and were injured because of the defects. It was held that the defendant was under a duty "not to be guilty of negligence with regard to the state and condition of the truck." There seems to have been a return to the doctrine of Winterbottom v. Wright in Earl v. Lubbock, [1905] 1 K. B. 253. In that case, however, as in the earlier one, the defendant was not the manufacturer. He had merely made a contract to keep the van in repair. A later case (White v. Steadman, [1913] 3 K. B. 340, 348) emphasizes the element. A livery stable keeper who sent out a vicious horse was held liable, not merely to his customer, but also to another occupant of the carriage, and Thomas v. Winchester was cited and followed, White v. Steadman, supra, at pages 348, 349. It was again cited and followed in Dominion Natural Gas Co. v Collins, [1909] A. C. 640, 646. From these cases a consistent principle is with difficulty extracted. The English courts, however, agree with ours in holding that one who invites another to make use of an appliance is bound to the exercise of reasonable care. Caledonian Ry. Co. v. Mulholland, [1898] A. C. 216, 227; Inderman v. Dames, L. R. [1 C. P.] 274. That at bottom is the underlying principle of Devlin v. Smith. The contractor who builds the scaffold invites the owner's workmen to use it. The manufacturer who sells the automobile to the retail dealer invites the dealer's customers to use it. The invitation is addressed in the one case to determinate persons and in the other to an indeterminate class, but in each case it is equally plain, and in each its consequences must be the same.

There is nothing anomalous in a rule which imposes upon A., who has contracted with B., a duty to C. and D. and others according as he knows or does not know that the subject-matter of the contract is intended for their use. We may find an analogy in the law which measures the liability of landlords. If A. leases to B. a tumble-down house, he is not liable, in the absence of fraud, to B.'s guests who enter it and are injured. This is because B. is then under the duty to repair it, the lessor has the right to suppose that he will fulfill that duty, and, if he omits to do so, his guests must look to him. Bohlen, supra, at page 276. But if A. lenses a building to be used by the lessee at once as a place of public entertainment, the rule is different. There injury to persons other than the lessee is to be foreseen, and foresight of the consequences involves the creation of a duty. Junkermann v. Tilyou R. Co., 213 N. Y. 404, 108 N. E. 190, L. R. A. 1915F, 700, and cases there cited.

[8] In this view of the defendant's liability there is nothing inconsistent with the theory of liability on which the case was tried. It is true that the court told the jury that "an automobile is not an inherently dangerous vehicle." The meaning, however, is made plain by the context. The meaning is that danger is not to be expected when the vehicle is well constructed. The court left it to the jury to say whether the defendant ought to have foreseen that the car, if negligently constructed, would become "imminently dangerous." Subtle distinctions are drawn by the defendant between things

inherently dangerous and things imminently dangerous, but the case does not turn upon these verbal niceties. If danger was to be expected as reasonably certain, there was a duty of vigilance, and this whether you call the danger inherent or imminent. In varying forms that thought was put before the jury. We do not say that the court would not have been justified in ruling as a matter of law that the car was a dangerous thing. If there was any error, it was none of which the defendant can complain.

[9, 10] We think the defendant was not absolved from a duty of inspection because it bought the wheels from a reputable manufacturer. It was not merely a dealer in automobiles. It was a manufacturer of automobiles. It was responsible for the finished product. It was not at liberty to put the finished product on the market without subjecting the component parts to ordinary and simple tests. Richmond & Danville R. R. Co. v. Elliott, 149 U. S. 266, 272, 13 Sup. Ct. 837, 37 L. Ed. 728. Under the charge of the trial judge nothing more was required of it. The obligation to inspect must vary with the nature of the thing to be inspected. The more probable the danger the greater the need of caution.

There is little analogy between this case and Carlson v. Phœnix Bridge Co., 132 N. Y. 273, 30 N. E. 750, where the defendant bought a tool for a servant's use. The making of tools was not the business in which the master was engaged. Reliance on the skill of the manufacturer was proper and almost inevitable. But that is not the defendant's situation. Both by its relation to the work and by the nature of its business, it is charged with a stricter duty.

Other rulings complained of have been considered, but no error has been found in them.

The judgment should be affirmed, with costs.

WILLARD BARTLETT, C. J. (dissenting). The plaintiff was injured in consequence of the collapse of a wheel of an automobile manufactured by the defendant corporation which sold it to a firm of automobile dealers in Schenectady, who in turn sold the car to the plaintiff. The wheel was purchased by the Buick Motor Company, ready made, from the Imperial Wheel Company of Flint, Mich., a reputable manufacturer of automobile wheels which had furnished the defendant with 80,000 wheels, none of which had proved to be made of defective wood prior to the accident in the present case. The defendant relied upon the wheel manufacturer to make all necessary tests as to the strength of the material therein, and made no such test itself. The present suit is an action for negligence, brought by the subvendee of the motor car against the manufacturer as the original vendor. The

evidence warranted a finding by the jury that the wheel which collapsed was defective when it left the hands of the defendant. The automobile was being prudently operated at the time of the accident, and was moving at a speed of only eight miles an hour. There was no allegation or proof of any actual knowledge of the defect on the part of the defendant, or any suggestion that any element of fraud or deceit or misrepresentation entered into the sale.

The theory upon which the case was submitted to the jury by the learned judge who presided at the trial was that, although an automobile is not an inherently dangerous vehicle, it may become such if equipped with a weak wheel; and that if the motor car in question, when it was put upon the market was in itself inherently dangerous by reason of its being equipped with a weak wheel, the defendant was chargeable with a knowledge of the defect so far as it might be discovered by a reasonable inspection and the application of reasonable tests. This liability, it was further held, was not limited to the original vendee, but extended to a subvendee like the plaintiff, who was not a party to the original contract of sale.

I think that these rulings, which have been approved by the Appellate Division, extend the liability of the vendor of a manufactured article further than any case which has yet received the sanction of this court. It has heretofore been held in this state that the liability of the vendor of a manufactured article for negligence arising out of the existence of defects therein does not extend to strangers injured in consequence of such defects, but is confined to the immediate vendee. The exceptions to this general rule which have thus far been recognized in New York are cases in which the article sold was of such a character that danger to life or limb was involved in the ordinary use thereof; in other words, where the article sold was inherently dangerous. As has already been pointed out, the learned trial judge instructed the jury that an automobile is not an inherently dangerous vehicle.

The late Chief Justice Cooley of Michigan, one of the most learned and accurate of American law writers, states the general rule thus:

"The general rule is that a contractor, manufacturer, vendor or furnisher of an article is not liable to third parties who have no contractual relations with him, for negligence in the construction, manufacture, or sale of such article." 2 Cooley on Torts (3d Ed.), 1486.

The leading English authority in support of this rule, to which all the later cases on the same subject refer, is Winterbottom v. Wright, 10 Meeson & Welsby, 109, which was an action by the driver of a stagecoach against a contractor who had agreed with the postmaster general to provide and keep the vehicle in repair for the purpose of conveying the royal mail over a prescribed route. The coach broke down and upset, injuring the driver, who sought to recover against the contractor on account of its defective construction. The Court of Exchequer denied him any right of recovery on the ground that there was not privity of contract between the parties, the agreement having been made with the postmaster general alone.

"If the plaintiff can sue," said Lord Abinger, the Chief Baron, "every passenger or even any person passing along the road who was injured by the upsetting of the coach might being a similar action. Unless we confine the operation of such contracts as this to the parties who enter into them the most absurd and outrageous consequences, to which I can see no limit, would ensue."

The doctrine of that decision was recognized as the law of this state by the leading New York case of Thomas v. Winchester, 6 N. Y. 397, 408, 57 Am. Dec. 455, which, however, involved an exception to the general rule. There the defendant, who was a dealer in medicines, sold to a druggist a quantity of belladonna, which is a deadly poison, negligently labeled as extract of dandelion. The druggist in good faith used the poison in filling a prescription calling for the harmless dandelion extract, and the plaintiff for whom the prescription was put up with poisoned by the belladonna. This court held that the original vendor was liable for the injuries suffered by the patient. Chief Judge Ruggles, who delivered the opinion of the court, distinguished between an act of negligence imminently dangerous to the lives of others and one that is not so, saying:

"If A. build a wagon and sell it to B., who sells it to C. and C. hires it to D., who is consequence of the gross negligence of A. in building the wagon is overturned and injured. D. cannot recover damages against A. , the builder. A.'s obligation to build the wagon faithfully arises solely out of his contract with B. The public have nothing to do with it. * * * So., for the same reason, if a horse be defectively shod by a smith, and a person hiring the horse from the owner is thrown and injured in consequence of the smith's negligence in shoeing, the smith is not liable for the injury."

In Torgesen v. Schultz, 192 N. Y. 156, 159, 84 N. E. 956, 18 L. R. A. (N. S.) 726, 127 Am. St. Rep. 894, the defendant was the vendor of bottles of aerated water which was charged under high pressure and likely to explode unless used with precaution when exposed to sudden changes of temperature. The plaintiff, who was a servant of the purchaser, was injured by the explosion of one of these bottles. There was evidence tending to show that it had not been properly tested in order to insure users against such accidents. We held that the defendant corporation was liable notwithstanding the absence of any contract relation between it and the plaintiff—

"under the doctrine of Thomas v. Winchester, supra, and similar cases based upon the duty of the vendor of an article dangerous in its nature, or likely to become so in the course of the ordinary usage to be contemplated by the vendor, either to exercise due care to warn users of the danger or to take reasonable care to prevent the article sold from proving dangerous when subjected only to customary usage."

The character of the exception to the general rule limiting liability for negligence to the original parties to the contract of sale, was still more clearly stated by Judge Hiscock, writing for the court in Statler v. Ray Manufacturing Co., 195 N. Y. 478, 482, 88 N. E. 1063, where he said that:

"In the case of an article of inherently dangerous nature, a manufacturer may become liable for a negligent construction which, when added to the inherent character of the appliance, makes it imminently dangerous, and causes or contributes to a resulting injury not necessarily incident to the use of such an article if properly constructed, but naturally following from a defective construction."

In that case the injuries were inflicted by the explosion of a battery of steam-driven coffee urns, constituting an appliance liable to become dangerous in the course of ordinary usage.

The case of Devlin v. Smith, 89 N. Y. 470, 42 Am. Rep. 311, is cited as an authority in conflict with the view that the liability of the manufacturer and vendor extends to third parties only when the article manufactured and sold is inherently dangerous. In that case the builder of a scaffold 90 feet high, which was erected for the purpose of enabling painters to stand upon it, was held to be liable to the administratrix of a painter who fell therefrom and was killed, being at the time in the employ of the person for whom the scaffold was built. It is said that the scaffold, if properly constructed, was not inherently dangerous, and hence that this decision affirms the existence of liability in the case of an article not dangerous in itself, but made so only in consequence of negligent construction. Whatever logical force there may be in this view it seems to me clear from the language of Judge Rapallo, we wrote the opinion of the court that the scaffold was deemed to be an inherently dangerous structure, and that the case was decided as it was because the court entertained that view. Otherwise he would hardly have said, as he did, that the circumstances seemed to bring the case fairly within the principle of Thomas v. Winchester.

I do not see how we can uphold the judgment in the present case without overruling what has been so often said by this court and other courts of like authority in reference to the absence of any liability for negligence on the part of the original vendor of an ordinary carriage to any one except his immediate vendee. The absence of such liability was the very point actually decided in the English case of Winterbottom v. Wright, supra, and the illustration quoted from the opinion of Chief Judge Ruggles in Thomas v. Winchester, supra, assumes that the law on the subject was so plain that the statement would be accepted almost as a matter of course. In the case at bar the defective wheel on an automobile, moving only eight miles an hour, was not any more dangerous to the occupants of the car than a similarly defective wheel would be to the occupants of a carriage drawn by a horse at the same speed, and yet, unless the courts have been all wrong on this question up to the present time, there would be no liability to strangers to the original sale in the case of the horsedrawn carriage.

The rule upon which, in my judgment, the determination of this case depends, and the recognized exceptions thereto, were discussed by Circuit Judge Sanborn, of the United States Circuit Court of Appeals in the Eighth Circuit, in Huset v. J. I. Case Threshing Machine Co., 120 Fed. 865, 57 C. C. A. 237, 61 L. R. A. 303, in an opinion which reviews all the leading American and English decisions on the subject up to the time when it was rendered (1903). I have already discussed the leading New York cases, but as to the rest I feel that I can add nothing to the learning of that opinion or the cogency of its reasoning. It have examined the cases to which Judge Sanborn refers, but if I were to discuss them at length, I should be forced merely to paraphrase his language, as a study of the authorities he cites has led me to the same conclusion; and the repetition of what has already been so well said would contribute nothing to the advantage of the bench, the bar, or the individual litigants whose case is before us.

A few cases decided since his opinion was written, however, may be noticed. In Earl v. Lubbock, [1905] L. R. 1 K. B. Div. 253, the Court of Appeal in 1904 considered and approved the propositions of law laid down by the Court of Exchequer in Winterbottom v. Wright, supra, declaring that the decision in that case, since the year 1842, had stood the test of repeated discussion. The Master of the Rolls approved the principles laid down by Lord Abinger as based upon sound reasoning; and all the members of the court agreed that his decision was a controlling authority which must be followed. That the federal courts still adhere to the general rule, as I have stated it, appears by the decision of the Circuit Court of Appeal in the Second Circuit, in March, 1915, in the case of Cadillac Motor Car Co. v. Johnson, 221 Fed. 801, 137 C. C. A. 279, L. R. A. 1915E, 287. That case, like this, was an action by a subvendee against a manufacturer of automobiles for negligence in failing to discover that one of its wheels was defective, the court holding that such an action could not be maintained. It is true there was a dissenting opinion in that case, but it was based chiefly upon the proposition that rules applicable to stage coaches are archaic when applied to automobiles, and that if the law did not afford a remedy to strangers to the contract, the law should be changed. If this be true, the change should be effected by the Legislature and not by the courts. A perusal of the opinion in that case and in the Huset Case will disclose how uniformly the courts throughout this country have adhered to the rule and how consistently they

have refused to broaden the scope of the exceptions. I think we should adhere to it in the case at bar, and therefore I vote for a reversal of this judgment.

HISCOCK, CHASE, and CUDDEBACK, JJ., concur with CARDOZO, J., and HOGAN, J., concurs in result. WILLARD BARTLETT, C. J., reads dissenting opinion. POUND, J., not voting.

Judgment affirmed.

========

(217 N. Y. 424)
PEOPLE ex. rel. CARLISLE, State Highway Com'r, v. BOARD OF SUP'RS OF ONONDAGA COUNTY.

(Court of Appeals of New York. March 14, 1916.)

MANDAMUS 🔑 97—STATE AND COUNTY HIGHWAYS—LEVY OF MAINTENANCE EXPENSE—DUTY OF BOARD OF SUPERVISORS—STATUTE.

Under Highway Law (Consol. Laws. C. 25), § 172, as amended by Laws 1912, c. 83, providing that each town shall pay for the maintenance of state and county highways, that each year the highway commission shall transmit to the clerk of the board of supervisors of each county a statement specifying the number of miles of improved state and county highways in each town and the amount which each must pay for their maintenance, and that the board of supervisors shall cause the amount to be paid by each town to be assessed, levied, and collected as other town charges, it is the duty of a county board of supervisors, compellable by mandamus, to cause towns within the county to assess, levy, and collect taxes for the maintenance of state and county highways, after service upon them by the state commissioner of highways of a statement in writing specifying the number of miles of improved highways in each town and the proportionate amount which each must pay for their maintenance; section 134 of the Highway Law, as amended by Laws 1911, c. 646, having no relation to the duty of a board of supervisors to raise the expenses of maintaining a highway, merely according to the board, before acceptance of a highway by the state, an opportunity to protest against the acceptance of the highway when it has not been properly completed, giving the board the opportunity to be heard upon its protest, and making it the duty of the board to maintain the highway after acceptance.

[Ed. Note.—For other cases, see Mandamus, Cent. Dig. § 203; Dec. Dig. 🔑 97.]

Appeal from Supreme Court, Appellate Division, Fourth Department.

Mandamus by the People on the relation of John N. Carlisle, as State Commissioner of Highways, against the Board of Supervisors of Onondaga County. From an order of the Appellate Division (164 App. Div. 922, 149 N. Y. Supp. 1103), affirming an order granting a motion for a peremptory writ, defendant appeals. Affirmed.

which are sufficient to jolt vehicles passing over them. The severity of the jolt would depend, of course, largely upon the speed at which the vehicle is moving at the time it passes over. There is no duty resting upon a railway company to keep the surface of the road, at the crossing, so smooth and free from all inequalities that no jar or jolt will be caused by vehicles passing over the crossing. We think the evidence as to the condition of the crossing does not establish such inequality in the surface of the crossing as to interfere with the safe use of the crossing when used in the usual and ordinary way. If this is not so, then the railroad company, in the maintenance of crossings, owes a higher duty in respect to crossings, than any one ever dreamed was due the public in the maintenance of public highways."

In the case of Gable v. Kriege, 221 Iowa 852, 860, 267 N.W. 86, 90, 105 A.L.R. 539, we stated: "A hole or depression of the extent that plaintiffs' testimony shows, 3 or 4 inches deep at its deepest point and not abrupt but cupped out by travel, would not render a highway unsafe for travel in the ordinary and reasonable manner of traveling thereon."

[4] Applying the foregoing pronouncements to the facts herein, it would appear that, under our holding in the Peterson case, supra, the fact that the holes complained of had a 2-inch drop around the edge would not render them so dangerous to vehicular travel as to constitute actionable negligence. And, under our holding in the Gable case, supra, the fact that the maximum depth of the larger hole was 4 inches would not support a claim of actionable negligence on the part of the city. Many other cases are cited but none of them is as analogous as the Peterson and Gable cases and none of them appear to minimize the effect of either as a precedent of this court. Both were correctly decided and persuade us that the ruling of the trial court herein was correct because actionable negligence on the part of the city had not been established. Such conclusion on our part renders it unnecessary to discuss or decide the other assignments of error presented by appellant.

The judgment is affirmed.

All the Justices concur but HALE, J., not sitting.

BLAKELEY v. SHORTAL'S ESTATE et al.

No. 46690.

Supreme Court of Iowa.

Oct. 16, 1945.

1. Abatement and revival ⊙50

The statute on survival of actions, although in derogation of the common law, is liberally construed. Code 1939, §§ 64, 10957.

2. Action ⊙1

A "cause of action" for damages is not damage suffered by plaintiff or the mere evidentiary facts showing defendant's wrong, but is the wrong itself done by defendant to plaintiff, the breach of duty by defendant to plaintiff, whether it be a duty arising out of contract or tort.

See Words and Phrases, Permanent Edition, for all other definitions of "Cause of Action".

3. Abatement and revival ⊙52

Where decedent, in his lifetime, willfully sets in motion a cause that after his death proximately operates to damage of plaintiff to whom he owes a duty, his estate should not be permitted to escape liability, and, for purpose of survival statute, cause of action arises before, and survives, decedent's death, the damage relating back to the willful act of decedent. Code 1939, § 10957.

4. Damages ⊙52

The rule denying liability for injuries resulting from fright where no physical injury is shown cannot be invoked where fright was due to a willful act.

5. Damages ⊙208(6)

Evidence that decedent committed suicide in plaintiff's kitchen, causing his body to fall where plaintiff would come upon it when she returned home, raised a jury question as to whether decedent's act was willful so as to authorize a recovery by plaintiff from decedent's estate for shock occasioned when she discovered body notwithstanding that there was no physical injury.

6. Damages ⊙52

The term "willful act", within meaning of exception in the case of fright due to a willful act to the rule denying liability for injuries resulting from fright caused

BLAKELEY v. SHORTAL'S ESTATE   Iowa   29
Cite as 20 N.W.2d 28

by negligence where no physical injury is shown, contemplates a voluntary or intentional act.

> See Words and Phrases, Permanent Edition, for all other definitions of "Willful Act".

7. Torts ☞4

A willful wrong may be committed without any intention to injure any one.

8. Negligence ☞11

To constitute a "willful injury", the act which produced it must have been intentional or it must have been done under such circumstances as evinced a reckless disregard for the safety of others and a willingness to inflict the injury complained of.

> See Words and Phrases, Permanent Edition, for all other definitions of "Willful Injury".

9. Damages ☞52

The right to recover damages for fright or shock as the result of a willful act by defendant without physical injury to plaintiff depends on facts of each case.

10. Coroners ☞22

Where coroner made an investigation of a violent death which formed basis of litigation but no coroner's jury was called and no inquest was had and coroner made and filed a report pursuant to statute, such report was not admissible as bearing on cause of death. Code 1939, § 5214.

Appeal from District Court, Jefferson County; Harold V. Levis, Judge.

Action based upon a claim against an estate for damages arising from shock to claimant caused by suicide of decedent in claimant's home. Directed verdict for estate.

Reversed and remanded.

Ralph H. Munro, of Fairfield, for appellant.

Richard C. Leggett, of Fairfield, for appellees.

MANTZ, Justice.

This action is based upon a claim in probate filed by Ella Blakeley against the estate of Martin Shortal, deceased, wherein damages are claimed for a shock which claimant alleges she suffered when she attempted to enter her home and found therein Martin Shortal, a neighbor, lying on the kitchen floor with blood on the floor and other parts of the room. Her claim is that Shortal by his own wilful act suicided in the kitchen of her home and that when she saw the body and the blood she suffered a physical shock to her nerves and that this condition has continued since that time.

The administrators of the Shortal estate denied the claim generally, admitted the finding of the body in claimant's kitchen, but specifically denied that claimant suffered any injury or damage because of the finding of the body.

When claimant rested, upon motion of the administrators of the estate, the jury, by direction of the court, returned a verdict for such defendants. Claimant appealed.

I. There is little dispute in the essential facts. For about four years claimant and her husband had lived close neighbors on adjoining farms in Jefferson County, Iowa, to Martin Shortal and wife. About September, 1943, Shortal and his wife separated, the latter securing a divorce. Shortal had a sale about March 1st, following, and the property was divided. Claimant and her family remained on good terms with Shortal. Shortal was 50 years of age. On March 3, 1944, at about 6 p.m. Shortal came to the Blakely home. It was raining hard, Shortal was soaking wet, and his clothes were muddy. He wanted to stay all night. Some of his wet and muddy clothing was removed and hung up to dry and he was provided with a bed. In the morning he ate breakfast and remained in the house visiting with claimant and her husband. He asked for a pencil and some paper to do some figuring, saying that he thought in the division of his property he had been beaten out of some money. About noon claimant and her husband went to town to trade leaving Shortal sitting at the table figuring. They came home about 4 p.m. that day and claimant started to enter the kitchen of the home. She pushed the door partly open and there saw Shortal lying on the floor with pools of blood about him. When claimant saw the body and the blood she exclaimed, "Oh, my God, Martin has killed hisself!" She started falling but her husband behind her prevented her fall. They at once drove to a neighbor's and called the sheriff and coroner. These officials came an hour or so later and upon entering the house found Martin Shortal lying on the floor of the kitchen. He was then dead. His throat had been cut and there was a considerable quantity of blood on the floor and about the room. By his side was a skinning knife which belonged to claimant's son. It had blood on it. When claimant left for town this knife was in a holder hanging on the kitchen wall.

Claimant was then taken to a physician who pronounced her condition as one of shock to the nerves caused by her discovery of the body. Since that time she finds difficulty in sleeping, is nervous and restless. She did not return to the home for some time.

Appellees' motion for a directed verdict in essence is that claimant's evidence failed to sustain the allegation of her claim; that if Shortal did commit suicide the evidence failed to show that such act was wilful from which a shock could have been suffered and was to be reasonably anticipated as a natural consequence of such act; and that as a whole the evidence failed to show a situation wherein the jury could find damages for the claimant.

The court in ruling on the motion, stated in part: "The nub of that proposition is the query whether or not a cause of action has been alleged and proven. The court is inclined to believe that there has been no cause of action alleged or proven. * * * It appears to the court that no cause of action existed at the time of the death of this wrong-doer, and therefore, no cause of action to survive. It is a general rule that a cause of action for tort does not arise, or is not complete, until there is an injury. The mere fact that Martin Shortal committed suicide in the home of this claimant was not the cause of action claimed in this case, but it was the injury to the claimant which she claims thereafter resulted. * * * Therefore, the cause of action did not come into existence until after, as she claims, she saw the body and suffered as a result of shock therefrom. The cause of action therefore was not complete until after the death of Martin Shortal. If it had existed before his death, it would have survived. The court feels that there was no cause of action in existence at his death, therefore there could be no survival thereof."

II. The correctness of the court's holding that no cause of action was in existence at the time of Shortal's death, and therefore there could be no survival thereof, is challenged by this appeal. We hold that the court erred in such ruling.

The ruling involves an interpretation of sections 10957 and 10959 of the Code of 1939, which provide as follows:

"10957. Actions survive. All causes of action shall survive and may be brought notwithstanding the death of the person entitled or liable to the same."

"10959. Actions by or against legal representatives—substitution. Any action contemplated in sections 10957 and 10958 may be brought, or the court, on motion, may allow the action to be continued, by or against the legal representatives or successors in interest of the deceased. Such action shall be deemed a continuing one, and to have accrued to such representative or successor at the time it would have accrued to the deceased if he had survived. If such is continued against the legal representative of the defendant, a notice shall be served on him as in case of original notices."

[1] Our statute on survival of actions, section 10957, provides: "All causes of action shall survive * * *."

This statute, although in derogation of the common law, should be liberally construed. Wood v. Wood, 136 Iowa 128, 113 N.W. 492, 12 L.R.A., N.S., 891, 125 Am.St. Rep. 223; section 64, Iowa Code, 1939; 1 C.J.S., Abatement and Revival, § 133, p. 181.

[2] The term, cause of action, has sometimes been held to mean: "the act on the part of the defendant which gives the plaintiff his cause of complaint." Williamson v. Chicago, R. I. & P. Co., 84 Iowa 583, 588, 51 N.W. 60, 62. See also, 1 C.J.S., Actions, § 8, at p. 985 et seq.

This court has said: "In an action to recover damages the cause of action is not on the one hand the damage suffered by plaintiff, nor on the other hand the mere evidentiary facts showing defendant's wrong. But it is the wrong itself done by defendant to plaintiff, that is the breach of duty by the defendant to the plaintiff, whether it be a duty arising out of contract or of tort." Cahill v. Illinois Cent. R. Co., 137 Iowa 577, 580, 115 N.W. 216, 217, citing cases.

[3] If Martin Shortal wilfully set in motion a cause that after his death proximately operated to the damage of plaintiff to whom he owed a duty, his estate should not be permitted to escape liability. For the purpose of the survival statute the cause of action arose before, and survived his

death. The damage, when it happened, related back to the wilful act of the decedent.

[4] III. This brings us to the question whether a cause of action was pleaded or proven because of the fact that the injury and damages were due to fright in the absence of other physical injury. The rule in such cases is well stated in Holdorf v. Holdorf, 185 Iowa 838, 169 N.W. 737, 738, as follows: "It is, however, contended by counsel for appellee that no physical injury was inflicted upon plaintiff, and that, if she suffered damages, it was due to fright alone, for which no recovery can be had. The authorities are not in harmony upon this point, and it has often been held that no recovery will be permitted for damages resulting solely from fright caused by the negligence of another, in the absence of some physical injury. * * * The rule, however, denying liability for injuries resulting from fright caused by negligence, where no physical injury is shown, cannot be invoked where it *is* shown that the fright was due to a willful act." (Italics supplied.)

To the same effect see Watson v. Dilts, 116 Iowa 249, 89 N.W. 1068, 57 L.R.A. 559, 93 Am.St.Rep. 239; Watson v. Dilts, 124 Iowa 344, 100 N.W. 50.

[5] Hence, our decision rests upon whether or not the court was warranted in holding as a matter of law that the evidence failed to show that Shortal's act was wilful. We hold that the facts presented a jury question on this issue.

[6] In State v. Meek, 148 Iowa 671, 127 N.W. 1023, 1024, 31 L.R.A., N.S., 566, Ann. Cas.1912C 1075, this court in discussing the term, speaking through Weaver, J., said: "The word 'willful,' like most other words in our language, is of somewhat varied signification according to its context and the nature of the subject under discussion or treatment. Frequently it is used as nearly or quite synonymous with 'voluntary' or 'intentional,' * * *."

[7, 8] A wilful wrong may be committed without any intention to injure anyone. A good statement of the rule is contained in Southern Ry. Co. v. McNeeley, Ind.App., 88 N.E. 710, at page 712: "The authorities, from the earliest years of the common law, recognize the rule that there may be a willful wrong without a direct design to do harm. This principle has been applied to furious driving; to collisions between vessels; to the taking of unruly animals into crowds; to carelessly laying out poison for rats; to want of caution toward drunken persons; and to the careless casting of logs and the like upon highways. * * * To constitute a willful injury the act which produced it must have been intentional, or it must have been done under such circumstances as evinced a reckless disregard for the safety of others, and a willingness to inflict the injury complained of."

In the case of Watson v. Dilts, supra, at page 253 of 116 Iowa, at page 1069 of 89 N.W., 57 L.R.A. 559, 93 Am.St.Rep. 239, we held: "It is undoubtedly true that the door should not be thrown wide open for trumped-up claims on account of injuries resulting from fright, and we do not intend to so open it in this case. Each case must, of necessity, depend on its own facts."

[9] We adhere to the foregoing pronouncement. Each case must of necessity depend on its own facts. The application of the rule herein is limited strictly to the facts presented by the record. There is in the record ample evidence to show that in committing the act of suicide Shortal was a wilful wrongdoer, that he failed to act properly in the premises, and that when claimant sought to reenter her home, the gory and ghastly sight confronting her caused a shock and that such shock was the natural, though not the necessary or inevitable, result of his wrongful act. We hold that it was for the jury to determine whether or not Shortal's act was wilful. If they should so determine, then, under the rule announced in Holdorf v. Holdorf, supra, recovery could be had notwithstanding the fact that plaintiff's injury was caused by fright.

[10] IV. Did the court err in sustaining appellees' objection to the report of the coroner? Following the death of Shortal the coroner came and made an investigation. No coroner's jury was called and no inquest was had. The coroner made and filed a report pursuant to Section 5214 of the Code. The coroner as a witness was not permitted to state his conclusions as to what had transpired in claimant's home. His report was offered and upon objection was rejected as evidence. This ruling of the court is urged as error. Without setting out the cases cited by the parties, we think the ruling of the court was correct. In Wilkinson v. National Life Assn., 203 Iowa 960, 211 N.W. 238, this court reviewed vari-

ous cases in which there was an issue as to the admissibility of the coroner's report Morling, J., made a rather comprehensive analysis of such cases. The court held that such report was not admissible as bearing on the cause of death—whether suicide or otherwise. The holding of that case was followed in the case of Morton v. Equitable Life Ins. Co., 218 Iowa 846, 254 N.W. 325, 96 A.L.R. 315. We find no error here.

We hold that the trial court erred in sustaining appellees' motion for a directed verdict and for that reason the case is reversed.

Reversed and remanded.

All Justices concur, except HALE, J., not sitting.

In re PARISH'S ESTATE.

PAULSEN v. PARISH et al.

No. 46704.

Supreme Court of Iowa.

Oct. 16, 1945.

1. Husband and wife ⟳34

Conflicting evidence as to time of execution of document designated as an antenuptial contract sustained finding that document was executed by parties prior to marriage ceremony, and that document was a binding and valid antenuptial contract.

2. Husband and wife ⟳34

Antenuptial contracts are in the same category as other contracts, are controlled by same rules, and are established by preponderance of evidence.

3. Husband and wife ⟳31(2)

Antenuptial contracts have for their purpose the protection of interest of children by former marriages and the fixing of interests of respective parties in property of other.

4. Husband and wife ⟳31(3)

Antenuptial contracts are looked upon with favor by the law and are to be liberally construed to carry out intention of parties.

5. Husband and wife ⟳29(9)

Where an antenuptial contract is not unfair, inequitable, or unconscionable on its face, and not obtained by fraud, overreaching, or deceit, it should stand.

6. Husband and wife ⟳34

The validity of an antenuptial contract is to be determined from contract and any facts in evidence, burden to show invalidity being on party asserting such invalidity.

7. Husband and wife ⟳34

Where an antenuptial contract is apparently unjust and unreasonable, burden is cast upon those claiming under husband to show that contract was fairly procured.

8. Husband and wife ⟳29(4)

The subsequent marriage of the parties to an antenuptial contract is sufficient consideration.

9. Husband and wife ⟳31(2)

In construing antenuptial agreements, there is to be considered intention of contracting parties, their status as regards age, former marriage, children, property of contracting parties, and their intentions in entering into such agreement.

10. Husband and wife ⟳34

Where widow admitted signing document, designated by its terms an antenuptial contract, and contract on its face was not unjust or unreasonable, widow had burden of showing its invalidity.

11. Fraud ⟳50

Fraud is never presumed.

12. Husband and wife ⟳29(9)

Construction of antenuptial contract by taking contract by its four corners, examining its provisions, considering evidence as to its execution, intention of its makers, their relationships, their then status, their ages and family background, and provisions for wife required conclusion that contract was valid, as against claim of fraud and concealment of husband's assets.

13. Contracts ⟳143

The court cannot make another contract for the parties.

Appeal from District Court, Black Hawk County; R. W. Hasner, Judge.

Application in probate by widow for the admeasurement and setting off of her dis-

4 Torts against Property: Intentional, Negligent, and Without Fault

Because torts are most commonly associated with personal injury, torts against property are often overlooked. However, as we discussed earlier, tort law is one of the core areas of law and is multifaceted.

In this chapter, we discuss torts against property, both personal property and real property. Personal property is just about everything we own: a car, a notebook, a coat, a watch, and so on. Real property includes a home, a store, or a plot of land. Let's begin by discussing torts against personal property.

Torts against Personal Property

Trespass to Chattel

Here we deal with two new words common to tort law: trespass and chattel.

Generally, to trespass is to unlawfully interfere with another's person or property. In other words, any time someone intrudes upon another's body, home, car, or briefcase without authorization, that is generally trespass. Many outside the legal community think trespass only occurs when a person enters another person's land without authorization. Visions of "No Trespassing" signs come to mind. While this is one form of trespass, it is not the only form. Trespass involves interference with a person's body and personal space, as well as with real or personal property.

Often, when students first hear the word *chattel,* they think of the word *cattle.* Interestingly, all cattle is chattel, but not all chattel is cattle. **Chattel is personal property** (as opposed to real property). Your pen, your watch, your hairbrush, your gold ring, your computer, your desk, and your calculator are all chattel. So why is all cattle chattel? Because *cattle* are animals used for grazing, producing milk, and so on *that are owned by humans* (as opposed to such animals in the wilderness). In tort law, *domesticated* animals are generally considered property. Although all animals, whether human or not, are living things, non-human domesticated animals (e.g., cats, dogs, elephants, fish, giraffes) are typically thought of as property items. Therefore, if Jackie's pet kitten is run over by a car, the driver would probably be liable to Jackie in the same manner as if he had run over her radio. Accordingly, cattle, like other animals, are chattel. But chattel generally involves not only animals; it also includes any other type of personal property.

Now that we have identified trespass and chattel, let's identify the tort of trespass to chattel: **Trespass to chattel is intentional interference with another's use or possession of chattel.**

You are driving around in your Porsche sportscar on a Saturday afternoon. Becoming thirsty, you decide to stop at a local convenience store to buy a soda. Because you're only running into the store for a minute, you leave the doors unlocked and leave the key in the ignition with the motor running. As soon as you enter the store, several teenagers jump inside your car and decide to take it for a joyride. Their intention is not to steal the car, merely to drive around town with it for awhile. If they are caught by the police, they can be criminally punished; they can even go to jail. Additionally, you can sue them, in tort, for trespass to chattel. They have intentionally interfered with your use and possession of your car.

In another example, suppose that you bring this textbook to class. Another student, Regina, has lost her own copy of the book. There is a test coming up next week and Regina needs the book as a study guide. She doesn't feel like buying another book, so Regina decides to take yours instead. When you are not looking, she slips the book into her bag and eventually takes it home. This, too, is trespass to chattel.

Suppose that Regina did not lose her book. Instead, she already packed it in her bag near the end of class. Mistakenly, she packed your book in her bag too, thinking it was hers (an easy mistake to make because the books look exactly alike). If Regina leaves with your book, is this trespass to chattel? No, because trespass to chattel requires **intent,** and in this case, Regina *accidentally* took your book.

Returning to our first scenario, in which Regina intentionally took your book, what if she decided to keep it beyond the test date—for the rest of the semester, or permanently? Such an act is a classic example of the next tort, conversion.

Conversion

It is often the case that a word in the English language has many meanings. One meaning may be of a *general* nature, whereas another is particularly linked to a specific area, such as the law. *Conversion* is one of those words. Generally, to convert means to change from one form to another, such as a *convertible* car that *converts* from closed-roof to open-roof mode and vice versa. In torts, **conversion is intentional substantial interference with another's use or possession of chattel.** Note that the definitions of *trespass to chattel* and *conversion* are almost identical, except that conversion requires **substantial** interference. In other words, conversion starts out as a trespass to chattel, but if the interference becomes substantial, the act becomes conversion.

What exactly, then, is "substantial?" Using the earlier example, if Regina were to keep your book for a long period of time, such as until the end of the semester, it would *substantially* interfere with your ability to use and enjoy it. You would not have a study guide for the rest of the semester. You'd probably have to buy another book. Therefore, such substantial interference would probably amount to conversion.

However, had Regina taken the book for, say, 15 minutes, the act would probably be trespass to chattel, not conversion.

Substantial interference, then, may be determined by *duration*. But it may also be determined by *degree* of interference. Suppose Elaine and Lisa are roommates and basically wear the same size in clothing. Lisa wants to borrow Elaine's black mink coat to wear to a formal banquet. Without telling Elaine, Lisa takes Elaine's coat from the closet and gets ready for the banquet. Lisa makes a change to the coat: She dyes it neon pink. Needless to say, Elaine and Lisa have different taste in clothing. After the dance, Elaine returns the coat to Lisa. At the point when Elaine borrowed the coat without permission, she probably committed trespass to chattel. Once she dyed the coat neon pink, she committed conversion. Although Lisa only had the coat for a few hours, the harm she did to it was so substantial, and probably irreversible, that it would probably amount to conversion.

For further information about what constitutes *substantial* harm regarding conversion, read some case law on the topic.

COMMERCIAL PROPERTY INTERESTS

Some torts, such as **slander of title or disparagement,** that interfere with a person's ability to conduct business are often referred to as torts against property. Insofar as they closely deal with reputation and other civil rights, we discuss them in Chapters 5 and 7.

TORTS AGAINST REAL PROPERTY

Now that we have examined torts against personal property, let's take a look at some torts against real property.

Trespass to Land

Trespass to land is intentionally entering or wrongfully remaining on another person's land. Let's talk about this definition, because there may be more to it than meets the eye.

Suppose you are walking past a building complex on a hot summer night. You notice that the complex swimming pool is filled with water, but there is nobody around. You climb over the fence and hop in the pool for a swim. A classic example of trespass, right? Yes, but what about the next example?

You go to Florida for a winter vacation. You rent a bungalow near the beach. There are 100 identical bungalows, each with a different number. Your bungalow is number 224. Mistakenly, you enter bungalow 242, which was rented by Mr. and Mrs. Smith. The Smiths have gone to the beach and have left their bungalow door open. Thinking that 242 is your bungalow, you settle in to the Smith's bungalow. Tired from your trip, you do not bother to unpack, but simply lie down on the bed and take a nap. Are you trespassing? Yes.

Remember, the definition of trespass to land is *intentionally entering* or *wrongfully remaining* on another person's land. Here, you have *intentionally* entered another person's land and wrongfully remained there. You are wrongfully in bungalow 242, which belongs to the owner, who has granted the Smiths the right to possess it. Although you mistakenly thought it was your bungalow, you nonetheless entered it intentionally. Nobody picked you up and threw you inside the bungalow. You entered it of your own volition.

Mistake, then, does not excuse trespass. Practically speaking, of course, mistake can often defuse a potential lawsuit. Most actions for trespass involve the type we talked about in the earlier example of the swimming pool. In any event, mistaken trespass to land is nonetheless trespass to land. Note that *intent* is treated differently with this tort than with the other intentional torts we have discussed.

Above and Below Ground

Trespass is not limited to land on the ground level. It can involve entry above or below ground. For instance, suppose that Barry and Dwight are next-door neighbors with joining backyards. If Barry's tree branches grow and extend into Dwight's yard above the ground, this is, generally, trespass. The same holds true if the tree's roots extend into Dwight's yard below the ground. Of course, Dwight would not be likely to sue unless he suffered some type of damage, for instance, if the tree branches interfered with the sitting area on his patio or if the underground roots damaged his water pipes.

Negligent Torts against Real Property

Torts against personal or real property generally require intent. Accordingly, there is no negligent trespass or conversion. In any event, possessors of real property owe a duty of reasonable care to various individuals who enter their land. Let's discuss some torts—not necessarily against property, but committed on property—that typically require negligence.

Duty to Licensees and Invitees

First, let's define *licensee* and *invitee*. **A licensee is a person who is on the land for a nonbusiness purpose, with the possessor's consent. An invitee is a person who is on the land to conduct business.** Examples of licensees include family, friends, and neighbors. Examples of invitees include clients, shoppers, and students.

Hint: Here's an easy way to remember the difference between *licensee* and *invitee*. Licensee starts with an L, as in Love. If you invite someone you love into your home, that person is a licensee (a social guest, not a business guest). Invitee starts with an I, as in Investment. When you go to the bank to make a deposit, or to shop at the mall, or to look at a house or apartment to buy or rent, you are considering an investment. You are an invitee (a business guest, not a social guest) in that bank, shopping mall, or home.

Licensee = love, Invitee = investment. Practice it, and you'll always know the difference between the two.

Obviously, you don't "love" all licensees, nor is there an "investment" connected with all invitees, but you get the idea. Now that you know the difference between a licensee and an invitee, let's take a look at the duties owed to each by the possessor of the land.

Duty to Licensee

Generally, a possessor of land has the duty to warn a licensee against any known dangerous conditions. For example, suppose that Suzanne invites her friend, Joanne, to stay at Suzanne's house for a weekend. Suzanne's house is a large, two-story colonial, but only has one bathroom, which is on the first floor. Joanne is staying in the guest room, on the second floor. The stairway has a wobbly third step that can be dangerous. Usually, Suzanne steps over it or steps along its edge. However, Suzanne forgot to warn Joanne about the dangerous step. Joanne wanted to use the bathroom and started to walk down the stairs. As her foot touched the third step, it went through the step.

Joanne fell through the staircase and sustained several injuries. If Joanne sues Suzanne for her injuries, she will probably recover damages, based on Suzanne's breach of duty to her (a licensee). The wobbly step was a dangerous condition known to Suzanne, but she failed to warn Joanne about it.

On the other hand, suppose Suzanne had no idea that the step was defective. Suppose that, due to moisture, the step had become weak, but Suzanne never realized it. In that case, Suzanne would not have breached a duty, because she was required to warn Joanne (a licensee) only about *known* dangerous conditions.

Note: As we discussed earlier, as the owner of the house Suzanne may be vicariously liable to Joanne. Ultimately, this means Joanne may be able to recover damages for her injury even though Suzanne may not have been negligent. As with every tort, keep in mind the concepts of intent, negligence, and liability without fault.

Duty to Invitee

Unlike a licensee, an invitee is on the land for a business purpose. That person is afforded an even higher degree of care under tort law. The possessor of land not only has a duty to warn the invitee of known hidden dangers, but also to make a reasonable inspection for hidden dangers.

In the example in which Joanne was a licensee, Suzanne would not be liable for Joanne's injury if Suzanne had not known about the wobbly step. However if Joanne had *rented* a room from Suzanne, Joanne would be an invitee, not a licensee. In that case, Suzanne would owe Joanne a duty to make a reasonable inspection of the property in order to detect any hidden dangers. If Suzanne failed to make such inspection, and if such inspection would have exposed the wobbly step, then Suzanne would probably be held liable for Joanne's injury.

Duty to Trespasser

Did you ever think that a possessor of land actually owes a duty to a *trespasser*? Well, believe it! However, the duty is neither absolute nor is it owed to every type of trespasser. Let's take a closer look.

The duty is owed only to *known* trespassers, and only when the dangerous condition is *known* to the possessor. A known trespasser is someone who trespasses on the land with the possessor's knowledge. Consider the following example: Marvin walks to the park in order to play basketball. When he gets there, Marvin notices that all of the baskets are taken. In fact, there is a basketball tournament that day, so the baskets will be taken for the entire afternoon. Disappointed, Marvin starts to walk home, dribbling his basketball as he walks.

Marvin walks past Al's house. He notices a beautiful tiled basketball court with a fiberglass backboard in Al's yard. It appears that nobody is home, so Marvin happily runs onto the court and begins shooting baskets. Within a few minutes, Marvin slips on a loose tile and falls to the ground face first, breaking his nose. In this case, Marvin is an *unknown trespasser*. Al has no reason to know that Marvin would have trespassed onto his property, and therefore owes him no duty of care.

What if, instead, Marvin was a *known* trespasser? What if Marvin routinely entered Al's yard and began playing basketball? What if Al was aware of this and sometimes tolerated it quietly, and other times asked Marvin to leave? In that case, Marvin would be a known trespasser. He would not quite be a licensee, since Al did not want him there. In all likelihood, Al merely tolerated Marvin's presence because he didn't want to cause a confrontation that could escalate the matter. Therefore, assuming the facts of the previous example, when Marvin was hurt, would Al owe Marvin a duty in that case?

First, Al would not owe Marvin a duty if Al was not aware of the loose tile. Generally, Al would not have a duty to anyone other than to an invitee to make a reasonable inspection for hidden dangers.

Second, suppose Al *did* know about the loose tile. The courts are mixed in their rulings about the duty to warn known trespassers about known dangerous conditions. Some courts take the view that a trespasser is a tortfeasor and should not be privileged to be warned. Other courts, however, hold that a trespasser who is *known* is tolerated, and therefore is not all that different from a licensee. Accordingly, there are circumstances when the possessor of land owes a duty to trespassers to warn against known dangerous conditions.

Attractive Nuisance

In addition to what we have already learned about a land possessor's duty to known trespassers, there is a special duty generally owed to such known trespassers if they are children. Specifically, possessors of land may be liable to trespassing children who are injured by an **attractive nuisance** that is on the property. Generally, if the possessor of land:

1. knows or has reason to know of a dangerous condition on the land;
2. knows the condition poses a risk to trespassing children;
3. knows that children who do not realize the risk are likely to trespass; and
4. the benefit of keeping this condition unsafe is slight compared to the risk it poses, then that person is liable for injuries caused to such trespassing children.

For example, suppose that Healy has a hammock in his backyard, tied between two oak trees. The ropes that fasten the hammock to the trees have become worn through the years and cannot hold a great deal of weight anymore. Healy weighs almost 200 pounds and the ropes have always held up when he lies on the hammock. Charlie is 8 years old and lives across the street. Charlie often sneaks into Healy's yard to lie on the hammock when Healy is not home. An 8-year-old boy, Charlie weighs less than half of what Healy weighs. Healy has caught Charlie on occasion, and asked him not to play in the yard. One day, while Charlie is lying on the hammock, the rope snaps and Charlie falls to the ground and is injured. Is Healy liable to Charlie under the theory of attractive nuisance? No.

Remember, Healy did not know of the dangerous condition, nor did he have reason to know. Healy believed that the ropes that supported the hammock were in fine condition. In fact, Healy would probably have used the hammock himself at the next opportunity had the ropes not snapped. In order for a tortfeasor to be liable under the theory of attractive nuisance, he or she must know of the dangerous condition.

Suppose instead that Healy keeps an old axe in his garage. The blade hangs loosely on the handle, so Healy hardly ever uses it anymore. Healy never locks the garage door, because he does not keep anything valuable in there and does not believe anyone would be interested in anything inside the garage. One day, Charlie was bored and decided to explore inside the garage. Charlie found the axe and decided to play with it. As Charlie picked up the axe, the blade fell from the handle and landed on Charlie's foot, injuring him. In that case, would Healy be liable to Charlie under the theory of attractive nuisance? Again, no. You see, although Healy knew that the axe was potentially dangerous, he had no reason to believe that it was in a place on his property where children would be likely to trespass. On the other hand, if Healy kept the axe in the middle of his yard, outdoors, then it is possible that he should reasonably know that a neighboring child would be likely to be "attracted" to the "nuisance."

Next, suppose that Betsy lives in a neighborhood where the homes have large surrounding property. Because Betsy loves horses, she decides to take advantage of her large piece of land by converting her front yard into a mini-ranch.

Betsy installed an eight-foot wire fence around the yard to prevent the horses from jumping over. Many people from miles around marveled at the horses Betsy kept. In time, Betsy decided to breed horses professionally. She kept the horses on her property and sold them for profit.

One day, Natalie, a 12-year-old girl, was riding her bicycle past Betsy's land. She saw the horses and tried to get their attention by blowing her bicycle horn. One horse approached the fence. As Natalie stuck her fingers through the wire fence opening, the horse raised its hoofs and struck Natalie's hand, injuring her.

Is Betsy likely to be liable for Natalie's injury under the theory of attractive nuisance? That depends on a number of things. Let's look at the elements. First of all, did Betsy have reason to know of the nuisance (i.e., the horse)? As a professional horse breeder, the answer is yes, she probably should have known. Next, did she have reason to know that children were likely to trespass and to be attracted to the nuisance? If the answer is no, then Betsy is probably not liable.

But even if the answer is yes, Betsy may still not be found liable, if the cost of curing the nuisance is not outweighed by the risk it poses, for example, if the fence must be a wire fence in order to allow potential buyers to look at the horses. An eight-foot solid fence would block the buyers' view from outside. This lack of visibility of the merchandise (horses) could hurt Betsy's sales. If the risk of a child trespassing, *and* placing her fingers through the fence opening, *and* her being injured by a horse that happened to strike the child at that particular time is so minimal, then Betsy would probably not be held liable.

Again, the answers to these questions—whether the land possessor would be liable or not—are not absolute. They are often decided based on the elements, on a case-by-case basis. Therefore, a careful reading of the elements along with some relevant cases will help you gain a thorough understanding of these laws.

Know versus Reason to Know

Remember, a possessor of land has a duty to warn trespassers of "known" dangers, but to warn trespassing *children* (in attractive nuisance matters) of "known" dangers *and* dangers of which the possessor has "reason to know." While jurisdictions vary on this point, it seems to create more protection for trespassing children than for trespassing adults. Keep in mind, however, the additional cost–benefit element in attractive nuisance cases.

NUISANCE

Generally, **a nuisance is an unreasonable interference in a person's right to use and enjoy his or her property.** The interference may be intentional, negligent, or without fault. There are two main types of torts dealing with nuisance: **private nuisance** and **public nuisance**.

Private Nuisance

A private nuisance is unreasonable, substantial interference with a person's right to use and enjoy his or her property. Such interference is typically created by an act that the tortfeasor commits on his or her own land.

For instance, suppose that Al opens a lumberyard next to Brian Smith's house. Every day, Al and his workers use electric saws to cut tree logs into smaller pieces. The saws make a great deal of noise and disrupt Brian and his family.

Quite often, the Smiths have trouble carrying on telephone conversations, reading, sleeping, or watching television during the day because of the noise from the lumberyard. Does this amount to a private nuisance by Al against the Smiths? Let's take a look at the elements of private nuisance and apply them to these facts.

The **interference** must be both **substantial and unreasonable.** It appears that the activities that Al conducts in his lumberyard clearly interfere with the Smiths' rights to enjoy their property. But is the interference *substantial*? Well, as you know by now, concepts like *substantial* are ultimately determined in court on a case-by-case basis.

A good way to determine whether or not a particular act would amount to substantial interference is to read court cases with similar circumstances. That way, you can use previous court decisions as a guideline to predict how a court may rule on the matter today. Therefore, if the noise is loud enough to prevent a person from conducting normal, day-to-day household activities, the interference will more than likely be considered to be substantial.

Next, keep in mind that the substantial interference must be **unreasonable.** In other words, the reasonable person would find the activity to be substantial interference. For instance, suppose that Connie and Julie live in wooden houses next door to each other. Julie decides to insulate her house with aluminum siding.

Connie believes that aluminum is bad for the environment and destroys the neighboring atmosphere. Fearing that the aluminum siding will pollute the air she breathes, Connie wants Julie to forget about the aluminum siding. If Julie does not listen to Connie and indeed has the aluminum siding installed, does that amount to a private nuisance against Connie? Probably not. In court, the jury will probably determine that aluminum siding is an acceptable form of house insulation and thereby is not unreasonable. However, when looking at the facts about Al and the Smiths, a lumberyard operating very closely to a residential area may constitute an unreasonable interference.

Public Nuisance

A public nuisance is unreasonable, substantial interference with the public's use and enjoyment of common rights. As with private nuisance, this tort usually involves unreasonable use of land.

For example, suppose that Wayne bought some land next to Sunnyside Park, a public park in the town of Brookville. Sunnyside Park has plenty of grass and trees, and is used for picnics, baseball games, bicycle riding, and other recreation by the residents of Brookville as well as by people from neighboring communities.

Suppose Wayne begins to breed pigs, goats, and chickens on his property. The odor created by these animals is driving many people away from Sunnyside Park. This is a classic example of a public nuisance. Wayne will probably not be permitted to maintain such animals on his land. This would be the case even if Wayne's farm was next to, say, a private home rather than a public park. In fact, there is not much difference regarding the elements.

However, the plaintiff in a public nuisance may often be the entire community, as represented by the local government. Quite often, then, there may be laws passed regarding particular nuisances. For example, there may already be an existing law specifically preventing pigs, goats, and chickens to be raised anywhere in Brookville. In that case, there is no need to examine whether Wayne's act constitutes *unreasonable, substantial* interference, because it already constitutes a nuisance by *statute.*

Nuisance: Nature of Liability

As we discussed earlier, a person may be liable for either a private or a public nuisance whether or not the nuisance was committed intentionally, negligently, or without fault. If Davis sprays poison on Johnson's crops, intending to destroy them, that is a classic example of an intentional private nuisance. If, however,

Davis *negligently* sprayed the crops with poison, thinking it was a nourishing fluid, Davis may have negligently committed the nuisance.

Finally, suppose Davis' poison is a dangerous noxious gas that he uses to conduct scientific experiments. Through no fault of Davis, the gas seeps through the air and is absorbed into the ground near Johnson's crops. As a result, the crops are destroyed. In that case, Davis may nonetheless be held strictly liable for the nuisance.

Nuisance versus Trespass

We discussed trespass earlier in this chapter. While some of the examples we discussed may amount to both nuisance and trespass, there is a difference: First, trespass interferes with a person's *possession* of the land, not merely *use and enjoyment of it.* Therefore, a loud noise or unpleasant odor may directly interfere with use and enjoyment of land, but not possession. Second, nuisance involves a *substantial* interference, whereas trespass does not. For instance, if Albert momentarily enters Kim's hotel room, thinking it is his, he has committed trespass. But if upon seeing Kim Albert immediately realizes that he is in the wrong room, apologizes to her, and leaves, he has not *substantially interfered* with her property (her hotel room). Accordingly, Albert has not created a nuisance, though he has committed trespass.

TOXIC TORTS

In Chapter 3 we discussed the growing concern over toxic torts. These are, essentially, various torts in which harm is caused by some toxic substance. When such substances do damage to land, it is typically accidental. Accordingly, this type of harm is usually not trespass to land, because that tort requires intent.

Of course, if Joe, a farmer, wanted to drive away Walt, a neighboring farmer, and take over Walt's farm, and he spread noxious fluids onto Walt's fields, that might constitute trespass to land. However, in most instances, the tortfeasor will either be negligent or strictly liable (when the toxic substance is ultrahazardous), and so the harm to the land will likely be a nuisance.

REVIEW QUESTIONS

1. What is the main difference between trespass to chattel and conversion?
2. Give an example of aboveground trespass to land.
3. What is a licensee and what is an invitee?
4. How do the duties owed to a licensee and those owed to an invitee differ?

5. What duties are owed to trespassing adults?

6. What duties are owed to trespassing children?

7. What is the difference between a private nuisance and a public nuisance?

8. Discuss the differences between a trespass to land and a nuisance.

9. Give an example of an intentional private nuisance.

10. Why would a toxic tort more likely be a nuisance than a trespass to land?

A TORT TALE

Kelly and Diana, who do not know each other, were at the beach on a Sunday. The beach was crowded, and their beach towels were very close together. When Kelly was ready to leave, she mistakenly placed Diana's sunglasses in her own bag, thinking they were her own. Diana, who was taking a nap, did not notice this. Kelly got to her car and put her bag in the trunk. She then threw her beach chair in the trunk, too. When Kelly got home, she realized that the sunglasses in the bag had been crushed by the chair. She was upset that she had been so careless. If Diana discovers that Kelly took her sunglasses and sues her, Kelly will not be liable either for trespass to chattel or for conversion. **Why?**

CASE LAW

Before we move on to Chapter 5, take a look at some cases about torts against property. Remember our discussion about case law when reading through the cases.

JOST v. DAIRYLAND POWER COOPERATIVE   Wis.   **647**
Cite as 172 N.W.2d 647

come of this appeal, it is equally clear that they are to be so considered. While the mere fact that the ward is unsuccessful at a hearing or on appeal is not to be the determining factor as to the necessity of legal services involved, a " * * * reasonable basis and hope for success"[10] are factors to be given weight. In the case before us, appellant appealed the portion of the trial court order denying a termination of the guardianship over her estate. Two issues of law were raised, and on both the essential position of appellant was sustained. Clearly the attorney fees involved in taking this appeal are to be considered necessaries, to be allowed and paid out of the guardianship estate. On this point, the case is remanded with instructions to the trial court to fix and allow reasonable attorney fees to be paid appellant's counsel out of the appellant's estate.

Order reversed and cause remanded for further proceedings consistent with this opinion.

Andrew D. JOST et al., Respondents,

v.

DAIRYLAND POWER COOPERATIVE, Appellant.

No. 135.

Supreme Court of Wisconsin.

Dec. 19, 1969.

Rehearing Denied March 3, 1970.

Action wherein plaintiffs sought to recover for injury to crops and loss of market value of farms allegedly resulting from discharge of sulfur fumes into atmosphere

by defendant electric cooperative. The Circuit Court, Buffalo County, John G. Bartholomew, J., entered judgment on verdict for plaintiffs as amended, and both parties appealed. The Supreme Court, Heffernan, J., held that injuries sustained by plaintiffs, where evidence was uncontradicted that value of crops raised had diminished in value and that certain types of vegetation were dying out or had died out completely, and where it was clear that nuisance had continued for several years and would continue for an indefinite period into future, was permanent, so that, as a matter of law, market value of land was diminished, and plaintiffs were entitled to recover for such.

Affirmed in part and reversed in part.

1. Pleading ⚖49

Failure of plaintiffs, who sought to recover for injury to crops and loss of market value of farms allegedly resulting from discharge of sulfur fumes into atmosphere by defendant electric cooperative, to denominate cause of action as either nuisance or negligence or to plead allegations that could be construed as giving rise to both theories did not result in a fatal error.

2. Pleading ⚖48, 49

If facts reveal an apparent right to recover under any legal theory, they are sufficient as a cause of action, and there is no violation of rules of pleading if facts lead to defendant's liability on more than one theory.

3. Nuisance ⚖49(2)

If conduct on part of defendant electric cooperative in discharging sulfur fumes into atmosphere created a nuisance, it was irrelevant whether defendant was conforming to industry standards of due care.

10. *Id.* at page 38, 98 N.W.2d at p. 433; *see also* 41 Am.Jur.2d, Incompetent Persons, sec. 102, p. 640, stating: "Attorney fees incurred in good faith in proceedings to restore the capacity of one pre-

viously adjudged to be incompetent have generally been held to be chargeable against such person or his estate as necessaries, whether or not the proceedings were successful."

4. Nuisance ⬅49(5)

Evidence supported finding of jury that conduct of defendant electric cooperative in discharging sulphur fumes into atmosphere constituted a "continuing nuisance" to plaintiff owners of farms in area.

See publication Words and Phrases for other judicial constructions and definitions.

5. Trial ⬅362

A trial court may not change the jury's answer to a question unless it appears that the answer is not supported by any credible evidence.

6. Nuisance ⬅54

In action to recover for damage to plaintiffs' crops allegedly resulting from emission of sulfur fumes into atmosphere by defendant electric cooperative, instruction defining "substantial damages" as a sum, assessed by way of damages, which is worth having, opposed to nominal damages, which are assessed to satisfy a bare legal right, was proper.

See publication Words and Phrases for other judicial constructions and definitions.

7. Nuisance ⬅50(7)

Sums found for crop damage sustained by plaintiffs as result of discharge of sulfur gases into atmosphere by defendant electric cooperative, namely $250 for each of two years as to one plaintiff and $145 for each year as to two other plaintiffs, were supported by evidence and, as such, constituted "substantial damages."

8. Torts ⬅4, 16

A continued invasion of a plaintiff's interest by nonnegligent conduct, when actor knows of nature of injury inflicted, is an intentional tort, and fact that hurt is administered nonnegligently is not a defense to liability.

9. Nuisance ⬅49(2)

Evidence tending to show that defendant had used due care in construction and operation of its plant and that social and economic utility of plant outweighed gravity of damage to plaintiffs' crops from sulfur fumes emitted by plant was properly excluded, inasmuch as facts tending to show freedom from negligence would not have constituted a defense to action.

10. Nuisance ⬅43

Doctrine of comparative injury does not apply in Wisconsin to damage suits for nuisance.

11. Nuisance ⬅43

Injuries caused by air pollution or other nuisance must be compensated for irrespective of utility of offending conduct as compared to injury.

12. Nuisance ⬅50(4)

Injury to plaintiffs' crops resulting from discharge of sulfur gases by defendant electric cooperative, where evidence was uncontradicted that value of crops raised had diminished in value and that certain types of vegetation were dying out or had died out completely and where it was clear that nuisance had continued for several years and would continue for an indefinite period into future, was permanent, so that, as a matter of law, market value of land was diminished, and plaintiffs were entitled to recover for such.

The action is one for damages for injury to crops and loss of market value of farm lands. The plaintiffs are farmers living within, or near, the city limits of Alma, Wisconsin. Their farms are located on the bluffs overlooking the Mississippi River. In 1947 the Dairyland Power Cooperative erected a coal burning electric generating plant at Alma. It is the contention of the farmers that consumption of high-sulfur-content coal at this plant has increased from 300 tons per day in 1948 to 1,670 tons per day in 1967. There was testimony that the 1967 coal consumption resulted in discharging approximately 90 tons of sulfur-

JOST v. DAIRYLAND POWER COOPERATIVE   Wis.   **649**
Cite as 172 N. W. 2d 647

dioxide gas into the atmosphere each day. There was substantial evidence to show that the sulphur-dioxide gas, under certain atmospheric conditions, settled on the fields, causing a whitening of the alfalfa leaves and a dropping off of some of the vegetation. There was also testimony to show that the sulphur compounds resulting from the industrial pollution killed pine trees, caused screens to rust through rapidly, and made flower raising difficult or impossible. There was some testimony to show that some of the sulphur came from locomotives or from river barges, but there was testimony that the power plant was the source of most of the contamination. Defendant's witness, a farmer who was "hit" less frequently by the sulphurous fumes, estimated his crop damage at 5 percent. There was also evidence of damage to apple trees, sumac, and wild grape, in addition to the alfalfa damage.

Each of the plaintiff farmers testified that his land had diminished in value as the result of the continuing crop loss.

Defendant offered testimony of realtors to the effect that there had been no diminution of market value. One of these witnesses was the assessor of the city of Alma. Two of the three farms were on the city's tax roll.

Defendant offered testimony of realtors to the effect that there had been no diminution of market value. One of these witnesses was the assessor of the city of Alma. Two of the three farms were on the city's tax roll.

The jury found that the alfalfa crop on the three farms sustained damage. In concluded, however, that the damage was not substantial. The jury found a diminution of the market value of the Andrew Noll farm but no loss in the market value of the farms of Andrew Jost or Norbert Noll.

The trial judge changed the jury's answer in regard to "substantial" damage from "no" to "yes." Judgment was entered upon the verdict as amended. Defendant has appealed from the whole of the judgment, and plaintiff have filed for a review

of the judgment which sustained the jury's finding in regard to loss of market value.

Hale, Skemp, Hanson, Schnurrer & Skemp, La Crosse, for appellant.

Fugina, Kostner, Ward, Kostner & Galstad, Arcadia, for respondents.

HEFFERNAN, Justice.

One of the defendant's principal objections to the judgment is that plaintiff's counsel was permitted to proceed until almost the close of his case before electing to rely on the theory of nuisance rather than negligence. Defendant before trial moved that the pleadings be made more definite and certain, apparently on the theory that the complaint purported to allege a cause of action both in negligence and in nuisance, and that plaintiffs must elect to rely on one cause of action or the other. The trial judge declined to order such election. Defendant contends that thereafter plaintiffs offered "voluminous" testimony in an attempt to show the defendant's negligence in permitting the emission of sulphur fumes into the atmosphere. Our review of the 900 page record gives no support to the defendant's contention. In the entire transcript only a very few questions could be construed as bearing upon negligence. Contrary to defendant's claim, Attorney Kostner almost immediately dispelled any question in regard to the legal theory on which he was relying. After a defense objection to questions posed to the first witness, Attorney Kostner stated:

> "If the Court please, our purpose in asking the question is to show that at the present time there is no control of the diffusion of sulphur dioxide gases from the Alma plant into the atmosphere. Whether or not it's possible, or whether or not there is no method of doing it, is not material because if the sulphur dioxide gases are diffused in the atmosphere and that causes damage to the property the question of whether or not it can, be proper scientific methods, be controlled to hot material. The question is did it."

It seems eminently clear that, from the very outset, the case was tried on the theory of nuisance and not on the ground that the defendant had failed to exercise due care.

[1, 2] Defendant apparently contends that the failure to denominate the cause of action as either nuisance or negligence or to plead allegations that could be construed as giving rise to both theories results in a fatal error. We do not agree—a cause of action is not constituted by labelling the operative facts with the name of a legal theory. The operative facts themselves, if they show the invasion of a protected right, constitute the cause of action. What they are called is immaterial. If the facts reveal an apparent right to recover under any legal theory, they are sufficient as a cause of action—and there is no violation of the rules of pleading if the facts lead to the defendant's liability on more than one legal theory.

Negligence and nuisance, of course, are not always mutually exclusive legal concepts. Prosser points out:

"Another fertile source of confusion is the fact that nuisance is a field of tort liability, rather than a type of tortious conduct. It has reference to the interests invaded, to the damage or harm inflicted, and not to any particular kind of act or omission which has led to the invasion. The attempt frequently made to distingish between nuisance and negligence, for example, is based upon an entirely mistaken emphasis upon what the defendant has done rather than the result which has followed, and forgets completely the well established fact that negligence is merely one type of conduct which may give rise to a nuisance." Prosser, Law of Torts (hornbook series, 3d ed.), Nuisance, p. 594, sec. 88.

[3] In the instant cause there was no reason for confusion. Plaintiffs' attorney from the outset made it clear that liability was predicated on the *fact* that sulphur dioxide gases were emitted into the atmosphere, despite complaints over a period of several years. There was no attempt to hinge plaintiffs' case on the theory that the defendant was not exercising due care. Under the plaintiffs' theory, which we deem

to be a correct one, it is irrelevant that defendant was conforming to industry standards of due care if its conduct created a nuisance. We see no error in plaintiffs' pleading of the case, nor can we conclude that the trial conduct of plaintiffs in any way misled defendant or prejudiced its defense by requiring it to prepare for trial on a theory subsequently abandoned.

[4] The jury found that Dairyland Power Cooperative produced its power in such a manner as to constitute a continuing nuisance to the plaintiffs. The following question was, however, answered "no" by the jury, "Did such nuisance cause substantial damage to their alfalfa crops and and lands?" Nevertheless, the jury found the damage to the Jost alfalfa crops amounted to $250 for each of the two years, the Andrew Noll damage to $145 for each year, and the Norbert Noll damage to $145 for each year. In addition, Andrew Noll's farm was found to have sustained a $500 diminution in market value.

[5] Appellant claims that the trial judge erred in changing the answer to the substantial damage question from "no" to "yes." It should be noted that this question posed more than one point for the jury's determination; one, did the nuisance cause the damage, and, two, was the damage substantial. The cause element of the question, however, is not argued; and all that defendant contends is that the damage, though caused by the nuisance, was not substantial and that, therefore, the court erred in changing the jury's answer. The rule is clear. A trial court may not change the jury's answer to a question unless it appears that the answer is not supported by any "credible evidence." Leatherman v. Garza (1968), 39 Wis.2d 378, 386, 159 N.W. 2d 18; Auster v. Zaspel (1955), 270 Wis. 368, 71 N.W.2d 417; Paul v. Hodd (1955), 271 Wis. 278, 73 N.W.2d 412.

The damage to the alfalfa crop was undisputed. Even Danzinger, the neighboring farmer who testified, ostensibly for the defendant, estimated the crop damage at 5 percent. Moreover, the jury found the damage to the alfalfa crop alone to be not less than $290 for the least damaged of the plaintiffs. The court defined substantial damage as:

"* * * a sum, assessed by way of damages, which is worth having; opposed to nominal damages, which are assessed to satisfy a bare legal right. Substantial damages are damages which are considerable in amount and intended as a real compensation for a real injury."

[6, 7] The jury was properly instructed. The sums found for crop damage, though meager, are supported by the evidence. Having found such sums to be justly owing, it appears that by no rationalization can it be concluded that the sums properly payable did not constitute "substantial damage." In the oft-quoted case, Pennoyer v. Allen (1883), 56 Wis. 502, 14 N.W. 609, the court points out that only a "substantial injury" is compensible or protected against by law. Substantial injury is defined as "tangible" injury, or as a "discomfort perceptible to the senses of ordinary people." The Restatement, 4 Torts, p. 246, sec. 827, follows the same rationale:

"* * * where the invasion involves physical damage to tangible property, the gravity of the harm is ordinarily regarded as great even though the extent of the harm is relatively small. But where the invasion involves only personal discomfort and annoyance, the gravity of the harm is generally regarded as slight unless the invasion is substantial and continuing." *See,* also, Prosser, *supra,* p. 599.

Here the damage was to tangible property. The damage was apparent and undisputed. The trial judge summarized the nature of the damage:

"Aside from this testimony [Danzinger, discussed *supra*], exhibits and testimony of the plaintiffs which showed that plants and vegetation were affected by the sulphur fumes; that flowers could not be raised; that screens became rusty within a short time and totally unusable within two years. To buy the defendant's theory that the plaintiffs were not ordinary sensitive people would mean that the ordinary common housewife likes rusty screens, enjoys barn insects in her home, does not like flowers, delights in buying all her garden vegetables in a store and that her farm husband says, 'so what' if alfalfa plants turn a little yellow and the leaves drop off."

We conclude that the injury was substantial as a matter of law, since under the reasoning of *Pennoyer, supra,* and the Restatement, the injury was obvious injury to tangible property. Moreover, it was, in fact, of such a nature that the jury placed more than a nominal value upon the injury done.

Defendant strenuously argues that it was prejudiced by the court's refusal to permit certain testimony, particularly testimony that tended to show that defendant had used due care in the construction and operation of its plant, and to show that the social and economic utility of the Alma plant outweighed the gravity of damage to the plaintiffs.

Defendant's contention that the evidence should have been admitted rests on two theories; one, that due care, if shown, defeats a claim for nuisance, and, two, that, if the social utility of the offending industry substantially outweighs the gravity of the harm, the plaintiffs cannot recover damages.

We can agree with neither proposition. As this court pointed out in Bell v. Gray-Robinson Construction Co. (1954), 265 Wis. 652, 657, 62 N.W.2d 390, 392:

"A nuisance does not rest on the degree of care used * * * but on the degree of danger existing even with the best of care. [Citing authority] To constitute a nuisance, the wrongfulness must have been in the acts themselves [*i.e.,* the consequence of the acts] rather than in the failure to use the requisite degree of care in doing them * * *."

Pennoyer v. Allen, *supra*, 56 Wis. at page 512, 14 N.W. at page 613, points out:

" * * * it is no defense to show that such business was conducted in a reasonable and proper manner * * *. It is the interruption of such enjoyment and the destruction of such comfort that furnishes the ground of action, and it is no satisfaction to the injured party to be informed that it might have been done with more aggravation."

Brown v. Milwaukee Terminal Railway Co. (1929), 199 Wis. 575, 224 N.W. 748, 227 N.W. 385, sets forth the same rule of law *i.e.*, that freedom from negligence is no defense if the consequences of the continued conduct nevertheless cause substantial injury to a claimant.

[8]   In any event it is apparent that a continued invasion of a plaintiff's interests by non-negligent conduct, when the actor knows of the nature of the injury inflicted, is an intentional tort, and the fact the hurt is administered non-negligently is not a defense to liability. *See Prosser, supra*, pp. 594 ff., sec. 88; *Restatement, supra*, p. 226, sec. 822.

[9]   It is thus apparent that the facts tending to show freedom from negligence would not have constituted a defense to plaintiffs' nuisance action. It was therefore proper that such evidence was excluded (the nominal character of plaintiffs' proof as to negligence has been commented on above).

While there are some jurisdictions that permit the balancing of the utility of the offending conduct against the gravity of the injury inflicted, it is clear that the rule, permitting such balancing, is not approved in Wisconsin where the action is for damages. We said in Pennoyer v. Allen, *supra*, 56 Wis. at p. 512, 14 N.W. at p. 613:

"When such comfort and enjoyment are so impaired, and compensation is de-

manded, it is no defense to show that such business was conducted in a reasonable and proper manner, and with more than ordinary cleanliness, and that the odors so sent over and upon such adjacent premises were only such as were incident to the business when properly conducted. It is the interruption of such enjoyment and the destruction of such comfort that furnishes the ground of action, and it is no satisfaction to the injured party to be informed that it might have been done with more aggravation. The business is lawful; but such interruption and destruction is an invasion of private rights, and to that extent unlawful. It is not so much the manner of doing as the proximity of such a business to the adjacent occupant which causes the annoyance. A business necessarily contaminating the atmosphere to the extent indicated should be located where it will not necessarily deprive others of the enjoyment of their property, or less their comfort while enjoying the same."

In Dolata v. Berthelet Fuel & Supply Co. (1949), 254 Wis. 194, 198, 36 N.W.2d 97, 8 A.L.R.2d 413, relying on *Pennoyer*, this court concluded that even though a coalyard was operated properly, nevertheless, it, a socially and economically useful business, would be abated if it caused substantial damage to the adjoining plaintiff.

[10]   It appears clear that the doctrine of comparative injury is not entertained in Wisconsin in damage suits for nuisance. In Abdella v. Smith (1967), 34 Wis.2d 393, 149 N.W.2d 537, the doctrine was alluded to by a citation from *Prosser*. The case involved not an action for damages, but an injunction to abate the nuisance. The same problem was discussed in the earlier case of Holman v. Mineral Point Zinc Co. (1908), 135 Wis. 132 115 N.W. 327, where, in an action for *damages* occasioned by *sulphurous* fumes, defendant sought to rely on the theory that injury to a socially and economically useful factory by the granting of relief would outweigh the possible or actual injury to the plaintiff. This court

JOST v. DAIRYLAND POWER COOPERATIVE   Wis.   653
Cite as 172 N.W.2d 647

stated, in discussing a case cited by the parties therein:

"That was a suit to enjoin the operation of a copper smelter as a nuisance, and for damages occasioned by the destruction of timber on near-by lands. It is there held that, where an owner of property cannot use the same at all without indirectly injuriously affecting the property of another, the sound discretion of a court of equity is invoked when it is appealed to and asked to abate such use as a nuisance, and in such case the court will consider the comparative injury which will result from the granting or refusing of an injunction, and that it will not be granted when it would cause a large loss to the defendant, while the injury to the plaintiff, if refused, will be comparatively slight and can be compensated by damages. That decision could only be applicable on the question of the abatement of the nuisance, as the right of the plaintiff to recover damages is distinctly recognized. As already stated, this is an action to abate the nuisance and for damages, and the complaint is not demurrable, if otherwise sufficient, simply because the court on final hearing might not grant all the relief that is prayed for. Sec. 3181, Stats. (1898), provides that if the plaintiff prevails, he shall have judgment for damages and costs, and also for an abatement of the nuisance, unless the court shall certify that such abatement is unnecessary.

"Whether the court may apply the doctrine of comparative injury to the respective parties in rendering the judgment is not before the court for decision on this appeal. The other grounds for demurrer were not urged upon the attention of the court and are treated as abandoned. We hold that the complaint states a cause of action, and that the demurrer was properly overruled." Pp. 137, 138, 115 N.W. at p. 329.

As in *Holman,* the question of comparative injury is not before us, since this is a suit for damages, not abatement of a nuisance. Defendant nevertheless urges us to adopt the rule of the Restatement, which he contends applies the rule to damage suits for nuisance. It should be pointed out, however, that the Restatement recognizes that:

"For the purpose of determining liability for damages for private nuisance, conduct may be regarded as unreasonable even though its utility is great and the amount of harm is relatively small * *. It may be reasonable to continue an important activity if payment is made for the harm it is causing, but unreasonable to continue it without paying." Restatement, 4 Torts, p. 224, ch. 40.

Prosser, *supra,* page 621, too, states:

"In an action for damages, the relative hardship upon the plaintiff and the defendant is not material, once the nuisance is found to exist."

We therefore conclude that the court properly excluded all evidence that tended to show the utility of the Dairyland Cooperative's enterprise. Whether its economic or social importance dwarfed the claim of a small farmer is of no consequence in this lawsuit. It will not be said that, because a great and socially useful enterprise will be liable in damages, an injury small by comparison should go unredressed. We know of no acceptable rule of jurisprudence that permits those who are engaged in important and desirable enterprises to injure with impunity those who are engaged in enterprises of lesser economic significance. Even the government or other entities, including public utilities, endowed with the power of eminent domain —the power to take private property in order to devote it to a purpose beneficial to the public good—are obliged to pay a fair market value for what is taken or damaged. To contend that a public utility, in the pursuit of its praiseworthy and legitimate enterprise, can, in effect, deprive others of the full use of their property without compensation, poses a theory un-

654   **Wis.**   **172 NORTH WESTERN REPORTER, 2d SERIES**

known to the law of Wisconsin, and in our opinion would constitute the taking of property without due process of law.

[11] We adhere to the rule of Pennoyer v. Allen. Although written in 1883, we believe it remains completely applicable under modern conditions. We conclude that injuries caused by air pollution or other nuisance must be compensated irrespective of the utility of the offending conduct as compared to the injury. Nor do we imply that a different rule should apply where the remedy sought is abatement rather than damages. That point is not considered herein. We consider that the rule of *Dolata* continues to be the law in Wisconsin where the action is for abatement.

We conclude, however, that the court erred in concluding that the evidence failed to show a diminution in the market value. The evidence was uncontradicted that the value of crops raised had diminished in value and that certain types of vegetation were dying out or had died out completely. It is clear that the nuisance has continued for several years and will continue for an indefinite period into the future.

[12] The jury found there was a continuing nuisance. Under these circumstances, we conclude that the injury was permanent and that, as a matter of law, the market value of the land was diminished. *See* McCormick, Damages (hornbook series), p. 500, sec. 127. How much it was diminished we need not determine, since we are satisfied that there should be a new trial on the issue of diminution of market value only in regard to the real property of all plaintiffs.

We see no basis for the jury's conclusion that the market value of one of the farms was reduced by $500 and the value of the others not at all. Such a result—although there could have been a differential—is completely unsupported by the evidence.

We conclude that the plaintiffs are entitled to recover for the crops and damage to vegetation for the years complained of—

1965 and 1966—as found by the jury, but after those years recovery cannot again be for specific items of damage on a year-by-year basis. Their avenue for compensation is for permanent and continuing nuisance as may be reflected in a diminution of market value. Of course, permitting a recovery now for a permanent loss of market value presupposes that the degree of nuisance will not increase. If such be the case, an award of damages for loss of market value is final. If, however, the level of nuisance and air pollution should be increased above the level that may now be determined by a jury, with a consequent additional injury the plaintiffs would have the right to seek additional permanent damage to compensate them for the additional diminished market value.

Judgment affirmed in part and reversed in part consistent with this opinion.

E. R. BEYER LUMBER CO., Inc., et al., Respondents,

v.

Robert B. BROOKS, Appellant.

No. 24.

Supreme Court of Wisconsin.

Dec. 19, 1969.

Payees brought suit to recover balance due on note. The Circuit Court, Dane County, Norris E. Maloney, J., entered summary judgment for payees, and defendant appealed. The Supreme Court, Connor T. Hansen, J., held that where defendant signed promissory note without receiving value therefor and for purpose of lending his name to some other person and there were no words in note limiting defendant's promise to pay or anything to indicate defendant was secondarily liable, defendant

The majority point out that class actions are not properly a subject for justice court practice, and I agree with this position. A refusal to allow aggregation for purposes of arriving at a jurisdictional amount does not mean that a class action is a proper remedy for a justice court. A.R.S. § 22–211 provides that the procedure and practices in the Superior Court "so far as applicable" govern procedure and practices in justice of the peace courts. It is clear and would be a proper holding that class actions are not applicable to the justice of the peace courts. The power to make procedural rules applicable to any court rests with this Court, Article 6, section 5(5).

The class action is a useful procedural device for bringing before the court a large number of persons who have similar issues to be decided, and in the interest of economy in time and expense to court and litigant the matters can be resolved in a single action. The jurisdiction of the Superior Court is broad enough to deal with almost every area of concern except those instances where the amount involved is less than $200.00 and the Superior Court does not otherwise have jurisdiction. It would seem that in those instances in which the only issue is the amount of money, a claim for less than $200.00 should be prosecuted in the justice court, and the fact that others may have a similar or identical claim should be of no consequence, and the parties should be left to their own individual decisions as to whether to seek recovery for the amount of their claim in the justice court.

The class action can be abused by persons, who for private motives, prosecute a claim for a very small amount on their own part but by aggregating other such small claims in a class action exaggerate the whole controversy all out of proportion to the amount and justice required. It appears to me that the Court's ruling today invites much mischief in the area of the class action. Matters of small consequence can by the device of the class action be made into major controversies by the ambitious, vengeful or ruthless, when, were it

not for such device, the claims would have been resolved in the justice courts or passed over by some claimants as not worth the effort. Requiring that each claim in a class action equal the jurisdictional requirement for Superior Court would avoid such mischief and still provide justice.

In my view the relief sought by the petitioner to prohibit further proceedings in the Superior Court as a class action in this cause should have been granted.

108 Ariz. 178

SPUR INDUSTRIES, INC., an Arizona corporation formerly Spur Feeding Co., an Arizona corporation, Appellant and Cross-Appellee,

v.

DEL E. WEBB DEVELOPMENT CO., an Arizona corporation, Appellee and Cross-Appellant.

No. 10410.

Supreme Court of Arizona,
In Banc.

March 17, 1972.
Rehearing Denied April 18, 1972.

Action was brought by real estate developer to enjoin cattle feeding operation. The Superior Court of Maricopa County, Cause No. C–207029, Kenneth C. Chatwin, J., entered a decree from which cross-appeals were taken. The Supreme Court, Cameron, V. C. J., held, inter alia, that where defendant commenced cattle feeding operations in agricultural area well outside boundaries of any city and subsequently real estate developer purchased land nearby and commenced an extensive retirement community development, developer was entitled to enjoin the cattle feeding opera-

SPUR INDUSTRIES, INC. v. DEL E. WEBB DEVELOPMENT CO.   Ariz.   **701**
Cite as 494 P.2d 700

tion as a nuisance but it was required to indemnify cattle feeder for the reasonable cost of moving or shutting down.

Affirmed in part, reversed in part and remanded.

1. Nuisance ⚖1

"Private nuisance" is one affecting a single individual or definite small number of persons in enjoyment of private rights not common to the public.

See publication Words and Phrases for other judicial constructions and definitions.

2. Nuisance ⚖59

"Public nuisance" is one affecting rights enjoyed by citizens as part of public and must affect a considerable number of people or an entire community or neighborhood.

See publication Words and Phrases for other judicial constructions and definitions.

3. Nuisance ⚖23(2)

Remedy for minor inconveniences caused by nuisance lies in an action for damages rather than one for an injunction.

4. Nuisance ⚖3(10), 21, 61, 75

As to residents of community, operation of cattle feeding lot with its accompanying odors, flies, etc., was both a public and private nuisance and the residents could have successfully maintained action to abate the nuisance. A.R.S. § 36–601, subsec. A.

5. Nuisance ⚖26

Developer of real estate adjacent to commercial cattle feeding operation which produced odors, flies, etc., having shown loss of lot sales because of such operation, had standing to bring suit to enjoin the nuisance. A.R.S. § 36–601, subsec. A.

6. Nuisance ⚖18

Suit to enjoin nuisance sounds in equity and while courts have a special responsibility to public they are also concerned with protecting operator of a lawful, albeit noxious, business from result of a knowing

and willful encroachment by others near his business.

7. Nuisance ⚖23(1), 35

Where defendant commenced cattle feeding operations in agricultural area well outside boundaries of any city and subsequently real estate developer purchased land nearby and commenced an extensive retirement community development, developer was entitled to enjoin the cattle feeding operation as a nuisance but it was required to indemnify cattle feeder for the reasonable cost of moving or shutting down.

———————

Snell & Wilmer, by Mark Wilmer, and John Lundin, Phoenix, for appellant and cross-appellee.

L. Dennis Marlowe, Tempe, for appellee and cross-appellant.

CAMERON, Vice Chief Justice.

From a judgment permanently enjoining the defendant, Spur Industries, Inc., from operating a cattle feedlot near the plaintiff Del E. Webb Development Company's Sun City, Spur appeals. Webb cross-appeals. Although numerous issues are raised, we feel that it is necessary to answer only two questions. They are:

1. Where the operation of a business, such as a cattle feedlot is lawful in the first instance, but becomes a nuisance by reason of a nearby residential area, may the feedlot operation be enjoined in an action brought by the developer of the residential area?

2. Assuming that the nuisance may be enjoined, may the developer of a completely new town or urban area in a previously agricultural area be required to indemnify the operator of the feedlot who must move or cease operation because of the presence of the residential area created by the developer?

702   Ariz.   494 **PACIFIC REPORTER, 2d SERIES**

The facts necessary for a determination of this matter on appeal are as follows. The area in question is located in Maricopa County, Arizona, some 14 to 15 miles west of the urban area of Phoenix, on the Phoenix-Wickenburg Highway, also known as Grand Avenue. About two miles south of Grand Avenue is Olive Avenue which runs east and west. 111th Avenue runs north and south as does the Agua Fria River immediately to the west. See Exhibits A and B below.

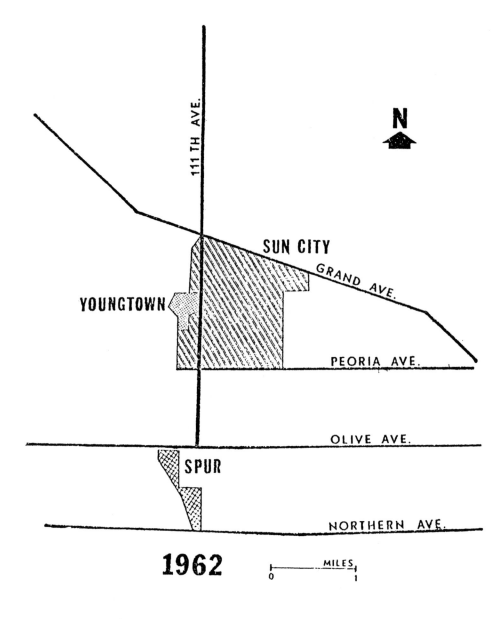

EXHIBIT A

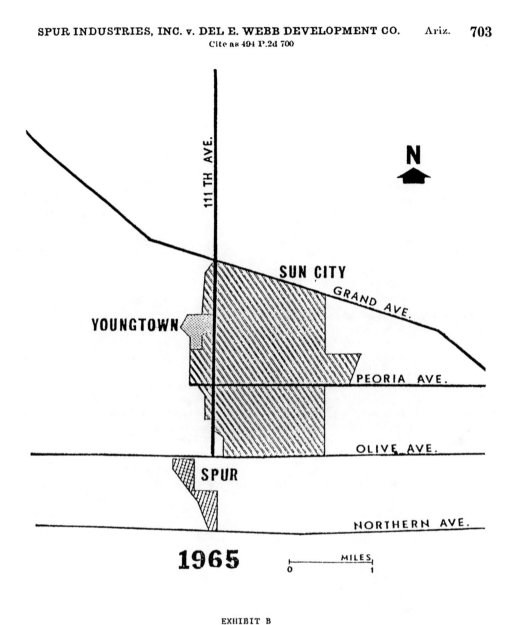

EXHIBIT B

Farming started in this area about 1911. In 1929, with the completion of the Carl Pleasant Dam, gravity flow water became available to the property located to the west of the Agua Fria River, though land to the east remained dependent upon well water for irrigation. By 1950, the only urban areas in the vicinity were the agriculturally related communities of Peoria, El Mirage, and Surprise located along Grand Avenue. Along 111th Avenue, approximately one mile south of Grand Avenue and 1½ miles north of Olive Avenue, the community of Youngtown was commenced in 1954. Youngtown is a retirement community appealing primarily to senior citizens.

In 1956, Spur's predecessors in interest, H. Marion Welborn and the Northside Hay Mill and Trading Company, developed feedlots, about ½ mile south of Olive Avenue, in an area between the confluence of the usually dry Agua Fria and New Rivers. The area is well suited for cattle feeding and in 1959, there were 25 cattle feeding pens or dairy operations within a 7 mile radius of the location developed by Spur's predecessors. In April and May of 1959, the Northside Hay Mill was feeding between 6,000 and 7,000 head of cattle and Welborn approximately 1,500 head on a combined area of 35 acres.

In May of 1959, Del Webb began to plan the development of an urban area to be known as Sun City. For this purpose, the Marinette and the Santa Fe Ranches, some 20,000 acres of farmland, were purchased for $15,000,000 or $750.00 per acre. This price was considerably less than the price of land located near the urban area of Phoenix, and along with the success of Youngtown was a factor influencing the decision to purchase the property in question.

By September 1959, Del Webb had started construction of a golf course south of Grand Avenue and Spur's predecessors had started to level ground for more feedlot area. In 1960, Spur purchased the property in question and began a rebuilding and expansion program extending both to the north and south of the original facilities. By 1962, Spur's expansion program was completed and had expanded from approximately 35 acres to 114 acres. See Exhibit A above.

Accompanied by an extensive advertising campaign, homes were first offered by Del Webb in January 1960 and the first unit to be completed was south of Grand Avenue and approximately 2½ miles north of Spur. By 2 May 1960, there were 450 to 500 houses completed or under construction. At this time, Del Webb did not consider odors from the Spur feed pens a problem and Del Webb continued to develop in a southerly direction, until sales resistance became so great that the parcels were difficult if not impossible to sell. Thomas E. Breen, Vice President and General Manager of the housing division of Del Webb, testified at deposition as follows:

"Q Did you ever have any discussions with Tony Cole at or about the time the sales office was opened south of Peoria concerning the problem in sales as the development came closer towards the feed lots?

"A Not at the time that that facility was opened. That was subsequent to that.

"Q All right, what is it that you recall about conversations with Cole on that subject?

"A Well, when the feed lot problem became a bigger problem, which, really, to the best of my recollection, commenced to become a serious problem in 1963, and there was some talk about not developing that area because of sales resistance, and to my recollection we shifted—we had planned at that time to the eastern portion of the property, and it was a consideration.

"Q Was any specific suggestion made by Mr. Cole as to the line of demarcation that should be drawn or anything of that type exactly where the development should cease?

"A I don't recall anything specific as far as the definite line would be, other than, you know, that it would be advisable to stay out of the southwestern portion there because of sales resistance.

"Q And to the best of your recollection, this was in about 1963?

"A That would be my recollection, yes.

*   *   *   *   *   *

"Q As you recall it, what was the reason that the suggestion was not

SPUR INDUSTRIES, INC. v. DEL E. WEBB DEVELOPMENT CO. Ariz. **705**
Cite as 494 P.2d 700

adopted to stop developing towards the southwest of the development?

"A Well, as far as I know, that decision was made subsequent to that time.

"Q Right. But I mean at that time?

"A Well, at that time what I am really referring to is more of a long-range planning than immediate planning, and I think it was the case of just trying to figure out how far you could go with it before you really ran into a lot of sales resistance and found a necessity to shift the direction.

"Q So the plan was to go as far as you could until the resistance got to the point where you couldn't go any further?

"A I would say that is reasonable, yes."

By December 1967, Del Webb's property had extended south to Olive Avenue and Spur was within 500 feet of Olive Avenue to the north. See Exhibit B above. Del Webb filed its original complaint alleging that in excess of 1,300 lots in the southwest portion were unfit for development for sale as residential lots because of the operation of the Spur feedlot.

Del Webb's suit complained that the Spur feeding operation was a public nuisance because of the flies and the odor which were drifting or being blown by the prevailing south to north wind over the southern portion of Sun City. At the time of the suit, Spur was feeding between 20,000 and 30,000 head of cattle, and the facts amply support the finding of the trial court that the feed pens had become a nuisance to the people who resided in the southern part of Del Webb's development. The testimony indicated that cattle in a commercial feedlot will produce 35 to 40 pounds of wet manure per day, per head, or over a million pounds of wet manure per day for 30,000 head of cattle, and that despite the admittedly good feedlot management and good housekeeping practices by Spur, the resulting odor and flies produced an annoying

494 P.2d—45

if not unhealthy situation as far as the senior citizens of southern Sun City were concerned. There is no doubt that some of the citizens of Sun City were unable to enjoy the outdoor living which Del Webb had advertised and that Del Webb was faced with sales resistance from prospective purchasers as well as strong and persistent complaints from the people who had purchased homes in that area.

Trial was commenced before the court with an advisory jury. The advisory jury was later discharged and the trial was continued before the court alone. Findings of fact and conclusions of law were requested and given. The case was vigorously contested, including special actions in this court on some of the matters. In one of the special actions before this court, Spur agreed to, and did, shut down its operation without prejudice to a determination of the matter on appeal. On appeal the many questions raised were extensively briefed.

It is noted, however, that neither the citizens of Sun City nor Youngtown are represented in this lawsuit and the suit is solely between Del E. Webb Development Company and Spur Industries, Inc.

MAY SPUR BE ENJOINED?

[1, 2] The difference between a private nuisance and a public nuisance is generally one of degree. A private nuisance is one affecting a single individual or a definite small number of persons in the enjoyment of private rights not common to the public, while a public nuisance is one affecting the rights enjoyed by citizens as a part of the public. To constitute a public nuisance, the nuisance must affect a considerable number of people or an entire community or neighborhood. City of Phoenix v. Johnson, 51 Ariz. 115, 75 P.2d 30 (1938).

[3] Where the injury is slight, the remedy for minor inconveniences lies in an action for damages rather than in one for an injunction. Kubby v. Hammond, 68 Ariz. 17, 198 P.2d 134 (1948). Moreover,

some courts have held, in the "balancing of conveniences" cases, that damages may be the sole remedy. See Boomer v. Atlantic Cement Co., 26 N.Y.2d 219, 309 N.Y.S.2d 312, 257 N.E.2d 870, 40 A.L.R.3d 590 (1970), and annotation comments, 40 A.L.R.3d 601.

Thus, it would appear from the admittedly incomplete record as developed in the trial court, that, at most, residents of Youngtown would be entitled to damages rather than injunctive relief.

We have no difficulty, however, in agreement with the conclusion of the trial court that Spur's operation was an enjoinable public nuisance as far as the people in the southern portion of Del Webb's Sun City were concerned.

§ 36–601, subsec. A read as follows:

"§ 36–601. Public nuisances dangerous to public health

"A. The following conditions are specifically declared public nuisances dangerous to the public health:

"1. Any condition or place in populous areas which constitutes a breeding place for flies, rodents, mosquitoes and other insects which are capable of carrying and transmitting disease-causing organisms to any person or persons."

By this statute, before an otherwise lawful (and necessary) business may be declared a public nuisance, there must be an "populous" area in which people are injured:

"* * * [I]t hardly admits a doubt that, in determining the question as to whether a lawful occupation is so conducted as to constitute a nuisance as a matter of fact, the locality and surroundings are of the first importance. (citations omitted) A business which is not per se a public nuisance may become such by being carried on a place where the health, comfort, or convenience of a populous neighborhood is affected. * * * What might amount to a

serious nuisance in one locality by reason of the density of the population, or character of the neighborhood affected, may in another place and under different surroundings be deemed proper and unobjectable. * * *." Mac-Donald v. Perry, 32 Ariz. 39, 49–50, 255 P. 494, 497 (1927).

[4,5] It is clear that as to the citizens of Sun City, the operation of Spur's feedlot was both a public and a private nuisance. They could have successfully maintained an action to abate the nuisance. Del Webb, having shown a special injury in the loss of sales, had a standing to bring suit to enjoin the nuisance. Engle v. Clark, 53 Ariz. 472, 90 P.2d 994 (1939); City of Phoenix v. Johnson, supra. The judgment of the trial court permanently enjoining the operation of the feedlot is affirmed.

MUST DEL WEBB INDEMIFY SPUR?

[6] A suit to enjoin a nuisance sounds in equity and the courts have long recognized a special responsibility to the pubic when acting as a court of equity:

§ 104. Where public interest is involved.

"Courts of equity may, and frequently do, go much further both to give and withhold relief in furtherance of the public interest than they are accustomed to go when only private interests are involved. Accordingly, the granting or withholding of relief may properly be dependent upon considerations of pubic interest. * *." 27 Am. Jr.2d, Equity, page 626.

In addition to protecting the public interest, however, courts of equity are concerned with protecting the operator of a lawfully, albeit noxious, business from the result of a knowing and willful encroachment by others near his business.

In the so-called "coming to the nuisance" cases, the courts have held that the residential landowner may not have relief if he knowingly came into a neighborhood reserved for industrial or agricultural endeavors and has been damaged thereby:

"Plaintiffs chose to live in a area uncontrolled by zoning laws or restrictive convenants and remote from urban development. In such an area plaintiffs cannot complain that legitimate agricultural pursuits are being carried on in the vicinity, nor can plaintiffs, having chosen to build in an agriculture area, complain that the agricultural pursuits carried on in the area depreciate the value of their homes. The area being primarily agricultural, any opinion reflecting the value of such property must take this factor into account. The standards affecting the value of residential property in an urban setting, subject to zoning controls and controlled planning techniques, cannot be the standards by which agricultural properties are judged.

"People employed in a city who build their homes in suburban areas of the county beyond the limits of a city and zoning regulations do so for a reason. Some do so to avoid the high taxation rate imposed by cities, or to avoid special assessment for street, sewer and water projects. They usually build on improved or hard surface highways, which have been built either at state or county expense and thereby avoid special assessment for these improvements. It may be that they desire to get away from the congestion of traffic, smoke, noise, foul air and the many other annoyances of city life. But with all these advantages in going beyond the area which is zoned and restricted to protect them in their homes, they must be prepared to take the disadvantages." Dill v. Excel Packing Company, 183 Kan. 513, 525, 526, 331 P. 2d 539, 548, 549 (1958). See also East St. Johns Shingle Co. v. City of Portland, 195 Or. 505, 246 P.2d 554, 560, 562 (1958).

And:

"* * * a party cannot justly call upon the law to make that place suitable for

his residence which was not so when he selected it. * * *." Gilbert v. Showerman, 23 Mich. 448, 455, 2 Brown 158 (1871).

Were Webb the only party injured, we would feel justified in holding that the doctrine of "coming to the nuisance" would have been a bar to the relief asked by Webb, and, on the other hand, had Spur located the feedlot near the outskirts of a city and had the city grown toward the feedlot, Spur would have to suffer the cost of abating the nuisance as to those people locating within the growth pattern of the expanding city:

"The case affords, perhaps, an example where a business established at a place remote from population is gradually surrounded and becomes part of a populous center, so that a business which formerly was not an interference with the rights of others has become so by the encroachment of the population * * *." City of Ft. Smith v. Western Hide & Fur Co., 153 Ark. 99, 103, 239 S.W. 724, 726 (1922).

We agree, however, with the Massachusetts court that:

"The law of nuisance affords no rigid rule to be applied in all instances. It is elastic. It undertakes to require only that which is fair and reasonable under all the circumstances. In a commonwealth like this, which depends for its material prosperity so largely on the continued growth and enlargement of manufacturing of diverse varieties, 'extreme rights' cannot be enforced. * * *." Stevens v. Rockport Granite Co., 216 Mass. 486, 488, 104 N.E. 371, 373 (1914).

[7] There was no indication in the instant case at the time Spur and its predecessors located in western Maricopa County that a new city would spring up, full-blown, alongside the feeding operation and that the developer of that city would ask the court to order Spur to move because of the new

city. Spur is required to move not because of any wrongdoing on the part of Spur, but because of a proper and legitimate regard of the courts for the rights and interests of the public.

Del Webb, on the other hand, is entitled to the relief prayed for (a permanent injunction), not because Webb is blameless, but because of the damage to the people who have been encouraged to purchase homes in Sun City. It does not equitably or legally follow, however, that Webb, being entitled to the injunction, is then free of any liability to Spur if Webb has in fact been the cause of the damage Spur has sustained. It does not seem harsh to require a developer, who has taken advantage of the lesser land values in a rural area as well as the availability of large tracts of land on which to build and develop a new town or city in the area, to indemnify those who are forced to leave as a result.

Having brought people to the nuisance to the foreseeable detriment of Spur, Webb must indemnify Spur for a reasonable amount of the cost of moving or shutting down. It should be noted that this relief to Spur is limited to a case wherein a developer has, with foreseeability, brought into a previously agricultural or industrial area the population which makes necessary the granting of an injunction against a lawful business and for which the business has no adequate relief.

It is therefore the decision of this court that the matter be remanded to the trial court for a hearing upon the damages sustained by the defendant Spur as a reasonable and direct result of the granting of the permanent injunction. Since the result of the appeal may appear novel and both sides have obtained a measure of relief, it is ordered that each side will bear its own costs.

Affirmed in part, reversed in part, and remanded for further proceedings consistent with this opinion.

HAYS, C. J., STRUCKMEYER and LOCKWOOD, JJ., and UDALL, Retired Justice.

---

108 Ariz. 186

Mark READER and Frances Reader, his wife, Albert Mayer and Jean Mayer, his wife, on behalf of themselves and all others similarly situated, Appellants,

v.

MAGMA–SUPERIOR COPPER COMPANY, an Arizona corporation, et al., Appellees.

No. 10414–PR.

Supreme Court of Arizona, In Banc.

March 15, 1972.

Proceeding on petition for review of an order of the Court of Appeals dismissing the appeal from an order of the Superior Court, Maricopa County. The Supreme Court, Struckmeyer, J., held that order determining that plaintiffs, bringing an action against six asserted owners or operators of copper smelters on behalf of the entire population of the county for compensatory and punitive damages, could not maintain lawsuit as a class action was an order which in effect terminated the litigation and was appealable under statute authorizing an appeal from any order affecting substantial rights when order in effect determines that action and prevents judgment from which an appeal might be taken.

Order of Court of Appeals vacated with directions.

Cameron, V. C. J., did not participate in determination of matter.

Appeal and Error ⇐93

Order determining that plaintiffs, bringing an action against six asserted owners or operators of copper smelters on behalf of the entire population of county for compensatory and punitive damages, could not maintain lawsuit as a class action was an order which in effect terminated the litigation and was appealable under statute authorizing an appeal from any order affecting substantial rights when order

5 Torts against Reputation: Intentional, Negligent, and Without Fault

Up to this point, we have dealt with torts to the person and to property. The harm we talked about was either physical, emotional, or financial. It would seem that harm to reputation would overlap emotional and financial harm. In any event, there is a large area of tort law, called defamation, that specifically involves harm to reputation. This chapter deals with the general principles of defamation and related torts.

Defamation is intentionally or negligently making a false statement about another person, which is heard or read by a third person and interpreted by that person to be true, and thereby harms or tends to harm the reputation of the person about whom the statement was made. If the statement is made about a public figure, it must be made with actual malice.

Quite a mouthful. Now let's sit back and examine it slowly, piece by piece.

First we see that defamation involves two mental states we have already discussed: **Intent** and **negligence.** We also examine the concept of actual malice, which applies to defamatory statements made against public figures.

In order for there to be defamation, there must be a **false statement.** Consider this example:

Lisa and Johnny are coworkers in a department store. Lisa saw Johnny stealing from a store cash register. Lisa told several employees about what Johnny did. As a result, Johnny was fired. Is Lisa liable to Johnny for defamation?

A. Yes, because Johnny was harmed by Lisa's statements.

B. Yes, because Johnny did not want anyone to know that he was stealing.

C. No, because Lisa's statements about Johnny were true.

D. More information is needed about defamation in order to answer this question.

What's the answer? C. Remember, a true statement cannot be defamatory, even if the statement is embarrassing and legally damaging. Only a false statement can possibly be defamatory. Of course, not every false statement is defamatory. Let's read on.

Suppose instead that Lisa and Johnny were the only people in the employee lounge. Johnny accused Lisa of falsifying her credentials in order to be hired. The statement is false. Is Johnny liable to Lisa for defamation?

A. Yes, because the statement is false.

B. Yes, because Johnny may have cause Lisa emotional distress.

C. No, because a third person did not hear or read Johnny's statement.

D. More information is needed about defamation in order to answer the question.

Have you figured out what the answer is? It is choice C. Although the statement was false, it was not heard or read by a third person. Now, had Johnny written a letter claiming this false accusation and posted the letter on a company bulletin board where one or several employees could see it, then Lisa could *potentially* have a claim of defamation against Johnny, subject to the other elements of this tort.

The act of making a false statement about someone that is heard or read by a third party is **publication**. In other words, if Alan makes a false statement about Marcia that is heard by Elaine, that is **publication**. However, if Alan makes the statement directly to Marcia, and nobody else hears or reads the statement, there is no publication and therefore no defamation.

Next, suppose that a bunch of friends gathered at Tony's house to watch the Super Bowl between the Green Bay Packers and the New England Patriots. "Hey, where's Bobby?" one of the friends remarked. "He'll be a little late," Tony joked. "He's planting a bomb in the Patriots' locker room as we speak." Tony's comment was intended to be a joke, because Bobby is a devoted Green Bay Packers fan. In any event, Tony made the comment in a room full of people. Is he liable to Bobby for defamation? No.

While the comment was a false statement intentionally made by Tony, it is not the type of statement that anyone in that setting would take seriously. It was merely Tony's attempt to emphasize Bobby's enthusiasm for the Packers. People would generally not believe that Bobby would actually plant a bomb in the opposing team's locker room. Therefore, the comment would not reasonably be interpreted by a third person to be true, and is therefore not defamation.

On the other hand, suppose Tony made a different comment explaining Bobby's lateness. Suppose Tony said that Bobby had been snorting cocaine late into the night before, and was feeling the aftereffects today. Suppose Tony said this with a straight face, and suppose there were people at Tony's house who didn't know Bobby well enough to know the story was not true.

Perhaps Tony had no intention to defame Bobby; maybe he just has an unusual sense of humor. In any event, that type of statement *could* reasonably be interpreted by a third person to be true. Whether or not it would be defamatory depends on whether it satisfies the remaining elements of defamation, to which we now turn.

Using the same setting, suppose that Marcia was another person on Tony's guest list but that she, too, was late. In the meantime, Tony was ordering food from a local delicatessen. "What should I order for Marcia," he asked? Frank replied, "Order a ham, salami, and provolone sandwich for her. She'd love one of those." Frank's comment was heard by all of Tony's guests. The statement was false. Although Frank did not intentionally make a false statement, he negligently believed that Marcia and anyone else would love that type of sandwich, because it was his own favorite as well.

The statement was false and was overheard by a number of people who could reasonably interpret it to be true. But was it defamatory? Probably not. Generally, such a comment would not harm or tend to harm Marcia's reputation. It is not likely that Marcia will suffer any embarrassment, criticism, or financial harm as a result of the comment. Will people think any less of Marcia if they believe that she loves ham, salami, and provolone sandwiches? It's very doubtful.

However, what if Marcia was the president of the American Vegetarians Association (AVA)? The AVA's primary rule is that no member will ever eat meat. In that case, Marcia's reputation as AVA president could be seriously harmed if people think that she eats sandwiches containing meat. In that case, Frank's statement could be defamatory.

INTENTIONAL VERSUS NEGLIGENT DEFAMATION

The previous example serves as a reminder of the difference between intentional and negligent defamation.

In either case, the intent to *make* the statement is there. With the exception of, say, people who talk in their sleep, a verbal statement is generally made intentionally. However, the intent of its effect may be in question. For instance, someone may make a statement in order to praise someone, or to condemn them. The statement may be made in jest, or in all seriousness.

In any event, if the person who makes the statement knows that it is false, then the intent to make a false statement is present. However, if the statement is made by a person who believes it to be true, then there is no intent to make a false statement.

As we learned earlier in the book, negligence involves harm resulting from a breach of duty of reasonable care when such duty of care is owed. Accordingly, a false statement may be made negligently if the person who made it did not use reasonable care in assessing its truth, and there was resulting harm.

For instance, suppose you heard that someone from your school named John was recently expelled for cheating. A different John, who is in your class, became sick with the flu that same day, and has not been to class for three sessions. When the instructor asks, "Has anyone seen John?" you yell out, "Yes, I heard that he was expelled for cheating." In that case, although you did not intend to make a false statement, you were probably negligent. You did not have enough information to conclude that your classmate was not the same John who was expelled. Because John is a very common name, it is highly likely that the person who was expelled was a different John. Suppose instead that the person who was expelled was named Wolfgang, and your classmate Wolfgang was missing from class for the same period of time. It is highly unlikely that there would be *two* people in an American school with as unique a first name as Wolfgang who were both absent from the school on the same day.

In that case, if you were to state that your classmate Wolfgang was absent because he had been expelled from cheating, you may not be liable for defamation, because your argument could be that you did not speak without using reasonable care. Remember, negligence requires *reasonable* care, not perfect care.

Another issue is whether a third person is reasonably likely to believe the statement. It is more likely that someone will believe a false statement that a married man is having an affair than that the same man is an alien from Mars. It is easier to believe that a woman with whom you work is an alcoholic than that she is an international terrorist. Therefore, statements made in jest may often be interpreted as true, depending on the nature and delivery of the statement. Accordingly, the person who made the statement may be negligent in not realizing that the statement could be interpreted as true.

PUBLIC FIGURES AND MALICE

When potentially harmful false statements are made about public figures, the statements can be defamatory only if they are made with the knowledge that they are false. Unlike false statements made about nonpublic figures, which may be defamatory whether made intentionally or negligently, such statements made about public figures may only be defamatory if they are made with **actual malice**.

Note: Actual malice does not necessarily mean made with ill will. Rather, it means that the statement was made, if not with a certain degree of certainty that it was false, then at least under serious doubt as to its truth. While the traditional definition of malice may imply ill will, that meaning is not applicable regarding defamation.

Suppose that Chester is a photojournalist working for a large, nationally known newspaper. Chester was covering a story about the opening of a new abortion clinic. Antiabortion demonstrators were expected to protest, so there was a great deal of action surrounding the clinic. Chester saw a man accompanying a woman to the clinic. The man held the woman in his arms, comforting her. Chester took a close-up photograph of the couple and added the caption: "Couple Decide to Give Up Baby at New Clinic."

Suppose that the man accompanying the pregnant woman was not the baby's father. Instead, he was a friend of hers who was there to provide moral support. Chester simply assumed that the man accompanying the woman was the father of her child. Whether Chester's caption was negligently written would be determined in court, based on whether Chester breached his duty of reasonable care. However, we can certainly conclude that Chester did not know that the statement was false.

If the man was not a public figure, he may have a valid cause of action against Chester for defamation, if Chester's statement was written negligently. But if the man was a public figure, say, a local politician, then he would not have a defamation action against Chester. Because Chester did not make the statement knowing it was false, or with a serious doubt about its truth, then Chester could not be liable to a public figure for defamation.

Now that we have covered the elements of defamation as well as the applicable mental states, let's take a look at the two main types of defamation: libel and slander.

LIBEL VERSUS SLANDER

Libel is written defamation; slander is verbal defamation. This is the most basic definition distinguishing libel from slander, although audio and video recordings are increasingly being classified as libel by some jurisdictions. Also, certain physical gestures without verbal expression may be considered slander.

Keeping this in mind, consider that it is generally easier to collect damages for libel than for slander. Indirectly, this appears to suggest that libel is a more serious form of defamation. Why do you think that would be the case? Why do you think that a person who writes a defamatory statement causes more harm than somebody who verbalizes one? Think about it for a few moments, then read ahead to find the answer.

Generally, the written or recorded word has a more lasting, permanent effect than its spoken counterpart. Shout a false rumor about someone and it may be heard but then forgotten. But write it on a note and pass it along, and that note may be read by hundreds of people, or maybe even more. Make a gesture that would tend to defame someone, such as a gesture indicating that someone is a drug user, and it is likely to be forgotten. But make such a statement on film and it is captured potentially forever, to be played over and over again to different audiences. These, then, are some examples of why libel tends to be considered more serious than slander, and why the process of collecting damages is different depending on the type of defamation.

In the case of libel, **special damages** need not be proven. Special damages are typically those of a monetary nature. In other words, a person may win an action for libel even without having suffered financial damage. However, to succeed in an action for slander, the victim must generally establish having suffered some type of financial damage. There is an exception to this general rule about slander if the slanderous remark is **slander per se.**

Slander per se applies if the defamatory statement alleges that the plaintiff (victim):

1. engaged in criminal behavior;
2. suffers from a loathsome communicable disease;
3. is unfit for his or her business or profession; or
4. has engaged in sexual misconduct.

Let's take a look at each allegation.

Criminal Behavior

For example, if Derek falsely tells Marvin that Jack sells stolen jewelry, Jack would likely have an action against Derek for slander per se.

Loathsome Communicable Disease

A loathsome communicable disease is one that is particularly dangerous and can be communicated from one person to another. For instance, while diabetes is certainly a dangerous disease, it is not communicable; and while the common cold is certainly communicable, it typically is hardly dangerous. But tuberculosis, for example, is both *loathsome* and *communicable*. Accordingly, if Jennifer falsely accuses Mark of having tuberculosis while both are talking with Stacey, then Mark probably has a good case of slander per se against Jennifer.

Unfit for Business or Profession

Suppose that Robert and Stanley own competing diners in the center of town. Robert is angry because Stanley's business has recently been growing. As a result, he begins telling people that Stanley's diner was recently condemned by the board of health. If this is false, it would be a perfect example of slander per se.

Sexual Misconduct

This is a very vague category, because it is difficult to determine exactly what sexual misconduct is, particularly in instances when it is not a crime. Acts such as rape or sexual assault certainly *are* sexual misconducts, but they are also crimes. Therefore, there would be no need for those acts to fall under the sexual misconduct category for slander per se, because they easily fit into the criminal behavior classification. Because there is a *separate* category specifically for sexual misconduct, it logically follows that there are acts that society considers to be sexual misconduct that may not necessarily be crimes. Adultery is a prime example that comes to mind.

Adultery involves a married person's extramarital sexual affair. While such an act is largely viewed as immoral, and therefore a prime candidate for sexual misconduct, it is not necessarily illegal.

Suppose, then, that Margaret stands up one day in her office building lunchroom and in front of a packed crowd falsely accuses Alonzo of cheating on his wife. Alonzo may have an action against Margaret for slander per se, based on Margaret's false accusation falling into the sexual misconduct category.

Note: How can you tell whether a particular statement alleges one of the four slander per se categories? Remember that the law is often vague, rather than straightforward. A good reading of relevant court cases will begin to unravel the mystery.

Accordingly, where the defamatory statement was either libel or slander per se, damages are generally *presumed*. In other words, the plaintiff does not have to actually prove the damages. In cases of slander, however, the plaintiff must prove the monetary loss.

Based on all that we have learned about defamation, let's take one more example, from start to finish, and apply each element—one by one—slowly and carefully:

Suppose that in a recent medical journal, Charles wrote that Sandra, who is a surgeon, has carelessly allowed many of her patients to die on the operating table: First, let's assume that the statement is false. Second, let's determine whether or not Charles knew whether it was true or not. Let's assume that Charles either definitely knew that the statement was false, or entertained serious doubts about the truth of the statement.

In that case, Sandra's status as a public figure or nonpublic figure would not matter.

Now, instead, let's suppose that Charles made the statement based on some evidence that he *thought* applied to Sandra, but instead referred to another doctor. If Charles' reading of the evidence was negligent, if all the other elements are met, then he may be liable for defamation—but only if Sandra is not a public figure.

Third, if Charles' false accusation appeared in a medical journal, *publication* has occurred as soon as a third person has read the statement. Fourth, the statement must be reasonably interpreted by a third person to be true. In other words, if it is likely that someone reading the journal would reasonably believe Charles' statement to be true, then that element of defamation is satisfied.

Finally, the statement must either have harmed or be likely to harm Sandra's reputation. For example, Sandra's reputation as a doctor may be harmed, and she may lose patients or career opportunities as a result. Keep in mind that Sandra could successfully sue Charles for libel without having to prove special damages. In other words, Sandra would not need to show that she did indeed, say, lose patients as a result of Charles' libelous statement.

Considering the elements we just reviewed, what if, instead of *writing* the false accusation, Charles merely said it in a room full of people? In that case, the statement would not be libel. Rather, it would be slander. Because the statement alleges that Sandra is unfit for her profession, the statement would be slander per se. Again, Sandra would be able to win a defamation lawsuit against Charles without needing to prove special damages.

However, suppose Charles had not criticized Sandra's ability as a doctor. What if, instead, Charles falsely accused Sandra of being a horrible cook? In that case, the statement is libel if written, or slander if spoken. But it is not slander per se, as it does not fall under one of those four categories.

Accordingly, if the statement were libel, Sandra would have to prove that she either was harmed by it or will likely be harmed by it. For instance, people who overheard the statement may politely refuse Sandra's invitations to parties at her house, fearing that she will force them to try her cooking.

Now, if the statement were spoken, it would be slander, and Sandra would prevail if she could demonstrate that she *was* actually financially harmed. For example, Sandra could try to establish that some patients who think she is a horrible cook feel that she cannot properly follow a recipe, which means she probably cannot follow instructions to perform an operation. As a result, they leave Sandra's care and find a new doctor. In that case, Sandra would be able to maintain an action against Charles for slander.

LIABILITY WITHOUT FAULT

So far in this chapter we have discussed intentional and negligent defamation. Keep in mind that with defamation, as with other areas of tort law that we have discussed, liability without fault may be imposed.

In earlier times, defamation was largely treated as a strict liability tort. In other words, as long as the other elements of defamation applied, it did not matter whether the person who made the statement knew it was false or even acted unreasonably in making it. We have discussed the law as it applies currently, namely, that a person is liable for defamation who makes the defamatory statement intentionally or negligently.

However, the notion of *vicarious liability* may apply to defamation. For example, suppose that Shelley works for a daily newspaper, the *American Press.* Shelley was covering a professional basketball game between the Boston Celtics and the New York Knicks, in New York City's Madison Square Garden. John McEnroe, the former tennis star who was known throughout his career for his on-court temper flare-ups, was at the game too. In fact, he was sitting only a few seats away from Shelley. On this night, the Celtics were on the verge of defeating the Knicks rather handily. Some fans were getting frustrated and started an argument. The argument led to a small brawl, not far from where both Shelly and McEnroe were sitting. McEnroe was not at all involved in the dispute.

That night, Shelley decided not to write about the one-sided game. Rather, her headline read: "McEnroe Still Can't Control His Temper." The article insinuated that McEnroe was involved in the brawl at the game. Although Shelley clearly knew that McEnroe was not involved, she realized that the juicy headline would sell many newspapers.

Shelley's act is a classic case of libel. Accordingly, McEnroe has a good chance of prevailing in a lawsuit. Nina is the publisher of the *American Press*. If McEnroe decides to sue the *Press*, Nina will likely be held *vicariously liable,* even though she had nothing to do with writing the story or deciding to print it. Remember that employers are often held vicariously liable for the tortious acts of their employees. This principle applies in defamation matters too.

OTHER TORTS INVOLVING FALSE STATEMENTS

Torts involving **disparagement** or **slander of title** do not affect the physical person. They are sometimes classified as property torts in the sense that a person's livelihood is his or her "property" right (as discussed in Chapter 4). Although there is usually no direct attack to reputation, the ultimate result may cause some harm to reputation. Because these torts are so closely related to defamation, it is best that we discuss them in detail in this chapter.

Disparagement is making a false statement about a person's business with the intent to cause harm to such business, when the statement is heard or read by a third person and interpreted by that person to be true. Slander of title requires the same elements, but specifically involves statements made about a person's title or ownership.

These torts, then, are very similar to defamation, except for three important differences:

First, you will notice that these torts are only *intentional,* whereas defamation may be made negligently as well.

Second, defamatory statements tend to harm the *reputation* of the individual, whereas disparaging statements do not, at least, not directly.

For example, suppose that Tom is a big fan of *Starsky & Hutch,* a popular 1970s television show. In that show, Detective Starsky owned a flashy sportscar, a 1975 Ford Gran Torino that was bright red with white stripes on the sides. The car, like the show, was a big hit in the seventies, and has since become a collector's item. Two car dealers, Taylor and Evans, each have one of these cars in stock, and both know that Tom is interested.

In order to make the sale himself, Taylor is thinking about making a false statement to Tom about Evans' car. Suppose that Taylor falsely tells Tom that Evans' car is a lemon, in bad mechanical shape, and not an authentic Gran Torino.

This could be defamatory, because it would tend to harm Evans' reputation as a car dealer; it would suggest that Evans' car is a fraud.

Instead, suppose that Taylor falsely tells Tom that Evans just sold the car to someone else. While this, too, may help Taylor be the one to make the sale to Tom, it would not tend to harm Evans' reputation. Accordingly, the statement would not be defamatory, though it could be disparaging.

Third, Plaintiffs in actions involving disparagement and slander of title must prove special damages. On the other hand, plaintiffs in defamation actions need to prove such damages only if the actions involve slander, not libel or slander per se.

In many jurisdictions, the torts of disparagement and slander of title are less common than defamation. Nonetheless, it is helpful for you to be aware of the distinction. In Chapter 6, we discuss other torts that may affect a person's ability to conduct business.

Note: In any event, persons may be liable for disparagement, without fault. For instance, in the above scenario, Taylor could be vicariously liable if one of his employees had made the disparaging comment.

REVIEW QUESTIONS

1. In defamation, what is publication?
2. What is the difference between libel and slander?
3. What are the different standards for defaming a private person versus defaming a public figure?
4. What are special damages, and in what type of defamation actions must they be proven?
5. What is slander per se?
6. Is libel presumably more damaging than slander? Why?
7. Give an example of a false statement that is not likely to be interpreted as being true.
8. Give an example of negligent defamation.
9. Give an example in which there is liability without fault for defamation.
10. Give an example of slander that is not slander per se.

A TORT TALE

Jason and Samantha are members of the Board of Directors of General Motors. At a recent Board luncheon, with three members present, Samantha said to

Jason, "I just got a box of some incredible Honduran cigars. I know you like to smoke Honduran cigars, so I'll give you a few."

Samantha was later shocked because Jason sued her for defamation. After all, she was just being friendly. After thinking about it, she realized that she had made a mistake. It wasn't Jason who liked cigars, it was another Board member.

But what was the harm? It is perfectly legal to smoke cigars from the Honduras. What was even more shocking to Samantha was that Jason *won* the case.

Why was this defamation? What would Jason have to prove in this situation to win his case?

Case Law

This, then, is the tortious harm to reputation, with defamation at its core. Before we move on to Chapter 6, take a look at some cases in order to gain an even better understanding of this type of tort law. As always, keep in mind everything we have discussed about case law.

BELLI v. ORLANDO DAILY NEWSPAPERS, INC.
579
Cite as 389 F.2d 579 (1967)

Melvin M. BELLI, Appellant,

v.

ORLANDO DAILY NEWSPAPERS, INC.,
et al., Appellees.

No. 23623.

United States Court of Appeals
Fifth Circuit.

Dec. 28, 1967.

Rehearing Denied Feb. 16, 1968.

Action for damages for libel and slander. The United States District Court for the Middle District of Florida, George C. Young, J., dismissed the complaint and appeal was taken. The Court of Appeals, Wisdom, Circuit Judge, held that publication in newspaper of article containing false statement that prominent attorney had "taken" association which had agreed to pay attorney's hotel bill during attorney's attendance at convention by charging clothing bills to hotel bill was capable of carrying defamatory meaning and whether publication was so understood by the "common mind" was for jury to determine.

Reversed and remanded.

1. Libel and Slander ⊜6(1), 19, 33

A libel per se is one that is defamatory on its face, including publication that is susceptible of several meanings, one of which is defamatory; it is actionable without proof of special harm.

2. Libel and Slander ⊜19

A libel per quod is one in which the defamatory meaning, or innuendo, is not apparent on the face of the publication, but must be established by proof of extrinsic facts.

3. Libel and Slander ⊜80

Where complaint in libel action did not allege defamation by extrinsic facts or plead special damages, sufficiency of claim would have to be determined solely on basis of whether it sufficiently alleged publication which was libelous per se.

4. Libel and Slander ⊜6(1)

Libel per se is not limited to statements imputing criminal offense, loathsome disease, matter incompatible with business, trade, profession or office, and unchastity on part of woman but includes libel whose defamatory innuendo is apparent from publication itself without reference to extrinsic facts by way of inducement.

5. Libel and Slander ⊜123(2)

Under Florida law, it is' for trial court in the first instance to determine whether words are reasonably capable of defamatory interpretation, or whether they are necessarily so; and it is then for jury to say whether they were in fact understood as defamatory.

6. Libel and Slander ⊜123(2)

Both judge and jury played part in determining whether language constitutes libel.

7. Libel and Slander ⊜123(2)

Newspaper story alleging that bar association agreed to reimburse prominent attorney for participating in panel discussion by paying attorney's hotel bill, and that attorney and his "well dressed wife" had "taken" association by charging hundreds of dollars in clothing purchases to hotel bill, was capable of carrying defamatory meaning and would have enabled jury to conclude that conduct imputed to attorney was incompatible with standards of ethical lawyer and as such constituted libel per se.

8. Libel and Slander ⊜123(2)

Under Florida law, any doubt as to defamatory effect of publication should be resolved by the common mind of the jury, and not by even the most carefully considered judicial pronouncement.

9. Libel and Slander ⊜33

Any allegedly slanderous statements not involving imputation as to crime, disease, particular unfitness for office, or unchastity may constitute slander per quod but are actionable only upon showing of special damages.

10. Libel and Slander ⬥6(1)

Under Florida law, scope of general class of slander per se includes statements holding another up to scorn, contempt and ridicule.

11. Libel and Slander ⬥123(2)

Whether defendant's statement to newspaper columnist that prominent attorney had agreed to attend state bar convention if bar association would pay attorney's hotel bill and that attorney and his wife had charged about $300 worth of clothing to hotel bill was defamatory was question for jury.

12. Conspiracy ⬥18

Complaint of prominent attorney who was subject of allegedly libelous newspaper article stated cause of action on theory that newspaper and other persons conspired to abuse, discredit and vilify attorney through publication of the article.

13. Libel and Slander ⬥48(1)

Before libelous newspaper article may be considered privileged commentary concerning public figure, matter covered by publication must be shown to be of legitimate and substantial public interest.

14. Libel and Slander ⬥123(8)

Whether prominent attorney was a public figure rendering privileged a libelous commentary if published without malice was issue for resolution by trial court.

15. Libel and Slander ⬥83

Complaint charging newspaper and other persons with malice in publication of allegedly libelous article was sufficient to establish basis for showing of actual malice. Fed.Rules Civ.Proc. rule 9(b), 28 U.S.C.A.

Paul A. Louis, Bertha Claire Lee, Murray Sams, Jr., Miami, Fla., J. P. Tonkoff, Yakima, Wash., for appellant.

Richard W. Bates, Joseph P. Baker, George T. Eidson, Jr., Robert Dyer, Orlando, Fla., for appellees.

Before WISDOM and GODBOLD, Circuit Judges, and McRAE, District Judge.

WISDOM, Circuit Judge.

This action for damages for libel and slander is based on a false statement relating to Mr. Melvin Belli. Belli, an attorney of national prominence, is well known in the legal profession for his pioneering in the development of demonstrative evidence as a trial tactic and his success in obtaining large judgments for plaintiffs in personal injury suits. He is well known to the general public because of his representation of Jack Ruby and others in the public eye.

In March 1964 Mr. Leon Handley, an attorney in Orlando, Florida, in a conversation with Miss Jean Yothers, a columnist for the Orlando Evening Star, repeated a story he had heard concerning Belli. Handley told Yothers that the Florida Bar Association had invited Belli to serve as a member of one of the panels on the program of the Association at its 1955 Convention in Miami Beach. Belli agreed, with the understanding that "since there were no funds provided in the budget for payment per se for his contribution as a lawyer to the program the Florida Bar instead would pick up the hotel tab for himself and his wife during their stay." According to Handley, after Mr. and Mrs. Belli left Florida, the Association discovered that the Bellis "ran up a bunch of [clothing] bills" which they charged to their hotel room.[1]

---

1. Handley's story, as recited in the complaint is as follows:

   [T]he Florida Bar wanted Belli to appear on a program and they informed him that they had—that they didn't have the money in the budget to pay him, but as a lawyer maybe he would agree to the plan of attending and participating and having his hotel bill paid for, and he agreed and came down here and was on the program, and after he

and his wife had gone they discovered the hotel bill, that they had charged some clothing to their hotel bill * * * about $300.00. * * *

* * * that the Florida Bar was embarrassed over it. * * * the whole thing was an embarrassment to every member that knew about it. * * *

* * * that although Belli had been informed of the scarcity of funds and

BELLI v. ORLANDO DAILY NEWSPAPERS, INC.   **581**
Cite as 389 F.2d 579 (1967)

The derogatory portion of the story was admittedly false: the Bellis had not charged any purchases to their hotel account. Unfortunately for all, Jean Yothers reported, with embellishments, this nine-year old story in her gossip column in the Orlando Evening Star for March 19, 1964. She commented, in part: " * * * Oops! * * * the plan backfired on the Florida Bar * * [Mr. Belli and 'his well-dressed wife' had charged] clothing bills amounting to hundreds of $s * * * to their hotel rooms. * * * The Florida Bar had been taken. * * * After all, that was the plan!" [2]

On these facts, Belli brought this diversity action. The complaint alleges that (1) Yothers, the Orlando Evening Star, and its editor libeled Belli through publication of the article, (2) that Handley slandered Belli in making the false statement to Yothers, and (3) that all of these parties, with others, participated in a conspiracy to defame Belli.

The district court dismissed Belli's complaint for failure to state a claim upon which relief could be granted. The court relied on the erroneous assumption that the determination whether a statement is a libel (or slander) per se is solely for the court. We consider it a close question whether the publication is so clearly defamatory that as a matter of law the case should not be submitted to the jury. We hold, however, that the publication itself, without reference to extrinsic facts, is capable of carrying a defamatory meaning. It is for a jury to determine whether it was so understood by the "common mind". We reverse and remand.

I.

[1–3] Historically, libel, as generally distinguishable from slander, was actionable without the necessity of pleading or proving that the plaintiff had suffered any damages as a result of it.[3] That is the accepted rule today in England[4] and in many jurisdictions in the United States[5] both as to libel per se and libel per quod.[6] A libel per se is one that is

---

had agreed to come down just for his transportation and hotel bill, he still ran up a bunch of bills. * * *

2. The article appeared in the Orlando Evening Star under the title "On the Town" by Jean Yothers and headed "Florida Bar Got the Bill". The full text is as follows:

Jack Ruby's flamboyant attorney Melvin Belli of San Francisco makes an indelible impression whither he goeth.

Consider the time he and Mrs. Belli were in Miami six or so years ago and Belli was a member of a panel at a program-meeting of the Florida Bar.

Here's what happened:

In making arrangements for Belli's participation it had been pointed out to him that since there were no funds provided in the budget for payment per se for his contribution as a lawyer to the program, the Florida Bar instead would pick up the hotel tab for himself and his wife during their stay. Belli agreed.

Oops!

A local attorney remembers, with embarrassed chagrin, how the plan backfired on the Florida Bar.

After the well-dressed Mr. Belli and his well-dressed wife left town, the ho-

tel where they had been staying received clothing bills amounting to hundreds of $s. The Bellis had shopped in Miami stores and charged clothing bills to their hotel rooms.

The Florida Bar had been taken.

It was hard to stomach but the Board of Governors of the Florida Bar picked up the Bellis' bill.

After all, that was the plan!

3. For a general discussion of the history of the law of defamation, see Veeder, The History and Theory of the Law of Defamation, 3 Colum.L.Rev. 546 (1903), 4 Colum.L.Rev. 33 (1904). See also Plucknett, A Concise History of the Common Law, 454 (4th ed. 1948); 2 Pollock & Maitland, The History of English Law 536–38 (2d ed. 1898).

4. Youssoupoff v. Metro-Goldwyn-Mayer Pictures, 1934, 50 T.L.R. 581.

5. See Prosser, The Law of Torts 781 (1964).

6. Dean Prosser asserts that this is now the rule only in a "small minority of the American Jurisdictions". Prosser, The Law of Torts 781 (1964); Prosser, Libel Per Quod, 46 Va.L.Rev. 839, 844–47 (1960); Prosser, More Libel Per Quod,

defamatory on its face, including a publication that is susceptible of several meanings, one of which is defamatory; it is actionable without proof of special harm. A libel per quod is one in which the defamatory meaning, or innuendo, is not apparent on the face of the publication, but must be established by proof of extrinsic facts. Here the district court held, correctly, that the Belli claim "must be determined solely on the basis of whether it sufficiently alleges a publication which is libelous per se"—since, as is evident from the complaint, the plaintiff did not allege defamation by extrinsic facts or plead special damages.[7]

A. In its opinion below the court recognized that there are four categories of defamatory imputations which traditionally have been considered actionable without proof of harm. As set out in the Restatement of Torts, Second, Tentative Draft 12, Section 569, these are statements which impute to another "(1) a criminal offense, (2) a loathsome disease, (3) matter incompatible with his business, trade, profession or office, and (4) unchastity on the part of a woman plaintiff". Such defamatory statements, whether the publication is in the form of libel or in the form of slander, are regarded as especially likely to cause harm to the reputation of the person defamed, although such harm is not and perhaps cannot be proved. See Restatement, Second, Tentative Draft 12, Sections 569–574; Prosser, Law of Torts § 107 (1963); I Harper and James, Law of Torts § 5.9 (1956). Florida law recognizes these four traditional categories of per se libel and slander. Richard v. Gray, Fla.S.Ct.1953, 62 So.2d 597, 598; Layne v. Tribune, 1933, 108 Fla. 177, 146 So. 234, 236, 86 A.L.R. 466; Adams v. News-Journal Corp., Fla.S.Ct.1955, 84

So.2d 549, 551; Miami Herald Pub. Co. v. Brautigan, Fla.App.1961, 127 So.2d 718, 722.

[4] Libel per se is not limited to these four categories: Courts use a stock formula to describe a general class of per se libel (but not per se slander). The Restatement's formula is:

One who publishes defamatory matter is subject to liability without proof of special harm or loss of reputation if the defamation is

(a) Libel whose defamatory innuendo is apparent from the publication itself without reference to extrinsic facts by way of inducement. Restatement, Second, Tentative Draft 12, Section 569.

In Florida and in many states the rubric runs: a libel per se is "any publication which exposes a person to distrust, hatred, contempt, ridicule, obloquy". For example, in Briggs v. Brown, 55 Fla. 417, 46 So. 325, 330 (1908) the court states the formula for libels per se as follows:

A civil action for libel will lie when there has been a false and unprivileged publication by letter or otherwise which exposes a person to distrust, hatred, contempt, ridicule, or obloquy * * * or which has a tendency to injure such person in his office, occupation, business, or employment. If the publication is false and not privileged, and is such that its natural and proximate consequence necessarily causes injury to a person in his personal, social, official, or business relations or life, wrong and injury are presumed and implied, and such publication is actionable per se.

This definition is in accord with earlier Florida cases and has been repeated with approval in many later decisions.[8]

---

79 Harv.L.Rev. 1629 (1966). But see Eldredge, The Spurious Rule of Libel Per Quod, 79 Harv.L.Rev. 733 (1966). See various tentative drafts of the A.L.I. Restatement of Torts, Second.

7. The district court granted the plaintiff leave to amend. The plaintiff stood by his contention that the publication was libelous per se.

8. E.g., Metropolis Co. v. Croasdell, 145 Fla. 455, 199 So. 568, 569 (1941); Layne v. Tribune Co., 108 Fla. 177, 146 So.2d 234, 236, 86 A.L.R. 466 (1933); McClellan v. L'Engle, 74 Fla. 581, 77 So. 270, 272 (1917); McCormick v. Miami Herald Publ. Co., 139 So.2d 197, 200 (Fla.Dist. Ct.App.1962).

BELLI v. ORLANDO DAILY NEWSPAPERS, INC.   583
Cite as 389 F.2d 579 (1967)

B. There is no dispute between the parties as to these fundamental principles. The dispute centers about the district court's conclusion that "whether a given writing is or is not libelous per se is a question of law for the Court to determine". The court below found that Florida "appellate decisions do not disclose any clear statement that the existence of libel per se is a question for the Court and not for the jury, [but] the Court interprets cases [throughout the United States] as establishing this as a sub silentio proposition of Florida law".

[5] We find that the general law and Florida law are in agreement with Dean Prosser's conclusion: "It is for the court *in the first instance* to determine whether the words are reasonably capable of a particular interpretation, or whether they are necessarily so; it is then for the jury to say whether they were in fact understood as defamatory. If the language used is open to two meanings * * * it is for the jury to determine whether the defamatory sense was the one conveyed." (Emphasis added.) Prosser, Law of Torts § 106, at 765 (1963). Similarly the Restatement, Second, Tentative Draft 12, Section 614, expresses the rule as follows:

(1) The Court determines

(a) Whether a communication is capable of bearing a particular meaning, and

(b) Whether that meaning is defamatory.

(2) The jury determines whether a communication, capable of a defamatory meaning, was so understood by its recipient.

Section 615 states:

(1) The Court determines

(a) Whether the defamatory meaning of libel is apparent from the publication itself without reference to extrinsic facts, and

(b) Whether an imputation of crime or disease or of unchastity to a woman, is of such a character as to make libel or slander actionable without proof of special harm.

(2) Subject to the control of the court whenever the issue arises, the jury determines whether language imputes to another conduct, characteristics or a condition incompatible with the proper conduct of his business, trade, profession or office.

[6] Both judge and jury play a part in determining whether language constitutes libel. The Supreme Court has delineated these roles in Washington Post Co. v. Chaloner, 1919, 250 U.S. 290, 39 S.Ct. 448, 63 L.Ed. 987:

A publication claimed to be defamatory must be read and construed in the sense in which the readers to whom it is addressed would ordinarily understand it. * * * When thus read, if its meaning is so unambiguous as to reasonably bear but one interpretation, it is for the judge to say whether that signification is defamatory or not. If, upon the other hand, it is capable of two meanings, one of which would be libelous and actionable and the other not, it is for the jury to say, under all the circumstances surrounding its publication, including extraneous facts admissible in evidence, which of the two meanings would be attributed to it by those to whom it is addressed or by whom it may be read.

In most of the Florida cases relied upon by all of the parties to this suit the trial court disposed of the libel issue summarily, so that in those cases the role of the jury was not discussed on appeal.[9]

9. E. g., Budd v. J. Y. Gooch Co., 157 Fla. 716, 27 So.2d 72 (Fla.1946); Adams v. News-Journal Corp., 84 So.2d 549 (Fla. 1956); Walsh v. Miami Herald Publ. Co., 80 So.2d 669 (Fla.1955); Richard v. Gray, 62 So.2d 597 (Fla.1953); Commander v. Pedersen, 116 Fla. 148, 156 So. 337 (1934); O'Neal v. Tribune Co., 176 So.2d 535 (Fla.Dist.Ct.App.1965); Hevey v. News-Journal Corp., 148 So.2d 543 (Fla. Dist.Ct.App.1963). See also Summit v. Zetterlund, 287 F. 759 (S.D.Fla.1923); Grayson v. Savannah News-Press Inc., 110 Ga.App. 561, 139 S.E.2d 347, 351

In cases in which jury trials were had the appellate decisions do not reflect whether the issue of libel per se was submitted to the jury. However, in Miami Herald Pub. Co. v. Brautigan, Fla.App.1961, 127 So.2d 718, cert. denied, 135 So.2d 741, cert. denied 369 U.S. 821, 82 S.Ct. 828, 7 L.Ed.2d 786 (1962) the trial court submitted to the jury the question whether a news story criticizing a state attorney for "muzzling" the grand jury was libelous per se; the District Court of Appeal affirmed. Some Florida decisions have specifically referred to the jury's role in determining libel per se. See Caldwell v. Cromwell-Collier Publ. Co., 5 Cir. 1947, 161 F.2d 333, 336 ("a jury might well conclude * * *"); Metropolis Co. v. Croasdell, 145 Fla. 455, 199 So. 568, 570 (1941) ("the evidence adduced by the plaintiff, if believed by the jury * * *"); McClellan v. L'Engle, 74 Fla. 581, 77 So. 270, 273 (1917) ("the language used may or may not be, by a jury, considered * * *."), but none of these cases involved the precise issue confronting this Court. In Jones v. Greeley, 25 Fla. 629, 6 So. 448, 450 (1885), the Florida Supreme Court approved the instruction, "It is a question for the jury to determine whether or not the alleged libel bears the construction which the plaintiff in his declaration seeks to put upon it * * *."

C. The district court in this case completely excised the jury's role, a position it could take only on the assumption that the publication unambiguously carried no defamatory meaning. Since the court did not spell out its reasons, the defendants in their briefs have attempted to articulate the rationale for the holding below.

The defendants argue that the article did not "hurt" Belli as an attorney, did not imply that he was "losing his touch with demonstrative evidence", did not affect his ability to "obtain those 'more adequate awards' for seamen and railroad workers for which he is so justly famous". In effect, so the argument runs, the article was nothing more than caustic comment on the acuteness of the Florida Bar Association. Belli simply "showed the Florida lawyers that their agreement was somewhat more favorable to him that they—in their naiveté—contemplated". In its harshest sense, they say, "the article implies no more than that Mr. Belli 'put one over' on the Florida Bar", which is "not quite the same as conning a destitute widow out of her homestead". In short, Mr. Belli just got "a little more out of the agreement than the Bar Association contemplated".

The defendants make a case—just barely—for the view that the article is capable of being reasonably interpreted as non-defamatory. But since the article on its face is also capable of carrying a defamatory meaning, it is for the jury to decide whether the words were in fact so understood.

The plaintiff contends, in his brief, "No person reading the headline and the article *sub judice* * * * could conclude other than that Melvin Belli, both as a lawyer and as a private citizen is grasping, conniving, contemptible, dishonest; a cheat, swindler, trickster, deceiver, defrauder; a person to be avoided, shunned and distrusted." Without benefit of the defendants' cavalier reading of the article or the plaintiff's retort hyperbolic, we consider that the bare bones of the article are capable of carrying the meaning that Belli tricked and deceived the Florida Bar Association out of hundreds of dollars worth of clothes.

The story alleges: (1) Belli knew that the Florida Bar Association's budget would enable him to be reimbursed only for his hotel bill; (2) subject to this limitation he agreed to participate in a

---

(1964); Walker v. Sheehan, 80 Ga.App. 606, 56 S.E.2d 628, 632 (1949); Hermann v. Newark Morning Ledger Co., 49 N.J. Super. 551, 140 A.2d 529, 530 (1958); Katapodis v. Brooklyn Spectator, 287 N.Y. 17, 38 N.E.2d 112, 137 A.L.R. 910

(1941); Appliance Buyers Credit Corp. v. Baxley, 241 S.C. 64, 127 S.E.2d 8, 10 (1962); Southern Publ. Co. v. Foster, 53 S.W.2d 1014, 1016 (Tex.Comm'n App. 1932); Frinzi v. Hanson, 30 Wis.2d 271, 140 N.W.2d 259 (1966).

BELLI v. ORLANDO DAILY NEWSPAPERS, INC.   585
Cite as 389 F.2d 579 (1967)

panel discussion; (3) he deliberately planned to "take" the Association for hundreds of dollars by charging clothing purchases to his hotel bill; (4) he and his well-dressed wife left Miami before the Association found out about their purchases; (5) the Association, to its embarrassment, had to pick up the tab. "The Florida Bar had been taken. * * After all that was the plan."

[7]   The author's comment seems intended to insure the common reader's understanding of what purportedly happened. The common reader is likely to understand "take", just as Miss Yothers must have understood it. A recent dictionary defines it: "To cheat, deceive"; [10] other dictionaries agree with this definition.[11] The man in the street is likely to understand that hotel expenses do not include "hundreds of dollars worth of clothing". But any doubts the reader might have as to what purportedly happened are likely to be resolved by the reference to Belli's "plan" to "take" the Florida Bar. We hold that a jury might reasonably conclude that the conduct imputed to Belli was incompatible with the standards of an ethical lawyer and as such violated one of the four traditional categories of libel per se. A jury might also conclude that such conduct subjected Belli to contempt and ridicule humiliating him socially and injuring him professionally.

The Court has some doubt whether the publication in question carries a nondefamatory meaning. The Court has very little doubt that it carries a defamatory meaning. The Court has concluded however that the final determination of the issue of defamation should be made by a jury.

[8]   The story is nine years old. It was not made within the context of a discussion of an important public issue. Nevertheless, the delimiting effect of the law of libel on First Amendment rights and a free press impels the Court not to excise the role of the jury. "Since one's reputation is the view which others take of him * * * [w]hether an idea injures a person's reputation depends upon the opinions of those to whom it is published." Developments in the Law: Defamation, 69 Harv.L.Rev. 875, 881–82 (1956). Thus, because it is impractical, even unreliable, to depend upon in-court testimony of recipients of the particular publication for determining whether that publication is defamatory, a logical function of the jury is to decide whether the plaintiff has been lowered in the esteem of those to whom the idea was published. As early as the seventeenth century, the court in Lord Townshend v. Dr. Hughes, 1693, 2 Mod. 150, 195, held that "words should not be construed in a rigid or in a mild sense, but according to the general and natural meaning, and agreeable to the common understanding of all men." Florida has adopted the common-mind test. Loeb v. Geronemus, Fla.1953, 66 So.2d 241. Any doubt as to the defamatory effect of a publication should be resolved by the common mind of the jury, and not by even the most carefully considered judicial pronouncement.

10.   The Reader's Digest Great Encyclopedia Dictionary 1365 (1967).

11.   See, for example, the Dictionary of American Slang 28 (1960) which defines "been taken" as "To have been taken advantage of, deceived, cheated or tricked, overcharged, sold misrepresented merchandise; swindled", or Webster's Third New International Dictionary 2330 (1966), which defines one of the meanings of the word "take" as "to impose upon, CHEAT, SWINDLE".

The seriousness of the charge of the newspaper article in this case, if inter-

preted by a jury as suggested by the above-cited possible dictionary definitions of one of the terms used therein, can be measured in part by reference to Rule 11.02 of the Integration Rules of the Florida Bar 3(a): "The commission by a lawyer of any act contrary to honesty, justice or good morals, whether the act is committed in the course of his relations as an attorney or otherwise * * * and whether or not the act is a felony or misdemeanor, constitutes a cause for discipline."

II.

Historically, the action for written defamation (libel) developed as a criminal action in the Star Chamber; the separate action for spoken defamation (slander) developed in the ecclesiastical courts. For the crime of libel, it was necessary to show harm only to the reputation; to recover on slander it was necessary to show pecuniary loss. The strict requirements for a slander action were rationalized on the ground that since libel is in a relatively permanent form and has a wider potential audience, pecuniary harm is so probable as to be presumed. See generally Veeder, The History and Theory of the Law of Defamation, 3 Colum.L.Rev. 546 (1903), 4 Colum.L.Rev. (1904). The difference between the law applicable to libel and that applicable to slander has been generally continued in the modern law of defamation. See Prosser, Law of Torts § 107 (1963); Developments in the Law: Defamation, 69 Harv.L.Rev. 876, 887 (1956); Harper and James, §§ 5.9, 5.10.

[9] With slander, as with libel, certain defamatory words are actionable without proof of any actual damage to the plaintiff. These fall into the same categories of libel per se. Pollard v. Lyon, 91 U.S. 225, 226, 23 L.Ed. 308 (1875). This classification was accepted by the Florida Supreme Court in Loeb v. Geronemus, 66 So.2d 241, 244 (1953): "Only certain well-defined classes of imputation as to crime, disease, particular unfitness for office, etc., or unchastity, have been deemed slanderous per se." Accord, e. g., Campbell v. Jacksonville Kennel Club, 66 So.2d 495 (Fla.1953); Carter v. Sterling, 132 So.2d 430 (Fla. Dist.Ct.App.1961). Any allegedly slanderous statements not falling within any of these categories may constitute slander per quod but are actionable only upon a showing of special damages. Loeb v. Geronemus, supra; Carter v. Sterling,

supra. Belli has not complained of special damage by reason of Handley's statement.

[10] In spite of language apparently limiting slander per se to four well-defined categories, Florida courts have adopted a broad view of what constitutes slander per se. In Sharpe v. Bussey, 1939, 137 Fla. 96, 187 So. 779, 780, 121 A.L.R. 1148, the court although emphasizing that "This action is for slander, not libel" quoted with approval the following language from Briggs v. Brown, 1908, 55 Fla. 417, 46 So. 325, 330, an action for libel and slander:

If the publication is false and not privileged, and is such that its natural and proximate consequence necessarily causes injury to a person in his personal, social, official or business relations of life, wrong and injury are presumed or implied and such publication is actionable per se.

Later cases approve this language. Joopanenko v. Gavagan, 67 So.2d 434 (Fla.1953); Carter v. Sterling, 132 So.2d 430 (Fla.Dist.Ct.App.1961). In *Sharp* the defendant was alleged to have said that the plaintiff was at a Negro dance hall, dancing with Negro "wenches". The Court found that the statement made by the defendant, if false, would cause injury to the plaintiff "in his social, official and business relations of life" because the plaintiff would have been viewed as having forfeited "respect and confidence" of the community (Jacksonville, Duval County) and would have been held "in contempt" and have been "despised by self-respecting" white and Negro citizens.[12] In *Joopanenko*, the plaintiff alleged that the defendant, addressing a crowd and speaking of the plaintiff, said "Don't let that man speak, I know him and he is a Communist". The Supreme Court of Florida refused to decide whether the statement accused the plaintiff of having committed a

---

12. The Court in *Sharp* relied extensively on the *libel* case of Briggs v. Brown, 55 Fla. 417, 46 So. 325 (1908). Furthermore, in *Sharp* a possible ground for the Court's holding, and one alluded to at least indirectly, was the injury to the plaintiff in his official capacity as mayor. This would place the case within one of the traditional categories of slander per se.

BELLI v. ORLANDO DAILY NEWSPAPERS, INC.   587

Cite as 389 F.2d 579 (1967)

crime, 67 So.2d at 437, and did not mention any effect of the statement on the plaintiff's business or profession. Instead, the Court held that "Such words hold him up to scorn, contempt and ridicule, causing such person to be shunned by his neighbors. * * *" In Florida then, the scope of a general class of slander per se includes statements holding another up to "scorn, contempt, and ridicule".

[11] Handley's oral statement to Yothers, as it is repeated in the record, does not contain all of the derogatory language of the printed column. There is no reference to a "plan" to "take" the Florida Bar Association. Handley referred to $300 of purchases, not to hundreds of dollars of clothing bills. The difference is in degree. We hold that it is for the jury to decide whether his account of the story was defamatory.

III.

Belli charges a conspiracy among Orlando Daily Newspapers, Inc., the Evening Star editor Martin Anderson, Jean Anderson, and other unnamed persons and corporations (but not Handley) to abuse, discredit, and vilify Belli through publication of the libelous article. The district court dismissed the conspiracy count as being too vague and indefinite to state a claim upon which relief may be granted. This dismissal is in error in light of our holding on the alleged libel.

[12] In Loeb v. Geronemus, 66 So.2d 241, 243 (Fla.1953), the court stated that "whether the complaint * * * alleges facts sufficient to state a cause of action [for conspiracy] must be determined from the standpoint of whether the complaint states a cause of action in either libel or slander." Additionally, the Florida Court of Appeals, referring to an earlier Supreme Court decision, observed that "A complaint alleging a conspiracy * * *, an overt act done in pursuance

with the conspiracy and damages resulting from such overt act was held to contain all the essential elements of a malicious conspiracy." Reagan v. Davis, 97 So.2d 324, 327 (Fla.Dist.Ct.App.1957). Since the alleged libel in the present case is actionable, the complaint alleging the conspiracy, the publication of the libelous article, and damages resulting therefrom is sufficient to state a cause of action.

IV.

The defendants, relying on New York Times Co. v. Sullivan, 376 U.S. 254, 84 S.Ct. 710, 11 L.Ed.2d 686 (1964), and the appellate decision in Curtis Publ. Co. v. Butts, 5 Cir. 1965, 351 F.2d 702, 705, aff'd 388 U.S. 130, 87 S.Ct. 1975, 18 L.Ed.2d 1094, and other lower court and appellate decisions,[13] assert that even if false the article in the Evening Star was a privileged commentary concerning a public figure; thus, if published without malice, the article could not give rise to liability for libel.

[13, 14] The New York Times doctrine has been expanded by the Supreme Court to encompass reporting of the conduct of "public figures". Curtis Publ. Co. v. Butts, 1967, 388 U.S. 130, 87 S.Ct. 1975, 18 L.Ed.2d 1094. Edwin A. Walker, commander of the federal troops during the school segregation confrontation at Little Rock in 1957 and an outspoken advocate against federal intervention in such matters, Coach Wallace Butts, one-time head football coach at the University of Georgia, and Linus Pauling,[14] scholar, scientist, and winner of two Nobel Prizes, have been classified as "public figures". Not only must Belli be considered a public figure before the defendants can avail themselves of the *New York Times* privilege; the matter covered by the publication must be of legitimate and substantial public interest. Thus a court confronted with a

13. Walker v. Courier-Journal & Louisville Times Co., 5 Cir., 1966, 368 F.2d 189, reversing 246 F.Supp. 231 (W.D.Ky.1965); Pauling v. Globe-Democrat Publ. Co., 8 Cir. 1966, 362 F.2d 188; Pauling v. National Review, Inc., 49 Misc.2d 975, 269 N.Y.S.2d 11 (Sup.Ct.1966).

14. See Pauling v. Globe-Democrat Publ. Co., 8 Cir. 1966, 362 F.2d 188.

defamation suit in which the defendant asserts the *New York Times* privilege is compelled to make the dual inquiry (1) whether the plaintiff is a public figure and (2) whether the alleged defamatory publication is directed towards his public conduct. In most cases it is a relatively simple matter to determine whether the plaintiff is a public *official* and whether the defamatory comment is directed toward his *official* capacity. But in the case of a public *figure* there is substantially more room for the interplay of facts concerning his entry into the public arena and the nature of the issue in which he has become embroiled. We conclude, therefore, that the trial court is the proper arena for development of the relevant facts and resolution of the crucial issues in the first instance.[15]

Although it may be conceded that the event purportedly covered by the Evening Star article was not a "public issue" or "public event", it may have been a matter of "public interest".[16] New York Times v. Sullivan, supra. Garrison v. Louisiana, 1964, 379 U.S. 64, 85 S.Ct. 209, 13 L.Ed.2d 125. We recognize, however, that we are here confronted with a case where the event reported was some nine years old and was reported in a gossip column. As the majority in Rosenblatt v. Baer, supra, 383 U.S. at 87, 86 S.Ct. at 677, recognized, concerning libel of a public official, "To be sure, there may be cases where a person is so far removed from a former position of authority that comment on the manner in which he performed his responsibilities no longer has the interest necessary to justify the New York Times rule." Furthermore, in a number of cases, some involving invasions of privacy, the privilege established in *New York Times* was not extended to public figures in circumstances concerning conduct or speech, however current, on matters of little or no public import.[17] We must leave it to the trial court, therefore, to determine whether Belli "was a public man in whose public conduct society and the press had a legitimate and substantial interest." Curtis Publ. Co. v. Butts, 388 U.S. at 165, 87 S.Ct. at 1997, 18 L.Ed.2d at 1117 (Warren, C. J., concurring).

[15] The opinion of Mr. Justice Harlan, joined by three other members of the Court, in the combined cases of *Walker* and *Butts* adopts a more narrow view of the privilege regarding defamation of public figures than that set out in *New York Times* regarding defamation of public officials.[18] A majority of

---

15. Cf. Rosenblatt v. Baer, 1966, 383 U.S. 75, 88, 86 S.Ct. 669, 677, 15 L.Ed.2d 597: "[A]s is the case with questions of privilege generally it is for the trial judge in the first instance to determine whether the proofs show respondent to be a 'public official.'"

16. See generally Comment, Defamation of the Public Official, 61 Nw.U.L.Rev. 614 (1966); Comment, The Scope of First Amendment Protection for Good-Faith Defamatory Error, 75 Yale L.J. 642 (1966); Note, Free Speech and Defamation of Public Persons: The Expanding Doctrine of New York Times Co. v. Sullivan, 52 Corn.L.Q. 419 (1967); Supreme Court, 1966 Term, 81 Harv.L.Rev. 69, 160 (1967). The danger of adopting a circular definition of the scope of the New York Times privilege is discussed in the Supreme Court, 1966 Term, supra at 163.

17. Lorillard v. Field Enterprises, Inc., 65 Ill.App.2d 65, 213 N.E.2d 1, 7 (1965) (socialite); Faulk v. Aware, Inc., 14 N.

Y.2d 954, 253 N.Y.S.2d 990, 202 N.E.2d 372 (1964), cert. denied, 380 U.S. 916, 85 S.Ct. 900, 13 L.Ed.2d 801 (radio and television performer); Dempsey v. Time, Inc., 43 Misc.2d 754, 252 N.Y.S.2d 186, 189 (Sup.Ct.1964), aff'd, 22 A.D.2d 854, 254 N.Y.S.2d 80 (1964) (prizefighter); Spahn v. Julian Messner, Inc., 43 Misc. 2d 219, 250 N.Y.S.2d 529, 535 (Sup.Ct. 1964), aff'd, 23 A.D.2d 216, 260 N.Y.S.2d 451 (1965) (baseball pitcher).

18. Compare the New York Times standard with the standard stated in Mr. Justice Harlan's opinion, 388 U.S. 130, 87 S.Ct. 1975, 1991, 18 L.Ed.2d 104.

We consider and would hold that a "public figure" who is not a public official may also recover damages for a defamatory falsehood whose substance makes substantial danger to reputation apparent, on a showing of highly unreasonable conduct constituting an extreme departure from the standards of investigation and reporting ordinarily

BELLI v. ORLANDO DAILY NEWSPAPERS, INC.   **589**
Cite as 389 F.2d 579 (1967)

the Court, however, extended the *New York Times* standards to encompass public figures. The Court in *New York Times* required "convincing clarity" of the proof presented to show actual malice, 376 U.S. at 285–286, 84 S.Ct. 710 (and found it lacking in that case); however, this requirement extends only to the proof required to meet the constitutional demands. As to the *complaint*, the Federal Rules of Civil Procedure require only that "Malice, intent, knowledge, and other condition of mind of a person * * * be averred generally." Rule 9(b). In his amended complaint Belli charged the defendants with actual malice in publication of the allegedly libelous article. This charge then, is sufficient on its face to establish a basis for a showing of actual malice by defendants in the perpetration of the alleged libel, as required by the *New York Times* decision.

We reverse the dismissal of the district court and remand the case for further proceedings consistent with this opinion.

GODBOLD, Circuit Judge (specially concurring):

I agree that the district court erred in dismissing the plaintiff's complaint for failure to state a claim upon which relief could be granted. But as to some of the principles that will guide the district court in further proceedings, my views differ from those stated in the careful and scholarly opinion of the majority.

There are two aspects to the complex problem of defining the provinces of judge and jury in a defamation case. The first involves a determination whether the publication complained of falls within one of the four categories which permit an action to be maintained without allegation or proof of special damages. Although the matter is not free from doubt, in Florida this question seems to be one for the court. McCormick v. Miami Herald Publishing Co.,

139 So.2d 197 (Fla.App.1962); see Adams v. News-Journal Corp., 84 So.2d 549 (Fla.1955). Compare Miami Herald Publishing Co. v. Brautigam, 127 So.2d 718 (Fla.App.1961). The second concerns whether the published statement is defamatory. On this point there is general agreement that it is for the judge in the first instance to determine whether the words are capable of defamatory meaning; if so it becomes the duty of the jury to decide whether they are defamatory in fact. 1 Harper & James, Torts § 5.29 (1956); Prosser, Torts § 106 (3d ed. 1964). This does not preclude the judge from ruling, in an appropriate case, that the meaning of the publication is so unambiguous when construed in the sense in which ordinary readers would understand it that it is defamatory as a matter of law. Washington Post Co. v. Chaloner, 250 U.S. 290, 39 S.Ct. 448, 63 L.Ed. 987 (1919). "If the article standing alone is plainly libelous, or manifestly wanting in any defamatory meaning, it is the duty of the court to declare either way and instruct the jury accordingly." Newell, Slander & Libel 362 (3d ed. 1914). I fail to see any way in which reasonable men could construe the statements, oral and written, in this case in a nondefamatory sense, and would therefore hold them defamatory as a matter of law. The expressed doubt of the majority whether the newspaper statements could carry a nondefamatory meaning is but little less firm than my view. The role of the jury is not to be excised. Nor is that of judges. If the content of language is defamatory beyond cavil, freedom does not call for allowing the defamer to make a second attack on the victim's reputation, though done in a judicial atmosphere, on the theory of showing that to the common mind the victim has not suffered in esteem. Judges deal regularly with questions of what ordinary and reasonable people do and think, in the field of constitutional liberties as well as elsewhere, and the properly exercisable judicial role is not diminished on

adhered to by responsible publishers. But see Rose v. Koch, Minn.1967, 154 N.W.2d 409, which interprets *Butts* as

setting out separate standards for public officials and public figures.

the ground that reputation is what is injured.

ON PETITION FOR REHEARING EN BANC

PER CURIAM:

The Petition for Rehearing is denied and no member of this panel nor Judge in regular active service on the Court having requested that the Court be polled on rehearing en banc, Rule 25(a), subpar. (b), the Petition for Rehearing En Banc is denied.

DRY CLIME LAMP CORPORATION and Henry S. Arnold, d/b/a Consolidated Engineering Company and Futorian Manufacturing Corporation of New York, Appellants,

v.

G. L. EDWARDS and James A. Hemphill, d/b/a Gulf Plastics Company, Appellees.

No. 23353.

United States Court of Appeals
Fifth Circuit.

Jan. 29, 1968.

Action by plastics company against manufacturer's representative and custom-built radiant oven manufacturer for breach of implied warranty of reasonable suitability in regard to plastic parts baking and curing system which was designed by representative and contained manufacturer's oven as one component but failed to operate satisfactorily. The United States District Court for the Southern District of Mississippi, William Harold Cox, J., entered judgment on verdict for plastics company, and manufacturer and representative appealed. The Court of Appeals, Godbold, Circuit Judge, held that evidence established that both defendants had breached implied war-

ranty, that manufacturer's express guarantee on oven did not prevent an implied warranty or limit the implied warranty to the narrower scope of the express warranty, and that court lacked power to enter judgment affecting representative if representative had no interest in attached funds or judgment against representative would have to be limited to extent of subjecting interest to plastics company's claim if representative did have an interest in attached funds, where action had been begun in Mississippi state court by attachment or garnishment directed to Mississippi residents allegedly indebted to representative and manufacturer.

Reversed for redetermination of damages and proceedings consistent with opinion.

1. Contracts ⚖️322(3)
   Sales ⚖️441(3)

Under Mississippi law, evidence in action by plastics company against manufacturer's representative and custom-built radiant oven manufacturer sustained trial judge's conclusion that representative and manufacturer had breached an implied warranty of reasonable suitability in regard to plastic parts baking and curing system designed by representative and containing manufacturer's oven.

2. Contracts ⚖️326

Under Mississippi law, where plastic parts baking and curing system failed to operate satisfactorily, manufacturer's representative which designed system for buyer was liable on implied warranty of reasonable suitability on basis of its oral undertaking to engineer, design, and supply drawings and specifications of system in connection with its sale of the major component to be incorporated into system.

3. Principal and Agent ⚖️101(1)

Under Mississippi law, in regard to plastic parts baking and curing system which failed to operate satisfactorily, manufacturer of radiant oven contained in system was liable as principal of manu-

294   ECONOMOPOULOS *v.* A. G. POLLARD CO.   [218

which it was founded, are decisive here. The reasoning on which that decision rested was that certificates for shares in the capital stock of a corporation are merely title deeds of the shares, and that the presence within the territorial limits of the Commonwealth of the title deeds of the shares does not bring the shares themselves within the Commonwealth. To the same effect see *In re James,* 144 N. Y. 6, 12. See also *Peabody* v. *Treasurer & Receiver General,* 215 Mass. 129. The case of *In re Kissel's Estate,* 121 N. Y. Supp. 1088, affirmed in 142 App. Div. (N. Y.) 934, is relied on by both parties. In that case the certificates of the foreign corporations were in New Jersey when the donee of the power died and the succession took effect. As we understand the decision it went on the ground that the shares were shares in a foreign corporation and not on the ground that the certificates for the shares were in New Jersey. The other case relied on by the respondent (*In re Fearing,* 200 N. Y. 340) was a decision as to the locality of bonds and does not bear on the question which we have to decide, namely, the locality of shares in a foreign corporation. In connection with *In re Fearing, ubi supra,* see *Wheeler* v. *New York,* 233 U. S. 434.

It follows that the amount of the tax due upon the estate passing under the will of Mary S. Dwight is $1,441.56. The decree of the Probate Court must be modified accordingly and, so modified, affirmed.

So ordered.

————

GEORGE ECONOMOPOULOS *vs.* A. G. POLLARD COMPANY.

Middlesex.   March 2, 1914. — June 17, 1914.

Present: RUGG, C. J., LORING, BRALEY, SHELDON, & CROSBY, JJ.

Slander, Publication.

In an action against the proprietor of a department store for slander, in accusing the plaintiff of the crime of larceny, there was evidence tending to show that the plaintiff, who could understand or talk little if any English, was addressed in English by a clerk, when no one else was within hearing, and was asked "if he didn't want to pay for what he had taken," that, the plaintiff not understanding, the clerk called a Greek clerk to whom he said in English, referring to the plaintiff, "I think he has taken a handkerchief. . . will you speak to him?" that the Greek clerk said to the plaintiff in Greek, "This gentleman here accuse you that you steal a handkerchief." The plaintiff testified that there "were fifty or sixty men around there." There was no evidence that any one other than the plaintiff and the Greek clerk understood the Greek language. *Held*, that, assuming, without deciding it, that the words spoken could have been found to have been accusations of larceny, there was no evidence warranting a finding of their publication.

Defamatory words, spoken in a foreign language in the presence of third persons, are not actionable if they are comprehensible only to the person using them and the person accused.

TORT against a corporation maintaining a department store in Lowell, the declaration alleging in the first and second counts that servants and agents of the defendant assaulted and illegally detained the plaintiff, and in a third count that they falsely and maliciously charged the plaintiff with the crime of larceny, saying, "You have stolen a handkerchief from us, and have it in your pocket." Writ dated December 15, 1911.

In the Superior Court the case was tried before *McLaughlin, J.* The testimony of the plaintiff, who could understand or talk little if any English, was as follows upon the issue of the slander alleged in the declaration: He had entered the defendant's store for the purpose of examining and purchasing goods. "Before I went two steps a hand grabbed me and I asked 'What is the matter?' He didn't give me no answer but called with the hand (indicating) to some other to come. I didn't understand what he said nor what language he spoke. He did not speak in Greek. There came a man to the men who were holding me and they were in conversation in English which I didn't understand. The Greek clerk (Miralos) said to me, 'This gentleman here accuse you that you steal a handkerchief and that you have it in your possession.' This is what the Greek salesman said to me. 'You have a hand-kerchief and have it in your possession, you steal it.' . . . There were fifty or sixty men around there."

The testimony of Joseph Carrier, a clerk of the defendant, on the same subject was as follows: "There wasn't anybody else around there when I came to where he was excepting him. I asked him if he did n't want to pay for what he had taken. I got no reply from him and I sent for the young Greek clerk (Miralos) and told him what I had seen. The Greek clerk talked Greek, which I could not understand. . . . Two women went by. . . .

When Miralos came up I said to him, 'I think he has taken a handkerchief from that box, will you speak to him?' And George (Miralos) spoke to him. I called his attention that I thought the man (the plaintiff) had taken the handkerchief in these words: 'I think that man has taken a handkerchief, ask him about it.'"

The testimony of George Miralos, the Greek salesman, on the same subject was as follows: "Mr. Carrier called me and I came nearer and he say, 'Ask this man if he took any handkerchief from this box that he did not pay for?' I asked him if he took any handkerchief from this box and he say 'Search me.' . . . Mr. Joe Carrier told me all about it. I say, 'You know what he said?' Well, he say, 'Yes, he says I take a handkerchief,' and he opened his coat and he say 'Search me.'"

At the conclusion of the evidence the plaintiff asked the judge to rule as follows: "If the salesman of the defendant (Carrier) acting in the belief that he was protecting the property of his employer, falsely and publicly accused the plaintiff of theft, in any words conveying that plain meaning, his act was that of his employer and makes the employer liable for all injuries to the plaintiff resulting naturally from his words."

The judge refused to give the ruling asked for, ruled that there was no evidence for the jury on the third count, and submitted the case to the jury on the first two counts only. The jury found for the defendant; and the plaintiff alleged exceptions.

W. H. Bent, for the plaintiff.

F. N. Wier, (*J. M. O'Donoghue* with him,) for the defendant.

LORING, J. We do not find it necessary to decide whether the two statements relied on by the plaintiff could have been found to be accusations of larceny. If it be assumed that such a finding could have been made, the judge was right in directing the jury to find a verdict for the defendant because there was no evidence of publication of either of them. See *Downs* v. *Hawley*, 112 Mass. 237; *Rumney* v. *Worthley*, 186 Mass. 144. There was no evidence that anybody but the plaintiff was present when Carrier spoke to the plaintiff in English. There was no publication of this statement made in English, because on the evidence the words could not have been heard by any one but the plaintiff. *Sheffill* v. *Van Deusen*, 13 Gray, 304.

Nor was there any evidence of publication of the Greek words spoken by Miralos. For, although there was evidence that they were spoken in the presence of others, there was no evidence that any one could understand them but the plaintiff. *Sheffill* v. *Van Deusen, ubi supra,* at page 305, and cases cited.

Under these circumstances we do not have to consider the question whether Carrier and Miralos could have been found to be acting within the scope of their employment by the defendant in making the two statements relied upon, as to which see *Kane* v. *Boston Mutual Life Ins. Co.* 200 Mass. 265, 269.

Exceptions overruled.

LAURENT REVEL *vs.* CORDELIA VEIN.

Middlesex.   March 3, 1914. — June 17, 1914.

Present: RUGG, C. J., LORING, BRALEY, SHELDON, & CROSBY, JJ.

Evidence, Relevancy and materiality.   *Witness,* Contradiction.

In an action of contract, where there was a declaration in set-off and the issues raised by the pleadings were as to amounts of money alleged to have been lent by the parties to each other, and where it appeared that the defendant was a woman and a hotel keeper with whom the plaintiff at times had lived, and no issue was raised by the pleadings as to any amounts due to the defendant from the plaintiff for board or lodging, if both parties introduce evidence in regard to personal relations of the parties, the defendant may testify in direct examination that, at a certain time when the plaintiff was living with her, he did not pay for his board, although previously the defendant had called the plaintiff as a witness and had asked him whether at that time he had paid for board and he had said that he had done so, because, the relations of the parties being in issue as affecting the probability of some of their financial dealings, the subject matter of the question was a material one, on which the defendant might contradict her own witness. *Whether,* if the subject matter had been immaterial, the testimony might have been admitted by the judge in the exercise of his discretion, was not decided.

CONTRACT for $5,463.81, alleged to have been lent by the plaintiff to the defendant. Writ dated August 25, 1911.

The defendant filed a declaration in set-off for $5,084.21, alleged to have been lent to the plaintiff by her.

The case was heard in the Superior Court by *Pratt,* J., who disallowed some and allowed others of the items of both declara-

6 Malpractice: Intentional, Negligent, and Without Fault

Malpractice is an area of tort law that often is not given as much attention as it deserves. In this chapter, we define malpractice and provide plenty of examples. We also talk about why malpractice is an important area of the law in itself, and how it relates to tort law in general.

Malpractice essentially means "bad practice." More specifically, it means professional misconduct. Some define malpractice as "professional negligence," but that definition is limited. Not all malpractice is based on negligence, though much of it is. Malpractice is professional misconduct that, like other areas of torts we've covered, may arise from intent, negligence, or liability without fault.

Many people outside the legal community associate malpractice with the field of medicine. This is probably because *medical malpractice* cases represent a large portion of all malpractice matters. However, malpractice is a tort that applies to professions in general, including the legal field. Just as lawyers may help clients to sue doctors, they may help clients to sue other lawyers too. But a lawyer is not necessarily the only legal professional who may be sued for malpractice. Paralegals may be liable for professional misconduct as well. Accordingly, it is important to learn about the general standards of care expected in each profession, and the consequences of failing to exercise such care.

Reasonable Care, Not Perfect Care

A professional is held to the standard of *reasonable* care in the profession. As we have already discussed, reasonable care does not necessarily mean perfect care.

For example, suppose that Susan began having stomach problems. She would have a mild stomachache almost every day. After about one week, she decided to go to Cliff, a doctor. Cliff told Susan that it was just nerves, and prescribed some medication to help Susan relax. A few weeks passed and Susan did not get any better.

Susan then decided to visit Dia, another doctor. Dia discovered that Susan's pain arose from a bacterial infection that Susan developed while on vacation. Apparently, Susan had eaten some contaminated food that resulted in the infection. Under Dia's care, Susan made a speedy recovery. Susan was very lucky that she went to Dia when she did. Had she delayed any longer, the infection may have caused irreversible damage. Is Cliff liable for malpractice? To answer this question, let's take a look at the facts and apply them to the law.

First, it is evident that Cliff *misdiagnosed* Susan's condition. In other words, Cliff did not properly explain to Susan the cause of her pain. For the moment, let's suppose the extreme—that Cliff actually knew how to properly treat Susan but *purposely* misled her, because he *wanted* Susan to remain ill. Cliff's motives may have been personal against Susan, or just general irrational behavior on his part.

In any event, if Cliff did indeed intentionally misdiagnose Susan, his action would certainly amount to malpractice.

A more common scenario, however, would be that Cliff made an honest mistake in failing to properly diagnose Susan's condition. As a doctor, Cliff certainly *wanted* to cure Susan, but he just didn't properly identify the cause of her pain. A nonintentional misdiagnosis does not automatically mean malpractice. If Cliff's misdiagnosis, though incorrect, was nonetheless *reasonable*, then he will probably not be liable for malpractice.

As it turned out, Dia made the proper diagnosis. But perhaps this was an unusually brilliant diagnosis, made because of Dia's outstanding training and access to superior technology. Perhaps the average doctor would have made the same diagnosis Cliff did. In that case, Cliff would probably not be liable for malpractice, because his diagnosis was reasonable, even if incorrect.

This example serves as a classic reminder of the fact that doctors are not necessarily liable because they do not cure a patient. They are only liable if they fail to use reasonable care. Therefore, even when patients die on the operating table, doctors are not liable if the medical care that they provided was reasonable.

The same holds true for other professionals, such as attorneys. Suppose that Hank was injured in an automobile accident and wants to sue Ralph, the other driver. Hank approaches Thomas, an attorney, and asks for legal advice.

Thomas agrees to represent Hank. However, Thomas does not realize that the applicable *statute of limitations* is about to expire. Hank must file his lawsuit before the deadline set by the statue of limitations or he will probably be barred from suing Ralph. Thomas continues to delay preparing the case, and the statute of limitations runs out. Hank is now *time-barred* from bringing a lawsuit against Ralph.

Generally, if an attorney fails to address as important an element of a lawsuit as the statute of limitations, this amounts to negligence. Accordingly, Hank may have a good cause of action against Thomas for malpractice.

Suppose instead that Thomas did in fact file the lawsuit before time ran out, and suppose that he sought $1 million in damages on Hank's behalf. A few weeks later, he received a telephone call from Ralph's insurance company, who offered to settle the lawsuit for $300,000. In other words, the company would pay Hank $300,000 if he would drop the lawsuit against Ralph. Being a responsible attorney, Thomas discussed the settlement offer with Hank.

Note: Generally, an attorney should discuss any settlement offer with a client. The attorney may, of course, offer his or her opinion about the offer, but it is ultimately the client's decision whether or not to accept it.

Thomas told Hank that the offer was low, and that Hank should not accept any settlement offer less than $500,000, because Thomas expected to recover at least that amount, if not more, by winning the trial. Thomas, fully confident that he would win at trial, convinced Hank to reject the offer. The insurance company never made another settlement offer.

At trial, Hank was awarded $100,000 in damages. If he had taken the settlement offer, he would have received $300,000. By electing instead to proceed with the trial, he received only $100,000. Essentially, he gambled and lost. In retrospect, Thomas' advice was flawed. Had Thomas convinced Hank to settle out of court, Hank would have collected more money. But Thomas' miscalculation does not necessarily amount to professional misconduct. If Thomas' estimation of victory at trial, though mistaken, was *reasonable*, then Thomas did not commit malpractice.

In fact, even if Thomas were to lose the case outright and recover no money at all for Hank, that still does not mean that Thomas committed malpractice. Just as doctors are not obligated to guarantee a medical cure, attorneys are not obligated to guarantee a courtroom victory.

INFORMED CONSENT

Generally, professionals are required to disclose all relevant information to those they serve. Accordingly, those served are **informed** when they give their ultimate **consent** for a particular service.

Generally speaking, who makes the ultimate decision about whether or not to proceed with an operation?

A. The doctor.

B. The patient.

Along the same lines, who makes the ultimate decision about whether or not to proceed with a lawsuit?

A. The attorney

B. The client

For both questions, the correct answer is B. It is *patients* and *clients* who ultimately decide their own fate, not the professionals who serve them. But you would be suprised how many people do not realize that. Think about it. When you seek professional help you are paying for the service. The service is being done on *your* behalf. It is either your body, your freedom, your car, your house, or any other aspect of *you*. Therefore, does it not make sense that *you* should have the final say?

Sometimes people are intimidated by the professionals' superior knowledge about a particular subject and do not actively participate in the matter at hand. A good professional, however, must have more than good knowledge; he or she must be able to *communicate* that knowledge effectively, and to encourage the patient or client to *participate* in the final decision.

For example, take the decision about whether or not to have an operation. Suppose that Melissa loves to play tennis. She is in her mid-twenties and has been playing tennis for about ten years. She will probably never be good enough to play professionally, but she enjoys tennis as a recreational sport. From time to time, Melissa plays in small tennis tournaments, and she has even won a couple of them. About two months ago, Melissa injured her knee during a tournament. She went to see Robert, an orthopedic surgeon who deals with many sports-related injuries. After a thorough examination, Robert told Melissa that she has two realistic options.

1. Melissa may rest the knee and undergo some physical therapy, at which point she can resume just about any physical activity, including recreational tennis. In that case, Melissa should never again play competitive tennis, as she may severely aggravate the injury.

2. Melissa may undergo knee surgery which, if successful, would result in a complete recovery, thereby permitting Melissa to resume playing competitive tennis. However, there is the risk that Melissa may suffer complications that could limit her ability to put pressure on her knee. This may prevent her from being able to play any type of tennis game, or to engage in any type of recreational exercise.

As any good professional would do, Robert explained the choices to Melissa clearly. He told her that his opinion was that she should have the surgery because the chances of a complete recovery were excellent, whereas the chances of complications were minimal. In any event, the decision is up to *Melissa*, not up to *Robert*.

Whether Melissa elects to undergo surgery or to not have the operation—thereby giving up playing competitive tennis—her decision will be **informed consent**. Either way, Melissa will know what the choices are and will be the one to make the ultimate decision.

The same type of scenario involving informed consent could easily arise in the legal field. Suppose that Grant owns an apartment building and Jason is one of his tenants. Jason is often late in paying the rent, and Grant has mentioned it to him on several occasions. Jason is always apologetic for the delay. In fact, Jason has begun looking for a less expensive apartment in another building, and has told Grant that. In any event, Grant is still considering evicting Jason.

Grant consults Lisa, an experienced landlord-tenant attorney, who outlines Grant's options for him. Lisa explains to Grant that the eviction process is often a lengthy one, and that the courts often have a great deal of sympathy for tenants who are about to be thrown out of their homes. She believes that Jason may opt to stay in the apartment for as long as he can, without paying *any* rent.

Alternatively, Lisa suggests that Grant work out a payment plan with Jason, and even help Jason to find a cheaper apartment. That way, Grant will get *some* of his money, and be rid of Jason more quickly. Grant fears that such an approach will set a precedent for other tenants and decides to begin eviction proceedings anyway. Regardless of the outcome, Lisa has informed Grant of his options. Therefore, it is on Grant's *informed consent* that Lisa begins the eviction process against Jason.

Malpractice against Paralegals

Paralegals can be liable for malpractice too. Although all legal professionals are generally governed by the American Bar Association's Code of Ethics (as well as other organizations to which these professionals may belong), paralegals are generally less regulated than attorneys. Nonetheless, they are capable of malpractice and are often held responsible for its consequences. Many of the criteria used to determine attorney malpractice are used to determine paralegal malpractice as well.

However, an act more applicable to paralegals is inaccurate representation, namely, when paralegals do not clearly establish that they are in fact paralegals, not attorneys.

Suppose, for example, that Marcia is a paralegal who works for a small law office. One afternoon, Marcia is the only person in the office. She is finishing up a project and is using one of the attorneys' computers. Sidney walks into the office and sees Marcia sitting behind a desk, with numerous law school diplomas and certificates hanging on the wall behind her.

Sidney has a legal dilemma. He has inherited his uncle's resort hotel in Hawaii, but Sidney's two brothers are trying to take it away from him. Marcia gives Sidney some advice about how to proceed. Sidney thanks her, says he'll think about it, and leaves the office.

At no time during the conversation did Marcia ever discuss her professional status. Although she did not lie and say she was an attorney, Marcia may very well have misled Sidney. After all, she was sitting behind a lawyer's desk in a law office. It would only be natural for Sidney to assume that she was in fact a lawyer.

As a legal professional, Marcia owed Sidney a duty of reasonable care. While her advice may have been excellent, she was nonetheless obligated to disclose to Sidney that she was a paralegal, not an attorney.

Of course, if her own law office has a policy that specifically prohibits paralegals from giving legal advice, then Marcia would have violated that as well.

Generally, paralegals are discouraged from giving legal advice, particularly when there are attorneys working in the same office. While there is no absolute rule forbidding paralegals to *ever* give legal advice, paralegals should always accurately disclose their professional status to the people to whom they give advice.

COMPETENCE

A great deal of professional malpractice occurs when there is a lack of professional competence, namely, when the professional assumes a task that he or she is not capable of performing effectively.

For instance, suppose that John is fresh out of law school and looking for a job. Discouraged by the available positions at some local law firms, John instead decides to open his own practice. In order to meet his business expenses, John diligently assumes almost every case that comes across his desk.

While the volume of cases helps John's practice to grow, John must be very careful to handle his clients' matters *competently*. In other words, suppose a client approaches John with a question about immigration law, and John does not know a thing about immigration law. John may tell the client:

1. "I'm sorry, but I don't deal with immigration matters. You'll have to find another attorney."
2. "Here is the name and address of an immigration attorney."
3. "I'll be happy to help you, but I will need to consult with an immigration attorney who has more experience in these types of matters. I'll discuss all arrangements, including fees, with you."
4. "Sure, I'll be happy to take your case."

Options 1, 2, and 3 are all examples of sound professionalism. Option 4, by itself, is not. If John assumes the case and then decides to "learn as he goes," he may not be providing the client with the type of care that an attorney is obligated to provide. In his eagerness to gain clients, John may be in over his head. If John's inexperience leads to poor legal service that harms the client, that would be a classic example of malpractice based on professional incompetence.

OTHER TYPES OF PROFESSIONAL MALPRACTICE

While medical and legal malpractice are prime examples of professional misconduct, there are certainly other fields in which professionals are held accountable for the services they provide.

Take, for example, public servants. Police officers, firefighters, and elected officials owe a standard of care to the public, but they are not liable for every unsolved crime, unextinguished fire, or unsuccessful government policy. If a bank is robbed and the police fail to capture the culprits, this by itself is not professional malpractice. However, if the police officers had been drinking alcoholic beverages while on duty, and were thereby too drunk to chase the criminals, that would be a prime example of malpractice.

In addition to other civil and criminal sanctions that could result from a public servant's misconduct, many inappropriate acts fall under the category of malpractice.

Educational Malpractice

Did you ever stop to question whether you received a good quality education? Could it have been better? If not you, what about a classmate of yours, or a friend or relative? Who, if anyone, is to blame if a student receives a poor education—the student, the teacher, or the school?

In recent years, a growing number of lawsuits have been brought against educational institutions for malpractice. While there are a great number of fine schools throughout the United States, there are also many that are substandard, to say the least.

The problems in delivering poor education are many, and may often involve lack of financial support, unmotivated faculty, or poor overall administration.

Other instances could involve relaxed standards. For example, a particular school may be interested in high enrollment and a high graduation rate. To gain these favorable statistics, the school may allow students to graduate without meeting as rigorous standards as do their counterparts in other schools. In the case of overcrowded schools, students often "slip through the cracks" and graduate without having fulfilled all the necessary requirements.

In any case, students may be happy to be done with their schooling without realizing that they have not gained the skills and knowledge befitting completion of a particular educational program. Unfortunately, the poor training and lack of knowledge may come back to haunt them in the future.

Think about it. Would you want a doctor who barely got through medical school to operate on you? Or an accountant who was mistakenly given passing grades to prepare your income tax returns? Or somebody who never passed a road test to drive your children to school? Fortunately, professional licenses are typically gained only after certain criteria have been fulfilled. However, a disturbingly large number of people still "slip through the cracks."

An educational institution may be liable in granting status (a license or diploma, for example) to students who have not met the necessary requirements.

Next, consider the student who fails senior year of high school two times and must attend the twelfth grade for a *third* time. What if that student and his parents complain to the school, or to the local or state department of education? The school is not automatically liable. That issue depends on whether the school, through its administrators, faculty, and staff, failed to provide the type of professional service that would have caused a student to complete high school in the normal course of time. After all, maybe the student did not attend class, refused to pay attention, or had personal problems or concerns outside of school that dominated his thoughts and distracted him from his studies.

Whatever the case, the academic field is yet another professional environment in which lawsuits have been filed for malpractice.

LIABILITY WITHOUT FAULT

We have discussed intentional and negligent professional misconduct. Now let's talk a little bit about malpractice liability without fault. Generally, a company, firm, hospital, or other employer may be vicariously liable for the negligent acts of one or more of its employees. Accordingly, while an employee may commit malpractice and be sued, the employer may be named in the lawsuit as well.

This notion is an expansion of the theory of *respondeat superior*, which we discussed in Chapter 2. An employer may not only be vicariously liable, thereby responsible for paying damages, but may suffer professional sanctions as well.

For example, suppose that Carla is a sole-practicing attorney. Adrienne is one of Carla's clients. Carla is preparing Adrienne's paperwork for an upcoming lawsuit against her former landlord. Marvin, who is Carla's paralegal, negligently misplaces the file. Carla is unable to gather all of the information she needs, and is unable to file the papers on time. Although she asks for an extension, the court refuses to grant Carla's request. As a result, Adrienne is unable to file her lawsuit because the *statute of limitations* has expired.

Adrienne then contacts Jim, an attorney who deals with professional malpractice. Jim sues Carla's firm for damages, including the amount Adrienne had expected to recover in her original lawsuit plus reasonable attorney's fees. Remember, Carla was not personally negligent. Her paralegal employee, Marvin, was. As a result of Marvin's negligence, Carla may not only be liable for the damages, but she may face sanctions by her state bar association for malpractice.

Malpractice liability without fault may result in all applicable damages *and* sanctions under *respondeat superior*.

MALPRACTICE CLAIMS

The debate about malpractice litigation (lawsuits) is a lively one. There are those who argue that such lawsuits are an excuse for frustrated individuals to take their revenge on innocent professionals, or that plaintiffs use such lawsuits as a quick way to collect an undeserved fortune. Others insist that without malpractice litigation, professionals would not feel the need to adhere to an acceptable set of standards, thereby doing a great disservice to the general public.

What is the truth about the threat of a malpractice lawsuit? Does it force doctors to practice "defensive medicine," or does it give them an incentive not to become careless? Is it an underhanded way for lawyers and clients to make a profit, or is it a way to ensure high-quality service? The answer is not absolute. There may be a little bit of truth in each of these arguments. With further study and reflection, you can become more familiar with these and other arguments about malpractice, and be better prepared to draw your own conclusions.

REVIEW QUESTIONS

1. What does malpractice mean?
2. Why is professional negligence a limited definition of malpractice?
3. Name three professions in which malpractice may apply, and give an example of each.
4. Explain the difference between reasonable care and perfect care.
5. What is informed consent?
6. Give an example of paralegal malpractice.
7. Give an example of malpractice based on incompetence.
8. Give an example of a student's poor education that is the fault of the teacher, one that it is the fault of the school, and one that is the fault of the student.
9. What does defensive medicine mean, in terms of malpractice?
10. What is the theory of *respondeat superior*?

A TORT TALE

Julio and Melanie met at a party. They started talking, and Julio told Melanie that he was involved in a child custody suit with his ex-wife. Julio said that the next phase would be to file a certain document with the court that has to be filed within 30 days. But Julio was complaining that he needed more time, because he had to find certain information that should be included in the document.

Melanie assured Julio that the court would not have a problem if Julio took an extra 30 days to file the document.

By the time Julio filed the document, 50 days had passed. He was 20 days late. The court refused to accept the document. This, in turn, resulted in Julio losing the case and not gaining custody of his children. As it turns out, Melanie gave Julio horrible advice—advice that fell well below the standard of reasonable care in the legal profession.

However, Melanie is not liable to Julio for malpractice. Why?

CASE LAW

Before we move on to Chapter 7, take a look at a couple of cases that deal with malpractice. Reading them will help you gain a better understanding of this hotly-debated topic. As always, keep in mind everything we have discussed about case law as you read.

construction of the applicable law. And it is for the Commission to say whether, on the showing made, considered in the light of the controlling statutory standard as here construed, Southern Bell should be permitted, at this time, to increase its schedule of rates for intrastate service.

It is the prerogative of that agency, to decide that question. It is an agency composed of men of special knowledge, observation, and experience in their field, and it has at hand a staff trained for this type of work. And the law imposes on it, not us, the duty to fix rates.

[14] Of course, in determining the net operating income of applicant the Commission must take into consideration the net income to be produced by the greater number of telephones in service at the end of any test period adopted by it. Of this fact we assume the Commission is fully aware. Perhaps that is why the court below declined to incorporate a direction to that effect in its judgment.

The judgment entered in the court below must be modified in accord with this opinion. Thereupon the cause will be remanded to the Commission for further proceedings in accord therewith. It is so ordered.

Modified and affirmed.

230 N.C. 517

HODGES v. CARTER et al.

No. 21.

Supreme Court of North Carolina.

Feb. 24, 1954.

Action by insured to recover compensation for losses resulting from alleged negligence in prosecuting insured's claim against insurers. The Superior Court, Beaufort County, Chester R. Morris, J., entered judgment of involuntary nonsuit and insured appealed. The Supreme Court, Barnhill, C. J., held that no breach of duty was shown by the evidence.

Affirmed.

1. Attorney and Client ☞107

An attorney, who engages in the practice of law and contracts to prosecute an action in behalf of his client, impliedly represents that he possesses the requisite degree of learning, skill, and ability necessary to practice of his profession and which others similarly situated ordinarily possess, that he will exercise his best judgment in the prosecution of the litigation entrusted to him, and that he will exercise reasonable and ordinary care and diligence in the use of his skill and in the application of his knowledge to his client's cause.

2. Attorney and Client ☞109

An attorney who acts in good faith and in an honest belief that his advice and acts are well founded and in the best interest of his client is not answerable for a mere error of judgment or for a mistake in a point of law which has not been settled by the court of last resort in his state and on which reasonable doubt may be entertained by well-informed lawyers.

3. Attorney and Client ☞129(2)

In action by insured to recover compensation for losses resulting from alleged negligence in prosecuting insured's claims against insurers, evidence did not disclose breach of duty. G.S. § 58–153.

———

Civil action to recover compensation for losses resulting from the alleged negligence of defendant D. D. Topping and H. C. Carter, now deceased, in prosecuting, on behalf of plaintiff, certain actions on fire insurance policies.

On 4 June 1948 plaintiff's drug store building located in Belhaven, N. C., together with his lunch counter, fixtures, stock of drugs and sundries therein contained, was destroyed by fire. At the time plaintiff was insured under four policies of fire insurance against loss of, or damage to, said mercantile building and its contents. He filed proof of loss with each of the four insurance companies which issued said pol-

HODGES v. CARTER
Cite as 80 S.E.2d 144   N. C.   145

icies. The insurance companies severally rejected the proofs of loss, denied liability, and declined to pay any part of the plaintiff's losses resulting from said fire.

H. C. Carter and D. D. Topping were at the time attorneys practicing in Beaufort and adjoining counties. As they were the ones from whom plaintiff seeks to recover, they will hereafter be referred to as the defendants.

On 7 April 1949 plaintiff entered into a written contract of employment with defendants to prosecute an action against each of the insurers on the policy issued by it. The compensation to be paid was fixed on a contingent basis and defendants bound themselves "to do whatever may be necessary in order to bring the matters to a successful conclusion, to the best of their knowledge and ability."

On 3 May 1949 defendants, in behalf of plaintiff, instituted in the Superior Court of Beaufort County four separate actions —one against each of the four insurers. Complaints were filed and summonses were issued, directed to the sheriff of Beaufort County. In each case the summons and complaint, together with copies thereof, were mailed to the Commissioner of Insurance of the State of North Carolina. The Commissioner accepted service of summons and complaint in each case and forwarded a copy thereof by registered mail to the insurance company named defendant therein.

Thereafter each defendant made a special appearance and moved to dismiss the action against it for want of proper service of process for that the Insurance Commissioner was without authority, statutory or otherwise, to accept service of process issued against a foreign insurance company doing business in this State. When the special appearance and motion to dismiss came on for hearing at the February Term 1950, the judge presiding concluded that the acceptance of service of process by the Insurance Commissioner was valid

and served to subject the movants to the jurisdiction of the court. Judgment was entered in each case denying the motion therein made. Each defendant excepted and appealed. This Court reversed. Hodges v. New Hampshire Fire Insurance Co., 232 N.C. 475, 61 S.E.2d 372. See also Hodges v. Home Insurance Co., 233 N.C. 289, 63 S.E.2d 819.

On 4 March 1952 plaintiff instituted this action in which he alleges that the defendants were negligent in prosecuting his said actions in that they failed to (1) have process properly served, and (2) sue out alias summonses at the time the insurers filed their motions to dismiss the actions for want of proper service of summons, although they then had approximately sixty days within which to procure the issuance thereof.

Defendants, answering, deny negligence and plead good faith and the exercise of their best judgment.

At the hearing in the court below the judge, at the conclusion of plaintiff's evidence in chief, entered judgment of involuntary nonsuit. Plaintiff excepted and appealed.

Allen, Allen & Langley, Kinston, for plaintiff-appellant.

Grimes & Grimes, Rodman & Rodman, and L. H. Ross, Washington, for defendant appellees.

BARNHILL, Chief Justice.

This seems to be a case of first impression in this jurisdiction. At least counsel have not directed our attention to any other decision of this Court on the question here presented, and we have found none.

[1] Ordinarily when an attorney engages in the practice of the law and contracts to prosecute an action in behalf of his client, he impliedly represents that (1) he possesses the requisite degree of learn-

ing, skill, and ability necessary to the practice of his profession and which others similarly situated ordinarily possess; (2) he will exert his best judgment in the prosecution of the litigation entrusted to him; and (3) he will exercise reasonable and ordinary care and diligence in the use of his skill and in the application of his knowledge to his client's cause. McCullough v. Sullivan, 102 N.J.L. 381, 132 A. 102, 43 A.L.R. 928; In re Woods, 158 Tenn. 383, 13 S.W.2d 800, 62 A.L.R. 904; Great American Indemnity Co. v. Dabney, Tex. Civ.App., 128 S.W.2d 496; Davis v. Associated Indemnity Corp., D.C., 56 F.Supp. 541; Gimbel v. Waldman, 193 Misc. 758, 84 N.Y.S.2d 888; Annotation 52 L.R.A. 883; 5 A.J. 287, § 47; Prosser Torts, p. 236, sec. 36; Shearman & Redfield Negligence, sec. 569.

[2] An attorney who acts in good faith and in an honest belief that his advice and acts are well founded and in the best interest of his client is not answerable for a mere error of judgment or for a mistake in a point of law which has not been settled by the court of last resort in his State and on which reasonable doubt may be entertained by well-informed lawyers. 5 A.J. 335, sec. 126; 7 C.J.S., Attorney and Client, § 142, page 979; McCullough v. Sullivan, supra; Hill v. Mynatt, Tenn.Ch.App., 59 S.W. 163, 52 L.R.A. 883.

Conversely, he is answerable in damages for any loss to his client which proximately results from a want of that degree of knowledge and skill ordinarily possessed by others of his profession similarly situated, or from the omission to use reasonable care and diligence, or from the failure to exercise in good faith his best judgment in attending to the litigation committed to his care. 5 A.J. 333, sec. 124; In re Woods, supra; McCullough v. Sullivan, supra; Annotation 52 L.R.A. 883.

[3] When the facts appearing in this record are considered in the light of these controlling principles of law, it immediately becomes manifest that plaintiff has failed to produce a scintilla of evidence tending to show that defendants breached any duty the law imposed upon them when they accepted employment to prosecute plaintiff's actions against his insurers or that they did not possess the requisite learning and skill required of an attorney or that they acted otherwise than in the utmost good faith.

The Commissioner of Insurance is the statutory process agent of foreign insurance companies doing business in this State, G.S. § 58–153, Hodges v. New Hampshire Insurance Co., 232 N.C. 475, 61 S.E.2d 372, and when defendants mailed the process to the Commissioner of Insurance for his acceptance of service thereof, they were following a custom which had prevailed in this State for two decades or more. Foreign insurance companies had theretofore uniformly ratified such service, appeared in response thereto, filed their answers, and made their defense. The right of the Commissioner to accept service of process in behalf of foreign insurance companies doing business in this State had not been tested in the courts. Attorneys generally, throughout the State, took it for granted that under the terms of G.S. § 58–153 such acceptance of service was adequate. And, in addition, the defendants had obtained the judicial declaration of a judge of our Superior Courts that the acceptance of service by the Commissioner subjected the defendants to the jurisdiction of the court. Why then stop in the midst of the stream and pursue some other course?

Doubtless this litigation was inspired by a comment which appears in our opinion on the second appeal, Hodges v. Home Insurance Co., 233 N.C. 289, 63 S.E.2d 819. However, what was there said was pure dictum, injected—perhaps ill advisedly—in explanation of the reason we could afford plaintiff no relief on that appeal. We did not hold, or intend to intimate, that defendants had been in any wise neglectful of their duties as counsel for plaintiff.

STATE v. CEPHUS
Cite as 80 S.E.2d 147

N. C.   **147**

The judgment entered in the court below is

Affirmed.

PARKER, J., took no part in the consideration or decision of this case.

239 N.C. 535

STATE   v.   DAWES.

No. 74.

Supreme Court of North Carolina.

Feb. 24, 1954.

Defendant was convicted for possessing nontax-paid whisky for purpose of sale. The Superior Court, Nash County, Walter J. Bone, J., entered judgment and defendant appealed. The Supreme Court found the record free of reversible error.

No error.

Criminal Law ⬅︎1182

Conviction for possession of nontax-paid whisky for purpose of sale was affirmed.

———◆———

Criminal prosecution tried on appeal from the County Recorder's Court upon a warrant charging the defendant with possession of nontax-paid whiskey for the purpose of sale.

From a verdict of guilty and judgment imposing penal servitude of six months, the defendant appeals, assigning errors.

Davenport & Davenport, C. C. Abernathy, Nashville, and T. A. Burgess, Rocky Mount, for defendant, appellant.

Harry McMullan, Atty. Gen., T. W. Bruton, Asst. Atty. Gen., and Charles G. Powell, Jr., Raleigh, Member of Staff, for the State.

PER CURIAM.

This case involves no new question requiring extended discussion. A careful examination of the record leaves us with the impression it is free of reversible or prejudicial error. The verdict and judgment will be upheld.

No error.

BARNHILL, C. J., took no part in the consideration or decision of this case.

239 N.C. 521

STATE   v.   CEPHUS.

No. 77.

Supreme Court of North Carolina.

Feb. 24, 1954.

Prosecution for assault with deadly weapon. The Superior Court, Edgecombe County, Walter J. Bone, J., upon verdict, entered judgment of conviction. Defendant appealed. The Supreme Court, Barnhill, C. J., held that trial court erred in instructing jury that burden of proof was on defendant to satisfy jury that he acted in self defense.

New trial.

1. Assault and Battery ⬅︎82

The rule in homicide cases that upon proof that defendant intentionally assaulted another with deadly weapon, inflicting wound which proximately caused death of person assaulted, defendant has burden of proving facts and circumstances which rebut presumption of malice or which excuse homicide on ground of self-defense, accident or misadventure, has no application in prosecution for assault with deadly weapon.

2. Criminal Law ⬅︎308

In criminal prosecutions, defendant's plea of not guilty clothes him with a preted afterwards to repudiate any of its obligations." Wiggins Ferry Co. v. Ohio & Mississippi R. Co., 142 U.S. 396, 408, 12 S.Ct. 188, 192, 35 L.Ed. 1055.

National Credit Co. v. Casco Co., *supra*, 173 Wash. at 276, 22 P.2d 670. The inescapable conclusion to be drawn from the facts presented is that it was the intention of the parties that Settle was to comply with the trust provisions of the successive AGC-union contracts.

[2] Settle argues that on several occasions the union supplied him with new compliance agreements which were never signed, thus proving that it had no intention of continuing the arrangement. After 15 years of operating under the terms of the collective bargaining agreements, Settle Construction Company is estopped to deny that its original promise did not bind it to successive AGC-union contracts. Leonard v. Washington Employers, Inc., 77 Wash. 2d 271, 461 P.2d 538 (1969); De-Britz v. Sylvia, 21 Wash.2d 317, 150 P.2d 978 (1944).

Finally, Settle argues that only federal law fashioned by federal courts is applicable because the Labor Management Relations Act of 1947, § 301 (Taft-Hartley) 29 U.S.C., § 185 (1947) requires it. Textile Workers Union of America v. Lincoln Mills, 353 U.S. 448, 77 S.Ct. 912, 1 L.Ed.2d 972 (1957). If this is so, the following federal cases support the position above adopted. Lewis v. Kepple, 185 F.Supp. 884 (W.D.Penn.1960); Lewis v. Kerns, 175 F. Supp. 115 (S.D.Ind.1959); Lewis v. Cable, 107 F.Supp. 196 (W.D.Penn.1952). *Also see* Weber v. Anspach, 256 Or. 479, 473 P. 2d 1011 (1970).

The judgment is reversed and the cause remanded for a trial on the issue of the actual amount that is due and owing by Settle Construction Company to the trusts.

FARRIS and CALLOW, JJ., concur.

---

11 Wash.App. 272

Richard R. MILLER, Appellant,

v.

John A. KENNEDY, M.D., Respondent.

No. 1766–I.

Court of Appeals of Washington,
Division 1.

May 20, 1974.

Rehearing Denied July 18, 1974.

Medical malpractice action. The Superior Court, Pierce County, Stanley W. Worswick, J., entered judgment for physician, and patient appealed. The Court of Appeals, Callow, J., held that patient was entitled to an instruction defining circumstantial evidence, direct evidence and res ipsa loquitur, and that instruction on informed consent was improper where it did not make clear that duty to inform patient of the risks inherent in the treatment existed as matter of law, and that patient would have to prove only that a reasonable person in the patient's position would not have consented if he had known the facts.

Reversed and remanded.

1. Negligence ⚫121.2(3)

The legal doctrine of "res ipsa loquitur" eliminates the need to prove negligence where the apparatus which caused injury was under the exclusive control of the defendant, the accident ordinarily would not have occurred unless defendant had been negligent, and the accident was not caused by any action of plaintiff.

See publication Words and Phrases for other judicial constructions and definitions.

2. Physicians and Surgeons ⚫18.60

If defendant physician is in exclusive control of the instrumentality, and there is no voluntary participation or contribution by plaintiff to acts producing injury, negligence may be deduced without further proof in three situations: (1) where act causing the injury is so obviously negligent that negligence may be inferred as matter of law, (2) when people would know from

MILLER v. KENNEDY   Wash.   853
Cite as, Wash.App., 522 P.2d 852

experience that the result would not have happened without negligence, and (3) when a physician testifies that the bad result would not have occurred if proper care had been used.

3. Physicians and Surgeons ⬦18.100

Plaintiff patient, in medical malpractice action, was entitled to an instruction defining circumstantial evidence, direct evidence and res ipsa loquitur, where testimony of patient's medical witness could have caused jury to infer that physician's negligence caused injury to patient.

4. Trial ⬦295(6)

Instruction in medical malpractice action, stating that "The law does not hold that physicians or surgeons guarantee results, nor does it require that the result of their treatment be what is desired.", was proper when considered in the context of all the instructions, since a bad result is not, of itself, evidence of negligence.

5. Physicians and Surgeons ⬦14(3)

A physician, unless he so contracts, does not guarantee or warrant that an illness or disease will be cured.

6. Physicians and Surgeons ⬦14(3)

Physician is not an insurer that health will return to a patient, and liability should not be imposed upon a physician for an unfavorable, unforeseeable outcome which was not the result of negligence.

7. Physicians and Surgeons ⬦15(1)

The efforts of a physician may be unsuccessful, or the exercise of his judgment may be in error, without the physician being negligent, so long as the physician acts within the standard of care of his peers.

8. Physicians and Surgeons ⬦15(1)

Physician is liable for medical malpractice only for misjudgment when physician arrived at such judgment through a failure to act in accordance with the care and skill required in the circumstances.

9. Physicians and Surgeons ⬦15(1)

Mistake by a physician is not actionable unless it is shown to have occurred be-

cause the physician did not perform within the standard of care of his practice.

10. Physicians and Surgeons ⬦18.100

Instruction in medical malpractice action, stating that "A physician is not liable for an honest error of judgment if, in arriving at that judgment, the physician exercised reasonable care and skill, within the standard of care he was obliged to follow.", was a proper abstract statement of the law.

11. Assault and Battery ⬦2
Physicians and Surgeons ⬦15(15)

Performance of an operation without first obtaining consent of patient thereto may fall within the concepts of assault and battery as an intentional tort, and failure of physician to tell patient about the perils he faces is the breach of a duty and is appropriately considered under negligence concepts.

12. Physicians and Surgeons ⬦15(8)

Due care requires a physician to alert his patient to abnormalities in patient's body.

13. Physicians and Surgeons ⬦15(8)

Relationship between a physician and his patient is one of trust calling for a recognition by the physician of the ignorance and helplessness of patient regarding the patient's own physical condition.

14. Physicians and Surgeons ⬦15(8)

Duty of a physician to inform patient is a fiduciary duty.

15. Physicians and Surgeons ⬦15(8)

A patient is entitled to rely upon his physician to tell patient what he needs to know about the condition of his own body, and physician must supply the patient with material facts the patient will need in order to intelligently chart his destiny with dignity.

16. Physicians and Surgeons ⬦15(8)

Scope of a physician's duty to disclose to patient information concerning the treatment proposed, other treatments, and the risks of each course of action and of no treatment at all, is measured by the patient's need to know.

17. Physicians and Surgeons ⟨⟩15(8)

It is the prerogative of the patient to choose his treatment, and a physician may not withhold from the patient the knowledge necessary for the exercise of that right, since, without it, the prerogative is valueless.

18. Physicians and Surgeons ⟨⟩18.60

Burden of proving that a physician failed to inform the plaintiff patient of the available courses of treatment, or failed to warn of consequential hazards of each choice of treatment, is on the patient.

19. Physicians and Surgeons ⟨⟩15(8)

Elements of cause of action based on the "informed consent doctrine" include the existence of a material risk unknown to the patient, the failure to disclose it, a showing that patient would have chosen a different course if the risk had been disclosed, and resulting injury.

> See publication Words and Phrases for other judicial constructions and definitions.

20. Physicians and Surgeons ⟨⟩18.60

Burden of proving a defense, when it is established that physician failed to inform patient under the informed consent doctrine, is on the physician.

21. Physicians and Surgeons ⟨⟩18.80(7)

Existence of risks and alternatives which were present in the particular physical condition of a patient would be beyond knowledge of the layman, and would have to be established, in a medical malpractice action, by medical testimony.

22. Physicians and Surgeons ⟨⟩15(8), 18.80(7)

Physician has a duty to disclose to patient the material risks of a medical procedure as a matter of law, and testimony of medical experts is not necessary to establish the duty to disclose that which the law requires.

23. Physicians and Surgeons ⟨⟩15(8)

When a reasonable person in the position of a patient probably would attach significance to a specific risk in deciding on course of treatment, such risk is material and must be disclosed to patient by physician.

24. Physicians and Surgeons ⟨⟩18.12

Existence of a situation where disclosure by physician to patient of a risk would be detrimental to the patient would be a matter of defense for physician in an action against physician arising out of his failure to obtain patient's informed consent.

25. Physicians and Surgeons ⟨⟩18.90

A jury, as lay people, are equipped to place themselves in position of a patient, in a medical malpractice action arising out of alleged failure of physician to obtain patient's informed consent, and to decide whether, under the circumstances, the patient should have been told.

26. Physicians and Surgeons ⟨⟩18.100

An instruction outlining the elements of the negligence doctrine of "informed consent" should set forth that it is the duty of a physician or surgeon to disclose to a patient all relevant, material information the patient will need to make an informed decision on whether to consent to or reject the proposed treatment or operation.

27. Physicians and Surgeons ⟨⟩18.100

Jury should be instructed, in an action arising out of alleged failure of physician to obtain patient's informed consent, that the plaintiff patient must prove by a preponderance of the evidence that physician failed to inform patient of a material risk involved in submitting to a proposed course of treatment, that patient consented to the proposed treatment without being aware of or fully informed of material risks of each choice of treatment and of no treatment at all, that a reasonably prudent patient probably would not have consented to the treatment when informed of the material risks, and that treatment chosen caused injury to the patient.

28. Physicians and Surgeons ⟨⟩18.100

It is appropriate to instruct jury, in action against physician arising out of al-

MILLER v. KENNEDY   Wash. **855**
Cite as, Wash.App., 522 P.2d 852

leged failure of physician to obtain patient's informed consent, that in the event a patient has consented to proposed treatment or operation, a failure of physician or surgeon to fully inform patient of all the material risks present in his medical situation before obtaining such consent is negligence, and that a physician or surgeon is liable for any injury proximately resulting from the treatment if a reasonably prudent person in the patient's position would not have consented to the treatment if adequately informed of all the significant perils.

29. Appeal and Error ⬤⟿1050.1(7)
Physicians and Surgeons ⬤⟿18.100

Instruction in medical malpractice action which, inter alia, apprised jury that physician had to disclose all material facts to patient, and which emphasized that the duty to inform existed regardless of negligence or exercise of due care by physician "in the procedure itself," and which also stressed that patient was required to prove that patient would not have consented to treatment had he been fully informed, was erroneous, and patient was entitled to new trial, where instruction did not make it clear that duty to inform of the risks inherent in the treatment existed as matter of law, and where it was not stated that patient was required to prove only that a reasonable person in patient's position would not have consented.

30. Appeal and Error ⬤⟿756

Assignments of error relating to the exclusion of exhibits would not have to be considered unless meritorious on their face, where such assignments were unsupported by cited authority.

31. Witnesses ⬤⟿311

Impeaching evidence affects only the credibility of the witness, and is incompetent to prove the substantive facts encompassed therein.

32. Witnesses ⬤⟿379(12)

Letter to defendant physician, from witness which discussed procedure followed by defendant physician in the biopsy was properly excluded in medical malpractice action where such could not be offered for purpose of impeachment of defendant physician, even though letter was inconsistent with his later testimony, since the letter did not contain his statements and, therefore, did not contain inconsistent pronouncements of physician whose credibility was sought to be impeached.

33. Trial ⬤⟿56

Exclusion from evidence, in medical malpractice action, of hand written answers to interrogatories proposed to defendant physician was within court's discretion relating to admission of cumulative evidence where nothing in such answer was inconsistent with his answers given to the interrogatories except as admitted by the physician.

34. Appeal and Error ⬤⟿760(2)
Physicians and Surgeons ⬤⟿18.80(2)

Evidence was insufficient, in medical malpractice action, to establish standard of care required as to postbiopsy treatment, where physicians who testified were not interrogated directly on this aspect of the case, and where reviewing court was not referred to any page in the record containing testimony establishing the postbiopsy standard of care or any breach thereof. CAROA 42(g)(2)(ii).

Murray, Scott, McGavick, Gagliardi, Graves, Lane & Lowry, Edward M. Lane, Tacoma, for appellant.

Davies, Pearson, Anderson, Gadbow & Hayes, P. S., Wayne J. Davies, Seattle, for respondent.

CALLOW, Judge.

The plaintiff, Richard R. Miller, appeals from the trial court's refusal to grant a motion for a new trial or judgment n.o.v. following a verdict for the defendant in a medical malpractice case. The issues concern instructions on res ipsa loquitur, the physician as a guarantor of results, the liability of a physician for a mistake in judgment and "informed consent." Also presented and discussed are issues regarding the rejection of certain proposed exhibits and the trial court's removal of the claim of faulty post-biopsy care from the jury.

Dr. Kennedy is a board certified specialist in internal medicine, with sub-specialties in heart and nephrology, practicing in Tacoma, Washington. The plaintiff first consulted with Dr. Kennedy on January 14, 1970, complaining of fatigue, lightheadedness, tiring out easily and becoming shortwinded with exercise. Dr. Kennedy examined Mr. Miller, wrote down his medical history and took an electrocardiogram. At that time, Dr. Kennedy found that Mr. Miller had first degree heart block. On January 20, 1970, Mr. Miller returned for futher examination and was found to have second and third degree heart block. Mr. Miller was immediately hospitalized and placed in intensive care. On January 26, 1970, Mr. Miller was removed from intensive care and placed in a ward.

Many tests were performed to assist Dr. Kennedy in his efforts to diagnose the cause of Mr. Miller's heart disease. Various tests showed evidence of a kidney problem, and therefore Dr. Kennedy felt that a kidney biopsy was necessary. Witnesses for both parties testified that the decision to perform the biopsy was not malpractice. However, Mr. Miller testified that Dr. Kennedy did not advise him of the risk of the loss of the kidney nor explain the alternative ways of performing biopsies. The plaintiff further testified that he would not have consented to the biopsy had he known there was a risk of loss of the kidney. Dr. Kennedy testified that he did so inform the patient, and this testimony is substantially corroborated by the hospital record and by the prior conduct of the doctor in which he diagramed and explained in detail to Mr. Miller what was happening in his heart.

In performing the biopsy, the biopsy needle was inserted some 3 or 4 centimeters above the intended biopsy site. The kidney is encased in an outer capsule covering, inside of which there is an area called the cortex. The cortex surrounds the medulla which contains the nephrons, which are filtering, absorbing and secreting units doing the essential work of the kidney. The process of forming urine begins when arterial blood flows into a tuft of capillaries, called the glomerulus. The glomerulus is enclosed in a double membrane which leads into a tubule. The glomerulus, membranes and tubule form a single nephron. The glomerulus initially filters out some of the passing blood as do the membranes. The blood fluid then enters the tubule of the nephron where useful sugars, salts and water are reabsorbed by small capillaries and returned to the main bloodstream. The capillaries in turn secrete ammonia through the tubule wall into the fluid remaining which is flowing into the collecting tubule. The resulting comparatively small amount of waste is urine. The medulla area of the kidney contains approximately two and a half million nephrons. Inside the medulla area is the calyceal area, the collecting system of the kidney.

The plaintiff alleged that the biopsy needle was negligently inserted penetrating the calyceal system of the kidney causing damage and injury which eventually resulted in loss of the kidney. The defendant contended that the calyceal area was not punctured and that a small artery may have been injured. There is no dispute in the testimony that the loss of the kidney proximately resulted from the kidney biopsy, that the kidney was healthy prior to the biopsy and that the biopsy specimens were negative as to any of the conditions for which the biopsy was performed. The position of the plaintiff is that the defendant violated the standard of care while the defendant states that the standard of care was met and claims that an unfortunate chance led to the result.

Following the biopsy, the plaintiff remained in the hospital from January 29, 1970, until February 26, 1970, suffering continual bleeding from his kidney and considerable pain. On February 26, 1970,

MILLER v. KENNEDY
Cite as, Wash.App., 522 P.2d 852
Wash. **857**

Dr. Kennedy called upon another physician, Dr. Osborne, to examine Mr. Miller. In spite of his weakened condition and extensive bleeding, Mr. Miller was released from the hospital. Mr. Miller was again, at his own insistence, examined by Dr. Osborne, who removed·blood clots from his bladder and returned him home. After the condition returned, Mr. Miller was again hospitalized on March 30, 1970. It was suggested that an operation be performed to see if the upper portion of the kidney, where the bleeding was taking place, could be surgically removed in an attempt to save the balance of the kidney. On April 4, the date set for the surgical procedure, Mr. Miller hemorrhaged, and the surgical procedure was expedited. Dr. Osborne performed this surgery, attempted to remove the upper portion of the kidney, but was unable to do so. Finally, he was required to do a complete nephrectomy, removing the entire kidney. Mr. Miller was released from the hospital on April 10, 1970.

[1] The plaintiff submits that the jury should have been instructed on res ipsa loquitur. The legal doctrine of res ipsa loquitur eliminates the need to prove negligence where (a) the apparatus which caused injury was under the exclusive control of the defendant, (b) the accident ordinarily would not have occurred unless the defendant had been negligent, and (c) the accident was not caused by any action of the plaintiff. Emerick v. Mayr, 39 Wash. 2d 23, 234 P.2d 1079 (1951); Ewer v. Goodyear Tire & Rubber Co., 4 Wash. App. 152, 480 P.2d 260 (1971).

[2, 3] In ZeBarth v. Swedish Hosp. Medical Center, 81 Wash.2d 12, 18, 499 P. 2d 1 (1972), as in this case, the instruction proposed defined circumstantial evidence, direct evidence and res ipsa loquitur.[1] The plaintiff-appellant challenges the failure of the trial court to give this instruction claiming that the evidence made the instruction imperative. We agree that, under *ZeBarth*, the instruction should have been given. ZeBarth v. Swedish Hosp., in adopting the classic statement respecting res ipsa loquitur as applied to medical malpractice from Horner v. Northern Pac. Beneficial Ass'n Hosps., Inc., 62 Wash.2d 351, 382 P.2d 518 (1963), observed that there must be exclusive control of the instrumentality in the defendant and no voluntary participation or contribution by the plaintiff to the acts producing the injury. If such circumstances exist, then negligence may be deduced[2] without further proof in three situations: (1) where the act causing the injury is so obviously negligent that negligence may be inferred as a matter of law, (2) when people would

---

1. The instruction proposed by the plaintiff was a direct reflection of that approved in Horner v. Northern Pac. Beneficial Ass'n Hosps., Inc., 62 Wash.2d 351, 354, 382 P.2d 518 (1963). It read:

   Evidence is of two kinds—direct and circumstantial. Direct evidence is that given by a witness who testifies directly of his own knowledge concerning facts to be proved. Circumstantial evidence consists of proof of facts or circumstances which a Court of competent experience of mankind or experts in a esoteric field give rise of reasonable inference of the truth of the fact sought to be proved.

   One kind of evidence is not necessarily more or less valuable than the other.

   In connection with the foregoing you are instructed that it is for you to determine whether the matter of the occurrence of the injuries sustained by Richard Miller, and the attendant circumstances connected therewith, are of such character as would in your judgment warrant an inference that the injury would not have occurred had Dr. Kennedy conformed to the standard of care required of him.

   The rule is that when an agency or instrumentality which produces injury is under the control of a defendant, and the injury which occurred would ordinarily not have resulted if the person in control had used proper care, then, in the absence of satisfactory explanation, you are at liberty to infer, though you are not required to so infer, that the defendant was at some point negligent, and that such negligence produced the injury complained of by the plaintiff.

2. The term "inferred" rather than "deduced" is most often used in this connection as connoting the drawing of a conclusion as opposed to "implying" or "intimating."

know from experience that the result would not have happened without negligence, (3) when a physician testifies that the bad result would not have occurred if proper care had been used. In this case, the doctor had exclusive control of the instrumentality, and the patient did not participate in the procedure. The circumstances present the inquiry whether an instruction on res ipsa loquitur should have been given. It cannot be said from the vantage point of an unskilled person that the insertion of a biopsy needle into the calyceal area was so palpably negligent that an inference of negligence follows, nor can it be said that the general experience of most people indicates this would not have happened without negligence.

This leaves only the inquiry whether the third situation as recognized under Washington law was present, to wit, an instruction should be given on res ipsa loquitur when medical doctors testify that the injury would not have happened but for some negligent action on the part of the treating physician. ZeBarth v. Swedish Hosp. Medical Center, *supra*, 81 Wash.2d at 19, 499 P.2d 1. The testimony of the doctors called as witnesses is in conflict. However, the jury was free to believe the testimony of one doctor and disregard the testimony of all the others. The testimony of the medical witness testifying on behalf of the plaintiff was such that the trier of the fact could deduce from that testimony

that the defendant was negligent. The law concerning the propriety of instructing on res ipsa loquitur has been the subject of controversy as reflected in ZeBarth v. Swedish Hosp. Medical Center, *supra*; Zukowsky v. Brown, 79 Wash.2d 586, 488 P. 2d 269 (1971); Douglas v. Bussabarger, 73 Wash.2d 476, 438 P.2d 829 (1968), and Pederson v. Dumouchel, 72 Wash.2d 73, 431 P.2d 973, 31 A.L.R.3d 1100 (1967). The currently prevailing trend of the Washington cases would instruct the jury that it could infer negligence when the plaintiff's evidence supports the deduction that the injury would not have occurred otherwise.[3] Siegler v. Kuhlman, 81 Wash.2d 448, 502 P.2d 1181 (1972). They were not so instructed here. As stated in *ZeBarth*, 81 Wash.2d on page 22, 499 P.2d on page 7:

> Res ipsa loquitur does not, and did not here, operate to deprive defendant hospital of its defense on the merits. Inferences of negligence arising from the doctrine and evidence were met with persuasive evidence to the contrary. But, although defendant presented weighty, competent and exculpatory proof of due and reasonable care and prudence, the ultimate issue of fact was one for the jury to decide.

An inference that negligence caused the injury to the patient may follow from the testimony of the plaintiffs' medical witness and Washington law[4] entitled the

---

3. The opposing view is that instructions from the court (that the jury may infer from the evidence that negligence caused the bad result) may insert the trial court into the jury's evaluation of that evidence (infringing upon their province) tilting the balance of decision by a controlling factor which is not evidence, but a rule of law. See the dissents in *ZeBarth* and *Zukowsky*.

4. Riedinger v. Colburn, 361 F.Supp. 1073 (D.Idaho 1973), held that Idaho law required a showing by a plaintiff that (1) the instrumentality causing injury was under the control of the physician and (2) the circumstances were such that common knowledge and experience would justify the inference that the accident would not have happened in the absence of negligence, for res ipsa loquitur to apply. The court restricted res

ipsa loquitur to cases where a layman is able to say that the consequences of professional treatment were not such as ordinarily would have followed if due care had been exercised. The case states on page 1079:

> In plaintiff's supplemental trial memorandum . . . reliance is placed on the case of Zebarth v. Swedish Hosp. Med. Center, . . . as establishing a more "equitable rule" of further use of the doctrine of *res ipsa* based on the testimony of expert witnesses to create inferences of negligence.

The court declined to follow *ZeBarth* on the ground that the Supreme Court of Idaho had not expanded the rule to permit the application of res ipsa loquitur to cases where medical testimony would lead to an inference of negligence.

plaintiff to an instruction that the jury could make that interference.

[4–6] The trial court instructed the jury:

> The law does not hold that physicians or surgeons guarantee results, nor does it require that the result of their treatment be what is desired.

The instruction was proper under the law when considered in the context of all the instructions. A bad result is not, of itself, evidence of negligence. Teig v. St. John's Hosp., 63 Wash.2d 369, 387 P.2d 527 (1963); Rundin v. Sells, 1 Wash.2d 332, 95 P.2d 1023 (1939); Brant v. Sweet Clinic, 167 Wash. 166, 8 P.2d 972 (1932); Hoffman v. Watkins, 78 Wash. 118, 138 P. 664 (1914). A physician, unless he so contracts, does not warrant or guarantee that an illness or disease will be cured. Eckleberry v. Kaiser Foundation Northern Hosps., 226 Or. 616, 359 P.2d 1090, 84 A.L.R.2d 1327 (1961); Derr v. Bonney, 38 Wash.2d 678, 231 P.2d 637, 54 A.L.R.2d 193 (1951); Fritz v. Horsfall, 24 Wash.2d 14, 163 P.2d 148 (1945). A doctor is neither an insurer that health will return to a patient nor should liability be imposed upon a doctor for an unfavorable, unforeseeable outcome which was not the result of negligence. Nelson v. Murphy, 42 Wash.2d 737, 258 P.2d 472 (1953); Crouch v. Wyckoff, 6 Wash.2d 273, 107 P.2d 339 (1940). The law does not hold a physician to a standard of infallibility. Hunt v. Bradshaw, 251 F.2d 103 (4th Cir. 1958).

[7–10] The instruction is likewise challenged which read:

> A physician is not liable for an honest error of judgment if, in arriving at that judgment, the physician exercised reasonable care and skill, within the standard of care he was obliged to follow.

The efforts of a physician may be unsuccessful or the exercise of one's judgment be in error without the physician being negligent so long as the doctor aimed within the standard of care of his peers. Dinner v. Thorp. 54 Wash.2d 90, 338 P.2d 137 (1959). A doctor is liable only for misjudgment when he arrived at such judgment through a failure to act in accordance with the care and skill required in the circumstances. A mistake is not actionable unless it is shown to have occurred because the doctor did not perform within the standard of care of his practice. Huffman v. Lindquist, 37 Cal.2d 465, 234 P.2d 34, 29 A.L.R.2d 485 (1951); Norden v. Hartman, 134 Cal.App.2d 333, 285 P.2d 977 (1955); Skeffington v. Bradley, 366 Mich. 552, 115 N.W.2d 303 (1962); Marsh v. Pemberton, 10 Utah 2d 40, 347 P.2d 1108 (1959). This instruction also was appropriate as an abstract statement of the law.

The plaintiff has objected to the instruction given on informal consent claiming it is inadequate under the criteria laid down by ZeBarth v. Swedish Hosp. Medical Center, 81 Wash.2d 12, 499 P.2d 1 (1972), wrongfully places the burden of proving the failure to inform upon the plaintiff and wrongfully imposes on the plaintiff the obligation to prove by medical testimony a breach of a medical standard of disclosure. The plaintiff claims his proposed instruction on informed consent should have been given. We have commented upon many of the cases in this area in the foregoing opinion of Holt v. Nelson, Wash.App., 523 P.2d 211 (1974). In 1972 at the time ZeBarth v. Swedish Hosp. was being decided, Canterbury v. Spence, 150 U.S.App.D.C. 263, 464 F.2d 722 (1972), Cobbs v. Grant, 8 Cal.3d 229, 104 Cal.Rptr. 505, 502 P.2d 1 (1972) and Wilkinson v. Vesey, 295 A.2d 676 (R.I.1972), as well as other cases, were also in the process of decision. We deem it appropriate to review the plaintiff's assignment of error guided primarily by the pronouncement of our highest court in *ZeBarth* but also to take notice of the decisions reached in other jurisdictions which enlighten this area. We review the instruction given, and the instruction proposed originally if the fact is that the time that this case was in trial in 1972, few of the decisions which now reflect the direction of this developing area of the law had yet been published. (Appendix I reflects the plaintiff's proposed instruction and the court's instruction. Both contain misleading flaws and neither is approved in toto.) It is suitable that the area be reevaluated and reconciled within the extent of our authority. *See* Greene v. Rothschild, 68 Wash.2d 1, 402 P.2d 356, 414 P.2d 1013 (1965); Stratton v. Department of Labor & Indus., 7 Wash.App. 652, 501 P.2d 1072 (1972).

[11, 12] The contest over whether the failure to inform a patient of the material risks of a medical procedure constitutes an assault upon the patient or a negligent breach of a physician's duty to acquaint the patient with the perils of each medical course of action has been laid to rest. The performance of an operation without first obtaining any consent thereto may fall within the concepts of assault and battery as an intentional tort, but the failure to tell the patient about the perils he faces is the breach of a duty and is appropriately considered under negligence concepts. Cobbs v. Grant, *supra*, 104 Cal.Rptr. at 512, 502 P.2d at 8; Wilkinson v. Vesey, *supra*, 295 A.2d at 686; ZeBarth v. Swedish Hosp. Medical Center, *supra*, 81 Wash.2d at 23, 29, 499 P.2d 1. Due care requires the physician to alert the patient to abnormalities in his body. Canterbury v. Spence, *supra*, 464 F.2d at 781. As stated in *Wilkinson* 295 A.2d on page 686:

> The prevailing view, however, classifies the physician's duty in this regard as a question of negligence because of the absence of the elements of any wilful intent by the physician to injure his patient.

The relationship between a doctor and his patient is one of trust calling for a recognition by the physician of the ignorance and helplessness of the patient regarding his own physical condition. Canterbury v. Spence, *supra*, 464 F.2d at 781. The duty of the doctor to inform the patient is a fiduciary duty. Hunter v. Brown, 4 Wash.App. 899, 905, 484 P.2d 1162 (1971), aff'd, 81 Wash.2d 465, 502 P. 2d 1194 (1972); Mason v. Ellsworth, 3 Wash.App. 298, 308, 474 P.2d 909 (1970). The patient is entitled to rely upon the physician to tell him what he needs to know about the condition of his own body. The patient has the right to chart his own destiny, and the doctor must supply the patient with the material facts the patient will need in order to intelligently chart that destiny with dignity. Canterbury v. Spence, *supra*, 464 F.2d at 782.

[16, 17] The scope of the duty to disclose information concerning the treatment proposed, other treatments and the risks of each course of action and of no treatment at all is measured by the patient's need to know.[5] The inquiry as to each item of information which the doctor knows or should know about the patient's physical condition is "Would the patient as a human being consider this item in choosing his or her course of treatment?"[6] Cobbs v. Grant referring to the *Canterbury* case states, 104 Cal.Rptr. on page 514, 502 P.2d on page 10:

> The court in Canterbury v. Spence, supra, 464 F.2d 772, 784, bluntly observed: "Nor can we ignore the fact that to bind the disclosure obligation to medical

---

5. Cobbs v. Grant states, 104 Cal.Rptr. on page 514, 502 P.2d on page 10: "[A]s an integral part of the physician's overall obligation to the patient there is a duty of reasonable disclosure of the available choices with respect to proposed therapy and of the dangers inherently and potentially involved in each."

6. Cobbs v. Grant states, 104 Cal.Rptr. on page 515, 502 P.2d on page 11: "In sum, the patient's right of self-decision is the

measure of the physician's duty to reveal. That right can be effectively exercised only if the patient possesses adequate information to enable an intelligent choice. The scope of the physician's communications to the patient, then, must be measured by the patient's need, and that need is whatever information is material to the decision. Thus the test for determining whether a potential peril must be divulged is its materiality to the patient's decision."

MILLER v. KENNEDY

Wash. **861**

Cite as, Wash.App., 522 P.2d 852

usage is to arrogate the decision on revelation to the physician alone. Respect for the patient's right of self-determination on particular therapy demands a standard set by law for physicians rather than one which physicians may or may not impose upon themselves." Unlimited discretion in the physician is irreconcilable with the basic right of the patient to make the ultimate informed decision regarding the course of treatment to which he knowledgeably consents to be subjected.

Indeed, it is the prerogative of the patient to chose his treatment. A doctor may not withhold from the patient the knowledge necessary for the exercise of that right. Without it, the prerogative is valueless. Canterbury v. Spence, *supra*, 464 F.2d at 781, 782, 786.

[18–20] The burden of proving that a physician failed to inform the plaintiff-patient of the available courses of treatment or failed to warn of the consequential hazards of each choice of treatment is on the plaintiff. It is the plaintiff who must initially establish the existence of the elements of an action based on the informed consent doctrine, i. e., the existence of a material risk unknown to the patient, the failure to disclose it, that the patient would have chosen a different course if the risk had been disclosed and resulting injury. Canterbury v. Spence, *supra*, 464 F.2d at 791; Mason v. Ellsworth, *supra*, 3 Wash. App. at 312, 474 P.2d 909; Trogun v. Fruchtman, 58 Wis.2d 596, 207 N.W.2d 297, 314 (1973). The burden of proving a defense when failure to disclose has been established is on the doctor. Canterbury v. Spence, *supra*, 464 F.2d at 791; Cobbs v.

Grant, *supra*, 104 Cal.Rptr. at 516, 502 P.2d at 12. *Trogun*, 207 N.W.2d on page 315 places the burden of proof upon the parties as follows:

> We conclude that the burden of proof is on the plaintiff to establish a physician's failure to disclose particular risk information in connection with contemplated treatment, the patient's lack of knowledge of that risk and the adverse effects upon him which followed that treatment. . . . Once the plaintiff has established a prima facie showing of a failure of the physician to inform the patient, the physician must come forward with his explanation of the reasons for not so informing the patient, including evidence that such advice was not customarily given.

(Footnote omitted.)

[21, 22] Those elements which are the province of the medical profession must be established by the testimony of medical experts in the field of inquiry. Thus, the existence of the risks and alternatives which were present in the particular physical condition would be beyond the knowledge of the layman and would have to be established by medical testimony. On the other hand, those matters which are not within the special province of the training and experience of doctors may be established by the testimony of any witness with knowledge of the particular inquiry, such as whether the patient knew of the risk or whether the average patient would consider the risk in making a decision. Trogun v. Fruchtman, *supra* at 315. There is no need to prove what other doctors might tell their patients in similar circumstances.[7]

7. "When there is medical testimony which establishes that a risk is material, that alternatives are feasible, and that disclosure of the risk will not be detrimental to the particular patient, we find no reason why expert medical testimony should be required to establish the existence of a duty to disclose such risks. This is not a medical matter. Once materiality, feasibility and the effect of a disclosure on the patient is established

by expert testimony, what physicians disclose or do not disclose in a particular locality about the risks and feasible alternatives of certain proposed treatment or surgery, must be a happenstance because medical training and experience would be of little assistance on this aspect of the problem." Getchell v. Mansfield, 260 Or. 174, 181, 489 P.2d 953, 956 (1971).

The doctor has a duty to disclose the material risks as a matter of law.[8] The testimony of medical experts is not necessary to establish the duty to disclose that which the law requires. Once the existence of a risk has been established by expert medical testimony, there is no need to take the next step and also prove by expert medical testimony that the doctor should have told the patient about the risk.[9] Once it has been established by expert medical testimony that a risk existed, then the existence of the risk is the patient's business; and it is not for the medical profession to establish a criteria for the dissemination of information to the patient based upon what doctors feel the patient should be told. Canterbury v. Spence, 150 U.S.App.D.C. 263, 464 F.2d 772 (1972); Mason v. Ellsworth, *supra*. *See also* Comment, A New Standard for Informed Consent in Medical Malpractice Cases—The Role of the Expert Witness, 18 St. Louis Univ.L.J. 256 (1973). The patient has a right to know and the doctor has the duty to inform the patient whether the doctor wants to or not. The fiduciary duty of the doctor requires disclosure. There is no room for paternalism or for overprotectiveness. Getchell v. Mansfield, 260 Or. 174, 489 P.2d 953, 957 (1971) said:

8. "The requirement that a patient obtain an expert to evaluate the disclosures made in the light of the prevailing practice in the locality undermines the very basis of the informed consent theory—the patient's right to be the final judge to do with his body as he wills. Blind adherence to local practice is completely at odds with the undisputed right of the patient to receive information which will enable him to make a choice—either to take his chances with the treatment or operation recommended by the doctor or to risk living without it. As will be noted later, the patient is entitled to receive material information upon which he can base an informed consent. The decision as to what is or is not material is a human judgment, in our opinion, which does not necessarily require the assistance of the medical profession. The patient's right to make up his mind should not be delegated to a local medical group—many of whom have no idea as to his informational needs. The doctor-patient relationship is a one-on-one affair. What is a reasonable disclosure in one instance may not be reasonable in another. This variability negates the need of the plaintiff showing what other doctors may tell other patients." Wilkinson v. Vesey, *supra*, 295 A.2d at 688.

9. *ZeBarth* cites Natanson v. Kline, 187 Kan. 186, 354 P.2d 670 (1960) for the proposition that the standards of the medical profession as established by expert medical testimony are those to be applied by the jury in deciding whether a patient was adequately informed to decide whether to accept or forgo a risk. In *Natanson* on rehearing, we find on page 673:

Whether or not a physician has advised his patient of the inherent risks and hazards in a proposed form of treatment is a *question of fact* concerning which lay witnesses are competent to testify, and the establishment of such fact is not dependent upon expert medical testimony. It is only when the facts concerning the actual disclosures made to the patient are ascertained, or ascertainable by the trier of the facts, that the expert testimony of medical witnesses is required to establish whether such disclosures are in accordance with those which a reasonable medical practitioner would make under the same or similar circumstances.

Wilkinson v. Vesey, 295 A.2d 676, 686 (R.I. 1972) commenting on *Natanson* states:

As explicated in Collins v. Meeker, 198 Kan. 390, 424 P.2d 488 (1967), the *Natanson* rule provides . . . that where a physician is silent and makes no disclosure whatever, he has failed in the duty owed to the patient and the patient is not required to produce expert testimony to show that the doctor's failure was contrary to accepted medical practice but rather that it devolves upon the doctor to establish that his failure to make any disclosure did in fact conform under the existing conditions to accepted medical standards; and that where actual disclosures have been made and are ascertainable, the patient then must produce expert medical testimony to establish that the disclosures made were not in accord with those which reasonable medical practitioners would have divulged under the same or like circumstances.

While there may be strength in numbers as one views the many courts which require expert testimony as to the community standard of revelation by one seeking to recover on the basis of informed consent, this view has come under increasing criticism.

(Footnote omitted.)

We hold, therefore, that a plaintiff who alleges that a physician failed to warn him of material risks inherent in his treatment, and to advise him of feasible alternatives, need not produce expert medical testimony that it is the custom of physicians in the same or similar localities to give such warnings in comparable cases. The duty to warn and to advise of alternatives does not arise from and is not limited by the custom of physicians in the locality. Rather, it exists as a matter of law if (1) the risk of injury inherent in the treatment is material; (2) there are feasible alternative courses available; and (3) the plaintiff can be advised of the risks and alternatives without detriment to his wellbeing. If there is evidence tending to prove all these elements, the plaintiff is entitled to have his case submitted to the jury under proper instructions. In most cases, expert medical testimony will be necessary to establish each of the three elements.

Harper and James write forcefully that there should be no need in most cases for expert medical testimony to establish that disclosure of certain risks and alternatives is the customary medical practice:

"Since the courts quite rightly recognize room for a doctor's therapeutic discretion in exercising his duty of disclosure, expert evidence of what is proper medical practice in that respect is relevant and is everywhere received. This is as it should be. But courts have generally gone much further and have *required* medical evidence that it is local professional practice to make the disclosure in question before a jury may find a doctor negligent in failing to make it, even where the treatment was an 'elective' one presenting no emergency. * * *

"Such a requirement in these circumstances is, it is submitted, an un-

warranted abdication of responsibility and of the individual's right to make an informed choice, to the medical profession. * * *." 2 Harper and James, Law of Torts, 60–61 (1956, Supp.1968).

[23] The patient is endowed with the right to know each hazard which the usual person would utilize in reaching his decision. When a reasonable person in the patient's position probably would attach significance to the specific risk in deciding on treatment, the risk is material and must be disclosed. Canterbury v. Spence, *supra*, 464 F.2d at 787. Wilkinson v. Vesey, 295 A.2d 676, 689 (R.I.1972), discusses materiality as follows:

[M]ateriality is to be the guide. It is our belief that, in due deference to the patient's right to self determination, a physician is bound to disclose all the known material risks peculiar to the proposed procedure. Materiality may be said to be the significance a reasonable person, in what the physician knows or should know is his patient's position, would attach to the disclosed risk or risks in deciding whether to submit or not to submit to surgery or treatment. (See Appendix II.)

[24] Situations may be envisioned where the disclosure of a risk to a patient would be detrimental to the patient. The existence of such a situation is a matter of defense for the doctor. The doctor may present evidence to justify the failure to disclose by his own testimony or by the testimony of other lay or expert witnesses. The doctor may establish the existence of a standard of nondisclosure by medical experts in his field or practice, but it is for the jury to accept or reject whether any standard of nondisclosure should deprive a patient of his right of self-determination. The situations where there was either no requirement of disclosure or where there was a reason for nondisclosure have been illustrated in Holt v. Nelson, Wash.App., 523 P.2d 211 (1974).[10] Included are men-

---

10. "By our absolving the patient of the need to present medical testimony reflecting a

community standard of disclosure, we do not mean to prevent the physician from intro-

tal incompetence, emergencies, and potential physical trauma or mental disturbance to the patient. Canterbury v. Spence, *supra*; Cobbs v. Grant, 8 Cal.3d 229, 104 Cal.Rptr. 505, 502 P.2d 1, 12 (1972). A review of the defenses reveals that the validity of a defense is considered from the standpoint of concern for the well-being of the patient.

[25] The jury is capable of deciding whether the doctor did not tell the patient about something that should have been revealed. The jury does not need testimony from physicians about the norm of disclosure in the community. The usual conduct of doctors in this matter is not relevant to the establishment of the liability which is imposed by law. The jury, as lay people, are equipped to place themselves in the position of a patient and decide whether, under the circumstances, the patient should have been told. Wilkinson v. Vesey stated, 295 A.2d on page 688:

> The jury can decide if the doctor has disclosed enough information to enable the patient to make an intelligent choice without the necessity of the plaintiff's expert. The plaintiff, of course, must present evidence as to the undisclosed facts and their materiality. If the jury finds the undisclosed information immaterial, the doctor has acted reasonably in withholding it. If it finds the nondisclosure is material, the doctor may have acted unreasonably and will be held lia-

ble for his failure to obtain the patient's informed consent.

[26–28] An instruction outlining the elements of the negligence doctrine of "informed consent" should set forth that it is the duty of a physician or surgeon to disclose to a patient all relevant, material information the patient will need to make an informed decision on whether to consent to or reject the proposed treatment or operation. The jury should also be instructed that the plaintiff-patient must prove by a preponderance of the evidence that (1) the physician failed to inform the patient of a material risk involved in submitting to the proposed course of treatment; (2) the patient consented to the proposed treatment without being aware of or fully informed of the material risks of each choice of treatment and of no treatment at all; (3) a reasonable, prudent patient probably would not have consented to the treatment when informed of the material risks; and (4) the treatment chosen caused injury to the patient. It is also appropriate to instruct the jury that in the event a patient has consented to a proposed treatment or operation, a failure of the physician or surgeon to fully inform the patient of all of the material risks present in his medical situation before obtaining such consent is negligence; and a physician or surgeon is liable for any injury proximately resulting from the treatment if a reasonably prudent person in the patient's position would not have consented to the treatment if adequately informed of all the significant perils.[11]

---

ducing evidence of such a standard, if one exists, nor does it eliminate the need for a witness with the proper expertise whose testimony will establish the known risks involved in the procedure in controversy. Mason v. Ellsworth, *supra*." Wilkinson v. Vesey, *supra*, 295 A.2d at 688.

11. The trial court's instruction was vague in its directive to the jury regarding a doctor's duty, imposed by law, to inform the patient of the risks of treatment. The instruction confused the issue by negating consideration of the concepts of negligence or due care in the performance of treatment,

a correct statement in the abstract; but a statement which placed the theory of informed consent before the jury in the negative rather than in the affirmative. The trial court's instruction was faulty also in telling the jury to consider whether the plaintiff would have consented rather than to consider whether a reasonably prudent patient in the patient's position would have consented.

The instruction proposed by the plaintiff affirmatively stated the duty of the doctor to inform the patient of material risks as a matter of law. This was proper. Its defect was to introduce the concept of sur-

MILLER v. KENNEDY   Wash.   **865**

Cite as, Wash.App., 522 P.2d 852

[29] The instruction given by the court apprised the jury that the physician must disclose all material facts to the patient. However, the instruction was misleading in emphasizing that the duty to inform existed regardless of negligence or the exercise of due care by the physician "in the procedure itself" without making it clear also that the duty to inform of the risks inherent in the treatment existed as a matter of law. The small but important transgression of the instruction is one of misdirection. The instruction also stressed that the plaintiff was required to prove that he, the plaintiff-patient, would not have consented to the treatment had he been fully informed; while the proper approach requires the plaintiff to prove instead that a reasonable person in the plaintiff-patient's position would not have consented. *See* Comment, Informed Consent: Alternatives for Illinois, 4 Univ. of Ill.L.F. 739 (1973). The instruction incorrectly stated the precepts of the law of informed consent. The plaintiff is entitled to a new trial with revised instructions given on res ipsa loquitur and informed consent.

[30–33] Since a new trial is indicated, we will indicate our views on questions which might arise again. Both of the assignments of error relating to the exclusion of exhibits were unsupported by cited authority and, therefore, need not have been considered unless meritorious on their face. Myers v. Harter, 76 Wash.2d 772, 459 P.2d 25 (1969); Northern State Constr. Co. v. Robbins, 76 Wash.2d 357, 457 P.2d 187 (1969); Brown v. Quick Mix Co., 75 Wash.2d 833, 454 P.2d 205 (1969); Myers v. Western Farmers Ass'n, 75 Wash.2d 133, 449 P.2d 104 (1969). Both exhibits were offered to impeach the testimony of the defendant-doctor. One excluded exhibit was a letter to the defendant-doctor from the witness Dr. Hickman

which discussed the procedure followed by the defendant-doctor in the kidney biopsy. Such an exhibit could not be offered for purposes of impeachment of the defendant-doctor even though the letter was inconsistent with his later testimony since the letter did not contain his statements and, therefore, did not contain inconsistent pronouncements of the person whose credibility was sought to be impeached. The letter, therefore, contained merely the contradictory statements of another, would be hearsay, and not available for impeachment purposes. As noted in Jacqueline's Washington, Inc. v. Mercantile Stores Co., 80 Wash.2d 784, 498 P.2d 870 (1972), impeaching evidence affects only the credibility of the witness and is incompetent to prove the substantive facts encompassed therein. The effort to introduce the letter was an impermissible attempt to rebut the testimony of the defendant-doctor through impeachment. The other excluded exhibit contained the handwritten answers to the interrogatories proposed to the defendant-doctor. Nothing in that document was inconsistent with the answers given to the interrogatories except as admitted by the doctor. The trial court was within its discretion in excluding the exhibit as cumulative.

[34] The trial court did not submit the issue of post-biopsy care to the jury on the ground that the evidence was insufficient to establish the standard of care required as to the post-biopsy treatment "coupled with requisite evidence showing a failure of the standard, a breach of the standard as a basis of liability, . . ." We have reviewed the record and concur with the trial court's ruling that the evidence must be found wanting on that issue. Absent special exceptions or situations, a plaintiff-patient must establish the standard of professional practice at the time of the al-

---

gery without informed consent as imposing liability on an assault and battery theory. That intentional tort theory is accepted currently only where treatment is performed in the absence of any consent at all.

Appropriately, neither the proposed nor the given instruction would have instructed the

jury to measure the duty of the doctor to inform his patient of the material risks of treatment against a standard of disclosure established by expert medical testimony.

leged injury by the testimony of the professional equals of the defendant-physician, a failure to meet that standard and resulting injury to himself. Hayes v. Hulswit, 73 Wash.2d 796, 440 P.2d 849 (1968); Douglas v. Bussabarger, 73 Wash.2d 476, 438 P.2d 829 (1968); Pederson v. Dumouchel, 72 Wash.2d 73, 431 P.2d 973, 31 A.L.R.3d 1100 (1967). The physicians who testified were not interrogated directly on this aspect of the case, and our attention has not been called to any evidence that would establish this contention. CAROA 42(g)(2)(ii) reads:

> Under this heading the following shall be included: A brief statement of the nature of the case; a short resume of the pleadings and proceedings; the nature of the judgment or appropriate ruling or order from which the appeal is taken; a clear and concise statement of the facts appropriate to an understanding of the nature of the controversy, with page references to the record.

We are not referred to any page in the record containing testimony establishing the post-biopsy standard of care or any breach thereof. We conclude from our review of the record and the absence of reference pursuant to the rule that such evidence does not exist. *See* State v. Day, 7 Wash.App. 965, 971, 503 P.2d 1098 (1972).

Reversed and remanded.

HOROWITZ and FARRIS, JJ., concur.

APPENDIX I

The plaintiff's proposed instruction reads:

> You are instructed that a patient has the right to determine what shall be done with his own body. A surgeon must obtain from the patient consent to perform a surgical procedure, such as a kidney biopsy. The consent of the patient must be an informed consent, that is, the physician must inform the patient of all material facts which are necessary to form the basis of an intelligent consent by the patient, and, in that regard, must inform

him of the nature and consequences of the procedure and the reasonably foreseeable risks. If the patient inquires further as to any or all risks involved, the physician must make a complete disclosure of all facts and risks. Surgery performed, without disclosure by the surgeon as above described, constitutes an assault and battery. If you find from the evidence that the defendant physician failed to properly inform the plaintiff as above described, and further find that the plaintiff would not have consented to the surgical procedure if he had been informed, and that the plaintiff was injured as a result of submitting to the procedure, then you should find the defendant liable to the plaintiff for the injuries and damages resulting from said surgical procedure.

The court's instruction reads:

> Under the legal doctrine of "informed consent," a patient may recover from a physician for damages proximately caused by a procedure performed without the patient's "informed consent," irrespective of any negligence or lack of negligence of the physician in the procedure itself.
>
> In order to recover on this basis in this case, plaintiff must prove by a preponderance of the evidence:
>
> 1. That he was not informed of a reasonably foreseeable risk or that he inquired of defendant as to all risks and was not informed thereof;
>
> 2. That he would not have consented to the procedure had he been so informed;
>
> 3. That he has been injured as a proximate result of the procedure.

APPENDIX II

The *Statement of a Patient's Bill of Rights* as promulgated in 1972 by the American Hospital Association includes the following provisions:

> 1. The patient has the right to considerate and respectful care.

114   **47 CALIFORNIA REPORTER**

sonable one, but whether it is reasonable to conclude that a verdict more favorable to * * * [the County] would have been reached but for the error." (Garden Grove School Dist. v. Hendler, 63 A.C. 137, 139–140, 45 Cal.Rptr. 313, 315, 403 P.2d 721, 723.)

Judgment reversed.

SHOEMAKER, P. J., concurs.

Edgar W. DUFF, Jr., and Christina V. Duff, Plaintiffs and Respondents,

v.

Dalton ENGELBERG and Ann Engelberg, Defendants and Appellants,

Lee McCoy et al., Defendants.

Civ. 10914.

District Court of Appeal, Third District, California.

Oct. 18, 1965.

Suit by purchasers for specific performance of executory contract to purchase real property and for damages against vendors and third persons who assertedly induced vendors to refuse to perform contract. From judgment for purchasers by the Superior Court of Sacramento County, William A. White, J., defendants appealed. The District Court of Appeal, Pierce, P. J., held that purchasers could recover, in addition to specific performance and consequential and incidental damages from vendors, compensatory and exemplary damages from third persons who induced vendors not to go forward with sale and that there was no showing of double recovery of compensatory damages.

Affirmed.

1. Damages ⟨⟩91(1)
   Torts ⟨⟩12

Purchasers under executory contract to purchase real property could recover, in addition to specific performance and consequential and incidental relief from vendors, compensatory and exemplary damages from third persons who induced vendor not to go forward with sale.

2. Appeal and Error ⟨⟩931(1)

On judgment roll appeal court must accept as supported by substantial evidence findings of trial court.

3. Damages ⟨⟩42

In light of intent and lack of justification necessary to tort of inducing another to break contract, recovery should be allowed for unforeseen expenses, as well as for mental suffering, damage to reputation, and punitive damages.

4. Judgment ⟨⟩631

Fact that purchasers recovered incidental damages as well as specific performance from vendors did not bar claim for compensatory and exemplary damages against third persons for harm resulting from act of intentionally inducing vendors to refuse to perform contract.

5. Conspiracy ⟨⟩8

Against conspirators committing intentional harm of inducing the breach of contract for sale of land, purchasers were entitled to recover damages for all harm resulting from conspirators' acts.

6. Damages ⟨⟩15

There can be no double recovery of compensatory damages

7. Appeal and Error ⟨⟩846(5)

Where purchasers of real estate were awarded, in addition to specific performance and incidental damages from vendors, compensatory damages from third persons who induced vendors to refuse to go along with sale and request for special finding showing basis for allowance of compensatory damages was not made, court on judgment roll appeal could not assume that there was allowance of double recovery of compensatory damages.

8. Conspiracy ⬡➔20

Where complaint alleged and court found that acts of persons conspiring to breach contract for sale of land were malicious, the allowance of punitive damages to purchasers was proper.

——————◆——————

Max H. Hoseit, Sacramento, for appellants.

Colley & McGhee, Sacramento, for respondents.

PIERCE, Presiding Justice.

[1] The sole question on this judgment-roll appeal by defendants Dalton Engelberg and Ann Engelberg from a plaintiffs' judgment against them is, as stated in defendants'-appellants' brief, "whether a vendee under an executory contract to purchase real property can recover in addition to specific performance of said contract along with consequential and incidental relief damages, both compensatory and exemplary, against a third party who induced the vendor not to go forward with the sale. * * *"

Affirming the trial court's judgment we hold that he can, that the measure of damages is not the same in the cause of action against the third party tort-feasors as it is in the count for specific performance against the vendor.

[2] We summarize the findings of the trial court which, since this is a judgment-roll appeal, we must accept as supported by substantial evidence. (See 3 Witkin, Cal.Procedure, Appeal, secs. 80, 81, pp. 2240–2241.)

Plaintiffs entered into a binding contract for the purchase of a lot in Carmichael, Sacramento County, from defendants McCoy. Defendants Engelberg and Campbell,

who did not want plaintiffs and their family to live in the neighborhood because plaintiffs are Negroes, maliciously caused the McCoys to refuse to perform the contract. Instead, the McCoys conveyed the property to the Campbells "as trustees." The conspirators had actual knowledge of the contract between the McCoys and plaintiffs and the conveyance was made for the express purpose of defeating plaintiffs' rights.

The court decreed specific performance with incidental damages against defendants McCoy. These damages consisted of interest at a higher rate that plaintiffs had to pay while they pursued their remedy of specific performance. The court also gave judgments against the Engelbergs and the Campbells for $1,000 compensatory damage and $500 punitive damages.

The thesis of appellants is that since plaintiffs were made whole by the judgment for specific performance (with incidental relief) they cannot have additional relief against the conspirators. They argue that since plaintiffs could not both obtain specific performance and have an action at law for damages for breach of contract against the vendor, neither can they sue and recover against the parties inducing the breach of contract after having sought and obtained specific performance.

Appellants cite cases, none of which are authority for the proposition for which they are cited. This case, on the precise question raised, appears to be one of first impression in California.

In California Auto Court Ass'n v. Cohn, 98 Cal.App.2d 145, 219 P.2d 511, a motel owner had a contract with plaintiff real estate broker employing him to sell the motel. Plaintiff showed the motel to Marks who was ready, willing and able to buy. To euchre plaintiff out of his commission, the vendor, Marks, and Ostroff, the latter's father-in-law, conspired. The scheme: The motel was sold to Ostroff as "trustee." Marks operated it and was the beneficial owner. A trial court judgment for defendants on demurrer was reversed. The reviewing court stated (per Justice White, on p. 149, 219 P.2d on p. 514): "* * * Each participant in the wrongful act is responsible as a joint tort-feasor for all damages ensuing from the wrong * * *." The court also stated (on p. 150, 219 P.2d on p. 515): "* * * In the various California cases wherein damages have been awarded or injuctive relief granted for unjustifiable interference with contractual relations, it is apparent that the plaintiff is not confined to an action ex contractu against the party with whom he contracted." See also dictum in Swift v. Beaty (1954) 39 Tenn.App. 292, 282 S.W.2d 655, which states at page 659: "[A] person's liability in tort for wrongfully inducing the breach of a contract is in no way affected by the fact that the injured party also has a right of action in contract against the defaulting party to the contract."

[3] Professor Prosser has this to say with reference to the question under discussion: "* * * Although older cases sometimes held to the contrary, it is now agreed that the fact that there is an available action against the party who breaks the contract is no defense to the one who induces the breach, since the two are joint wrongdoers, and each is liable for the loss. Even a judgment in such an action, returned unsatisfied, is no defense. Where substantial loss has occurred, one line of cases tends to adopt the contract measure of damages, limiting recovery to those damages which were within the contemplation of the parties when the original contract was made. Another, apparently somewhat more uncertain of its ground, has applied a tort measure, but has limited the damages to those which are sufficiently 'proximate,' with some analogy to the rules as to negligent torts. A third, perhaps the most numerous, has treated the tort as an intentional one, and has allowed recovery for unforeseen expenses, as well as for mental suffering, damage to reputation, and puni-

tive damages, by analogy to the cases of intentional injury to person or property. *In the light of the intent and the lack of justification necessary to the tort, this seems the most consistent result.* [Citations.] (Emphasis added.) (Prosser, Torts (3d ed.) ch. 26, sec. 123, pp. 972–973.) We accept the rule last stated as being the proper one for the reasons quoted in italics.

[4] The vice of appellants' reasoning (stated above) is that specific performance, plus incidental relief does not really make the plaintiff whole. The suit for specific performance gives to plaintiff the property he was entitled to receive and the incidental expenses and other damages to which he was subjected in his efforts to pursue and recover that property. Those are the expectable-Hadley v. Baxendale[1]-type of damages. They are not necessarily the total damages suffered when the tort is intentional.

"A person who commits a tort against another for the purpose of causing a particular harm to the other is liable for such harm if it results, whether or not it is expectable, except * * *" (Rest., Torts, sec. 915—exception stated not applicable.)

[5] The court awarded plaintiffs only incidental damages against defendant vendors. Plaintiffs had not charged them as members of the conspiracy. Against the conspirators committing the intentional harm, plaintiffs were entitled to recover damages for all harm resulting from their acts. (Rest., Torts, supra, sec. 915; Civ. Code, sec. 3333; 2 Witkin, Summary of Cal. Law (7th ed.) sec. 391, p. 1596.)

[6, 7] Of course, there can be no double recovery of compensatory damages. (Ash v. Mortensen (1944) 24 Cal.2d 654, 658, 660, 150 P.2d 876; Dodds v. Bucknum (1963) 214 Cal.App.2d 206, 212, 29 Cal. Rptr. 393.) There was no showing that a double recovery occurred here. This is a judgment-roll appeal. The findings of the court show that the award of incidental

---

1. Hadley v. Baxendale (1854) 9 Ex. 341, 156 Eng.Rep. 145.

damages against defendant vendors was the difference between the rate of interest plaintiffs had to pay on moneys borrowed and the normal bank rate. There is no showing as to what the basis was for the allowance of compensatory damages in the sum of $1,000 against the defendant conspirators. The finding that plaintiffs were damaged in that sum by said defendants was a sufficient finding of ultimate fact. (Foster v. Keating (1953) 120 Cal.App.2d 435, 453, 261 P.2d 529.) There was no request for special findings. We cannot assume that there was an allowance of a double recovery of damages.

[8] The allowance of punitive damages was proper. The complaint had alleged, and the court found, that the acts of the conspirators were malicious. (Civ.Code, sec. 3294.)

The judgment is affirmed.

FRIEDMAN and REGAN, JJ., concur.

In re James Milton SMITH on Habeas Corpus.

Cr. 3822.

District Court of Appeal, Third District, California.

Oct. 21, 1965.

Hearing Granted Dec. 15, 1965.

Habeas corpus proceeding by prisoner convicted under statute prescribing punishment for assault on guard by prisoner serving sentence in state prison. The District Court of Appeal, Regan, J., held that petitioner who had been committed to Youth Authority and later transferred to state prison on direction of Youth Authority without resentencing by court remained ward of Youth Authority and, although a prisoner confined in state prison, was not undergoing sentence in state prison within meaning of statute under which he had been convicted.

Petition granted.

Friedman, J., dissented.

1. Infants ⬅69
Person convicted of felony and committed to Youth Authority was person serving sentence.

2. Statutes ⬅230
Ordinarily, any essential change in phraseology of statute indicates intention of legislature to change its meaning rather than to interpret it.

3. Convicts ⬅5
Prisoner who had been committed to Youth Authority and later transferred to state prison on direction of Youth Authority without resentencing by court remained ward of Youth Authority and, although a prisoner confined in state prison, was not undergoing sentence in state prison, and his conviction under statute prescribing punishment for assault on guard by prisoner serving sentence in state prison was invalid. West's Ann.Pen.Code, § 4501.

———◆———

Robert K. Patch, Sacramento, Court-Appointed, for appellant.

Thomas C. Lynch, Atty. Gen., by Doris H. Maier, Asst. Atty. Gen., and Raymond M. Momboisse, Deputy Atty. Gen., for respondent.

REGAN, Justice.

Smith, who was convicted of a violation of Penal Code section 4501 (aggravated assault by a prisoner serving a sentence of less than life), petitions for a writ of habeas corpus seeking his discharge from custody. Smith contends his conviction was

7 Torts against Other Civil Rights: Intentional, Negligent, and Without Fault

This chapter deals with some other torts that are important enough to mention as we continue learning the basics. They do not necessarily belong in one common category, but like all other civil wrongs they are violations of our **civil rights.** Our civil rights are those rights guaranteed to all Americans by the United States Constitution, and at times expanded by the individual states.

Invasion of Privacy

Suppose that a famous movie star has begun drinking heavily, and is spotted sleeping in an alley near some garbage cans. An eager reporter takes a photograph of the sleeping star and writes an accompanying story. The headline reads: Star Hits Skid Row. The story describes how the star was found drunk and sleeping it off in an alley. In Chapter 5, we asked whether this type of story is defamation. We know that is not, because the facts are true. However, does this give the reporter the right to print the story? To answer this question, we must look at the four types of torts that deal with invasion of privacy: **unreasonable intrusion, public disclosure of private facts, false light,** and **appropriation.**

Unreasonable Intrusion

Unreasonable intrusion is intentional intrusion into a person's private affairs in a highly offensive manner. Let's examine these elements, one by one.

First, the intrusion into another person's private affairs must be **intentional.** For example, Domingo returns to his old neighborhood to make a documentary film about how the neighborhood has changed in the last 25 years. He plans to show the videotape at the neighborhood's annual Summerfest celebration. The Summerfest takes place in the local park, and audio and video equipment is provided for live music and videos.

Late one evening, Domingo returns to the apartment building where he was born and begins taping in the hallway leading to his former apartment door. At that moment, Joseph opens his own apartment door to throw some garbage into the incinerator a few feet away. Because it is late at night, Joseph is wearing only his underwear. Domingo does not realize that his camera has taped Joseph.

When Domingo shows the video to the entire neighborhood, there is a roar of laughter when the tape features Joseph in his underwear taking out the garbage. Joseph, who is there, is highly embarrassed. Is Domingo liable to Joseph for unreasonable intrusion?

A. Yes, because Joseph was embarrassed.

B. Yes, because Domingo negligently taped Joseph.

C. No, because Joseph did not suffer physical harm.

D. No, because Domingo did not intentionally tape Joseph.

The correct answer is D. Remember, unreasonable intrusion is an *intentional* tort. Because Domingo did not intentionally tape Joseph, he will not be liable for that tort.

What if, instead, Domingo intentionally videotaped Gary and Victor playing basketball in the park on a Sunday afternoon? While other people were waiting to use the court, Gary and Victor played an intense game of one-on-one. On this particular day, Gary played terribly. He missed almost every shot and looked very tired. Victor easily coasted to a lopsided victory. Neither Gary nor Victor knew that Domingo had taped their game.

If Domingo shows the video of the game in front of the entire neighborhood and Gary is very embarrassed, will Domingo be liable to Gary for unreasonable intrusion? Generally, no. You see, the game was not played behind closed doors. Rather, it was played in a public park, where multiple spectators could easily have viewed the event. Accordingly, it is not an intrusion into Gary's **private affairs.**

Of course, if Domingo had planted a small but powerful microphone somewhere on the basketball court, and the microphone captured Gary's conversation with Victor, which may have been private, there may be a different result. However, given the original set of facts, Domingo will probably not be found liable for unreasonable intrusion against Gary.

The final element of this tort is that the intrusion must be **highly offensive** to the reasonable person. If you recall, in Chapter 2 we discussed the subjective nature of the *reasonable person* standard. In other words, a person may be liable if the intrusion would be highly offensive to the reasonable person, not necessarily only to the person whose privacy was intruded on.

Suppose that Jake has numerous unpaid credit card bills. Representatives from the banks who issued the credit cards, who wish to discuss payment arrangements with Jake, routinely call his house in the early evening, hoping to catch him at home. Jake finds the phone calls to be a highly offensive intrusion. A court of law probably would not. It would appear that a creditor seeking to collect a debt may make a diligent effort to speak to the debtor. Calling the debtor's house in the early evening would probably not be considered highly offensive by the reasonable person.

Now, if the bank representatives called Jake at 3 o'clock in the morning, or called him five times in one evening, that type of conduct would more likely be considered highly offensive. Also, if the callers used foul language when speaking with Jake, or if they threatened him with physical violence, such behavior would amount to being highly offensive and thereby an unreasonable intrusion.

Public Disclosure of Private Facts

Public disclosure of private facts is the intentional communication of private information to the public, in a highly offensive manner. Basically, this tort may be the actual *publicizing* of an unreasonable intrusion, though it may also be independent of the original intrusion.

For instance, suppose that Brenda is jealous of Cassie and wants to know whether Cassie is a natural blonde. Brenda sneaks into Cassie's house and discovers hair care products that Cassie uses to color her hair. Also, Brenda discovers photos of Cassie as a brunette. To this point, Brenda's actions most likely amount to an *unreasonable intrusion*. If Brenda decides to share the information about Cassie's hair products and photos, this will probably amount to *public disclosure of private facts*. To illustrate the difference, suppose instead that Brenda tells the information only to Linda. In addition to Brenda's liability for the unreasonable intrusion, if Linda publicizes the information, Linda may be liable for *public disclosure of private facts*, but not for the original *unreasonable intrusion*.

False Light

False Light is intentionally portraying a person to the public in a way that creates a false impression, in a highly offensive manner.

Notice that, as with unreasonable intrusion and public disclosure of private facts, false light contains the elements of **intent** and **highly offensive**. This tort, however, does not necessarily deal with privacy. Rather, it deals with creating a false impression that would be highly offensive to the reasonable person.

Suppose that Claudia is a reporter for the *American Hawk,* a weekly news-magazine. Claudia covers a story about citizens of San Antonio, Texas, who are upset about a work-release program involving violent criminals. Specifically, the program is designed to permit criminals who are nearing the end of their prison sentences to work for government-sponsored programs as a way to accomplish something productive and to ease their return to the world outside of prison. Part of their work involves repairing some roads in San Antonio.

Claudia arrives at the site where the prisoners are working. Her camera crew takes a picture of Curtis, who to Claudia looks like the perfect worker. The article headline, which features a close-up picture of Curtis, reads: Criminals Doing an Honest Day's Work. However, Curtis was never a prisoner. He was one of the many road workers who were not part of the work-release program. When Curtis found out about the article, he sued Claudia for false light. Has she placed Curtis in false light? Generally, yes, but only if she knew that Curtis was not really a prisoner. Otherwise, Claudia would not be liable for false light.

Note: Keep in mind that Claudia may nonetheless be liable to Curtis for, say, defamation. However, she cannot be liable for false light unless she created the false impression intentionally.

Now suppose that Claudia placed a photograph of Curtis in another article titled, San Antonio Sports Fans Want a Football Team. The article is a feature story about the many sports fans in San Antonio who are hoping for a National Football League (NFL) team for their city. If Curtis does not particularly care about there being an NFL team in San Antonio, or is not really even a football fan, then the photograph is certainly misleading. Suppose Claudia knew this, but thought that Curtis looked like a typical sports fan and decided to use the photo anyway. In that case, would she be liable for placing Curtis in false light? Generally, no. Even though her act was intentionally misleading, it was probably not **highly offensive** under the reasonable person standard.

In the first example, Curtis would likely be mistaken for a *criminal.* Here, he would merely be mistaken for a *football fan.* Regarding the misrepresentation, Curtis may be flattered, insulted, or indifferent. In any event, Claudia's conduct will probably not reach the *highly offensive* level necessary to commit the tort of placing someone in false light.

Appropriation

Appropriation is intentional and unconsented use of a person's name or likeness for gain. Again, this tort requires **intent.** Specifically, the tortfeasor must intentionally and for personal benefit use another person's name or likeness, without having received consent to do so.

For example, suppose Bill Brown, a tailor, is eager to increase his business. He obtains a publicity photo of Robert De Niro, the famous actor, wearing a designer suit. Bill has the photo enlarged and places it in his storefront window with a sign that reads: Bill Brown—Tailor to the Stars! Bill did not make either the suit that De Niro was wearing in the photo or any of his other suits, for that matter. In fact, De Niro has never even been to Bill's tailor shop.

Accordingly, Bill has committed the tort of *appropriation*. He has intentionally and without De Niro's consent, used De Niro's picture for personal gain. Moreover, suppose that the photo that Bill used was from one of De Niro's motion picture roles. In that case, whoever owns legal rights to that character may sue Bill as well.

Suppose instead that Bill never used De Niro's photo. Instead, Bill created a false advertisement that read: Robert De Niro Buys His Suits at Bill Brown's Tailor Shop; Why Don't You? In that case, De Niro's *likeness* is not used, but his *name* is. That, too, is a classic example of appropriation.

NEGLIGENT INVASION OF PRIVACY

The four torts of **invasion of privacy—unreasonable intrusion, public disclosure of private facts, false light, and appropriation**—all share the common element of *intent*. While a person who was negligent cannot be held liable for committing these specific torts, he or she may be liable for the resulting *harm* in any event.

The acts that lead to invasion of privacy torts do not generally result in physical harm. However, they may result in emotional or financial harm. As a result, a tortfeasor remains liable for harm caused by *negligence,* even though the tortfeasor will not be specifically liable for an invasion of privacy tort unless the actions were intentional.

Take the example about false light involving Claudia, the reporter for the *American Hawk.* Suppose that Claudia negligently places Curtis' photo underneath another headline titled: Serial Killer Released on Technicality. Suppose that Curtis' employer sees the photo, thinks that the article is about Curtis, and fires him. While Claudia did not place Curtis in false light (because her act was not intentional), she may be liable for harm caused to him by her negligence.

LIABILITY WITHOUT FAULT FOR INVASION OF PRIVACY

Persons who commit invasion of privacy acts cannot be held strictly liable; the acts must be intentional. However, there may be others who are ultimately *vicariously liable* for the harm caused by such torts. For instance, take two of the earlier examples:

1. In the example about false light, suppose that the *American Hawk* is owned and published by Margaret. In that case, if Claudia places Curtis in false light or causes him harm through her negligence, Margaret may be vicariously liable.

2. In the example about appropriation, suppose that it was Jake, one of Bill's employees, who placed the photo of De Niro in the store window. Bill may even have been vacationing in another part of the country at the time, thousands of miles away. Nonetheless, Bill may be vicariously liable for Jake's tortious act.

These, then, are the four torts that comprise invasion of privacy. Now let's take a look at some other areas of torts.

MALICIOUS PROSECUTION

We have already discussed the difference between *civil* and *criminal* law, and the fact that certain acts may fall into both categories. We have also stated that private persons may only institute civil lawsuits. In criminal lawsuits, the complaint is brought by all of the people through their representative, namely, the district attorney (DA) or a prosecutor from the DA's office. The tort of **malicious prosecution** deals with yet another interaction between civil and criminal law.

Malicious prosecution is intentionally filing a groundless criminal complaint against another person, thereby causing harm to such person, who is ultimately acquitted from the charges or against whom the charges are dismissed.

This definition sounds like quite a mouthful, but it's not really as complicated as it sounds. Let's examine each element, slowly and carefully.

First of all, *malicious prosecution* is an **intentional** tort. This means that a person cannot be charged for negligently or without fault committing malicious prosecution.

Next, it arises from filing a **groundless criminal complaint**. As we discussed, a criminal complaint is brought by the prosecutor. A crime is deemed to be conducted not only against the direct victim, but against all of the people. For example, if James steals Vanessa's car, James has committed a crime.

Note: Of course, given your knowledge of torts, you know that in addition to committing one or several crimes, James has committed trespass to chattel or conversion, as well as other possible torts, depending on the circumstances.

To the extent that James' act is criminal, he has committed the crime not only against Vanessa, but against all the people (of the state, typically) as a whole. Therefore, if the crime took place in New York, then the people of the State of New York would collectively bring an action against James. The people would be represented by the district attorney's office.

Even though Vanessa is not the only victim in the case, her role is a very important one for practical purposes. Most likely, it is Vanessa's decision to press charges against James, and her subsequent testimony, that will help to convict James in criminal court.

Therefore, if Vanessa calls the police to report that her car has been stolen, and she identifies James as the culprit, it is on this information that the police will likely make the arrest that will begin the procedure leading to James' conviction.

Suppose, then, that Vanessa had driven to a dance club and had parked her car in the club's lot. She noticed James lurking in the parking lot alone. Vanessa entered the club and began to look for her friends. Once she found her friends, Vanessa decided to go to the bar and order a drink. At that point, she realized that she forgot her wallet inside her car.

Vanessa went out to the parking lot and discovered that her car was not there. Immediately, she suspected James. Based on Vanessa's description of James, he was arrested a few days later and charged with the crime. But suppose that while James is in criminal proceedings, the police continue their investigation and discover that Steve, not James, stole Vanessa's car.

In fact, Steve makes a full confession and tells the police that neither James nor anyone else helped him to steal the car. All the charges against James are dropped. Is Vanessa liable to James for malicious prosecution? No.

Remember, malicious prosecution must be intentional. Here, Vanessa erroneously but *not intentionally* led the police to arrest James. Though James was innocent, Vanessa had made a mistake. She actually *did* believe that James was the person who stole her car. She did not knowingly mislead the police. Accordingly, she did not commit malicious prosecution.

Suppose, instead, that Vanessa has known James for a long time. She was angry with James and wanted to frame him for a crime.

Vanessa stored her car in a friend's garage, claimed it was stolen, and then falsely told the police that she saw James stealing it. In that case, Vanessa would be liable for malicious prosecution *if* the following also occurred:

1. James was ultimately acquitted of the charges or the charges were dropped; and
2. James was harmed by Vanessa's false charges (for instance, his reputation in the community was tarnished).

It is necessary for all of the elements to be present in order for Vanessa to be liable for malicious prosecution.

It is not enough, then, for a person to maliciously attempt to bring about a false prosecution, in order to be liable for malicious prosecution. The person falsely accused must not be convicted, and must suffer some type of harm. Certainly, this does not mean Vanessa or anyone else may attempt to mislead law enforcement agencies and only be liable if the accused is exonerated and suffers harm. However, while the mere attempt to bring about a groundless prosecution may be a violation of both civil and criminal law, it does not by itself amount to malicious prosecution.

TORTIOUS INTERFERENCE WITH CONTRACT

Earlier in the book we discussed the fact that civil law is mainly comprised of **torts** and **contracts**. We defined a contract as an agreement enforceable by law. Accordingly, two parties who enter into a contract are generally protected by that contract. The contract, though beneficial to the contracting parties, may be to another person's detriment. In certain circumstances, if a person attempts to interfere with an existing contract, such interference may be a tortious act.

Tortious interference with a contract is intentionally attempting to induce another party to breach a contract.

For example, suppose Marcia is interested in buying a house and has narrowed her choices to two: Jeff's house and Roger's house. After careful consideration, Marcia decided on Jeff's house and entered into a contract with him. Marcia called Roger and told him that she already entered into a contract with Jeff and was no longer interested in buying Roger's house.

Determined to induce Marcia to change her mind, Roger calls Marcia the following day and offers to lower the price for his house. He also offers to include some adjoining land as part of the deal. At this point, Roger has tortiously interfered with Marcia and Jeff's contract. Roger is, in effect, attempting to plant a seed in Marcia's mind to *breach* (break) her contract with Jeff. In other words, Roger is trying to get Marcia to renege on her decision to buy Jeff's house and buy Roger's house instead.

Even if Roger is successful in getting Marcia to *want* to change her mind, legally she cannot. She has a contractual *obligation* to buy Jeff's house, just as Jeff has the obligation to sell the house to Marcia. Of course, if Marcia can think of some way to convince Jeff to break the contract, then the contract may be legally broken upon the consent of *both* parties (Marcia and Jeff).

All the while, this plotting is to Jeff's detriment, because Roger, a third party, is trying to interfere with Marcia and Jeff's contractual relations. This, then, is tortious interference with contract.

Another common example of tortious interference with contract happens in the workplace. For instance, suppose Fiorello is a world-renowned chef of Italian cuisine. Michael owns Amore, a popular Italian restaurant. Fiorello and Michael enter into a contract whereby Fiorello agrees that if he resigns or is terminated from Amore, he will not work in any restaurant within five miles of Amore within one year of leaving Amore. After six months of working at Amore, Fiorello decides to resign. A few weeks later, Fiorello is hired by Giovanni's restaurant, which is across the street from Amore. The sign in the window of Giovanni's reads: Now featuring the legendary master chef Fiorello.

When Michael finds out that Fiorello is now working for Giovanni, he sues Fiorello for breach of contract, and also sues Giovanni for *tortious interference with contract.*

Is Giovanni liable for that tort? Only if he knew about Fiorello's contract with Michael. Otherwise, Giovanni would not be liable for tortious interference with contract, because that is an *intentional* tort.

Nonintentional Liability for Malicious Prosecution and Tortious Interference with Contract

Both **malicious prosecution** and **tortious interference with contract** are *intentional* torts. Therefore, a person may only be held specifically liable for these torts if he or she committed the acts *intentionally*. However, a person may be liable for harm caused as a result of those acts if they were committed negligently or even without fault, without being specifically liable for those torts.

Sound confusing? Look at these examples and it will make better sense to you.

Suppose Michelle negligently assumes that Ralph has robbed her grocery store and convinces the police to prosecute Ralph. Even if all of the other elements necessary for malicious prosecution suffice, Michelle cannot be liable for that tort because she did not intentionally mislead the police. However, Ralph may nonetheless sue Michelle for any harm he suffered that was proximately caused by her negligence.

Next, even if Michelle had nothing to do with Ralph's erroneous prosecution, Michelle may nonetheless owe Ralph damages if she was vicariously liable for someone who intentionally or negligently caused the prosecution.

The same reasoning applies to tortious interference with contract. If a person negligently interferes with another's contract, the damaged party may not have an action for tortious interference with contract, but may sue for harm based on negligence.

For instance, take the example involving Fiorello, Michael, and Giovanni, in which Fiorello was legally obligated under contract not to work within a five-mile radius of Michael's restaurant, Amore, for at least one year after leaving Amore. Suppose Giovanni's restaurant was not across the street from Amore but was actually four miles away. Suppose Giovanni was negligent in thinking that Giovanni's was six miles away from Amore, and thus thought that hiring Fiorello would not cause a breach of Fiorello's contract with Michael. In that case, Michael may be able to sue for damages for harm suffered as a result of Giovanni's negligence.

Next, suppose that when Giovanni's restaurant hired Fiorello, Giovanni was vacationing in Europe. Giovanni's assistant manager, Joseph, hired Fiorello, even though Joseph was fully aware of Fiorello's contract with Michael. In that case, Michael may not only successfully sue Fiorello and Joseph, but he may also sue *Giovanni*, even though Giovanni had nothing to do with the hiring.

Keep in mind that while Giovanni may be liable for damages, that would be based on liability without fault (in this case, vicarious liability), not tortious interference with contract. However, Joseph, who knowingly ignored the restriction in Fiorello and Michael's contract, would be liable for tortious interference with contract.

REVIEW QUESTIONS

1. What are civil rights?
2. What is unreasonable intrusion?
3. What is public disclosure of private facts?
4. Give an example in which public disclosure of private facts is committed, based on an unreasonable intrusion committed by someone else.
5. What is false light?
6. What is appropriation?
7. What is malicious prosecution?
8. What is tortious interference with contract?
9. Give an example showing how someone may be liable for negligently interfering with someone else's privacy.
10. Give an example showing how someone may be vicariously liable for harm resulting from appropriation committed by someone else.

A TORT TALE

One afternoon, Jessica was on her way to the shopping mall. She stopped off at the bank, where she noticed Jason. She remembers that her eye caught Jason particularly because he was wearing a white cowboy hat. Jessica then drove to the mall, which was two miles further along the road.

As she was entering the mall, Jessica was almost knocked over by Steve, who bumped into her as he was running out of the mall. Unknown to Jessica, Steve had just robbed a jewelry store in the mall. Jessica entered the mall, did her shopping, and went home.

That night, Jessica turned on the television and watched the evening news. That is when she saw the news report about the store being robbed at about the same time she was entering the mall. She thought back and realized that the man who bumped into her may have been the culprit.

Jessica went to the police the next day and gave them a full description of the man who bumped into her, including the fact that he was wearing a white cowboy hat. Jessica mistakenly thought that *Jason*, whom she saw at the bank earlier that day, was *Steve*, the robber running out of the mall.

That afternoon, Jason was again wearing his cowboy hat and was arrested by the police. Jessica, still mistaken, identified him as the man from the mall. At trial, Jason was acquitted of all charges. **Jessica is not liable to Jason for malicious prosecution. Why?**

CASE LAW

Before we move on to Chapter 8, let's take a look at some cases regarding some of the torts we have learned about in this chapter. As always, keep in mind what we have discussed about case law.

We have now covered many of the basic torts. In Chapter 8, we look at some defenses that apply to these torts.

beneficiaries, petitioned the court, laid the entire matter before it and refused to act except with its approval.

The order appealed from should be affirmed, with costs.

BURKE, SCILEPPI, BERGAN, BREITEL, JASEN and GIBSON, JJ., concur.

Order affirmed.

25 N.Y.2d 560

Ralph NADER, Respondent,

v.

GENERAL MOTORS CORPORATION, Appellant, et al., Defendants.

Court of Appeals of New York.

Jan. 8, 1970.

Action by author and lecturer on automobile safety against automobile manufacturer and others for two causes of invasion of right to privacy, intentional infliction of severe emotional distress and interference with plaintiff's economic advantage. The Supreme Court, Special Term, New York County, Joseph A. Brust, J., 57 Misc.2d 301, 292 N.Y.S.2d 514, denied defendant's motion to dismiss first, second and fourth causes of action and appeal was taken. The Supreme Court, Appellate Division, 31 A.D.2d 392, 298 N.Y.S.2d 137, affirmed. On appeal by permission of the Appellate Division on certified question, the Court of Appeals, Fuld, C. J., held that fact that defendants may have interviewed many persons who knew plaintiff and asked questions about him and cast aspersions on his character did not constitute invasion of privacy under District of Columbia law, notwithstanding that inquiries may have uncovered information of a personal nature but that complaint that defendants en-

gaged in unauthorized wiretapping and eavesdropping by mechanical and electronic means stated cause of action for invasion of privacy.

Affirmed.

1. Pleading ⬦360(14)

Bill of particulars is to be read in connection with complaint, on motion to dismiss.

2. Torts ⬦2

District of Columbia had most significant relationship with subject matter of action for invasion of privacy, so that District of Columbia law governed, where it was in that jurisdiction that most of acts relied on to support recovery allegedly occurred and plaintiff lived and suffered impact of those acts in the District.

3. Torts ⬦8

Common-law action for invasion of privacy is recognized in District of Columbia.

4. Torts ⬦8

Some intrusions into one's privacy are inevitable concomitants of life in an industrial and densely populated society, and not all such acts are proscribed, even if it were possible to do so, as invasions of privacy.

5. Torts ⬦8

Under District of Columbia law, right of privacy encompasses merely right to protect one's self from having one's affairs known to others and to keep secret intimate facts about one's self from prying eyes or ears of others and does not encompass broad right to be let alone.

6. Torts ⬦24

Under District of Columbia law, mere gathering of information about a particular individual does not give rise to cause of action for invasion of privacy, since there can be no such invasion where information sought is open to public view and where it has been voluntarily revealed to others.

7. Torts ⟜27

To sustain cause of action for invasion of privacy under District of Columbia law, it must be shown that defendant's conduct was truly intrusive and that it was designed to elicit information which would not be available through normal inquiry or observation.

8. Torts ⟜8

Fact that automobile corporation through its agents or employees may have interviewed many persons who knew author of book on automobile safety and asked questions about him and cast aspersions on his character did not constitute invasion of privacy under District of Columbia law, notwithstanding that inquiries may have uncovered information of personal nature; if questions tended to disparage author's character his remedy would be by way of action for defamation.

9. Torts ⟜8

Any conduct of automobile corporation in causing author of book on automobile safety to be accosted by girls with illicit proposals or causing author to receive large number of threatening and harassing telephone calls at his home at odd hours did not involve intrusion for purpose of gathering information of a private and confidential nature and thus did not constitute actionable invasion of privacy under District of Columbia law.

10. Torts ⟜4, 8

Where severe mental pain or anguish is inflicted through a deliberate and malicious campaign of harassment and intimidation, a remedy is available under District of Columbia law in the form of an action for intentional infliction of emotional distress; however, elements of such action are decidedly different from those governing tort of invasion of privacy and case cannot be cast in form of recovery for the latter so as to avoid more stringent plead-

ing and proof requirements applicable to the former.

11. Torts ⟜26(1)

Complaint by author of book on automobile safety that automobile corporation or its agents engaged in unauthorized wiretapping and eavesdropping by mechanical and electronic means stated cause of action under District of Columbia law for invasion of privacy.

12. Torts ⟜26(1)

Allegation in complaint by author of book on automotive safety that automobile corporation hired people to shadow author and keep him under surveillance and particularly that agent followed him into bank and positioned himself sufficiently close to observe denominations of bills author was withdrawing from account stated cause of action under District of Columbia law to recover for invasion of privacy; defense that author acted in such a way as to reveal funds to any casual observer could be established at trial.

13. Torts ⟜8

Although under District of Columbia law mere observation of one in a public place does not amount to an invasion of privacy, under certain circumstances surveillance may be so overzealous as to render it actionable; a person does not automatically make public everything he does by being in a public place.

14. Pleading ⟜354(16)

Fact that three of five allegations of invasion of privacy failed to state cause of action did not subject entire complaint to dismissal where remaining two allegations were sufficient.

15. Pleading ⟜354(16)

So long as a pleading sets forth allegations which suffice to spell out a claim for relief, it is not subject to dismissal by reason of inclusion therein of additional nonactionable allegations.

Simon H. Rifkind, New York City, Martin Kleinbard, Rye, and Allan Blumstein, New York City, for appellant.

Alfred W. Gans., Stuart M. Speiser and Paul D. Rheingold, New York City, for respondent.

FULD, Chief Judge.

On this appeal, taken by permission of the Appellate Division on a certified question, we are called upon to determine the reach of the tort of invasion of privacy as it exists under the law of the District of Columbia.

The complaint, in this action by Ralph Nadar, pleads four causes of action against the `appellant, General Motors Corporation, and three other defendants allegedly acting as its agents. The first two causes of action charge an invasion of privacy, the third is predicated on the intentional infliction of severe emotional distress and the fourth on interference with the plaintiff's economic advantage. This appeal concerns only the legal sufficiency of the first two causes of action, which were upheld in the courts below as against the appellant's motion to dismiss (CPLR 3211, subd. [a], par. 7).

The plaintiff, an author and lecturer on automotive safety, has, for some years, been an articulate and severe critic of General Motors' products from the standpoint of safety and design. According to the complaint—which, for present purposes, we must assume to be true—the appellant, having learned of the imminent publication of the plaintiff's book "Unsafe at any Speed," decided to conduct a campaign of intimidation against him in order to "suppress plaintiff's criticism of and prevent his disclosure of information" about its products. To that end, the appellant authorized and directed the

other defendants to engage in a series of activities which, the plaintiff claims in his first two causes of action, violated his right to privacy.[1]

[1] Specifically, the plaintiff alleges that the appellant's agents (1) conducted a series of interviews with acquaintances of the plaintiff, "questioning them about, and casting aspersions upon [his] political, social * * * racial and religious views * * *; his integrity; his sexual proclivities and inclinations; and his personal habits" (Complaint, par. 9 [b]; (2) kept him under surveillance in public places for an unreasonable length of time (par. 9 [c]); (3) caused him to be accosted by girls for the purpose of entrapping him into illicit relationships (par 9[d]); (4) made threatening, harassing and obnoxious telephone calls to him (par. 9[e]); (5) tapped his telephone and eavesdropped, by means of mechanical and electronic equipment, on his private conversations with others (par. 9[f]; and (6) conducted a "continuing" and harassing investigation of him (par.9[g]). These charges are amplied in the plaintiff's bill of particulars, and those particulars are, of course, to be taken into account in considering the sufficiency of the challenged causes of action. (See Bolivar v. Monnat, 232 App. Div. 33, 34, 248 N.Y.S. 722, 725; see, also, 4 Weinstein-Korn-Miller, N.Y.Civ.Prac.; par. 3211.43.)

[2] The threshold choice of law question requires no extended discussion. In point of fact, the parties have agreed—at least for purposes of this motion—that the sufficiency of these allegations is to be determined under the law of the District of Columbia. The District is the jurisdiction in which most of the acts are alleged to have occurred, and it was there, too, that the plaintiff lived and suffered the impact

---

1. The first cause of action contains allegations of several types of activity which took place, for the most part, in the District of Columbia, while the second charges the appellant with engaging in similar activity in New York. It appears that, at least to some

extent, both counts are premised on the same conduct and should be treated as stating alternative rather than cumulative claims for damages. In any event, however, the substantive nature of the two counts is the same.

of those acts. It is, in short, the place which has the most significant relationship with the subject matter of the tort charged. (See, e. g., Babcock v. Jackson, 12 N.Y.2d 473, 240 N.Y.S.2d 743, 191 N.E. 2d 279, 95 A.L.R.2d 1.)

[3] Turning, then, to the law of the District of Columbia, it appears that its courts have not only recognized a common-law action for invasion of privacy but have broadened the scope of that tort beyond its traditional limits. (See Pearson v. Dodd, 133 U.S.App.D.C. 279, 410 F.2d 701; Afro-American Pub. Co. v. Jaffe, 125 U.S.App.D.C. 70, 366 F.2d 649; Peay v. Curtis Pub. Co., D.C., 78 F.Supp. 305; see, also Bloustein, Privacy as an Aspect of Human Dignity, 39 N.Y.U.L.Rev. 962, 977; Prosser, Privacy, 48 Cal.L.Rev. 383, 389 et seq.) Thus, in the most recent of its cases on the subject, Pearson v. Dodd (133 U.S. App.D.C. 279, 410 F.2d 701, *supra*), the Federal Court of Appeals for the District of Columbia declared (p. 704):

> "We approve the extension of the tort of invasion of privacy to instances of *intrusion*, whether by physical trespass or not, into spheres from which an ordinary man in a plaintiff's position could reasonably expect that the particular defendant should be excluded." (Italics supplied.)

It is this form of invasion of privacy—initially termed "intrusion" by Dean Prosser in 1960 (Privacy, 48 Cal.L.Rev. 383, 389 et seq.; Torts, § 112)—on which the two challenged causes of action are predicated.

[4] Quite obviously, some intrusions into one's private sphere are inevitable concomitants of life in an industrial and densely populated society, which the law does not seek to proscribe even if it were possible to do so. "The law does not provide a remedy for every annoyance that occurs in everyday life." (Kelley v. Post Pub. Co., 327 Mass. 275, 278, 98 N.E.2d 286, 287.) However, the District of Columbia courts have held that the law should and does protect against certain

types of intrusive conduct, and we must, therefore, determine whether the plaintiff's allegations are actionable as violations of the right to privacy under the law of that jurisdiction. To do so, we must, in effect, predict what the judges of that jurisdiction's highest court would hold if this case were presented to them. (See, e. g., Cooper v. American Airlines, 2 Cir., 149 F.2d 355, 359, 162 A.L.R. 318, per Frank, J.) In other words, what would the Court of Appeals for the District of Columbia say is the character of the "privacy" sought to be protected? More specifically, would that court accord an individual a right, as the plaintiff before us insists, to be protected against any interference whatsoever with his personal seclusion and solitude? Or would it adopt a more restrictive view of the right, as the appellant urges, merely protecting the individual from intrusion into "something secret," from snooping and prying into his private affairs?

The classic article by Warren and Brandeis (The Right to Privacy, 4 Harv.L.Rev. 193)—to which the court in the *Pearson* case referred as the source of the District's common-law action for invasion of privacy (410 F.2d, at p. 703)—was premised, to a large extent, on principles originally developed in the field of copyright law. The authors thus based their thesis on a right granted by the common law to "each individual * * * of determining, ordinarily, to what extent his thoughts, sentiments and emotions shall be communicated to others" (4 Harv.L.Rev., at p. 198). Their principal concern appeared to be not with a broad "right to be let alone" (Cooley, Torts [2d ed.], p. 29) but, rather, with the right to protect oneself from having one's private affairs known to others and to keep secret or intimate facts about oneself from the prying eyes or ears of others.

[5] In recognizing the existence of a common-law cause of action for invasion of privacy in the District of Columbia, the Court of Appeals has expressly adopted this latter formulation of the nature of the right. (See, e. g., Afro-American Pub. Co.

v. Jaffe, 125 U.S.App.D.C. 70, 366 F.2d 649, 653, *supra*.) Quoting from the Restatement, Torts (§ 867), the court in the *Jaffe* case (366 F.2d, at p. 653) has declared that "[l]iability attaches to a person 'who unreasonably and seriously interferes with another's interest in *not having his affairs known to others.*'" (Emphasis supplied.) And, in *Pearson*, where the court extended the tort of invasion of privacy to instances of "intrusion," it again indicated, contrary to the plaintiff's submission, that the interest protected was one's right to keep knowledge about oneself from exposure to others, the right to prevent *"the obtaining of the information* by improperly intrusive means" (410 F.2d, at p. 704; emphasis supplied). In other jurisdictions, too, the cases which have recognized a remedy for invasion of privacy founded upon intrusive conduct have generally involved the gathering of private facts or information through improper means. (See, e. g., Hamberger v. Eastman, 106 N.H. 107, 206 A.2d 239, 11 A.L.R.3d 1288; Ford Motor Co. v. Williams, 108 Ga.App. 21, 132 S.E.2d 206; LeCrone v. Ohio Bell Tel. Co., 120 Ohio App. 129, 201 N.E.2d 533; see, also, Bloustein, Privacy as an Aspect of Human Dignity, 39 N.Y.U.L.Rev. 962, 972. But cf. Housh v. Peth, 165 Ohio St. 35, 133 N.E.2d 340.)

[6,7] It should be emphasized that the mere gathering of information about a particular individual does not give rise to a cause of action under this theory. Privacy is invaded only if the information sought is of a confidential nature and the defendant's conduct was unreasonably intrusive. Just as a common-law copyright is lost when material is published, so, too, there can be no invasion of privacy where the information sought is open to public view or has been voluntarily revealed to others. (See Forster v. Manchester, 410 Pa. 192,

189 A.2d 147; Tucker v. American Employers' Ins. Co., 171 So.2d 437, 13 A.L.R. 3d 1020 [Fla.App.]; see, also, Prosser, Torts [3d ed.], p. 835; Restatement, 2d, Torts, Tent. Draft No. 13, § 652B, comment c.) In order to sustain a cause of action for invasion of privacy, therefore, the plaintiff must show that the appellant's conduct was truly "intrusive" and that it was designed to elicit information which would not be available through normal inquiry or observation.

The majority of the Appellate Division in the present case stated that *all of* "[t]he activities complained of" in the first two counts constituted actionable invasions of privacy under the law of the District of Columbia (31 A.D.2d, at p. 394, 298 N.Y. S.2d, at p. 139).[2] We do not agree with that sweeping determination. At most, only two of the activities charged to the appellant are, in our view, actionable as invasions of privacy under the law of the District of Columbia (*infra*, pp. 568–571). However, since the first two counts include allegations which are sufficient to state a cause of action, we could—as the concurring opinion notes (p. 571)—merely affirm the order before us without further elaboration. To do so, though, would be a disservice both to the judge who will be called upon to try this case and to the litigants themselves. In other words, we deem it desirable, nay essential, that we go further and, for the guidance of the trial court and counsel, indicate the extent to which the plaintiff is entitled to rely on the various allegations in support of his privacy claim.

In following such a course, we are prompted not only by a desire to avoid any misconceptions that might stem from the opinion below but also by recognition of the fact that we are dealing with a new and developing area of the law. Indeed,

---

2. "The activities complained of:" wrote the Appellate Division majority, "the shadowing, the indiscriminate interviewing of third persons about features of his intimate life, the wiretapping and eavesdropping, the prying into his bank ac-

counts, taxes, the alleged accosting by young women and the receipt of threatening phone calls, all are within the purview of these cases" (31 A.D.2d, at p. 394, 298 N.Y.S.2d, at p. 139).

we would fail to meet our responsibility if we were to withhold determination—particularly since the parties have fully briefed and argued the points involved—and thereby thrust upon the trial judge the initial burden of appraising the impact of a doctrine still in the process of growth and of predicting its reach in another jurisdiction.

[8] Turning, then, to the particular acts charged in the complaint, we cannot find any basis for a claim of invasion of privacy, under District of Columbia law, in the allegations that the appellant, through its agents or employees, interviewed many persons who knew the plaintiff, asking questions about him and casting aspersions on his character. Although those inquiries may have uncovered information of a personal nature, it is difficult to see how they may be said to have invaded the plaintiff's privacy. Information about the plaintiff which was already known to others could hardly be regarded as private to the plaintiff. Presumably, the plaintiff had previously revealed the information to such other persons, and he would necessarily assume the risk that a friend or acquaintance in whom he had confided might breach the confidence. If, as alleged, the questions tended to disparage the plaintiff's character, his remedy would seem to be by way of an action for defamation, not for breach of his right to privacy. (Cf. Morrison v. National Broadcasting Co., 19 N.Y.2d 453, 458–459, 280 N.Y.S.2d 641, 643–644, 227 N.E.2d 572, 573–574.)

[9] Nor can we find any actionable invasion of privacy in the allegations that the appellant caused the plaintiff to be accosted by girls with illicit proposals, or that it was responsible for the making of a large number of threatening and harassing telephone calls to the plaintiff's home at odd hours. Neither of these activities, howsoever offensive and disturbing, involved intrusion for the purpose of gathering information of a private and confidential nature.

[10] As already indicated, it is manifestly neither practical nor desirable for the law to provide a remedy against any and all activity which an individual might find annoying. On the other hand, where severe mental pain or anguish is inflicted through a deliberate and malicious campaign of harassment or intimidation, a remedy is available in the form of an action for the intentional infliction of emotional distress—the theory underlying the plaintiff's third cause of action. But the elements of such an action are decidedly different from those governing the tort of invasion of privacy, and just as we have carefully guarded against the use of the prima facie tort doctrine to circumvent the limitations relating to other established tort remedies (see Morrison v. National Broadcasting Co., 19 N.Y.2d 453, 458–459, 280 N.Y.S.2d 641, 643–644, 227 N.E.2d 572, 573–574, *supra*), we should be wary of any attempt to rely on the tort of invasion of privacy as a means of avoiding the more stringent pleading and proof requirements for an action for infliction of emotional distress. (See, e. g., Clark v. Associated Retail Credit Men, 70 App.D.C. 183, 105 F.2d 62, 65).

[11] Apart, however, from the foregoing allegations which we find inadequate to spell out a cause of action for invasion of privacy under District of Columbia law, the complaint contains allegations concerning other activities by the appellant or its agents which do satisfy the requirements for such a cause of action. The one which most clearly meets those requirements is the charge that the appellant and its codefendants engaged in unauthorized wiretapping and eavesdropping by mechanical and electronic means. The Court of Appeals in the *Pearson* case expressly recognized that such conduct constitutes a tortious intrusion (133 U.S.App.D.C. 279, 410 F.2d 701, 704, *supra*), and other jurisdictions have reached a similar conclusion. (See, e. g., Hamberger v. Eastman, 106 N.H. 107, 112, 206 A.2d 239, *supra*; Roach v. Harper, 143

W.Va. 869, 877, 105 S.E.2d 564; Fowler v. Southern Bell Tel. & Tel. Co., 5 Cir., 343 F.2d 150, 156.) [3] In point of fact, the appellant does not dispute this, acknowledging that, to the extent the two challenged counts charge it with wiretapping and eavesdropping, an actionable invasion of privacy has been stated.

[12, 13] There are additional allegations that the appellant hired people to shadow the plaintiff and keep him under surveillance. In particular, he claims that, on one occasion, one of its agents followed him into a bank, getting sufficiently close to him to see the denomination of the bills he was withdrawing from his account. From what we have already said, it is manifest that the mere observation of the plaintiff in a public place does not amount to an invasion of his privacy. But, under certain circumstances, surveillance may be so "overzealous" as to render it actionable. (See Pearson v. Dodd, 133 U.S.App.D.C. 279, 410 F.2d 701, 704, *supra*; Pinkerton Nat. Detective Agency, Inc. v. Stevens, 108 Ga.App. 159, 132 S.E.2d 119.) Whether or not the surveillance in the present case falls into this latter category will depend on the nature of the proof. A person does not automatically make public everything he does merely by being in a public place, and the mere fact that Nader was in a bank did not give anyone the right to try to discover the amount of money he was withdrawing. On the other hand, if the plaintiff acted in such a way as to reveal that fact to any casual observer, then, it may not be said that the appellant intruded into his private sphere. In any event, though, it is enough for present purposes to say that the surveillance allegation is not insufficient as a matter of law.

[14, 15] Since, then, the first two causes of action do contain allegations which are adequate to state a cause of action for invasion of privacy under District of Col-

umbia law, the courts below properly denied the appellant's motion to dismiss those causes of action. It is settled that, so long as a pleading sets forth allegations which suffice to spell out a claim for relief, it is not subject to dismissal by reason of the inclusion therein of additional nonactionable allegations. (See Spano v. Perini Corp., 25 N.Y.2d 11, 18, 302 N.Y.S.2d 527, 532, 250 N.E.2d 31, 35; see, also, Tompkins v. State of New York, 7 N.Y.2d 906, 907, 197 N.Y.S.2d 475, 476, 165 N.E.2d 424, 425; Rager v. McCloskey, 305 N.Y. 75, 80, 111 N.E.2d 214, 217.)

We would but add that the allegations concerning the interviewing of third persons, the accosting by girls and the annoying and threatening telephone calls, though insufficient to support a cause of action for invasion of privacy, are pertinent to the plaintiff's third cause of action—in which those allegations are reiterated—charging the intentional infliction of emotional distress. However, as already noted, it will be necessary for the plaintiff to meet the additional requirements prescribed by the law of the District of Columbia for the maintenance of a cause of action under that theory.

The order appealed from should be affirmed, with costs, and the question certified answered in the affirmative.

BREITEL, Judge (concurring in result).

There is no doubt that the first and second causes of action are sufficient in alleging an invasion of privacy under what appears to be the applicable law in the District of Columbia (Pearson v. Dodd, 133 U.S.App.D.C. 279, 410 F.2d 701, 704; Afro-American Pub. Co. v. Jaffe, 125 U.S.App.D.C. 70, 366 F.2d 649, 653–654). This should be the end of this court's proper concern with the pleadings, the only matter before the court being a motion to

3. Indeed, although the question whether wiretapping affords a predicate for an invasion of privacy action has not yet arisen in our own jurisdiction, we note that our

Penal Law—in an article entitled "Offenses Against the Right to Privacy"—makes eavesdropping by such means a felony (Penal Law, art. 250, § 250.05).

dismiss specified causes of action for insufficiency.

Thus it is not proper, it is submitted, for the court directly or indirectly to analyze particular allegations in the pleadings, once the causes of action are found sufficient, in order to determine whether they would alternatively sustain one cause of action or another, or whether evidence offered in support of the allegations is relevant only as to one rather than to another cause of action. Particularly, it is inappropriate to decide that several of the allegations as they now appear are referable only to the more restricted tort of intentional infliction of mental distress rather than to the common-law right of privacy upon which the first and second causes of action depend. The third cause of action is quite restricted. Thus many of the quite offensive acts charged will not be actionable unless plaintiff succeeds in the very difficult, if not impossible, task of showing that defendants' activities were designed, actually or virtually, to make plaintiff unhappy and not to uncover disgraceful information about him. The real issue in the volatile and developing law of privacy is whether a private person is entitled to be free of certain grave offensive intrusions unsupported by palpable social or economic excuse or justification.

True, scholars, in trying to define the elusive concept of the right of privacy, have, as of the present, subdivided the common law right into separate classifications, most significantly distinguishing between unreasonable intrusion and unreasonable publicity (Restatement, 2d, Torts, Tent. Draft No. 13 [April 27, 1967], §§ 652A, 652B, 652D; Prosser, Torts [3d ed.], pp. 832–837). This does not mean, however, that the classifications are either frozen or exhausted, or that several of the classifications may not overlap.

Concretely applied to this case, it is suggested, for example, that it is premature to hold that the attempted entrapment of plaintiff in a public place by seemingly promiscuous ladies is no invasion of any of the categories of the right to privacy and is restricted to a much more limited cause of action for intentional infliction of mental distress. Moreover, it does not strain credulity or imagination to conceive of the systematic "public" surveillance of another as being the implementation of a plan to intrude on the privacy of another. Although acts performed in "public", especially if taken singly or in small numbers, may not be confidential, at least arguably a right to privacy may nevertheless be invaded through extensive or exhaustive monitoring and cataloguing of acts normally disconnected and anonymous.

These are but illustrations of the problems raised in attempting to determine issues of relevancy and allocability of evidence in advance of a trial record. The other allegations so treated involve harassing telephone calls, and investigatory interviews. It is just as important that while allegations treated singly may not constitute a cause of action, they may do so in combination, or serve to enhance other violations of the right to privacy.

It is not unimportant that plaintiff contends that a giant corporation had allegedly sought by surreptitious and unusual methods to silence an unusually effective critic. If there was such a plan, and only a trial would show that, it is unduly restrictive of the future trial to allocate the evidence beforehand based only on a pleader's specification of overt acts on the bold assumption that they are not connected causally or do not bear on intent and motive.

It should be observed, too, that the right to privacy, even as thus far developed, does not always refer to that which is not known to the public or is confidential. Indeed, the statutory right of privacy in this State and perhaps the most traditional right of privacy in the "common law sense" relates to the commercialized publicity of one's face or name, perhaps the two most public aspects of an individual (see Civil Rights Law, §§ 50, 51; Restatement,

2d, Torts, Tent. Draft No. 13 [April 27, 1967], § 652C).

There is still further difficulty. In this State thus far there has been no recognition of a common law right of privacy, but only that which derives from a statute of rather limited scope (Civil Rights Law, §§ 50, 51; Flores v. Mosler Safe Co., 7 N.Y. 2d 276, 280, 196 N.Y.S.2d 975, 977, 164 N. E.2d 853, 854; Roberson v. Rochester Folding Box Co., 171 N.Y. 538, 556–557, 64 N.E. 442, 447–448, 59 L.R.A. 478). Consequently, this court must undertake the hazardous task of applying what is at present the quite different law of the District of Columbia. True, this may be the court's burden eventually, if the case were to return to it for review after trial, especially if the plaintiff were to prevail upon such a trial. However, there is no occasion to advance, now, into a complicated, subtle and still-changing field of law of another jurisdiction, solely to determine before trial the relevancy and allocability among pleaded causes of action or projected but not yet offered items of evidence. It is not overstatement to say that in the District of Columbia the law of the right of privacy is still inchoate in its development, perhaps more so than in many other jurisdictions that accept this newly coined common-law cause of action, despite unequivocal acceptance as a doctrine and extension by dictum

to cases of intrusion (Pearson v. Dodd, *supra*, 410 F.2d, at p. 704).* In the absence of a trial record, the court should avoid any unnecessary extrapolation of what the District of Columbia Court of Appeals has characterized as "an untried and developing area of tort law" (Pearson v. Dodd, *supra*, p. 705).

Nor does Rager v. McCloskey, 305 N.Y. 75, 111 N.E.2d 214 offer support for the excursion in this case into the allocation in advance of trial and an evidentiary record of the functional relevancy of evidence perhaps to be offered in the future and perhaps not. In the *Rager* case, plaintiff had urged throughout the proceedings an alternative, independent, and unsustainable legal theory based allegedly on the accordion doctrine of "prima facie" tort (see Morrison v. National Broadcasting Co., 24 A.D.2d 284, 289–292, 266 N.Y.S.2d 406, 411–414, 16 A.L.R.3d 1175, revd. on narrow grounds, 19 N.Y.2d 453, 280 N.Y.S.2d 641, 227 N.E.2d 572). Quite appropriately, although perhaps not necessarily, the court in sustaining the complaint pointed out that the cause of action could not survive on the alternative theory in the absence of allegation and proof of special damages. This was accomplished by a simple reference to the theory of "prima facie" tort and the patent vital omission of an allegation of special damages in the pleading.

---

* This is what the latest pronouncement from the Court of Appeals in the District of Columbia has to say about this "new" tort, as applied to intrusion: "Unlike other types of invasion of privacy, intrusion does not involve as one of its essential elements the publication of the information obtained. The tort is completed with the obtaining of the information by improperly intrusive means.
" 'Intrusion' has not been either recognized or rejected as a tort in the District of Columbia. It has been recognized by a number of state courts, most recently by the New Hampshire Supreme Court in Hamberger v. Eastman, 106 N.H. 107 [206 A.2d 239] *Hamberger* found liable a defendant who eavesdropped upon the marital bedroom of plaintiffs by electronic means, holding that 'the invasion of the plaintiffs' solitude or seclusion

* * * was a violation of their right of privacy.'
"We approve the extension of the tort of invasion of privacy to instances of intrusion, whether by physical trespass or not, into spheres from which an ordinary man in a plaintiff's position could reasonably expect that the particular defendant should be excluded. Just as the Fourth Amendment has expanded to protect citizens from government intrusions where intrusion is not reasonably expected, so should tort law protect citizens from other citizens. The protection should not turn exclusively on the question of whether the intrusion involves a technical trespass under the law of property. The common law, like the Fourth Amendment, should 'protect people, not places.' " (footnotes omitted).

Notably, and so relevant to the policy to be followed in this case, the court otherwise limited its analysis of the pleading. Having found that the *Rager* complaint stated a cause of action against each of the defendants, the court declined to consider whether allegations of additional false statements, and recitals of conspiracy, were still relevant or admissible on any further cause of action. It stated: "Since, then, the complaint does state a cause of action against each of the defendants, it is immune from attack for insufficiency, even though it may contain additional allegations that are inadequate to charge any further cause of action. See Abrams v. Allen, 297 N.Y. 52, 54, 74 N.E.2d 305, 306, 173 A.L.R. 671; Advance Music Corp. v. American Tobacco Co., 296 N.Y. 79, 84, 70 N.E.2d 401, 403; Abbey v. Wheeler, 170 N.Y. 122, 127, 62 N.E. 1074, 1076. Accordingly, we postpone for possible future consideration the question whether other allegedly false statements—attributed to one or another of defendants—may be ruled defamatory and slanderous per se, as well as the further question whether the recitals of conspiracy are sufficient to charge each of the defendants with liability for the acts of the others." (Rager v. McCloskey, *supra,* 305 N.Y. at p. 80, 111 N.E.2d at p. 217.)

The plaintiff, naturally enough, is trying to broaden his warrant, and defendant-appellant is correspondingly trying to narrow that warrant. But the eagerness of the parties in briefing hypothetical problems does not require an advisory opinion or a declaratory judgment by the highest court of the State without the benefit of a trial judge's rulings on relevancy, and an Appellate Division's review of those rulings on a trial record. There is no justification, on the present record, for giving an illiberal and restrictive scope to a cause of action based on the right of privacy as that right is likely to be defined under the applicable law of another jurisdiction.

The broad statements in the opinion of the Appellate Division can be met, as this court has done so often, by declaring that they are not necessarily adopted in concluding that a cause or causes of action have been stated.

Accordingly, because of the prematurity of ruling on any other question but the sufficiency of the causes of action, I concur in result only.

SCILEPPI, BERGAN and GIBSON, JJ., concur with FULD, C. J.

BREITEL, J., concurs in result in an opinion in which BURKE and JASEN, JJ., concur.

Order affirmed, etc.

25 N.Y.2d 576

In the Matter of the Arbitration between A/S J. LUDWIG MOWINCKELS REDERI, Appellant,

and

DOW CHEMICAL COMPANY et al., Respondents.

Court of Appeals of New York.

Jan. 22, 1970.

Proceeding on petition to stay arbitration demanded in connection with maritime charter party. The Supreme Court, Special Term, New York County, Arthur Markewich, J., entered a judgment denying motion for stay and an appeal was taken. The Appellate Division of the Supreme Court in the First Judicial Department, 31 A.D.2d 372, 297 N.Y.S.2d 1011, affirmed and an appeal was taken. The Court of Appeals, Fuld, C. J., held that maritime charter party containing broad arbitration clause was solely federal in character and governed exclusively by federal law including Federal Arbitration Act, precluding

8 DEFENSES, REMEDIES, AND DAMAGES

We have covered many basic concepts of torts themselves. Now we take a look at defenses, remedies, and damages.

DEFENSES

Defense is yet another of the many words used in legal and nonlegal circles alike. Unlike some of the other words, the meaning of defense basically remains the same. Generally, to *defend* means to protect or to justify. A defense may be a shield against a physical attack, such as during a battle in war, on the playing field, or on a chessboard. A defense could also be used to thwart a verbal attack, such as during an argument.

In the legal sense, **a defense is a legal justification for a particular act that would otherwise be illegal.** Even if all the elements of a particular civil or criminal violation are present, the person who committed the violation may not be held responsible if he or she can successfully raise an appropriate defense.

Defense Distinguished from Missing Element

A *defense* to a tort is not the same thing as an act that is not really a tort because of a missing element. For example, we know that for there to be *battery* there must be *contact*. If Alan swings at Bob and misses, Bob cannot successfully sue Alan for battery, because the element of contact is missing.

To say that Alan would raise a defense of "no contact" would be inaccurate. Instead, Alan's argument that there was no contact would indicate that all of the elements for the tort of battery were never established. However, if Alan *did* in fact make contact with Bob, as well as fulfill all the other elements of battery, then Alan would have to establish why his action was justified. In that case, Alan would need to raise a *defense*.

Let's take a look at some defenses that negate liability for acts that are otherwise considered torts.

Self-Defense

If you reasonably believe that you or a third person are threatened by unjustified imminent bodily harm, you may use the amount of force reasonably necessary to defend against that harm.

Did you already know the full meaning of self-defense? Unlike other tort concepts, *self-defense* is a notion with which many people both in and out of the legal community are familiar. However, you should examine the definition carefully, as there may be some points that are different from what you may have thought the term really means.

First of all, the belief that there is a threat of harm must be **reasonable.** Suppose that Chester was walking along and noticed Jason approaching him. Jason was wearing a sweatshirt with the letters KC in bright red across the middle. Actually, KC was an abbreviation for Kansas City.

Chester, however, thought that the letters meant "Kill Chester." Accordingly, Chester attacked Jason and threw him to the ground.

As we have already learned, this act would normally be battery. If Jason was aware of the attack, it would be assault as well. But would Chester be successful in claiming that he acted in self-defense?

A. Yes, because he honestly believed that Jason was going to kill him.

B. Yes, because the letters KC assume there will be an attack.

C. No, because Chester's belief about imminent harm was not reasonable.

D. More information is needed to answer this question.

The correct answer is C. Chester's belief will most likely not be considered reasonable. That the letters KC might mean Kill Chester, thereby subjecting Chester to imminent harm at Jason's hands, would not justify Chester's actions. Although Chester's belief may have been *genuine*, it was not *reasonable* under the circumstances.

As you know by now, a reasonable belief need not be perfect. For example, suppose that Bob points a water gun at Lester. Believing that the gun is real, Lester picks up a brick and throws it at Bob, knocking Bob unconscious. If Lester's belief that the gun is real is a *reasonable* belief, then Lester will probably succeed in a claim of self-defense.

If Bob and Lester were good friends and the gun was plastic and bright orange, then Lester probably should have realized that the gun was a toy. However, if they were strangers and the water gun looked genuine, then the reasonable person may have thought it to be real, too.

Let's return to Jason and Chester. Imagine that Jason *did* in fact threaten Chester, but over the telephone. Jason called Chester and told him: "If I see you next week, I will hurt you." If Chester physically attacks Jason at their next meeting, may Chester successfully claim self-defense? No, because the threat of harm was not **imminent.** As we discussed when learning about *assault,* a threat of harm may not necessarily mean that the harm will occur immediately. Chester may not physically attack Jason in anticipation of *future* harm and then claim self-defense.

Of course, Chester may have various legal recourses available to him, such as notifying the police, hiring a bodyguard, or bringing an action against Jason for *infliction of emotional distress,* among other things. However, Chester may not preemptively attack Jason and then successfully claim self-defense, because the threat of harm was not *imminent.*

Next, the force used in self-defense must be the amount **reasonably necessary** to defend against the imminent harm. For instance, if one punch is all it would reasonably take to repel an attacker, then throwing additional punches may be *unreasonable.*

Suppose that Ricky is walking home from the subway station. Tony jumps Ricky from behind, attempting to steal Tony's wallet. Ricky manages to overpower Tony, throwing him to the ground. When Tony realizes that he is overmatched, he gets up and attempts to run away. Ricky chases him, catches him, and begins to hit Tony with repeated blows. At this point, Ricky is committing assault and battery upon Tony, and may not successfully claim that he is acting in self-defense. Think about that entire scenario, and let's discuss it in more detail.

Public opinion may vary about what Ricky *should* be allowed to do. For instance, some may argue that Ricky should have every right to beat Tony up, because Tony attacked Ricky and tried to steal Ricky's wallet. Note that the key word is *should.* What Ricky *should* be permitted to do in some persons' opinion and what Ricky *is* permitted to do by law are two different things.

Ricky may argue that he was attempting to subdue Tony in order to turn Tony over to the police. In effect, Ricky would be making a citizen's arrest. Even if Ricky were entitled to make such an arrest, he would not be entitled to use more than a reasonable amount of force to arrest Tony. In fact, even if Ricky were actually a police officer, he would not be entitled to use more force than that reasonably necessary to place Tony under arrest. Any additional force over what would be reasonably necessary is **excessive force.**

In any event, in this scenario Ricky clearly would not be entitled to claim self-defense for the excessive force that he used against Tony.

Next, remember that the defense of self or a third person must be against **unjustified harm.** Imagine that Tony has in fact grabbed Ricky's wallet and starts running away. Ricky chases Tony, catches him, and tries to take the wallet back by force. Kevin is walking along the street, sees Ricky using force against Tony, and tries to help Tony. Kevin will *not* be entitled to come to Tony's defense because Ricky's force against Tony is **justified**—Ricky is trying to get his wallet back. (See additional information about using force to recover property later in this chapter).

What if, instead, Tony had tried to mug Jenny, and Ricky rushed to her defense? The same principles would apply, except that instead of self-defense, Ricky would be defending a third person.

Deadly Force

Consistent with the elements of self-defense that we have discussed, **a person may use deadly force in self-defense if that person has a reasonable belief that she is about to be harmed by deadly force.** Accordingly, a person may kill another person to save himself or a third party from being killed.

Duty to Retreat and the Castle Exception

In some jurisdictions, a person has a duty to retreat, if such act is a reasonable alternative to defending oneself. In other words, if a person can get out of harm's way by retreating rather than by using force, some courts require the person to retreat.

However, even those courts make an exception if the threat of harm occurs in a person's home. Consider this example to illustrate the difference.

While inside a sports bar, George gets into an argument with the Benson brothers, Nick and Ray. The Bensons wait for George across the street from the sports bar in order to attack him when he leaves. George may exit from the front and defend himself, or exit from the back, enter his car, and drive away safely. In many jurisdictions, George has the option to do either. In other jurisdictions, however, George may be required by law to retreat (take the back door) rather than fight. In any event, if the threat was *in George's home*, then George would have the option to stay and defend himself and his home.

We refer to this exception, which brings to mind the expression "a home is a person's castle," as the **castle exception.**

Defense of Property

A person may use the amount of force reasonably necessary, short of deadly force, to protect or recover property. This definition is very similar to the one for self-defense. The focal difference is that deadly force may generally not be used to recover property. Consider this example to illustrate.

Theresa is sleeping one evening when Simon breaks into her home. He opens the door to her bedroom, causing Theresa to wake. Simon pulls out a knife and charges Theresa. Fearing for her life, she reaches into the drawer of her night table, picks up her gun, and shoots Simon. In this case, Theresa has used deadly force to thwart deadly force.

Imagine instead that Theresa did not wake until she heard Simon rummaging through the living room. Theresa grabbed her pistol and headed down the stairs. When Simon saw her, he ran out of the house. Theresa chased him but he was too fast for her. She noticed that he was holding her diamond watch and running away. In order to recover her property, Theresa shot Simon.

In the second instance, Theresa would generally be prohibited from using deadly force. Unlike the scenario in her bedroom, when Simon charged at her with a knife, Theresa was not encountering deadly force while Simon was running away from her. She would not be legally permitted to use deadly force against him solely to recover property.

Deadly Traps

Deadly traps that are set in order to protect property are generally not permissible by law. Consider this example.

You own a vacation cabin in the woods. You stay in the cabin for only a few weeks and weekends each year. The cabin remains unoccupied the rest of the time. Because people realize that your cabin, which is isolated from other cabins, is empty, they see it as an easy place from which to steal. As a result, your cabin was burglarized twice last year.

You become upset and you want this to stop. You set up a trap for whoever opens the door. If any person opens the door without first deactivating the trap, he or she will be struck by an arrow that you have aimed at the door. Most likely, the arrow will kill or seriously injure the person.

Although that device would be on *your* property, and would probably only serve to harm those who are illegally present in your cabin, the device is nonetheless against the law. Using that type of trap is a classic example of using deadly force to protect property.

A person has the right to use force to recover property, even if the force can lead to physical harm. However, the force must stop short of being deadly force.

Consent

If a person legally consents to a particular act, then that act is not a tort. This definition, though brief, may not be as simple as it looks.

First, let's deal with the general concept of consent, that is, to agree to something. For instance, you would think that if Mack and Ray chased Walter, caught him, and violently threw him to the ground, this would certainly be a tort. But if the three were playing a game of tackle football, to which Walter consented, then Mack and Ray would be justified in their action.

Also, if Sally agrees to have sexual relations with Calvin, then generally she has consented. But there are exceptions to the rule. Consider the concept of *capacity to consent.*

Capacity to Consent

Although a person may verbally consent to a particular act, that person may lack the **capacity to consent.** For instance, if Sally is a minor, she may not be *legally* capable of consenting to sexual relations with Calvin, even if she verbally and physically consented.

In that case, Calvin may be liable for assault and battery, and may not successfully raise the defense of consent.

Note: You may think that Calvin will be charged with statutory rape, and he very well may be. But remember, that is a crime, and we are dealing with torts.

In addition to minors, persons who are deemed to be mentally incompetent may also lack the capacity to consent. Such mental incompetence may be a medical condition or a temporary state of mind.

Minors As Tortfeasors

Generally, a minor will be held to the standard of reasonable care of a minor of similar age, intelligence, and experience, except when that minor conducts adult activity. In that case, the minor will be held to the standard of an adult.

For example, if while riding a bicycle a minor accidentally crashes into a pedestrian, the minor will be held to the standard of a reasonable minor of the same age, intelligence, and experience in riding a bicycle. However, if the minor injured the pedestrian while the minor was driving a car (an adult activity), the minor would be held to the reasonable standard of an adult.

Intoxication

A person who is drunk or drugged may not be capable of legally consenting to a particular act. Also, a person may not be able to form the intent to commit a particular act. Therefore, in the case of date rape, the level of intoxication of either the aggressor or the victim may play a role in determining liability.

Voluntary versus Involuntary Intoxication

Persons who voluntarily consume drugs or alcohol may be less successful in raising intoxication as a defense than those who are made drunk or drugged against their will or without their knowledge.

For instance, if Derek goes to a bar after work, gets drunk, and gets into a car accident while driving home, Derek will have a very difficult time trying to excuse his liability because of his drunkedness. However, suppose someone placed a tasteless, odorless drug into Derek's drink while he was not looking; or, in trying to mug Derek, someone forcibly injected him with a drug. In those cases, Derek would be intoxicated either without his knowledge or against his will. Thus, Derek may be less responsible for his actions than if he had voluntarily placed himself in that position. Intoxication, then, may be a factor in determining a person's mental state.

Assumption of Risk

With many torts, a person may raise the defense that the victim assumed the risk. For instance, if Carl lends his car to Janet, but Janet is injured in an accident because the brakes are faulty, Carl may be liable for negligence if Carl failed to warn Janet about the faulty brakes. However, suppose that Carl did in fact warn Janet but Janet decided to take her chances anyway. If Janet is injured and she sues Carl, Carl may raise the defense of assumption of risk.

This defense is often used in liability without fault cases as well. Consider the following illustration: Alicia visits her friend Jackie at Jackie's house. Jackie owns a pit bull terrier, which she keeps locked in the basement.

While giving Alicia a tour of the house, Jackie warns Alicia to stay out of the basement, telling her that the pit bull is dangerous and may bite strangers. Ignoring the consequences, Alicia ventures into the basement on her own and is bitten by the pit bull. In that case, if Alicia sues Jackie, Jackie may successfully raise the defense that Alicia assumed the risk.

Necessity

A person who commits a tort as a reasonable effort to prevent a greater harm may raise the defense of necessity. Generally, the greater harm must not have been originated by the same person. To illustrate, consider this example: Cliff owns a sporting goods store that is closed on Sundays. One Sunday afternoon, Emma is driving past Cliff's store when she realizes that her engine is overheating.

Once she turns the engine off, Emma is horrified to realize that her engine is on fire. She looks through Cliff's store window and notices a fire extinguisher inside. In order to save her car from burning, Emma breaks the window, enters the store, and uses the extinguisher to put out the fire.

Emma's act generally brings three torts to mind that we learned about in Chapter 4: *conversion,* when she broke the window; *trespass,* when she entered the store; and *trespass to chattel,* when she used the fire extinguisher.

Given the circumstances, however, Emma could probably raise the defense of necessity. Arguably, it would be a greater harm for her car to burn as compared to the damage she caused to Cliff's store. There is a question, however, about how the fire started in the first place. Was Emma at fault for her engine overheating? If she was not, then her defense claim is valid. However, if the engine overheated because she neglected to properly maintain it, then Emma's defense claim may not necessarily relieve her of liability.

Private Necessity versus Public Necessity

Emma's situation is an example of a **private necessity.** A tort committed to prevent a greater harm to one person or a few individuals is a private necessity. A tortfeasor who raises a private necessity defense is generally responsible for paying compensatory damages for the resulting harm. In the example, then,

Emma would probably have to reimburse Cliff for the damage she did to his store window, and for any damage done to his fire extinguisher.

On the other hand, a tort committed to prevent a greater harm to the public at large is a **public necessity.** Using the same example, suppose that Emma broke into Cliff's store and used his fire extinguisher to put out a fire at a chemical factory. Had the factory fire spread, dangerous fumes might have poisoned the environment for many miles around. In that case, Emma's actions would amount to a public necessity, and she would not be required to pay damages to Cliff.

What about Cliff? Does this mean that nobody will help pay for his broken window? If the necessity is for the public good, then the community at large is usually required to pay the damages. For instance, Cliff may be reimbursed by the town whose citizens Emma benefitted by putting out the fire at the factory.

Truth

In actions for defamation, truth is a defense. As we discussed in Chapter 5, defamation involves a number of elements about statements that are actually or potentially damaging to a person's reputation. In order to be defamatory, such statements must be *false.* Accordingly, truth is a defense.

For example, if Jack *truthfully* reveals that Herbert, an accountant, routinely steals money from his clients without their knowing it, such a statement may certainly damage Herbert's professional reputation. But Herbert will probably not be able to successfully sue Jack for defamation because the statement is *true.* By proving the truth of the statement, Jack may successfully raise the defense of truth to thwart Herbert's claim of defamation.

Contributory and Comparative Negligence

In an action for negligence, a negligent tortfeasor may be partially or wholly relieved of liability if there is **contributory** or **comparative** negligence on the part of the plaintiff. Whether or not such a defense may be used depends on the *jurisdiction* in which the action is brought.

Contributory Negligence

A plaintiff who is at all negligent may not prevail in an action for negligence against the tortfeasor. Imagine that Gina and Vic are involved in a car accident. Vic's car is damaged but Gina's is not. Vic claims that Gina was negligent and sues her for $10,000 in damages. Suppose that a jury determines that Vic was about 80% negligent while Gina was about 20% negligent. If the court is in a **contributory negligence jurisdiction,** then Vic will not be able to recover any damages, because he was partially negligent. Essentially, he would only be able to recover damages if he was not at all negligent.

The Last Clear Chance

In many contributory negligence jurisdictions, a plaintiff may nonetheless recover if the defendant had the **last clear chance** to prevent the harm to the plaintiff. For instance, suppose that Lenny wanders onto a construction site, even though he noticed several signs warning about danger at the site. Roger, a construction worker, notices Lenny, but continues some minor blasting to loosen some old concrete. Lenny is injured by the blasting. In that case, many courts will permit Lenny to recover because, even though he was contributorily negligent, Roger had the last clear chance to prevent the harm.

Note: Suppose instead that Roger blasted without seeing Lenny. In that case, it would be difficult for Lenny to recover damages, particularly in a contributory negligence jurisdiction.

Pure Comparative Negligence

In a pure comparative negligence jurisdiction, the plaintiff may recover damages to the extent that he or she is not negligent. Let's return to the car accident example to illustrate. Vic sued Gina for $10,000 and the jury determined that Vic was 80 percent negligent while Gina was 20 percent negligent. Therefore, if the court is in a **pure comparative negligence** jurisdiction, Vic will be able to recover $2,000, which is the entire amount ($10,000) minus 80 percent ($8,000), the extent to which he was negligent.

50 Percent Comparative Negligence

This category of sharing the liability for negligence is somewhat a combination of contributory negligence and pure comparative negligence. **In a 50 percent comparative negligence jurisdiction, a plaintiff may recover damages to the extent that he or she is not negligent. A plaintiff who is more than 50 percent negligent may not recover any damages.**

Returning to the example of Gina and Vic, because Vic was more than 50 percent negligent, he would not be able to recover any damages. However, if Vic were 50 percent negligent or less, he would be able to recover damages to the extent that he was not negligent, as with pure comparative negligence.

Take a look at these examples in order to better understand the differences between these three categories.

Facts: Angela and Diane accidentally set fire to Diane's home. The damages amount to $20,000. Diane sues Angela for damages. Angela is found to be 70 percent negligent, and Diane is 30 percent negligent.

1. How much would Angela be required to pay Diane in a contributory negligence jurisdiction? **Nothing.**

2. How much would Angela be required to pay Diane in a pure comparative negligence jurisdiction? **$14,000.**

3. How much would Angela be required to pay Diane in a 50 percent comparative negligence jurisdiction? **$14,000.**

4. Suppose instead that Angela was found to be 40 percent negligent and Diane 60 percent negligent. In that case, how much would Angela be required to pay Diane in a 50 percent comparative negligence jurisdiction? **Nothing.**

Remedies

Generally, the word *remedy* has various meanings. For instance, drinking plenty of liquids and taking Vitamin C are popular *remedies* to help fight a cold. In legal matters, however, **a remedy is the method by which a person may enforce his or her rights.** Such remedies are usually either *at law* or *in equity.*

In tort law, the most common types of remedies are remedies at law, whereby the plaintiff seeks monetary compensation, known as *damages.* (We discuss some types of damages later in this chapter.) However, sometimes there are *equitable remedies* in tort law, too. These remedies often bar the tortfeasor from continuing a particular action.

For instance, when a tortfeasor is creating a *nuisance,* the court may require the tortfeasor to stop the action. If Keith, for example, opens a pig farm next to a nursery school, the court may require Keith to permanently shut down his pig farm. This is called a *permanent injunction.* Sometimes, the court may issue a *temporary injunction* against a defendant, pending the outcome of the trial.

Res Ipsa Loquitur

The term *res ipsa loquitur* is a Latin term that means "the thing speaks for itself." In some cases, a plaintiff may not be able to prove the (tortfeasor) defendant's negligence. In those instances, under the remedy of res ipsa loquitur, a plaintiff may recover damages if:

1. The instrument causing the harm was exclusively under the defendant's control;
2. The type of harm that the plaintiff suffered normally occurs through negligence; and
3. The plaintiff did not contribute to his or her own harm.

Actually, the third element is, in effect, contributory or comparative negligence, which we have already discussed. However, in this context, it is an element for a remedy rather than a defense. Some courts also require that the defendant be in a better position than the plaintiff to explain the circumstances resulting in the harm.

Consider this example: Acme Construction Company is constructing a building in a busy neighborhood. One afternoon, Greg is walking by the construction site when a brick falls on his shoulder, injuring him.

Suppose Greg wants to sue Acme for damages, but there is not sufficient evidence to prove Acme's negligence. In that case, Greg may have a good chance of recovering damages under res ipsa loquitur if:

1. The brick was exclusively under Acme's control;
2. The circumstances resulting in Greg's injury normally occur due to negligence; and
3. Greg did not cause his own injuries.

Res ipsa loquitur is often a last-resort remedy for plaintiffs who cannot otherwise prove a defendants' negligence.

Joint and Several Liability

When more than one tortfeasor are liable, damages may be collected from any or all of the tortfeasors, in any combination, but not to exceed the total damages allowed. For example, Donna, Frank, and Louise were all held responsible for destroying Rhonda's antique vase. If the vase was worth $50,000, Rhonda may collect the entire $50,000 from Donna, or from either of the other two defendants. Instead, Rhonda may collect $15,000 each from Donna and Frank, and $20,000 from Louise, or any other combination. However, Rhonda may not collect a total of more than $50,000. Once Rhonda has collected $50,000, she has received legal **satisfaction.**

Suppose that Rhonda has collected the entire amount, $50,000, from Donna. Donna, in turn, may sue Frank and Louise for their **contribution,** or their fair share of paying the damages.

Survival Statutes

A survival statute entitles a plaintiff's claim to survive the plaintiff's death. Consider this example: Dominick is badly injured in a fire negligently started by Norman. Dominick sues Norman, but dies in the middle of the lawsuit. Despite Dominick's death, the lawsuit may continue and Dominick's estate may recover any *damages.*

DAMAGES

Generally, **damages are monetary compensation awarded to the plaintiff in a civil lawsuit.** Various types of damages may be applicable to the particular case in question.

Compensatory Damages

The most common types of damages are **compensatory damages.** These are awarded to a plaintiff as compensation for a loss. For instance, suppose Melanie injures her leg while falling on a slippery floor inside a restaurant. If Melanie sues for damages and the jury returns a verdict in her favor, the money awarded to Melanie for her loss would generally be *compensatory.*

Compensatory damages are either **general** (*direct*) or **special** (*consequential*). General damages are those that are usually awarded for direct loss. For instance, a money amount determining the value for which to compensate Melanie for her injured leg would be a general, direct damage.

Typically, there is a set value amount placed on each type of injury. However, if Melanie must miss work for a certain period of time as a result of the injury, then the amount of money for which she should be compensated will probably depend on the amount of earnings that she will likely lose. Thus, compensation for loss of earnings is a special damage, and it varies depending on each plaintiff's special circumstances.

Such damages are also called *consequential,* because they are indirectly related to the actual harm or loss.

Punitive Damages

Because torts are part of civil law, tort damages are usually designed to compensate the plaintiff, not to punish the defendant. However, when a tortfeasor has acted with particular ill will, malice, or conscious disregard, **punitive damages** may be awarded in order to punish the defendant and deter others from engaging in similar conduct.

For instance, suppose Walter intentionally causes Roy to suffer a severe injury. In addition to compensatory damages, Walter may be required to pay punitive damages as punishment for his conduct toward Roy. Again, keep in mind that punitive damages are far less common than are compensatory damages.

Nominal Damages

When the plaintiff has proven that the defendant has committed a tort, but little or no harm or loss is incurred, the plaintiff may be entitled only to **nominal damages.** Nominal damages are comparatively small and are awarded in order to confirm the tortfeasor's wrongdoing and to deter others from engaging in similar tortious conduct.

Have you ever read or heard about a case in which the plaintiff was awarded, say, one dollar in damages? That is a prime example of *nominal damages.* Like punitive damages, nominal damages are not very common.

Wrongful Death

Generally, when a person dies who was the victim of a tort, that person's spouse, parents, and children may recover damages for that family member's wrongful death.

Loss of Consortium

A person who is harmed as the victim of a tort, when such harm causes his or her spouse to suffer loss of love, affection, companionship, or financial support, may receive damages as a result. In some cases, the tort victim's minor children may also receive damages. Thus, unlike wrongful death actions, a person may recover for loss of consortium when the plaintiff remains alive.

Duty to Mitigate Damages

Generally, a plaintiff has a duty to mitigate damages. Though not an actual defense to a tort claim, plaintiff's failure to mitigate damages may result in a reapportioning of damages payable by the defendant.

For example, imagine that Robert negligently drops a bowling ball on Stacey's foot. Stacey sees a doctor, who informs her that she has a severe sprain. The doctor advises Stacey to stay off her feet for two weeks and then begin some exercises to strengthen the foot. Stacey's medical expenses and other compensatory damages total $5,000.

After one week of staying off her feet, Stacey becomes impatient. Feeling a great deal better, she decides to go dancing, which she loves to do. As a result, Stacey aggravates the injury to her foot and will now require extensive treatment to prevent irreversible damage. This treatment will cost another $15,000.

Stacey sues Robert for $20,000, to cover her entire damages. Robert, however, claims that Stacey failed to mitigate her damages by not following the doctor's advice. Accordingly, the court may award only $5,000 to Stacey, for the original injury.

REVIEW QUESTIONS

1. What is a defense?
2. How is a defense of a tort different from a missing element in a tort?
3. Give an example of self-defense.
4. What is the castle exception rule?
5. May force be used to recover property?
6. What does capacity to consent mean?
7. What is the difference between private necessity and public necessity?

8. What is contributory negligence?
9. What is res ipsa loquitur?
10. What is the duty to mitigate damages?

A TORT TALE

Jordan and Riley were involved in a car accident. Jordan's car was not damaged, but Riley's was. Riley's damages were about $10,000. Riley sued Jordan in court. The jury determined that Jordan was liable for $4,000 worth of the damages. The trial was held in a comparative negligence jurisdiction, not a contributory negligence jurisdiction. Even so, Jordan was not required to pay for any of the damages. **Why?**

CASE LAW

Before you move on to Chapter 9, take a look at a couple of cases involving damages. As always, keep in mind everything we have discussed about reading case law while you are reading.

PACIFIC REPORTER

VOL. 199, SECOND SERIES

SUMMERS v. TICE et al.
L. A. 20650, 20651.

Supreme Court of California, in Bank.
Nov. 17, 1948.
Rehearing Denied Dec. 16, 1948.

1. Weapons ⊂⊃18(2)

Evidence that defendants shot uphill at a quail in the direction of plaintiff, though knowing his location, authorized finding of negligence.

2. Weapons ⊂⊃18(1)

Members of a hunting party do not necessarily assume risk of their companions' negligence.

3. Weapons ⊂⊃18(1)

Where plaintiff suggested that all members of hunting party "stay in line" while hunting, and went uphill at right angle to hunting line, but cautioned other hunters to use care, and other hunters knew plaintiff's position, court could find that plaintiff did not act negligently nor assume risk of being shot by other hunters.

4. Weapons ⊂⊃18(2)

Where evidence did not clearly show which of two defendants' shot struck plaintiff, finding that pellets lodged in plaintiff's eye and lip as result of shots fired "by defendants and each of them" was a sufficient finding that defendants were jointly liable and that negligence of both was cause of injury.

5. Weapons ⊂⊃18(2)

Where evidence showed that two defendants, while hunting, shot at about same time at quail and that two birdshot struck plaintiff, who was in the hunting party, burden of proving which defendant's shot struck plaintiff shifted to defendants, and in absence of further evidence judgment against both defendants was proper.

199 P.2d—1

6. Damages ⊂⊃163(1)

If defendants are independent tort feasors and thus each liable for damage caused by him alone, but matter of apportionment is incapable of proof, innocent wronged party should not be deprived of redress but wrongdoers should be left to work out between themselves any apportionment.

7. Weapons ⊂⊃18(1)

Where member of hunting party was shot when two other hunters shot at quail at about the same time, each was liable for the whole damage whether they be deemed to have acted in concert or independently, in absence of direct evidence as to which hunter's shot struck plaintiff.

Appeal from Superior Court, Los Angeles County; John A. Holland, Judge pro tem.

Actions by Charles A. Summers against Harold W. Tice and against Ernest Simonson for negligently shooting plaintiff while hunting. From judgments for plaintiff, defendants appeal, and the appeals were consolidated pursuant to stipulation.

Affirmed.

Prior opinion, 190 P.2d 963.

Gale & Purciel, of Bell, Joseph D. Taylor, of Los Angeles, and Wm. A. Wittman, of South Gate, for appellants.

Werner O. Graf, of Los Angeles, for respondent.

CARTER, Justice.

Each of the two defendants appeals from a judgment against them in an action for personal injuries. Pursuant to stipulation the appeals have been consolidated.

Plaintiff's action was against both defendants for an injury to his right eye and face as the result of being struck by bird shot discharged from a shotgun. The case was tried by the court without a jury and the court found that on November 20, 1945, plaintiff and the two defendants were hunting quail on the open range. Each of the defendants was armed with a 12 gauge shotgun loaded with shells containing 7½ size shot. Prior to going hunting plaintiff discussed the hunting procedure with defendants, indicating that they were to exercise care when shooting and to "keep in line." In the course of hunting plaintiff proceeded up a hill, thus placing the hunters at the points of a triangle. The view of defendants with reference to plaintiff was unobstructed and they knew his location. Defendant Tice flushed a quail which rose in flight to a ten foot elevation and flew between plaintiff and defendants. Both defendants shot at the quail, shooting in plaintiff's direction. At that time defendants were 75 yards from plaintiff. One shot struck plaintiff in his eye and another in his upper lip. Finally it was found by the court that as the direct result of the shooting by defendants the shots struck plaintiff as above mentioned and that defendants were negligent in so shooting and plaintiff was not contributorily negligent.

[1] First, on the subject of negligence, defendant Simonson contends that the evidence is insufficient to sustain the finding on that score, but he does not point out wherein it is lacking. There is evidence that both defendants, at about the same time or one immediately after the other, shot at a quail and in so doing shot toward plaintiff who was uphill from them, and that they knew his location. That is sufficient from which the trial court could conclude that they acted with respect to plaintiff other than as persons of ordinary prudence. The issue was one of fact for the trial court. See, Rudd v. Byrnes, 156 Cal. 636, 105 P. 957, 26 L.R.A., N.S., 134, 20 Ann. Cas. 124.

Defendant Tice states in his opening brief, "we have decided not to argue the insufficiency of negligence on the part of defendant Tice." It is true he states in his answer to plaintiff's petition for a hearing in this court that he did not concede this point but he does not argue it. Nothing more need be said on the subject.

[2, 3] Defendant Simonson urges that plaintiff was guilty of contributory negligence and assumed the risk as a matter of law. He cites no authority for the proposition that by going on a hunting party the various hunters assume the risk of negligence on the part of their companions. Such a tenet is not reasonable. It is true that plaintiff suggested that they all "stay in line," presumably abreast, while hunting, and he went uphill at somewhat of a right angle to the hunting line, but he also cautioned that they use care, and defendants knew plaintiff's position. We hold, therefore, that the trial court was justified in finding that he did not assume the risk or act other than as a person of ordinary prudence under the circumstances. See, Anthony v. Hobbie, 25 Cal.2d 814, 818, 155 P. 2d 826; Rudd v. Byrnes, supra. None of the cases cited by Simonson are in point.

The problem presented in this case is whether the judgment against both defendants may stand. It is argued by defendants that they are not joint tort feasors, and thus jointly and severally liable, as they were not acting in concert, and that there is not sufficient evidence to show which defendant was guilty of the negligence which caused the injuries—the shooting by Tice or that by Simonson. Tice argues that there is evidence to show that the shot which struck plaintiff came from Simonson's gun because of admissions allegedly made by him to third persons and no evidence that they came from his gun. Further in connection with the latter contention, the court failed to find on plaintiff's allegation in his complaint that he did not know which one was at fault—did not find which defendant was guilty of the negligence which caused the injuries to plaintiff.

[4] Considering the last argument first, we believe it is clear that the court sufficiently found on the issue that defendants were jointly liable and that thus the negligence of both was the cause of the injury or to that legal effect. It found that both defendants were negligent and "That as a direct and proximate result of the shots fired by *defendants, and each of them,* a

birdshot pellet was caused to and did lodge in plaintiff's right eye and that another birdshot pellet was caused to and did lodge in plaintiff's upper lip." In so doing the court evidently did not give credence to the admissions of Simonson to third persons that he fired the shots, which it was justified in doing. It thus determined that the negligence of both defendants was the legal cause of the injury—or that both were responsible. Implicit in such finding is the assumption that the court was unable to ascertain whether the shots were from the gun of one defendant or the other or one shot from each of them. The one shot that entered plaintiff's eye was the major factor in assessing damages and that shot could not have come from the gun of both defendants. It was from one or the other only.

It has been held that where a group of persons are on a hunting party, or otherwise engaged in the use of firearms, and two of them are negligent in firing in the direction of a third person who is injured thereby, both of those so firing are liable for the injury suffered by the third person, although the negligence of only one of them could have caused the injury. Moore v. Foster, Miss., 180 So. 73; Oliver v. Miles, Miss., 110 So. 666, 50 A.L.R. 357; Reyher v. Mayne, 90 Colo. 856, 10 P.2d 1109; Benson v. Ross, 143 Mich. 452, 106 N.W. 1120, 114 Am.St.Rep. 675. The same rule has been applied in criminal cases (State v. Newberg, 129 Or. 564, 278 P. 568, 63 A.L.R. 1225), and both drivers have been held liable for the negligence of one where they engaged in a racing contest causing an injury to a third person. Saisa v. Lilja, 1 Cir., 76 F.2d 380. These cases speak of the action of defendants as being in concert as the ground of decision, yet it would seem they are straining that concept and the more reasonable basis appears in Oliver v. Miles, supra. There two persons were hunting together. Both shot at some partridges and in so doing shot across the highway injuring plaintiff who was travelling on it. The court stated they were acting in concert and thus both were liable. The court then stated [110 So. 668]: "We think that * * * each is liable for the resulting injury to the boy, although no one

can say definitely who actually shot him. *To hold otherwise would be to exonerate both from liability, although each was negligent, and the injury resulted from such negligence."* [Emphasis added.] 110 So. p. 668. It is said in the Restatement: "For harm resulting to a third person from the tortious conduct of another, a person is liable if he * * * (b) knows that the other's conduct constitutes a breach of duty and gives substantial assistance or encouragement to the other so to conduct himself, or (c) gives substantial assistance to the other in accomplishing a tortious result and his own conduct, separately considered, constitutes a breach of duty to the third person." (Rest., Torts, sec. 876(b) (c).) Under subsection (b) the example is given: "A and B are members of a hunting party. Each of them in the presence of the other shoots across a public road at an animal, this being negligent as to persons on the road. A hits the animal. B's bullet strikes C, a traveler on the road. A is liable to C." (Rest., Torts, Sec. 876(b), Com., Illus. 3.) An illustration given under subsection (c) is the same as above except the factor of both defendants shooting is missing and joint liability is not imposed. It is further said that: "If two forces are actively operating, one because of the actor's negligence, the other not because of any misconduct on his part, and each of itself is sufficient to bring about harm to another, the actor's negligence may be held by the jury to be a substantial factor in bringing it about." (Rest., Torts, sec. 432.) Dean Wigmore has this to say: "When two or more persons by their acts are possibly the sole cause of a harm, or when two or more acts of the same person are possibly the sole cause, and the plaintiff has introduced evidence that the one of the two persons, or the one of the same person's two acts, is culpable, then the defendant has the burden of proving that the other person, or his other act, was the sole cause of the harm. (b) * * * The real reason for the rule that each joint tortfeasor is responsible for the whole damage is the practical unfairness of denying the injured person redress simply because he cannot prove how much damage each did, when it is certain that between them they did all; let them be the ones to apportion it among themselves. Since, then, the difficulty of proof is the reason, the rule should apply whenever the harm has plural causes, and not merely when they acted in conscious concert. * * * * (Wigmore, Select Cases on the Law of Torts, sec. 153.) Similarly Professor Carpenter has said: "[Suppose] the case where A and B independently shoot at C and but one bullet touches C's body. In such case, such proof as is ordinarily required that either A or B shot C, of course fails. It is suggested that there should be a relaxation of the proof required of the plaintiff * * * where the injury occurs as the result of one where more than one independent force is operating, and it is impossible to determine that the force set in operation by defendant did not in fact constitute a cause of the damage, and where it may have caused the damage, but the plaintiff is unable to establish that it was a cause." (20 Cal.L.Rev. 406.)

[5] When we consider the relative position of the parties and the results that would flow if plaintiff was required to pin the injury on one of the defendants only, a requirement that the burden of proof on that subject be shifted to defendants becomes manifest. They are both wrongdoers—both negligent toward plaintiff. They brought about a situation where the negligence of one of them injured the plaintiff, hence it should rest with them each to absolve himself if he can. The injured party has been placed by defendants in the unfair position of pointing to which defendant caused the harm. If one can escape the other may also and plaintiff is remediless. Ordinarily defendants are in a far better position to offer evidence to determine which one caused the injury. This reasoning has recently found favor in this Court. In a quite analogous situation this Court held that a patient injured while unconscious on an operating table in a hospital could hold all or any of the persons who had any connection with the operation even though he could not select the particular acts by the particular person which led to his disability. Ybarra v. Spangard, 25 Cal. 2d 486, 154 P.2d 687, 162 A.L.R. 1258. There the Court was considering whether the patient could avail himself of res ipsa loquitur, rather than where the burden of proof lay, yet the effect of the decision is that plaintiff has made out a case when he has produced evidence which gives rise to an inference of negligence which was the proximate cause of the injury. It is up to defendants to explain the cause of the injury. It was there said: "If the doctrine is to continue to serve a useful purpose, we should not forget that 'the particular force and justice of the rule, regarded as a presumption throwing upon the party charged the duty of producing evidence, consists in the circumstance that the chief evidence of the true cause, whether culpable or innocent, is practically accessible to him but inaccessible to the injured person.'" 25 Cal. 2d at page 490, 154 P.2d at page 689, 162 A.L.R. 1258. Similarly in the instant case plaintiff is not able to establish which of defendants caused his injury.

The foregoing discussion disposes of the authorities cited by defendants such as Kraft v. Smith, 24 Cal.2d 124, 148 P.2d 23, and Hernandez v. Southern California Gas Co., 213 Cal. 384, 2 P.2d 360, stating the general rule that one defendant is not liable for the independent tort of the other defendant, or that ordinarily the plaintiff must show a causal connection between the negligence and the injury. There was an entire lack of such connection in the Hernandez case and there were not several negligent defendants, one of whom must have caused the injury.

Defendants rely upon Christensen v. Los Angeles Electrical Supply Co., 112 Cal.App. 629, 297 P. 614, holding that a defendant is not liable where he negligently knocked down with his car a pedestrian and a third person then ran over the prostrate person. That involves the question of intervening cause which we do not have here. Moreover it is out of harmony with the current rule on that subject and was properly questioned in Hill v. Peres, 136 Cal.App. 132, 28 P.2d 946 (hearing in this Court denied), and must be deemed disapproved. See, Mosley v. Arden Farms Co., 26 Cal.2d 213, 157 P.2d 372, 158 A.L.R. 872; Sawyer v. Southern California Gas Co., 206 Cal. 366, 274 P. 544; 6 Cal.Jur. Ten Yr.Supp., Automobiles, sec. 349; 19 Cal.Jur. 570-572.

Cases are cited for the proposition that where two or more tort feasors acting independently of each other cause an injury to plaintiff, they are not joint tort feasors and plaintiff must establish the portion of the damage caused by each, even though it is impossible to prove the portion of the injury caused by each. See, Slater v. Pacific American Oil Co., 212 Cal. 648, 300 P. 31; Miller v. Highland Ditch Co., 87 Cal. 430, 25 P. 550, 22 Am.St.Rep. 254; People v. Gold Run D. & M. Co., 66 Cal. 138, 4 P. 1152, 56 Am.Rep. 80; Wade v. Thorsen, 5 Cal.App.2d 706, 43 P.2d 592; California Orange Co. v. Riverside P. C. Co., 50 Cal. App. 522, 195 P. 694; City of Oakland v. Pacific Gas & E. Co., 47 Cal.App.2d 444, 118 P.2d 328. In view of the foregoing discussion it is apparent that defendants in cases like the present one may be treated as liable on the same basis as joint tort feasors, and hence the last cited cases are distinguishable inasmuch as they involve independent tort feasors.

[6] In addition to that, however, it should be pointed out that the same reasons of policy and justice shift the burden to each of defendants to absolve himself if he can—relieving the wronged person of the duty of apportioning the injury to a particular defendant, apply here where we are concerned with whether plaintiff is required to supply evidence for the apportionment of damages. If defendants are independent tort feasors and thus each liable for the damage caused by him alone, and, at least, where the matter of apportionment is incapable of proof, the innocent wronged party should not be deprived of his right to redress. The wrongdoers should be left to work out between themselves any apportionment. See, Colonial Ins. Co., v. Industrial Acc. Com., 29 Cal.2d 79, 172 P.2d 884. Some of the cited cases refer to the difficulty of apportioning the burden of damages between the independent tort feasors, and say that where factually a correct division cannot be made, the trier of fact may make it the best it can, which would be more or less a guess, stressing the factor that the wrongdoers are not in a position to complain of uncertainty. California Orange Co. v. Riverside P. C. Co., supra.

[7] It is urged that plaintiff now has changed the theory of his case in claiming a concert of action; that he did not plead or prove such concert. From what has been said it is clear that there has been no change in theory. The joint liability, as well as the lack of knowledge as to which defendant was liable, was pleaded and the proof developed the case under either theory. We have seen that for the reasons of policy discussed herein, the case is based upon the legal proposition that, under the circumstances here presented, each defendant is liable for the whole damage whether they are deemed to be acting in concert or independently.

The judgment is affirmed.

GIBSON, C. J., and SHENK, EDMONDS, TRAYNOR, SCHAUER, and SPENCE, JJ., concur.

Walter TROMBLEY, Petitioner, v. JUSTICE'S COURT OF TOWNSHIP 15, COUNTY OF CONTRA COSTA et al., Respondents.

S. F. 17549.

Supreme Court of California, In Bank.

May 3, 1948.

Proceeding for a writ of certiorari.

Judgment affirmed.

Francis T. Cornish, of Berkeley, for petitioner.

Fred N. Howser, Atty. Gen., Herbert E. Wenig, Deputy Atty. Gen., Francis W. Collins, Dist. Atty., of Martinez, and Douglas M. Quinlan, Deputy Dist. Atty., of Richmond, for respondents.

Samuel S. Berman, of San Francisco, Harold J. Fisher, of Los Angeles, and Leon E. Gold, of San Francisco, as amici curiæ on behalf of respondents.

KATKO v. BRINEY   Iowa   657
Cite as 183 N.W.2d 657

Marvin KATKO, Appellee,

v.

Edward BRINEY and Bertha L. Briney,
Appellants.

No. 54169.

Supreme Court of Iowa.

Feb. 9, 1971.

Action for damages resulting from injury suffered by trespassing plaintiff when he triggered a spring gun placed in uninhabited house by defendants. The Mahaska District Court, Harold Fleck, J., gave judgment for plaintiff for both actual and punitive damages, and defendants appealed. The Supreme Court, Moore, C. J., held that instructions properly stated that one may use reasonable force for protection of property but that such right is subject to qualification that one may not use such means of force as will take human life or inflict great bodily injury, that fact that trespasser may be acting in violation of law would not change the rule, and that only time when setting of a spring gun is justified would be if trespasser was committing a felony of violence or a felony punishable by death, or where trespasser was endangering human life by his act.

Affirmed.

Larson, J., dissented and filed opinion.

1. Appeal and Error ⬤⇒837(2)

In civil action arising out of injury to plaintiff caused by spring gun set in uninhabitated house it was not prerogative of Supreme Court to review disposition made of criminal charge against plaintiff arising out of the same incident.

2. Weapons ⬤⇒18(2)

Instructions properly stated, in civil action arising out of setting of spring gun in uninhabited house which injured plaintiff, that one may use reasonable force for protection of property but that such right is subject to qualification that one may not use such means of force as will take human life or inflict great bodily injury, that fact that trespasser may be acting in violation of law would not change the rule, and that only time when setting of a spring gun is justified would be if trespasser was committing a felony of violence or a felony punishable by death, or where trespasser was endangering human life by his act.

3. Appeal and Error ⬤⇒221

Supreme Court would express no opinion as to whether punitive damages were allowable in case involving action by plaintiff for damages arising out of injury inflicted by spring gun set in uninhabited house, under rule that reviewing court would not consider a contention not raised in trial court.

4. Damages ⬤⇒87(1), 91(1)

Punitive damages are not allowed as a matter of right; when malice is shown or when a defendant acts with wanton and reckless disregard of rights of others, punitive damages may be allowed as punishment to defendant and as a deterrent to others.

———◆———

Bruce Palmer and H. S. Life, Oskaloosa, for appellants.

Garold Heslinga, Oskaloosa, for appellee.

MOORE, Chief Justice.

The primary issue presented here is whether an owner may protect personal property in an unoccupied boarded-up farm house against trespassers and thieves by a spring gun capable of inflicting death or serious injury.

We are not here concerned with a man's right to protect his home and members of his family. Defendants' home was several miles from the scene of the incident to which we refer infra.

Plaintiff's action is for damages resulting from serious injury caused by a shot from a 20-gauge spring shotgun set by defendants in a bedroom of an old farm house which had been uninhabited for several years. Plaintiff and his companion, Marvin McDonough, had broken and entered the house to find and steal old bottles and dated fruit jars which they considered antiques.

At defendants' request plaintiff's action was tried to a jury consisting of residents of the community where defendants' property was located. The jury returned a verdict for plaintiff and against defendants for $20,000 actual and $10,000 punitive damages.

After careful consideration of defendants' motions for judgment notwithstanding the verdict and for new trial, the experienced and capable trial judge overruled them and entered judgment on the verdict. Thus we have this appeal by defendants.

I. In this action our review of the record as made by the parties in the lower court is for the correction of errors at law. We do not review actions at law de novo. Rule 334, Rules of Civil Procedure. Findings of fact by the jury are binding upon this court if supported by substantial evidence. Rule 344(f), par. 1, R.C.P.

II. Most of the facts are not disputed. In 1957 defendant Bertha L. Briney inherited her parents' farm land in Mahaska and Monroe Counties. Included was an 80-acre tract in southwest Mahaska County where her grandparents and parents had lived. No one occupied the house thereafter. Her husband, Edward, attempted to care for the land. He kept no farm machinery thereon. The outbuildings became dilapidated.

For about 10 years, 1957 to 1967, there occurred a series of trespassing and housebreaking events with loss of some household items, the breaking of windows and "messing up of the property in general". The latest occurred June 8, 1967, prior to the event on July 16, 1967 herein involved.

Defendants through the years boarded up the windows and doors in an attempt to stop the intrusions. They had posted "no trespass" signs on the land several years before 1967. The nearest one was 35 feet from the house. On June 11, 1967 defendants set "a shotgun trap" in the north bedroom. After Mr. Briney cleaned and oiled his 20-gauge shotgun, the power of which he was well aware, defendants took it to the old house where they secured it to an iron bed with the barrel pointed at the bedroom door. It was rigged with wire from the doorknob to the gun's trigger so it would fire when the door was opened. Briney first pointed the gun so an intruder would be hit in the stomach but at Mrs Briney's suggestion it was lowered to hit the legs. He admitted he did so "because I was mad and tired of being tormented" but "he did not intend to injure anyone". He gave no explanation of why he used a loaded shell and set it to hit a person already in the house. Tin was nailed over the bedroom window. The spring gun could not be seen from the outside. No warning of its presence was posted.

Plaintiff lived with his wife and worked regularly as a gasoline station attendant in Eddyville, seven miles from the old house. He had observed it for several years while hunting in the area and considered it as being abandoned. He knew it had long been uninhabited. In 1967 the area around the house was covered with high weeds. Prior to July 16, 1967 plaintiff and McDonough had been to the premises and found several old bottles and fruit jars which they took and added to their collection of antiques. On the latter date about 9:30 p.m. they made a second trip to the Briney property. They entered the old house by removing a board from a porch window which was without glass. While McDonough was looking around the kitchen area plaintiff went to another part of the house. As he started to open the north bedroom door the shotgun went off striking him in the right leg above the ankle bone. Much of his leg, including part of the tibia, was blown away. Only by Mc-

KATKO v. BRINEY   Iowa **659**
Cite as 183 N.W.2d 657

Donough's assistance was plaintiff able to get out of the house and after crawling some distance was put in his vehicle and rushed to a doctor and then to a hospital. He remained in the hospital 40 days.

Plaintiff's doctor testified he seriously considered amputation but eventually the healing process was successful. Some weeks after his release from the hospital plaintiff returned to work on crutches. He was required to keep the injured leg in a cast for approximately a year and wear a special brace for another year. He continued to suffer pain during this period.

There was undenied medical testimony plaintiff had a permanent deformity, a loss of tissue, and a shortening of the leg.

The record discloses plaintiff to trial time had incurred $710 medical expense, $2056.85 for hospital service, $61.80 for orthopedic service and $750 as loss of earnings. In addition thereto the trial court submitted to the jury the question of damages for pain and suffering and for future disability.

[1] III. Plaintiff testified he knew he had no right to break and enter the house with intent to steal bottles and fruit jars therefrom. He further testified he had entered a plea of guilty to larceny in the nighttime of property of less than $20 value from a private building. He stated he had been fined $50 and costs and paroled during good behavior from a 60-day jail sentence. Other than minor traffic charges this was plaintiff's first brush with the law. On this civil case appeal it is not our prerogative to review the disposition made of the criminal charge against him.

IV. The main thrust of defendants' defense in the trial court and on this appeal is that "the law permits use of a spring gun in a dwelling or warehouse for the purpose of preventing the unlawful entry of a burglar or thief". They repeated this contention in their exceptions to the trial court's instructions 2, 5 and 6. They took

no exception to the trial court's statement of the issues or to other instructions.

In the statement of issues the trial court stated plaintiff and his companion committed a felony when they broke and entered defendants' house. In instruction 2 the court referred to the early case history of the use of spring guns and stated under the law their use was prohibited except to prevent the commission of felonies of violence and where human life is in danger. The instruction included a statement breaking and entering is not a felony of violence.

Instruction 5 stated: "You are hereby instructed that one may use reasonable force in the protection of his property, but such right is subject to the qualification that one may not use such means of force as will take human life or inflict great bodily injury. Such is the rule even though the injured party is a trespasser and is in violation of the law himself."

Instruction 6 stated: "An owner of premises is prohibited from willfully or intentionally injuring a trespasser by means of force that either takes life or inflicts great bodily injury; and therefore a person owning a premise is prohibited from setting out 'spring guns' and like dangerous devices which will likely take life or inflict great bodily injury, for the purpose of harming trespassers. The fact that the trespasser may be acting in violation of the law does not change the rule. The only time when such conduct of setting a 'spring gun' or a like dangerous device is justified would be when the trespasser was committing a felony of violence or a felony punishable by death, or where the trespasser was endangering human life by his act."

Instruction 7, to which defendants made no objection or exception, stated: "To entitle the plaintiff to recover for compensatory damages, the burden of proof is upon him to establish by a preponderance of the evidence each and all of the following propositions:

"1. That defendants erected a shotgun trap in a vacant house on land owned by defendant, Bertha L. Briney, on or about June 11, 1967, which fact was known only by them, to protect household goods from trespassers and thieves.

"2. That the force used by defendants was in excess of that force reasonably necessary and which persons are entitled to use in the protection of their property.

"3. That plaintiff was injured and damaged and the amount thereof.

"4. That plaintiff's injuries and damages resulted directly from the discharge of the shotgun trap which was set and used by defendants."

The overwhelming weight of authority, both textbook and case law, supports the trial court's statement of the applicable principles of law.

Prosser on Torts, Third Edition, pages 116–118, states:

"* * * the law has always placed a higher value upon human safety than upon mere rights in property, it is the accepted rule that there is no privilege to use any force calculated to cause death or serious bodily injury to repel the threat to land or chattels, unless there is also such a threat to the defendant's personal safety as to justify a self-defense. * * * spring guns and other man-killing devices are not justifiable against a mere trespasser, or even a petty thief. They are privileged only against those upon whom the landowner, if he were present in person would be free to inflict injury of the same kind."

Restatement of Torts, section 85, page 180, states: "The value of human life and limb, not only to the individual concerned but also to society, so outweighs the interest of a possessor of land in excluding from it those whom he is not willing to admit thereto that a possessor of land has, as is stated in § 79, no privilege to use force intended or likely to cause death or serious harm against another whom the possessor sees about to enter his premises or meddle

with his chattel, unless the intrusion threatens death or serious bodily harm to the occupiers or users of the premises. * * * A possessor of land cannot do indirectly and by a mechanical device that which, were he present, he could not do immediately and in person. Therefore, he cannot gain a privilege to install, for the purpose of protecting his land from intrusions harmless to the lives and limbs of the occupiers or users of it, a mechanical device whose only purpose is to inflict death or serious harm upon such as may intrude, by giving notice of his intention to inflict, by mechanical means and indirectly, harm which he could not, even after request, inflict directly were he present."

In Volume 2, Harper and James, The Law of Torts, section 27.3, pages 1440, 1441, this is found: "The possessor of land may not arrange his premises intentionally so as to cause death or serious bodily harm to a trespasser. The possessor may of course take some steps to repel a trespass. If he is present he may use force to do so, but only that amount which is reasonably necessary to effect the repulse. Moreover if the trespass threatens harm to property only—even a theft of property—the possessor would not be privileged to use deadly force, he may not arrange his premises so that such force will be inflicted by mechanical means. If he does, he will be liable even to a thief who is injured by such device."

Similar statements are found in 38 Am. Jur., Negligence, section 114, pages 776, 777, and 65 C.J.S. Negligence § 62(23), pages 678, 679; Anno. 44 A.L.R.2d 383, entitled "Trap to protect property".

In Hooker v. Miller, 37 Iowa 613, we held defendant vineyard owner liable for damages resulting from a spring gun shot although plaintiff was a trespasser and there to steal grapes. At pages 614, 615, this statement is made: "This court has held that a mere trespass against property other than a dwelling is not a sufficient justification to authorize the use of a dead-

KATKO v. BRINEY   Iowa   661
Cite as 183 N.W.2d 657

ly weapon by the owner in its defense; and that if death results in such a case it will be murder, though the killing be actually necessary to prevent the trespass. The State v. Vance, 17 Iowa 138." At page 617 this court said: "[T]respassers and other inconsiderable violators of the law are not to be visited by barbarous punishments or prevented by inhuman inflictions of bodily injuries."

The facts in Allison v. Fiscus, 156 Ohio 120, 100 N.E.2d 237, 44 A.L.R.2d 369, decided in 1951, are very similar to the case at bar. There plaintiff's right to damages was recognized for injuries received when he feloniously broke a door latch and started to enter defendant's warehouse with intent to steal. As he entered a trap of two sticks of dynamite buried under the doorway by defendant owner was set off and plaintiff seriously injured. The court held the question whether a particular trap was justified as a use of reasonable and necessary force against a trespasser engaged in the commission of a felony should have been submitted to the jury. The Ohio Supreme Court recognized plaintiff's right to recover punitive or exemplary damages in addition to compensatory damages.

In Starkey v. Dameron, 96 Colo. 459, 45 P.2d 172, plaintiff was allowed to recover compensatory and punitive damages for injuries received from a spring gun which defendant filling station operator had concealed in an automatic gasoline pump as protection against thieves.

In Wilder v. Gardner, 39 Ga.App. 608, 147 S.E. 911, judgment for plaintiff for injuries received from a spring gun which defendant had set, the court said: "A person in control of premises may be responsible even to a trespasser for injuries caused by pitfalls, mantraps, or other like contrivances so dangerous in character as to imply a disregard of consequences or a willingness to inflict injury."

In Phelps v. Hamlett, Tex.Civ.App., 207 S.W. 425, defendant rigged a bomb inside his outdoor theater so that if anyone came through the door the bomb would explode. The court reversed plaintiff's recovery because of an incorrect instruction but at page 426 said: "While the law authorizes an owner to protect his property by such reasonable means as he may find to be necessary, yet considerations of humanity preclude him from setting out, even on his own property, traps and devices dangerous to the life and limb of those whose appearance and presence may be reasonably anticipated, even though they may be trespassers."

In United Zinc & Chemical Co. v. Britt, 258 U.S. 268, 275, 42 S.Ct. 299, 66 L.Ed. 615, 617, the court states: "The liability for spring guns and mantraps arises from the fact that the defendant has * * * expected the trespasser and prepared an injury that is no more justified than if he had held the gun and fired it."

In addition to civil liability many jurisdictions hold a land owner criminally liable for serious injuries or homicide caused by spring guns or other set devices. See State v. Childers, 133 Ohio 508, 14 N.E.2d 767 (melon thief shot by spring gun); Pierce v. Commonwealth, 135 Va. 635, 115 S.E. 686 (policeman killed by spring gun when he opened unlocked front door of defendant's shoe repair shop); State v. Marfaudille, 48 Wash. 117, 92 P. 939 (murder conviction for death from spring gun set in a trunk); State v. Beckham, 306 Mo. 566, 267 S.W. 817 (boy killed by spring gun attached to window of defendant's chili stand); State v. Green, 118 S.C. 279, 110 S.E. 145, 19 A.L.R. 1431 (intruder shot by spring gun when he broke and entered vacant house. Manslaughter conviction of owner-affirmed); State v. Barr, 11 Wash. 481, 39 P. 1080 (murder conviction affirmed for death of an intruder into a boarded up cabin in which owner had set a spring gun).

In Wisconsin, Oregon and England the use of spring guns and similar devices is specifically made unlawful by statute. 44 A.L.R., section 3, pages 386, 388.

[2] The legal principles stated by the trial court in instructions 2, 5 and 6 are well established and supported by the authorities cited and quoted supra. There is no merit in defendants' objections and exceptions thereto. Defendants' various motions based on the same reasons stated in exceptions to instructions were properly overruled.

V. Plaintiff's claim and the jury's allowance of punitive damages, under the trial court's instructions relating thereto, were not at any time or in any manner challenged by defendants in the trial court as not allowable. We therefore are not presented with the problem of whether the $10,000 award should be allowed to stand.

[3] We express no opinion as to whether punitive damages are allowable in this type of case. If defendants' attorneys wanted that issue decided it was their duty to raise it in the trial court.

The rule is well established that we will not consider a contention not raised in the trial court. In other words we are a court of review and will not consider a contention raised for the first time in this court. Ke-Wash Company v. Stauffer Chemical Company, Iowa, 177 N.W.2d 5, 9; In re Adoption of Moriarty, 260 Iowa 1279, 1288, 152 N.W.2d 218, 223; Verschoor v. Miller, 259 Iowa 170, 176, 143 N.W.2d 385, 389; Mundy v. Olds, 254 Iowa 1095, 1100, 120 N.W.2d 469, 472; Bryan v. Iowa State Highway Commission, 251 Iowa 1093, 1096, 104 N.W.2d 562, 563, and citations.

In our most recent reference to the rule we say in Cole v. City of Osceola, Iowa, 179 N.W.2d 524, 527: "Of course, questions not presented to and not passed upon by the trial court cannot be raised or reviewed on appeal."

[4] Under our law punitive damages are not allowed as a matter of right. Sebastian v. Wood, 246 Iowa 94, 100, 101, 66 N.W.2d 841, 844. When malice is shown or when a defendant acted with wanton and reckless disregard of the rights of others, punitive damages may be allowed as punishment to the defendant and as a deterrent to others. Although not meant to compensate a plaintiff, the result is to increase his recovery. He is the fortuitous beneficiary of such an award simply because there is no one else to receive it.

The jury's findings of fact including a finding defendants acted with malice and with wanton and reckless disregard, as required for an allowance of punitive or exemplary damages, are supported by substantial evidence. We are bound thereby.

This opinion is not to be taken or construed as authority that the allowance of punitive damages is or is not proper under circumstances such as exist here. We hold only that question of law not having been properly raised cannot in this case be resolved.

Study and careful consideration of defendants' contentions on appeal reveal no reversible error.

Affirmed.

All Justices concur except LARSON, J., who dissents.

LARSON, Justice.

I respectfully dissent, first, because the majority wrongfully assumes that by installing a spring gun in the bedroom of their unoccupied house the defendants intended to shoot any intruder who attempted to enter the room. Under the record presented here, that was a fact question. Unless it is held that these property owners are liable for any injury to a intruder from such a device regardless of the intent with which it is installed, liability under these pleadings must rest upon two definite issues of fact, i. e., did the defendants intend to shoot the invader, and if so, did they employ unnecessary and unreasonable force against him?

It is my feeling that the majority oversimplifies the impact of this case on the law, not only in this but other jurisdictions,

KATKO v. BRINEY   Iowa   663
Cite as 183 N.W.2d 657

and that it has not thought through all the ramifications of this holding.

There being no statutory provisions governing the right of an owner to defend his property by the use of a spring gun or other like device, or of a criminal invader to recover punitive damages when injured by such an instrumentality while breaking into the building of another, our interest and attention are directed to what should be the court determination of public policy in these matters. On both issues we are faced with a case of first impression. We should accept the task and clearly establish the law in this jurisdiction hereafter. I would hold there is no absolute liability for injury to a criminal intruder by setting up such a device on his property, and unless done with an intent to kill or seriously injure the intruder, I would absolve the owner from liability other than for negligence. I would also hold the court had no jurisdiction to allow punitive damages when the intruder was engaged in a serious criminal offense such as breaking and entering with intent to steal.

It appears to me that the learned trial court was and the majority is now confused as to the basis of liability under the circumstances revealed. Certainly, the trial court's instructions did nothing to clarify the law in this jurisdiction for the jury. Timely objections to Instructions Nos. 2, 5 and 6 were made by the defendants, and thereafter the court should have been aware of the questions of liability left unresolved, i. e., whether in this jurisdiction we by judicial declaration bar the use in an unoccupied building of spring guns or other devices capable of inflicting serious injury or death on an intruder regardless of the intent with which they are installed, or whether such an intent is a vital element which must be proven in order to establish liability for an injury inflicted upon a criminal invader.

Although the court told the jury the plaintiff had the burden to prove "That the force used by defendants was in excess of that force reasonably necessary and which persons are entitled to use in the protection of their property", it utterly failed to tell the jury it could find the installation was not made with the intent or purpose of striking or injuring the plaintiff. There was considerable evidence to that effect. As I shall point out, both defendants stated the installation was made for the purpose of scaring or frightening away any intruder, not to seriously injure him. It may be that the evidence would support a finding of an intent to injure the intruder, but obviously that important issue was never adequately or clearly submitted to the jury.

Unless, then, we hold for the first time that liability for death or injury in such cases is absolute, the matter should be remanded for a jury determination of defendant's intent in installing the device under instructions usually given to a jury on the issue of intent.

I personally have no objection to this court's determination of the public policy of this state in such a case to ban the use of such devices in *all* instances where there is no intruder threat to human life or safety, but I do say we have never done so except in the case of a mere trespasser in a vineyard. Hooker v. Miller, 37 Iowa 613 (1873). To that extent, then, this is a case of first impression, and in any opinion we should make the law in this jurisdiction crystal clear. Although the legislature could pronounce this policy, as it has in some states, since we have entered this area of the law by the Hooker decision, I believe it proper for us to declare the applicable law in cases such as this for the guidance of the bench and bar hereafter. The majority opinion utterly fails in this regard. It fails to recognize the problem where such a device is installed in a building housing valuable property to ward off criminal intruders, and to clearly place the burden necessary to establish liability.

My second reason for this dissent is the allowance of an award of punitive damages herein. Plaintiff claimed a remedy which our law does not allow, and the trial court should not have submitted that issue to the jury. Like the law establishing liability for installing a spring gun or other similar device, the law recognizing and allowing punitive or exemplary damages is court-made law, not statutory law. As to the property owner's liability for exemplary damages where one is engaged in a serious criminal offense at the time of his injury, we also have a case of first impression. We have never extended this right to such a claimant, and I would not do so now. Unless we do, or there is a compelling reason or authority for such a right, which I fail to find, the trial court erred in submitting that issue to the jury. Like the case where a judgment is entered without jurisdiction of the subject matter, I would hold the award of $10,000 to plaintiff is void.

I do not wish to criticize, but believe the factual statement of the majority fails to give a true perspective of the relative facts and issues to be considered.

Plaintiff's petition at law asking damages alleged willful and malicious setting of a trap or device for the purpose of killing or inflicting great bodily harm upon any trespasser on defendants' property. We are, therefore, factually concerned with how such force may be properly applied by the property owner and whether his intent is relevant to liability. Negligent installation of a dangerous device to frighten and ward off an intruder or thief is not alleged, so unless the proof submitted was sufficient to establish a willful setting of the trap with a purpose of killing or seriously injuring the intruder, no recovery could be had. If the evidence submitted was such that a jury could find defendants had willfully set the spring gun with a purpose to seriously injure the plaintiff intruder, unless they were privileged under the law to set the gun under these circumstances, liability for the injury would follow.

From the record we learn that plaintiff and a companion made a second trip to a furnished but uninhabited house on defend-ants' farmland in Mahaska County on the night of July 16, 1967. They tore a plank from a porch window, entered the house with an intent to steal articles therein, and in search of desired articles plaintiff came to a closed bedroom door where he removed a chair braced under the door knob and pulled the door toward him. This action triggered a single shot 20-gauge shotgun which defendants had wired to the bottom of a bed. The blast went through the door and struck plaintiff two or three inches above the right ankle.

The Mahaska County Grand Jury issued a true bill charging plaintiff with breaking and entering in the nighttime, but the county attorney accepted a plea of guilty to the lesser offense of larceny in the nighttime of property of a value of less than $20 and did not press the greater charge.

At the trial of this case Mr. Briney, one of the defendants, testified that the house where plaintiff was injured had been the home of Mrs. Briney's parents. He said the furniture and other possessions left there were of considerable value and they had tried to preserve them and enjoy them for frequent visits by Mrs. Briney. It appeared this unoccupied house had been broken into repeatedly during the past ten years and, as a result, Mr. Briney said "things were pretty well torn up, a lot of things taken." To prevent these intrusions the Brineys nailed the doors and some windows shut and boarded up others. Prior to this time Mr. Briney testified he had locked the doors, posted seven no trespassing signs on the premises, and complained to the sheriffs of two counties on numerous occasions. Mr. Briney further testified that when all these efforts were futile and the vandalism continued, he placed a 20-guage shotgun in a bedroom and wired it so that it would shoot downward and toward the door if anyone opened it. He said he first aimed it straight at the door but later, at his wife's suggestion, reconsidered the aim and pointed the gun down in a way he thought would only scare

KATKO v. BRINEY

Cite as 183 N.W.2d 657

Iowa   665

someone if it were discharged. On cross-examination he admitted that he did not want anyone to know it was there in order to preserve the element of surprise.

Plaintiff testified he knew the house was unoccupied and admitted breaking into it in the nighttime without lawful reason or excuse. He claimed he and his companion were seeking old bottles and dated fruit jars. He also admitted breaking in on one prior occasion and stated the reason for the return visit was that "we decided we would go out to this place again and see if there was something we missed while we was out there the first time." An old organ fascinated plaintiff. Arriving this second time, they found that the window by which they had entered before was now a "solid mass of boards" and walked around the house until they found the porch window which offered less resistance. Plaintiff said they crawled through this window. While searching the house he came to the bedroom door and pulled it open, thus triggering the gun that delivered a charge which struck him in the leg.

Plaintiff's doctor testified that he treated the shotgun wound on the night it was sustained and for some period thereafter. The healing process was successful and plaintiff was released after 40 days in the hospital. There was medical testimony that plaintiff had a permanent deformity, a loss of tissue, and a shortening of the leg.

That plaintiff suffered a grievous wound is not denied, and that it constituted a serious bodily injury cannot be contradicted.

As previously indicated, this appeal presents two vital questions which are as novel as they are difficult. They are, (1) is the owner of a building in which are kept household furniture, appliances, and valuables, but not occupied by a person or persons, liable in damages to an intruder who in the nighttime broke into and entered the building with the intent to steal and was shot and seriously injured by a spring gun allegedly set by the owner to frighten in-

truders from his property, and (2) if he is liable for compensatory damages, is this a proper case for the allowance of exemplary or punitive damages?

The trial court overruled all objections to the instructions and denied defendants' motion for a new trial. Thus, the first question to be resolved is the status of the law in this jurisdiction as to the means of force a property owner is privileged to use to repel (1) a mere trespasser, (2) a criminal invader, thief or burglar, where he presents no threat to human life or safety, and (3) an intruder or criminal breaking and entering a dwelling which poses a threat to human life and safety. Overlooked by the majority is the vital problem relating to the relevancy and importance of the owner's intent in placing the device.

I have been unable to find a case exactly like the case at bar, although there have been many cases which consider liability to a mere trespasser for injuries incurred by a spring gun or other dangerous instruments set to protect against intrusion and theft. True, some of these cases seem to turn on the negligence of the party setting the trap and an absence of adequate warning thereof, but most of them involve an alleged intentional tort. It is also true some hold as a matter of public policy there is liability for any injury following the setting of a device which is intended to kill or inflict great bodily injury on one coming on the owner's property without permission, unless the invader poses a threat to human life, and this is so even though there is no statutory prohibition against the setting of spring guns in the jurisdiction.

Since our decision in Hooker v. Miller, supra, we have recognized in this state the doctrine that the owner of a premise is liable in damages to a mere trespasser coming upon his property for any injury occasioned by the unsafe condition of the property which the owner has intentionally permitted to exist, such as installed spring guns, unless adequate warning is given thereof. In

Hooker, which involved stealing grapes from a vineyard, we held a property owner had no right to resist such a trespass by means which may kill or inflict great bodily injury to the trespasser. But it does appear therein that we recognized some distinction between a mere trespass against property and a trespass involving a serious crime or involving a dwelling. Except when the trespass involves a serious crime, a crime posing a threat to human life, it may be argued that the law in this jurisdiction should limit the right of one to protect his property, that he does not have a privilege to resist a mere trespass by using a spring gun or other device which poses a threat to life.

However, left unsettled by this and other court pronouncements is the means which may be used to repel, prevent, or apprehend a trespasser engaged in a more serious criminal offense. True, there is a line of cases which seem to apply the same rule to all criminal trespasses except those involving arson, rape, assault, or other acts of violence against persons residing on the property invaded. State v. Vance, 17 Iowa 138 (1864); State v. Plumlee, 177 La. 687, 149 So. 425 (1933); Pierce v. Commonwealth, 135 Va. 635, 115 S.E. 686 (Virginia, 1923); Simpson v. State, 59 Ala. 1, 31 Am. Rep. 1 (1877); State v. Barr, 11 Wash. 481, 39 P. 1080 (1895); Starkey v. Dameron, 96 Colo. 459, 21 P.2d 1112 (1933); State v. Beckham, 306 Mo. 566, 267 S.W. 817 (1924); Bird v. Holbrook, 4 Bingham's Reports 628 (England, 1828). Also see annotation, 44 A.L.R.2d 391, § 5, and citations. There are others which at least infer that any serious law violation by the trespasser might permit the reasonable use of dangerous instrumentalities to repel the intruder and prevent loss or damage to one's valuable property. Scheuermann v. Scharfenberg, 163 Ala. 337, 50 So. 335; Marquis v. Benfer, Tex.Civ.App., 298 S.W.2d 601 (Texas 1956); Grant v. Hass, 31 Tex.Civ. App. 688, 75 S.W. 342 (1903); Gray v. Combs, 7 J.J. Marshall 478 (Ky., 1832), 23

Am.Dec. 431; Ilott v. Wilkes, 3 B. & A. 304 (1820 K.B.).

Also see the following articles on this subject: 68 Yale Law Journal 633, Duties to Trespassers: A Comparative Survey and Revaluation; 35 Yale Law Journal 525, The Privilege to Protect Property by Dangerous Barriers and Mechanical Devices; annotation, 44 A.L.R.2d 383, Use of Set Gun, Trap, or Similar Device on Defendant's Own Property.

Most of these discussions center around what should be public policy regarding a property owner's right to use a dangerous weapon or instrumentality to protect his premises from intruders or trespassers, and his duty to protect the trespasser from serious injury while upon his premises.

Some states, including Wisconsin, have statutes which announce the jurisdiction's public policy. Often they prohibit the use of spring guns or such devices to protect real and personal property, and of course in those instances a property owner, regardless of his intent or purpose, has no right to make use of them and is liable to anyone injured thereby. Since there has been no such statutory prohibition or direct judicial pronouncement to that effect prior to this time in this state, it could not be said as a matter of law that the mere placing of a spring gun in a building on one's premises is unlawful. Much depends upon its placement and purpose. Whether an owner exceeds his privilege to reasonably defend his property by such an installation, and whether liability is incurred in a given case, should therefore depend upon the circumstances revealed, the intent of the property owner, and his care in setting the device. In any event, I question whether it should be determined solely by the results of his act or its effect upon the intruder.

It appears there are cases and some authority which would relieve one setting a spring gun on his premises of any liability if adequate warning had been given an intruder and he ignores the warning. In all of these cases there is a question as to

KATKO v. BRINEY
Cite as 183 N.W.2d 657   **Iowa**   **667**

the *intent* of the property owner in setting the device. Intent, of course, may be determined from both direct and indirect evidence, and it is true the physical facts may be and often are sufficient to present a jury issue. I think they were here, but no clear instruction was given in this regard.

If, after proper instructions, the finder of fact determines that the gun was set with an intent and purpose to kill or inflict great bodily injury on an intruder, then and only then may it be said liability is established unless the property so protected is shown to be an occupied dwelling house. Of course, under this concept, if the finder of fact determines the gun set in an unoccupied house was intended to do no more than to frighten the intruder or sting him a bit, no liability would be incurred under such pleadings as are now presented. If such a concept of the law were adopted in Iowa, we would have here a question for the fact-finder or jury as to whether the gun was willfully and intentionally set so as to seriously injure the thief or merely scare him away.

I feel the better rule is that an owner of buildings housing valuable property may employ the use of spring guns or other devices intended to repel but not seriously injure an intruder who enters his secured premises with or without a criminal intent, but I do not advocate its general use, for there may also be liability for negligent installation of such a device. What I mean to say is that under such circumstances as we have here the issue as to whether the set was with an intent to seriously injure or kill an intruder is a question of fact that should be left to the jury under proper instructions, and that the mere setting of such a device with a resultant serious injury should not as a matter of law establish liability.

In the case of a mere trespass able authorities have reasoned that absolute liability may rightfully be fixed on the landowner for injuries to the trespasser because very little damage could be inflicted upon the property owner and the danger is great that a child or other innocent trespasser might be seriously injured by the device. In such matters they say no privilege to set up the device should be recognized by the courts regardless of the owner's intent. I agree.

On the other hand, where the intruder may pose a danger to the inhabitants of a dwelling, the privilege of using such a device to repel has been recognized by most authorities, and the mere setting thereof in the dwelling has not been held to create liability for an injury as a matter of law. In such cases intent and the reasonableness of the force would seem relevant to liability.

Although I am aware of the often-repeated statement that personal rights are more important than property rights, where the owner has stored his valuables representing his life's accumulations, his livelihood business, his tools and implements, and his treasured antiques as appears in the case at bar, and where the evidence is sufficient to sustain a finding that the installation was intended only as a warning to ward off thieves and criminals, I can see no compelling reason why the use of such a device alone would create liability as a matter of law.

For cases considering the devices a property owner is or is not privileged to use to repel a mere trespasser, see Hooker v. Miller, supra, 37 Iowa 613 (trap gun set in orchard to repel); State v. Vance, supra, 17 Iowa 138 (1864); Phelps v. Hamlett, Tex.Civ.App., 207 S.W. 425 (1918) (bomb set in open air theater); State v. Plumlee, supra, 177 La. 687, 149 So. 425 (1933) (trap gun set in open barn); Starkey v. Dameron, supra, 96 Colo. 459, 21 P.2d 1112 (1933) (spring gun in outdoor automatic gas pump); State v. Childers, 133 Ohio St. 508, 14 N.E.2d 767 (1938) (trap gun in melon patch); Weis v. Allen, 147 Or. 670, 35 P.2d 478 (1934) (trap gun in junkyard); Johnson v. Patterson, 14 Conn. 1 (1840) (straying poultry poisoned); Bird v. Holbrook, supra, 4 Bingham's Reports 628 (England, 1828) (spring gun in garden enclosed by wall of undisclosed height).

For cases apparently holding dangerous devices may be used to ward off and prevent a trespasser from breaking and entering into an inhabited dwelling, see State v. Vance, supra; Grant v. Hass, supra; Scheuermann v. Scharfenberg, supra; Simpson v. State, supra; United States v. Gilliam, 1 Hayw. & H. 109, 25 Fed.Cas. 1319, p. 1320, No. 15,205 a (D.C. 1882); State v. Childers, supra; Gramlich v. Wurst, 86 Pa. 74, 80 (1878).

Also, for cases considering the devices a property owner is privileged to use to repel an invader where there is no threat to human life or safety, see Allison v. Fiscus, 156 Ohio St. 120, 100 N.E.2d 237, 44 A.L.R.2d 369; State v. Barr, 11 Wash. 481, 39 P. 1080 (1895); State v. Childers, supra; Weis v. Allen, supra; Pierce v. Commonwealth, supra; Johnson v. Patterson, supra; Marquis v. Benfer, supra.

In Allison v. Fiscus, supra, at page 241 of 100 N.E.2d, it is said: "Assuredly, * * * the court had no right to hold as a matter of law that defendant was liable to plaintiff, as the *defendant's good faith* in using the force which he did to protect his building and the good faith of his belief as to the nature of the force he was using were questions for the jury to determine under proper instructions." (Emphasis supplied.)

In State v. Barr, supra, at page 1081 of 39 P., the court said: "* * * whether or not what was done in a particular case was justified under the law must be a question of fact, or mixed law and fact, and not a pure question of law."

In State v. Childers, supra, it is said at page 768 of 14 N.E.2d: "Of course the act in question must be done maliciously * * * and *that fact must be proved and found by the jury to exist.*" (Emphasis supplied.)

Also see State v. Metcalfe, 203 Iowa 155, 212 N.W. 382, where this court discussed the force that a property owner may use to oppose an unlawful effort to carry away his goods, and held the essential issue in such matters which must be explained to the jury is not the nature of the weapon employed but whether the defendant employed only that degree of force to accomplish such purpose which a reasonable person would deem reasonably necessary under the circumstances as they appeared in good faith to the defendant.

Like the Ohio Supreme Court in Allison v. Fiscus, supra, I believe that the basis of liability, if any, in such a case should be either the intentional, reckless, or grossly negligent conduct of the owner in setting the device.

If this is not a desirable expression of policy in this jurisdiction, I suggest the body selected and best fitted to establish a different public policy would be the State Legislature.

The next question presented is, which view of the law set out above did the trial court take, the view that the mere setting of a spring gun or like device in defendants' building created liability for the resulting injury, or the view that there must be a setting of the device with an intent to shoot, kill, or seriously injure one engaged in breaking and entering this house? Appellants argue this was not made clear in the court's instructions to the jury and, being material, is error. I agree.

They contend Instructions Nos. 2, 5 and 6, to which proper and timely exceptions were taken, are improper, that they were so inadequate and confusing as to constitute reversible error and required the trial court to grant their motion for a new trial.

Instruction No. 5 provides:

"You are hereby instructed that one may use reasonable force in the protection of his property, but such right is subject to the qualification that one may not *use such means of force* as will take human life or inflict great bodily injury. Such is the rule even though the injured party is a trespasser and is in violation of the law himself." (Emphasis supplied).

Instruction No. 6 provides:

"An owner of premises is prohibited from willfully or intentionally injuring a trespasser by means of force that either takes life or inflicts great bodily injury; and therefore a person owning a premise is prohibited from setting out 'spring guns' and like dangerous devices which will likely take life or inflict great bodily injury, *for the purpose of harming trespassers.* The fact that the trespasser may be acting in violation of the law does not change the rule. The only time when such conduct of setting a 'spring gun' or a like dangerous device is justified would be when the trespasser was committing a felony of violence or a felony punishable by death, or where the trespasser was endangering human life by his act." (Emphasis supplied.)

Specific objections were made to Instruction No. 2, inter alia, to the statement that is this jurisdiction the use of force which may take life or inflict serious bodily injury might be used was restricted to occupied dwellings or where specific statutes permitted its use; to the reference to an Iowa case wherein the subject related to a *simple trespass* in a vineyard where no breaking and entry of a building was involved, without pointing out the difference as to permissible force permitted to repel one entering the owner's buildings with intent to ravish and steal valuable personal property; and to the error resulting when the court wrongfully directed the jury to find defendants' acts were illegal by stating "that in so doing he violated the law and became liable for injuries sustained by the plaintiff."

In other words, defendants contended that this instruction failed to tell the jury the extent of defendant's rights to defend against burglary in buildings other than their dwelling, inferring they have no

right to employ a device which is dangerous to life and limb, regardless of its intended purpose only to ward off or scare the intruder.

Defendants also specifically objected to Instruction No. 5 because it also limited the right or privilege of one to use dangerous devices in any way to protect his property, and made it applicable to cases where the invader was in violation of the law, without classifying his offense.

Instruction No. 6 was specifically objected to as not being a proper statement of the law, as being inadequate, confusing, and misleading to the jury in regard to the vital issues in this case, because it would not be possible for a jury to understand the court when it told the jurors an owner of premises is prohibited from willfully or intentionally injuring a trespasser by means of force that either takes life or inflicts great bodily injury, and then told them a person owning premises is prohibited from setting out spring guns and like dangerous devices which will "likely" take life or inflict great bodily injury, *for the purpose of harming trespassers.*

Appellants argue from these instructions the jury could conclude it must find any setting of a spring gun or such other device to protect his property from a burglar or other criminal invader made the owner *absolutely liable* for injuries suffered by the intruder, unless the building being so protected was a dwelling, regardless of the owner's intent and purpose in setting the device in his building. On the other hand, in Instruction No. 6 the court refers to such a *setting with the intent and purpose* of killing or seriously injuring the intruder in order to make the owner liable for damages.

I too find these instructions are confusing. If the court was telling the jury, as appellants contend, that an owner of a premise may not set a spring gun to protect his property unless the trespasser's act amounts to a felony of violence and endangers human life, the phrase used, "for the purpose of harming trespassers", introduces the element of intent and would tend to confuse the jury as to the law on that issue. If the issue here was that such an intent was necessary to establish liability, the instruction was erroneous and confusing; otherwise the error was without prejudice.

I would, therefore, conclude there is merit in appellants' contention that the law was not made clear to the jury as to whether the act of placing a spring gun on this premise was prohibited by law, or whether the act of placing such a device requires a finding of intention to shoot the intruder or cause him great bodily injury to establish liability. I cannot tell whether the jury found liability on the mere act of placing the gun as Mr. Briney did in this house or on the fact that he did so with the intent to seriously harm a trespasser.

In the case at bar, as I have pointed out, there is a sharp conflict in the evidence. The physical facts and certain admissions as to how the gun was aimed would tend to support a finding of intent to injure, while the direct testimony of both defendants was that the gun was placed so it would "hit the floor eventually" and that it was set "low so it couldn't kill anybody." Mr. Briney testified, "My purpose in setting up the gun was not to injure somebody. I thought more or less that the gun would be at a distance of where anyone would grab the door, it would scare them", and in setting the angle of the gun to hit the lower part of the door, he said, "I didn't think it would go through quite that hard."

If the law in this jurisdiction permits, which I think it does, an explanation of the setting of a spring gun to repel invaders of certain private property, then the intent with which the set is made is a vital element in the liability issue.

In view of the failure to distinguish and clearly give the jury the basis upon which it should determine that liability issue, I would reverse and remand the entire case for a new trial.

As indicated, under these circumstances the trial court should not have submitted the punitive damage issue to the jury in this case. By Instruction No. 14 the learned trial judge wrongfully instructed the jury that the law of Iowa allows a jury in such a case to award exemplary damages if it is found that the act complained of is wanton and reckless or where the defendants are guilty of malice. True, this instruction was in accordance with certain past pronouncements of this court and no objection was taken to the substance of the instruction, but defendants have always contended under these circumstances the court should not have submitted the question of exemplary damages to the jury. We have never extended the exemplary damage law to cover such cases and I maintain we should not do so now, directly or indirectly. Without such a pronouncement to that extent, or some legislation extending that right to a person engaged in a serious criminal offense at the time of his injury, I believe the trial court possessed no jurisdiction to permit the jury to pass on such a claim, even though no objections thereto were made by the defendants.

Although this subject has been considered and discussed in several Iowa cases, including Sebastian v. Wood, 246 Iowa 94, 66 N.W.2d 841, and citations, granting exemplary damages for injury due to alleged reckless driving, and Amos v. Prom, 115 F.Supp. 127, relating to alleged mental suffering and humiliation when denied admission to a public dance hall, none seem to consider whether punitive damages are permitted where the injured party was, as here, engaged in a criminal act such as breaking and entering, burglary, or other serious offense. Also see Morgan v. Muench, 181 Iowa 719, 156 N.W. 819, and Stricklen v. Pearson Construction Co., 185 Iowa 95, 169 N.W. 628, and citations in each.

KATKO v. BRINEY
Cite as 183 N.W.2d 657

Iowa   **671**

Although I have found no authority to assist me in my view, I am convinced it is correct in principle and should be adopted in this jurisdiction. In so doing, I adhere to the rule recognized in Amos v. Prom, supra, at 137, et seq., where it is stated: "* * * the principle that intentional wrongful action in disregard for the rights of others amounts to conduct to which the law will attach a penalty and deterrent by way of exemplary damages." However, I would not extend this privilege to a case where the injured party's conduct itself was criminal and extremely violative of good public behavior.

From a general review of the subject of exemplary or punitive damages beginning with Wilkes v. Wood (1763), Lofft 1, 98 English Rep. 489, 498, which stated such "Damages are designed not only as a satisfaction to the injured person, but likewise as a punishment to the guilty, to deter from any such proceeding for the future, * * *", I find that both in England and the United States the purpose of this law was to restrain arbitrary and outrageous use of power. See 70 Harvard L.Rev. 517, 519 (1957), Exemplary Damages in the Law of Torts.

In Hawk v. Ridgway, 33 Ill. 473, 475 (1864), the Illinois court said, "Where the wrong is wanton, or it is willful, the jury are authorized to give an amount of damages beyond the actual injury sustained, as a punishment, and to preserve the public tranquillity."

Some courts rationalize punitive damages on the basis that they provide an outlet for the injured party's desire for revenge and thereby help keep the peace. Some others rationalize it as a punishment to defendant and to deter him and others from further antisocial conduct. It has also been said punitive damages are ordinarily a means of increasing the severity of the admonition inherent in the compensatory award. See 44 Harvard L.Rev. 1173 (1931).

A further study of this law indicates punitive damages have a direct relation to the criminal law. Historically, it was undoubtedly one of the functions of tort law *to deter* wrongful behavior. However, in modern times its priority has become that of compensating the victim of the injury. The business of punishing wrongdoers has increasingly become the exclusive purview of the criminal law. See Pollock and Maitland, History of English Law, Vol. II, 2d Ed. (1898), § 1, pp. 449–462.

The award of punitive damages in modern tort law gives rise to considerable anomalies. Such damages, of course, go to the private purse of the individual plaintiff and may be classified a windfall as to him in excess of his actual losses due entirely to a social judgment about defendant's conduct.

In properly applying this law Professor McCormick, in his treatise on damages found on pages 276 and 277 in McCormick on Damages (1935), said, "Perhaps the principal advantage is that it does tend to bring to punishment a type of cases of oppressive conduct, such as slanders, assaults, minor oppressions, and cruelties, which are theoretically criminally punishable, but which in actual practice go unnoticed by prosecutors occupied with more serious crimes. * * * The self-interest of the plaintiff leads to the actual prosecution of the claim for punitive damages, where the same motive would often lead him to refrain from the trouble incident to appearing against the wrongdoer in criminal proceedings."

So understood, punitive damages are an adjunct to the criminal law, yet one over which the criminal law has no control, and in the United Kingdom, the land of its birth, punitive damages are close to extinct. In Rookes v. Barnard, Appeal Cases (House of Lords, 1964) 1129, at 1221 et seq., the English court of last resort confined the award of punitive damages to a very narrow range of situations. It ruled in an intentional tort case that exemplary damages could be awarded only in cases (1) for oppressive arbitrary, or unconstitutional acts by government servants, (2) for defendant's conduct which had been calculated by him to make a profit for himself which might well exceed the compensation payable to the injured party, and (3) where expressly authorized by statute.

In the case at bar the plaintiff was guilty of serious criminal conduct, which event gave rise to his claim against defendants. Even so, he may be eligible for an award of compensatory damages which so far as the law is concerned redresses him and places him in the position he was prior to sustaining the injury. The windfall he would receive in the form of punitive damages is bothersome to the principle of damages, because it is a response to the conduct of the defendants rather than any reaction to the loss suffered by plaintiff or any measurement of his worthiness for the award.

When such a windfall comes to a criminal as a result of his indulgence in serious criminal conduct, the result is intolerable and indeed shocks the conscience. If we find the law upholds such a result, the criminal would be permitted by operation of law to profit from his own crime.

Furthermore, if our civil courts are to sustain such a result, it would in principle interfere with the purposes and policies of the criminal law. This would certainly be ironic since punitive damages have been thought to assist and promote those purposes, at least so far as the conduct of the defendant is concerned.

We cannot in good conscience ignore the conduct of the plaintiff. He does not come into court with clean hands, and attempts to make a claim to punitive damages in part on his own criminal conduct.

In such circumstances, to enrich him would be unjust, and compensatory damages in such a case itself would be a sufficient deterrent to the defendant or others who might intend to set such a device.

The criminal law can take whatever action is appropriate in such cases, but the civil law should not compound the breach of proper social conduct by rewarding the plaintiff for his crime. I conclude one engaged in a criminal activity is an unworthy object of largesse bestowed by punitive damages and hold the law does not support such a claim to enrichment in this case.

The admonitory function of the tort law is adequately served where the compensatory damages claimed are high and the granted award itself may act as a severe punishment and a deterrence. In such a case as we have here there is no need to hold out the prospect of punitive damages as an incentive to sue and rectify a minor physical damage such as a redress for lost dignity. Certainly this is not a case where defendants might profit in excess of the amount of reparation they may have to pay.

In a case of this kind there is no overwhelming social purpose to be achieved by punishing defendants beyond the compensatory sum claimed for damages.

Being convinced that there was reversible error in the court's instructions, that the issue of intent in placing the spring gun was not clearly presented to the jury, and that the issue as to punitive damages should not have been presented to the jury, I would reverse and remand the matter for a new trial.

The majority seem to ignore the evident issue of punitive policy involved herein and uphold the punitive damage award on a mere technical rule of civil procedure.

9 Careers in Tort Law

You have come a long way in learning all about torts. Now that you've learned so much, maybe even more than you realize, let's talk a little about how to put that knowledge to good use.

What type of career can you expect as a torts legal professional? The field of torts, along with contracts, is at the core of civil law. Therefore, it is a broad, diverse field. There are many roads to travel and many opportunities to explore.

Negligence and Personal Injury

Thankfully, there are more people in this country and on this earth who are peaceful than violent; more people who will resist physically harming another person than will commit such violence. Most torts that result in a physical injury are accidental rather than purposeful.

Of course, you already know that even an accidental injury can be a tort when there is *negligence*. The field of personal injury is vast. Let's think about a possible personal injury situation, and how the parties involved would need legal representation.

Suppose that Jim is walking through a large shopping mall, and a loose lighting fixture falls from the ceiling onto Jim's head. Jim is seriously injured and needs a great deal of medical attention.

Fortunately, Jim makes a complete recovery, but only after months of hospitalization and rehabilitation, which cause Jim to miss time from work. The fixture was loose because David, a mall maintenance person, neglected to fasten it properly.

Jim certainly has a good case for negligence against David. But David earns only a small income. Even if he loses the lawsuit, he cannot afford to pay damages to Jim. It may take Jim years until he can collect all of the money from David.

Instead, Jim's best chance to recover damages would be to sue the owners of the mall, who employ David. Remember, David's employers will likely be held vicariously liable for David's work-related negligence.

Next, keep in mind that the owners of the mall probably carry liability insurance. In other words, they pay a certain amount of money for an insurance policy to cover them in case of such lawsuits. Therefore, the insurance company will likely defend the owners against Jim's claim. Jim, the mall's owners, and the insurance company all will need assistance from legal professionals.

A lawsuit typically requires a great deal of preparation before the actual trial. The preparation includes going through the required process of *litigation*, as well as preparing an effective strategy for the trial.

Pretrial tasks often include client interviewing, creating and maintaining a client file, contacting witnesses, and researching the law. Lawyers often employ paralegals to perform many of these tasks. The tasks are often greatly varied from one case to another. Even the same type of task may vary, depending on the type of case or the size and style of the law firm.

In-House Legal Staff

In our example, the owners of the mall as well as the insurance company probably have an *in-house legal staff*. This means that, rather than hiring legal professionals whenever there is a legal problem, lawyers and paralegals are hired as employees and called upon for their legal services when needed.

An in-house staff is often valuable, especially when the employer legal issues and problems on a regular basis. Let's take a look at two particular types of employers that often maintain an in-house legal staff: hospitals and the media.

HOSPITALS

We discussed malpractice earlier in the book. Even before we did so, you were probably aware of the concept, especially in the medical profession. Doctors and other medical professionals are often sued when the plaintiff is unsatisfied with the services rendered. Because hospitals often involve matters of life and death, you can imagine that they are often the targets of lawsuits.

Accordingly, hospitals often maintain in-house legal professionals. The legal staff may include both lawyers and paralegals. Though the central area of concern is malpractice defense, there are many other issues to deal with.

Like any other business entity, a hospital has income and expenses. There are human resources (people who work there) as well as physical resources (hospital buildings, equipment, etc.). In short, there are a number of legal issues outside of malpractice surrounding the operation of a hospital, and legal professionals are needed to address them.

THE MEDIA

Newspapers, radio and television stations, and movie studios—particularly large ones—often maintain in-house legal staffs as well. Like hospitals and other business entities, there are various legal issues to handle. Of particular concern are issues of defamation. Just as hospitals have to worry about malpractice lawsuits, the media often worry about defamation. Just as patients who are unsatisfied with medical services may sue a hospital, subjects of media coverage who are unsatisfied with the publicity may sue a newspaper, television station, or movie studio.

If you prefer one area of tort law to another, say, personal injury, malpractice, or defamation, there is certainly plenty of opportunity for you to concentrate in the area you prefer.

QUALITY OF WORK LIFE

Generally, the larger the law firm or employer, the longer the working hours. While this is not always the case, it is a good rule of thumb. Working for a large firm may also involve plush surroundings and attractive perks such as an expense account, luxurious office space, and travel. On the other hand, working for a smaller firm may result in more hands-on experience and a more relaxed, informal setting. The hours may also be shorter.

Litigation work in particular often involves long hours. While some legal professionals relish the intensity and thrive on the pressure, others prefer a less strenuous work atmosphere. Fortunately, there is enough of a variety of legal employment to satisfy many tastes and preferences.

As in law firms, the atmosphere for legal professionals in companies or other business entities often varies based on the size and type of such employer. Quite often, legal professionals may wear many different hats within such an entity. For instance, in addition to providing legal services, an in-house lawyer or paralegal may be involved in personnel management, public relations, or financial consulting, all within that same entity.

EARNINGS

How much do lawyers or paralegals make? That's a question a great number of students ask. You are probably wondering that yourself; it is certainly a valid question. But there really *is* no exact answer. In fact, the range is very, very wide.

Some legal professionals earn millions of dollars per year, while others earn barely above minimum wage. Those in business for themselves may strike it rich or go bankrupt. While most fall somewhere in the middle rather than at the extremes, the range indeed appears limitless. Asking, "How much do lawyers or paralegals make?" is like asking, "What's the weather like in the United States?" Obviously, your answer will be very different depending on whether you're talking about Minneapolis or Miami.

JUSTICE

Would you rather be a legal professional for the plaintiff or for the defendant? Would you rather initiate lawsuits or defend against them? While many legal professionals do both, some only concentrate on one area.

Many people have a driving force, a motivation, to enter the legal profession in order to champion justice. Of those people, those who represent plaintiffs may gain satisfaction in helping the "little person" prevail over big, greedy conglomerates. Helping people enforce their legal rights rather than be unjustly harmed often brings a great deal of satisfaction to the legal professional who helped to champion those rights.

On the other hand, our society has been crippled by frivolous lawsuits. People who bring lawsuits for no reason other than a chance to get lucky and receive generous damages abuse the system designed to compensate the truly deserving. Even more unfortunate, there are legal professionals who encourage such frivolous lawsuits, caring only about making profits and not about who gets hurt in the process. Those members of the legal community are the reason for many "lawyer jokes." But beyond the jokes, they shame the profession and all the decent people in it.

Many legal professionals are determined to stamp out frivolous lawsuits, and to prevent innocent people or companies from falling victim to greedy plaintiffs and unethical attorneys.

In any event, protecting the rights of victims who need to bring a lawsuit or victims of a frivolous lawsuit often involves highly rewarding duties that a legal professional undertakes with pride.

CONCLUSION

When making a career decision, consider what exactly is important to you. While this chapter focuses on careers in *torts,* some of the points apply to careers in law generally. Are you mostly interested in quality of life, money, or justice? Do you thrive on pressure, enjoy travel, and like working with other people?

Do you like to write, talk, advise, and solve problems? Are you better at taking orders or giving them? What type of law interests you the most?

These are questions you should think about in choosing your career path. You may also want to try working in various legal settings, even as an intern, to get a taste for what each area is all about.

Remember, if you're still not sure, that's normal. Many people wonder what career is right for them, even years after completing their education. At this stage, it's perfectly reasonable for you to have some questions and doubts.

REVIEW QUESTIONS

These questions are designed to help you think about what type of legal career you might like to pursue.

1. When you think about the ideal career, how much of it involves money?
2. Again thinking of the ideal career, how much of it involves a flexible work schedule?
3. What do you prefer: dealing with people, or working on projects alone?
4. When you talk to people, do you prefer to talk one on one, or to a group of people?
5. Do you like working in a small, private area or a wide, open space?
6. As a legal professional, would you prefer to do a variety of tasks, or just one or two types?
7. Would you like to have one client and perform many legal services for that client, or would you rather have many clients?
8. Would you like to work in a school, a hospital, or a government agency?
9. Would you prefer to talk to people about injuries they suffered, or about violations to their civil rights?
10. Would you like to work with celebrities in the sports and entertainment fields?

A TORT TALE

Throughout this book, you've been exposed to tales for which you supplied some of the facts. Here, you're asked to do it again, with an interesting personal twist.

Five years have passed since you finished school and became a legal professional. You've been contacted by some of your friends from school, who are having a five-year class reunion. When you arrive at the reunion, people ask you about your career and how you like it. You say: "It's a great job. I have everything that I want. I'm really happy that I'm being paid to do something I really enjoy. It really is a dream come true."

What exactly do you do?

PALSGRAF v. LONG ISLAND R. CO.   **(N. Y.)**   09

(162 N.E.)

(248 N. Y. 339)

PALSGRAF v. LONG ISLAND R. CO.

Court of Appeals of New York. May 29, 1928.

1. Negligence ⬡103—Negligence is not actionable unless it involves invasion of legally protected interest.

Negligence is not actionable unless it involves invasion of legally protected interest or the violation of a right.

2. Negligence ⬡1—Negligence is absence of care according to circumstances.

"Negligence" is the absence of care according to the circumstances.

[Ed. Note.—For other definitions, see Words and Phrases, First and Second Series, Negligence.]

3. Carriers ⬡283(2)—Where railroad company's guard pushed passenger aboard, and package containing fireworks fell upon rails and exploded, and scales on platform many feet away fell on plaintiff, plaintiff could not recover.

Where railway company's guard pushed passenger boarding car, and package covered by newspaper and containing fireworks fell on rails and exploded, and shock of explosion threw down scales at the other end of platform many feet away, and scale struck plaintiff, plaintiff could not recover for injury sustained, since no negligence was shown in relation to plaintiff, and to recover plaintiff must show wrong to herself and not merely a wrong to some one else.

4. Torts ⬡1—Negligence is not a tort unless it results in commission of wrong.

Negligence is not a tort unless it results in the commission of a wrong, which imports violation of a right.

Andrews, Crane, and O'Brien, JJ., dissenting.

Appeal from Supreme Court, Appellate Division, Second Department.

Action by Helen Palsgraf against the Long Island Railroad Company. Judgment entered on the verdict of a jury in favor of the plaintiff was affirmed by the Appellate Division by a divided court (222 App. Div. 166, 225 N. Y. S. 412), and defendant appeals. Reversed, and complaint dismissed.

William McNamara and Joseph F. Keany, both of New York City, for appellant.

Mathew W. Wood, of New York City, for respondent.

CARDOZO, C. J. Plaintiff was standing on a platform of defendant's railroad after buying a ticket to go to Rockaway Beach. A train stopped at the station, bound for another place. Two men ran forward to catch it. One of the men reached the platform of the car without mishap, though the train was already moving. The other man, carrying a package, jumped aboard the car, but seemed unsteady as if about to fall. A guard on the car, who had held the door open, reached forward to help him in, and another guard on the platform pushed him from behind. In this act, the package was dislodged, and fell upon the rails. It was a package of small size, about fifteen inches long, and was covered by a newspaper. In fact it contained fireworks, but there was nothing in its appearance to give notice of its contents. The fireworks when they fell exploded. The shock of the explosion threw down some scales at the other end of the platform many feet away. The scales struck the plaintiff, causing injuries for which she sues.

[1-3] The conduct of the defendant's guard, if a wrong in its relation to the holder of the package, was not a wrong in its relation to the plaintiff, standing far away. Relatively to her it was not negligence at all. Nothing in the situation gave notice that the falling package had in it the potency of peril to persons thus removed. Negligence is not actionable unless it involves the invasion of a legally protected interest, the violation of a right. "Proof of negligence in the air, so to speak, will not do." Pollock, Torts (11th Ed.) p. 455; Martin v. Herzog, 228 N. Y. 164, 170, 126 N. E. 814. Cf. Salmond, Torts (6th Ed.) p. 24. "Negligence is the absence of care, according to the circumstances." Willes, J., in Vaughan v. Taff Vale Ry. Co., 5 H. & N. 679, 688; 1 Beven, Negligence (4th Ed.) 7; Paul v. Consol. Fireworks Co., 212 N. Y. 117, 105 N. E. 795; Adams v. Bullock, 227 N. Y. 208, 211, 125 N. E. 93; Parrott v. Wells-Fargo Co., 15 Wall. [U. S.] 524, 21 L. Ed. 206. The plaintiff, as she stood upon the platform of the station, might claim to be protected against intentional invasion of her bodily security. Such invasion is not charged. She might claim to be protected against unintentional invasion by conduct involving in the thought of reasonable men an unreasonable hazard that such invasion would ensue. These, from the point of view of the law, were the bounds of her immunity, with perhaps some rare exceptions, survivals for the most part of ancient forms of liability, where conduct is held to be at the peril of the actor. Sullivan v. Dunham, 161 N. Y. 290, 55 N. E. 923, 47 L. R. A. 715, 76 Am. St. Rep. 274. If no hazard was apparent to the eye of ordinary vigilance, an act innocent and harmless, at least to outward seeming, with reference to her, did not take to itself the quality of a tort because it happened to be a wrong, though apparently not one involving the risk of bodily insecurity, with reference to some one else. "In every instance, before negligence can be predicated of a given act, back of the act must be sought and found a duty to the individual complaining,

the observance of which would have averted or avoided the injury." McSherry, C. J., in West Virginia Central & P. R. Co. v. State, 96 Md. 652, 666, 54 A. 669, 671 (61 L. R. A. 574). Cf. Norfolk & W. Ry. Co. v. Wood, 99 Va. 156, 158, 159, 37 S. E. 846; Hughes v. Boston R. R. Co., 71 N. H. 279, 284, 51 A. 1070, 93 Am. St. Rep. 518; U. S. Express Co. v. Everest, 72 Kan. 517;[1] Emry v. Roanoke Navigation & Water Power Co., 111 N. C. 94, 95, 16 S. E. 18, 17 L. R. A. 699; Vaughan v. Transit Development Co., 222 N. Y. 79, 118 N. E. 219; Losee v. Clute, 51 N. Y. 494; Di Caprio v. New York Cent. R. Co., 231 N. Y. 94, 131 N. E. 746, 16 A. L. R. 940; 1 Shearman & Redfield on Negligence, § 8, and cases cited; Cooley on Torts (3d Ed.) p. 1411; Jaggard on Torts, vol. 2, p. 826; Wharton, Negligence, § 24; Bohlen, Studies in the Law of Torts, p. 601. "The ideas of negligence and duty are strictly correlative." Bowen, L. J., in Thomas v. Quartermaine, 18 Q. B. D. 685, 694. The plaintiff sues in her own right for a wrong personal to her, and not as the vicarious beneficiary of a breach of duty to another.

A different conclusion will involve us, and swiftly too, in a maze of contradictions. A guard stumbles over a package which has been left upon a platform. It seems to be a bundle of newspapers. It turns out to be a can of dynamite. To the eye of ordinary vigilance, the bundle is abandoned waste, which may be kicked or trod on with impunity. Is a passenger at the other end of the platform protected by the law against the unsuspected hazard concealed beneath the waste? If not, is the result to be any different, so far as the distant passenger is concerned, when the guard stumbles over a valise which a truckman or a porter has left upon the walk? The passenger far away, if the victim of a wrong at all, has a cause of action, not derivative, but original and primary. His claim to be protected against invasion of his bodily security is neither greater nor less because the act resulting in the invasion is a wrong to another far removed. In this case, the rights that are said to have been violated, the interests said to have been invaded, are not even of the same order. The man was not injured in his person nor even put in danger. The purpose of the act, as well as its effect, was to make his person safe. If there was a wrong to him at all, which may very well be doubted it was a wrong to a property interest only, the safety of his package. Out of this wrong to property, which threatened injury to nothing else, there has passed, we are told, to the plaintiff by derivation or succession a right of action for the invasion of an interest of another order, the right to bodily security. The diversity of interests emphasizes the futility of the effort to build the plaintiff's right upon the basis of a wrong to some one else. The gain is one of emphasis, for a like result would follow if the interests were the same. Even then, the orbit of the danger as disclosed to the eye of reasonable vigilance would be the orbit of the duty. One who jostles one's neighbor in a crowd does not invade the rights of others standing at the outer fringe when the unintended contact casts a bomb upon the ground. The wrongdoer as to them is the man who carries the bomb, not the one who explodes it without suspicion of the danger. Life will have to be made over, and human nature transformed, before prevision so extravagant can be accepted as the norm of conduct, the customary standard to which behavior must conform.

The argument for the plaintiff is built upon the shifting meanings of such words as "wrong" and "wrongful," and shares their instability. What the plaintiff must show is a wrong" to herself; i. e., a violation of her own right, and not merely a wrong to some one else, nor conduct "wrongful" because unsocial, but not "a wrong" to any one. We are told that one who drives at reckless speed through a crowded city street is guilty of a negligent act and therefore of a wrongful one, irrespective of the consequences. Negligent the act is, and wrongful in the sense that it is unsocial, but wrongful and unsocial in relation to other travelers, only because the eye of vigilance perceives the risk of damage. If the same act were to be committed on a speedway or a race course, it would lose its wrongful quality. The risk reasonably to be perceived defines the duty to be obeyed, and risk imports relation; it is risk to another or to others within the range of apprehension. Seavey, Negligence, Subjective or Objective, 41 H. L. Rv. 6; Boronkay v. Robinson & Carpenter, 247 N. Y. 365, 160 N. E. 400. This does not mean, of course, that one who launches a destructive force is always relieved of liability, if the force, though known to be destructive, pursues an unexpected path. "It was not necessary that the defendant should have had notice of the particular method in which an accident would occur, if the possibility of an accident was clear to the ordinarily prudent eye." Munsey v. Webb, 231 U. S. 150, 156, 34 S. Ct. 44, 45 (58 L. Ed. 162); Condran v. Park & Tilford, 213 N. Y. 341, 345, 107 N. E. 565; Robert v. United States Shipping Board Emergency Fleet Corp., 240 N. Y. 474, 477, 148 N. E. 650. Some acts, such as shooting are so imminently dangerous to any one who may come within reach of the missile however unexpectedly, as to impose a duty of prevision not far from that of an insurer. Even to-day, and much oftener in earlier stages of the law, one acts

[1] 83 P. 817.

sometimes at one's peril. Jeremiah Smith, Tort and Absolute Liability, 30 H. L. Rv. 328; Street, Foundations of Legal Liability, vol. 1, pp. 77, 78. Under this head, it may be, fall certain cases of what is known as transferred intent, an act willfully dangerous to A resulting by misadventure in injury to B. Talmage v. Smith, 101 Mich. 370, 374, 59 N. W. 656, 45 Am. St. Rep. 414. These cases aside, wrong is defined in terms of the natural or probable, at least when unintentional. Parrot v. Wells-Fargo Co. (The Nitro-Glycerine Case) 15 Wall. 524, 21 L. Ed. 206. The range of reasonable apprehension is at times a question for the court, and at times, if varying inferences are possible, a question for the jury. Here, by concession, there was nothing in the situation to suggest to the most cautious mind that the parcel wrapped in newspaper would spread wreckage through the station. If the guard had thrown it down knowingly and willfully, he would not have threatened the plaintiff's safety, so far as appearances could warn him. His conduct would not have involved, even then, an unreasonable probability of invasion of her bodily security. Liability can be no greater where the act is inadvertent.

[4] Negligence, like risk, is thus a term of relation. Negligence in the abstract, apart from things related, is surely not a tort, if indeed it is understandable at all. Bowen, L. J., in Thomas v. Quartermaine, 18 Q. B. D. 685, 694. Negligence is not a tort unless it results in the commission of a wrong, and the commission of a wrong imports the violation of a right; in this case, we are told, the right to be protected against interference with one's bodily security. But bodily security is protected, not against all forms of interference or aggression, but only against some. One who seeks redress at law does not make out a cause of action by showing without more that there has been damage to his person. If the harm was not willful, he must show that the act as to him had possibilities of danger so many and apparent as to entitle him to be protected against the doing of it though the harm was unintended. Affront to personality is still the keynote of the wrong. Confirmation of this view will be found in the history and development of the action on the case. Negligence as a basis of civil liability was unknown to mediæval law. 8 Holdsworth, History of English Law, p. 449; Street, Foundations of Legal Liability, vol. 1. pp. 189, 190. For damage to the person, the sole remedy was trespass, and trespass did not lie in the absence of aggression, and that direct and personal. Holdsworth, op. cit. p. 453; Street, op. cit. vol. 3, pp. 258, 260, vol. 1, pp. 71, 74. Liability for other damage, as where a servant without orders from the master

does or omits something to the damage of another, is a plant of later growth. Holdsworth, op. cit. 450, 457; Wigmore, Responsibility for Tortious Acts, vol. 3, Essays in Anglo-American Legal History, 520, 523, 526, 533. When it emerged out of the legal soil, it was thought of as a variant of trespass, an offshoot of the parent stock. This appears in the form of action, which was known as trespass on the case. Holdsworth, op. cit. p. 449; cf. Scott v. Shepard, 2 Wm. Black. 892; Green, Rationale of Proximate Cause, p. 19. The victim does not sue derivatively, or by right of subrogation, to vindicate an interest invaded in the person of another. Thus to view his cause of action is to ignore the fundamental difference between tort and crime. Holland, Jurisprudence (12th Ed.) p. 328. He sues for breach of a duty owing to himself.

The law of causation, remote or proximate, is thus foreign to the case before us. The question of liability is always anterior to the question of the measure of the consequences that go with liability. If there is no tort to be redressed, there is no occasion to consider what damage might be recovered if there were a finding of a tort. We may assume, without deciding, that negligence, not at large or in the abstract, but in relation to the plaintiff, would entail liability for any and all consequences, however novel or extraordinary. Bird v. St. Paul Fire & Marine Ins. Co., 224 N. Y. 47, 54, 120 N. E. 86, 13 A. L. R. 875; Ehrgott v. Mayor, etc., of City of New York, 96 N. Y. 264, 48 Am. Rep. 622; Smith v. London & S. W. R. Co., [1870–1871] L. R. 6 C. P. 14; 1 Beven, Negligence, 106; Street, op. cit. vol. 1, p. 90; Green, Rationale of Proximate Cause, pp. 88, 118; cf. Matter of Polemis, L. R. 1921, 3 K. B. 560; 44 Law Quarterly Review, 142. There is room for argument that a distinction is to be drawn according to the diversity of interests invaded by the act, as where conduct negligent in that it threatens an insignificant invasion of an interest in property results in an unforeseeable invasion of an interest of another order, as, e. g., one of bodily security. Perhaps other distinctions may be necessary. We do not go into the question now. The consequences to be followed must first be rooted in a wrong.

The judgment of the Appellate Division and that of the Trial Term should be reversed, and the complaint dismissed, with costs in all courts.

ANDREWS, J. (dissenting). Assisting a passenger to board a train, the defendant's servant negligently knocked a package from his arms. It fell between the platform and the cars. Of its contents the servant knew and could know nothing. A violent explosion followed. The concussion broke some scales standing a considerable distance away. In falling, they injured the plaintiff, an intending passenger.

Upon these facts, may she recover the damages she has suffered in an action brought against the master? The result we shall reach depends upon our theory as to the nature of negligence. Is it a relative concept—the breach of some duty owing to a particular person or to particular persons? Or, where there is an act which unreasonably threatens the safety of others, is the doer liable for all its proximate consequences, even where they result in injury to one who would generally be thought to be outside the radius of danger? This is not a mere dispute as to words. We might not believe that to the average mind the dropping of the bundle would seem to involve the probability of harm to the plaintiff standing many feet away whatever might be the case·as to the owner or to one so near as to be likely to be struck by its fall. If, however, we adopt the second hypothesis, we have to inquire only as to the relation between cause and effect. We deal in terms of proximate cause, not of negligence.

Negligence may be defined roughly as an act or omission which unreasonably does or may affect the rights of others, or which unreasonably fails to protect one's self from the dangers resulting from such acts. Here I confine myself to the first branch of the definition. Nor do I comment on the word "unreasonable." For present purposes it sufficiently describes that average of conduct that society requires of its members.

There must be both the act or the omission, and the right. It is the act itself, not the intent of the actor, that is important. Hover v. Barkhoof, 44 N. Y. 113; Mertz v. Connecticut Co., 217 N. Y. 475, 112 N. E. 166. In criminal law both the intent and the result are to be considered. Intent again is material in tort actions, where punitive damages are sought, dependent on actual malice—not on merely reckless conduct. But here neither insanity nor infancy lessens responsibility. Williams v. Hays, 143 N. Y. 442, 38 N. E. 449, 26 L. R. A. 153, 42 Am. St. Rep. 743.

As has been said, except in cases of contributory negligence, there must be rights which are or may be affected. Often though injury has occurred, no rights of him who suffers have been touched. A licensee or trespasser upon my land has no claim to affirmative care on my part that the land be made safe. Meiers v. Fred Koch Brewery, 229 N. Y. 10, 127 N. E. 491, 13 A. L. R. 633. Where a railroad is required to fence its tracks against cattle, no man's rights are injured should he wander upon the road because such fence is absent. Di Caprio v. New York Cent. R. Co.,

231 N. Y. 94, 131 N. E. 746, 16 A. L. R. 940. An unborn child may not demand immunity from personal harm. Drobner v. Peters, 232 N. Y. 220, 133 N. E. 567, 20 A. L. R. 1503.

But we are told that "there is no negligence unless there is in the particular case a legal duty to take care, and this duty must be one which is owed to the plaintiff himself and not merely to others." Salmond Torts (6th Ed.) 24. This I think too narrow a conception. Where there is the unreasonable act, and some right that may be affected there is negligence whether damage does or does not result. That is immaterial. Should we drive down Broadway at a reckless speed, we are negligent whether we strike an approaching car or miss it by an inch. The act itself is wrongful. It is a wrong not only to those who happen to be within the radius of danger, but to all who might have been there—a wrong to the public at large. Such is the language of the street. Such the language of the courts when speaking of contributory negligence. Such again and again their language in speaking of the duty of some defendant and discussing proximate cause in cases where such a discussion is wholly irrelevant on any other theory. Perry v. Rochester Line Co., 219 N. Y. 60, 113 N. E. 529, L. R. A. 1917B, 1058. As was said by Mr. Justice Holmes many years ago:

"The measure of the defendant's duty in determining whether a wrong has been committed is one thing, the measure of liability when a wrong has been committed is another." Spade v. Lynn & B. R. Co., 172 Mass. 488, 491, 52 N. E. 747, 748 (43 L. R. A. 832, 70 Am. St. Rep. 298).

Due care is a duty imposed on each one of us to protect society from unnecessary danger, not to protect A, B, or C alone.

It may well be that there is no such thing as negligence in the abstract. "Proof of negligence in the air, so to speak, will not do." In an empty world negligence would not exist. It does involve a relationship between man and his fellows, but not merely a relationship between man and those whom he might reasonably expect his act would injure; rather, a relationship between him and those whom he does in fact injure. If his act has a tendency to harm some one, it harms him a mile away as surely as it does those on the scene. We now permit children to recover for the negligent killing of the father. It was never prevented on the theory that no duty was owing to them. A husband may be compensated for the loss of his wife's services. To say that the wrongdoer was negligent as to the husband as well as to the wife is merely an attempt to fit facts to theory. An insurance company paying a fire loss recovers its payment of the negligent incendiary. We speak of subrogation—of suing in the right of the insured. Behind the cloud of words is the fact they hide, that the act, wrongful as to the insured, has also injured the company. Even if it be true that the fault of father, wife, or insured will prevent recovery, it is because we consider the original negligence, not the proximate cause of the injury. Pollock, Torts (12th Ed.) 463.

In the well-known Polhemis Case, [1921] 3 K. B. 560, Scrutton, L. J., said that the dropping of a plank was negligent, for it might injure "workman or cargo or ship." Because of either possibility, the owner of the vessel was to be made good for his loss. The act being wrongful, the doer was liable for its proximate results. Criticized and explained as this statement may have been, I think it states the law as it should be and as it is. Smith v. London & S. W R. Co. R. R. (1870–71) L. R. 6 C. P. 14.; Anthony v. Staid, 52 Mass. (11 Metc.) 290; Wood v. Pennsylvania R. Co., 177 Pa. 306, 35 A. 699, 35 L. R. A. 199, 55 Am. St. Rep. 728; Trashansky v. Hershkovitz, 239 N. Y. 452, 147 N. E. 63.

The proposition is this: Every one owes to the world at large the duty of refraining from those acts that may unreasonably threaten the safety of others. Such an act occurs. Not only is he wronged to whom harm might reasonably be expected to result, but he also who is in fact injured, even if he be outside what would generally be thought the danger zone. There needs be duty due the one complaining, but this is not a duty to a particular individual because as to him harm might be expected. Harm to some one being the natural result of the act, not only that one alone, but all those in fact injured may complain. We have never, I think, held otherwise. Indeed in the Di Caprio Case we said that a breach of a general ordinance defining the degree of care to be exercised in one's calling is evidence of negligence as to every one. We did not limit this statement to those who might be expected to be exposed to danger. Unreasonable risk being taken, its consequences are not confined to those who might probably be hurt.

If this be so, we do not have a plaintiff suing by "derivation or succession." Her action is original and primary. Her claim is for a breach of duty to herself—not that she is subrogated to any right of action of the owner of the parcel or of a passenger standing at the scene of the explosion.

The right to recover damages rests on additional considerations. The plaintiff's rights must be injured, and this injury must be caused by the negligence. We build a dam, but are negligent as to its foundations. Breaking, it injures property down stream.

We are not liable if all this happened because of some reason other than the insecure foundation. But, when injuries do result from our unlawful act, we are liable for the consequences. It does not matter that they are unusual, unexpected, unforeseen, and unforeseeable. But there is one limitation. The damages must be so connected with the negligence that the latter may be said to be the proximate cause of the former.

These two words have never been given an inclusive definition. What is a cause in a legal sense, still more what is a proximate cause, depend in each case upon many considerations, as does the existence of negligence itself. Any philosophical doctrine of causation does not help us. A boy throws a stone into a pond. The ripples spread. The water level rises. The history of that pond is altered to all eternity. It will be altered by other causes also. Yet it will be forever the resultant of all causes combined. Each one will have an influence. How great only omniscience can say. You may speak of a chain, or, if you please, a net. An analogy is of little aid. Each cause brings about future events. Without each the future would not be the same. Each is proximate in the sense it is essential. But that is not what we mean by the word. Nor on the other hand do we mean sole cause. There is no such thing.

Should analogy be thought helpful, however, I prefer that of a stream. The spring, starting on its journey, is joined by tributary after tributary. The river, reaching the ocean, comes from a hundred sources. No man may say whence any drop of water is derived. Yet for a time distinction may be possible. Into the clear creek, brown swamp water flows from the left. Later, from the right comes water stained by its clay bed. The three may remain for a space, sharply divided. But at last inevitably no trace of separation remains. They are so commingled that all distinction is lost.

As we have said, we cannot trace the effect of an act to the end, if end there is. Again, however, we may trace it part of the way. A murder at Serajevo may be the necessary antecedent to an assassination in London twenty years hence. An overturned lantern may burn all Chicago. We may follow the fire from the shed to the last building. We rightly say the fire started by the lantern caused its destruction.

A cause, but not the proximate cause. What we do mean by the word "proximate" is that, because of convenience, of public policy, of a rough sense of justice, the law arbitrarily declines to trace a series of events beyond a certain point. This is not logic. It is practical politics. Take our rule as to fires. Sparks from my burning haystack set on fire my house and my neighbor's. I may recover from a negligent railroad He may not. Yet the wrongful act as directly harmed the one as the other. We may regret that the line was drawn just where it was, but drawn somewhere it had to be. We said the act of the railroad was not the proximate cause of our neighbor's fire. Cause it surely was. The words we used were simply indicative of our notions of public policy. Other courts think differently. But somewhere they reach the point where they cannot say the stream comes from any one source.

Take the illustration given in an unpublished manuscript by a distinguished and helpful writer on the law of torts. A chauffeur negligently collides with another car which is filled with dynamite, although he could not know it. An explosion follows. A, walking on the sidewalk nearby, is killed. B, sitting in a window of a building opposite, is cut by flying glass. C, likewise sitting in a window a block away, is similarly injured. And a further illustration: A nursemaid, ten blocks away, startled by the noise, involuntarily drops a baby from her arms to the walk. We are told that C may not recover while A may. As to B it is a question for court or jury. We will all agree that the baby might not. Because, we are again told, the chauffeur had no reason to believe his conduct involved any risk of injuring either C or the baby. As to them he was not negligent.

But the chauffeur, being negligent in risking the collision, his belief that the scope of the harm he might do would be limited is immaterial. His act unreasonably jeopardized the safety of any one who might be affected by it. C's injury and that of the baby were directly traceable to the collision. Without that, the injury would not have happened. C had the right to sit in his office, secure from such dangers. The baby was entitled to use the sidewalk with reasonable safety.

The true theory is, it seems to me, that the injury to C, if in truth he is to be denied recovery, and the injury to the baby, is that their several injuries were not the proximate result of the negligence. And here not what the chauffeur had reason to believe would be the result of his conduct, but what the prudent would foresee, may have a bearing— may have some bearing, for the problem of proximate cause is not to be solved by any one consideration. It is all a question of expediency. There are no fixed rules to govern our judgment. There are simply matters of which we may take account. We have in a somewhat different connection spoken of "the stream of events." We have asked whether that stream was deflected—whether it was

forced into new and unexpected channels. Donnelly v. H. C. & A. I. Piercy Contracting Co., 222 N. Y. 210, 118 N. E. 605. This is rather rhetoric than law. There is in truth little to guide us other than common sense.

There are some hints that may help us. The proximate cause, involved as it may be with many other causes, must be, at the least, something without which the event would not happen. The court must ask itself whether there was a natural and continuous sequence between cause and effect. Was the one a substantial factor in producing the other? Was there a direct connection between them, without too many intervening causes? Is the effect of cause on result not too attentuated? Is the cause likely, in the usual judgment of mankind, to produce the result? Or, by the exercise of prudent foresight, could the result be foreseen? Is the result too remote from the cause, and here we consider remoteness in time and space. Bird v. St. Paul & M. Ins. Co., 224 N. Y. 47, 120 N. E. 86, 13 A. L. R. 875, where we passed upon the construction of a contract—but something was also said on this subject. Clearly we must so consider, for the greater the distance either in time or space, the more surely do other causes intervene to affect the result. When a lantern is overturned, the firing of a shed is a fairly direct consequence. Many things contribute to the spread of the conflagration—the force of the wind, the direction and width of streets, the character of intervening structures, other factors. We draw an uncertain and wavering line, but draw it we must as best we can.

Once again, it is all a question of fair judgment, always keeping in mind the fact that we endeavor to make a rule in each case that will be practical and in keeping with the general understanding of mankind.

Here another question must be answered. In the case supposed, it is said, and said correctly, that the chauffeur is liable for the direct effect of the explosion, although he had no reason to suppose it would follow a collision. "The fact that the injury occurred in a different manner than that which might have been expected does not prevent the chauffeur's negligence from being in law the cause of the injury." But the natural results of a negligent act—the results which a prudent man would or should foresee—do have a bearing upon the decision as to proximate cause. We have said so repeatedly. What should be foreseen? No human foresight would suggest that a collision itself might injure one a block away. On the contrary, given an explosion, such a possibility might be reasonably expected. I think the direct connection, the foresight of which the courts speak, assumes prevision of the explosion, for the immediate results of which, at least, the chauffeur is responsible.

It may be said this is unjust. Why? In fairness he should make good every injury flowing from his negligence. Not because of tenderness toward him, we say he need not answer for all that follows his wrong. We look back to the catastrophe, the fire kindled by the spark, or the explosion. We trace the consequences, not indefinitely, but to a certain point. And to aid us in fixing that point we ask what might ordinarily be expected to follow the fire or the explosion.

This last suggestion is the factor which must determine the case before us. The act upon which defendant's liability rests is knocking an apparently harmless package onto the platform. The act was negligent. For its proximate consequences, the defendant is liable. If its contents were broken to the owner; if it fell upon and crushed a passenger's foot, then to him; if it exploded and injured one in the immediate vicinity, to him also as to A. in the illustration. Mrs. Palsgraf was standing some distance away. How far cannot be told from the record—apparently 25 or 30 feet, perhaps less. Except for the explosion, she would have not injured. We are told by the appellant in his brief, "It cannot be denied that the explosion was the direct cause of the plaintiff's injuries." So it was a substantial factor in producing the result—there was

here a natural and continuous sequence—direct connection. The only intervening cause was that, instead of blowing her to the ground, the concussion smashed the weighing machine which in turn fell upon her. There was no remoteness in time, little in space. And surely, given such as explosion as here, it needed no great foresight to predict that the natural result would be to injure one on the platform at no greater distance from its scene than was the plaintiff. Just how no one might be able to predict. Whether by flying fragments by broken glass, by wreckage of machines or structures no one could say. But injury in some form was most probable.

Under these circumstances, I cannot say as a matter of law that the plaintiff's injuries were not the proximate result of the negligence. That is all we have before us. The court refused to so charges. No request was made to submit the matter to the jury as a question of fact, even would that have been proper upon the record before us.

The judgment appealed from should be affirmed, with costs.

POUND, LEHMAN, and KELLOGG, JJ., concur with CARDOZO, C.J.

ANDREWS, J.; dissents in opinion in which CRANE and O'BRIEN, JJ., concur.

Judgment reversed, etc.

NEW YORK TIMES CO. v. SULLIVAN

CERTIORARI TO THE SUPREME COURT OF ALABAMA.

No. 39. Argued January 6, 1964.—Decided March 9, 1964.*

Respondent, an elected official in Montgomery, Alabama, brought suit in a state court alleging that he had been libeled by an advertisement in corporate petitioner's newspaper, the text of which appeared over the names of the four individual petitioners and many others. The advertisement included statements, some of which were false, about police action allegedly directed against students who participated in a civil rights movement; respondent claimed the statements referred to him because his duties included supervision of the police department. The trial judge instructed the jury that such statements were "libelous per se," legal injury being implied without proof of actual damages, and that for the purpose of compensatory damages malice was presumed, so that such damages could be awarded against petitioners if the statements were found to have been published by them and to have related to respondent. As to punitive damages, the judge instructed that mere negligence was not evidence of actual malice and would not justify an award of punitive damages; he refused to instruct that actual intent to harm or recklessness had to be found before punitive damages could be awarded, or that a verdict for respondent should differentiate between compensatory and punitive damages. The jury found for respondent and the State Supreme Court affirmed. *Held:* A State cannot under the First and Fourteenth Amendments award damages to a public official for defamatory falsehood relating to his official conduct unless he proves "actual malice"—that the statement was made with knowledge of its falsity or with reckless disregard of whether it was true or false. Pp. 265–292.

(a) Application by state courts of a rule of law, whether statutory or not, to award a judgment in a civil action, is "state action" under the Fourteenth Amendment. P. 265.

(b)   Expression does not lose constitutional protection to which it would otherwise be entitled because it appears in the form of a paid advertisement. Pp. 265–266.

---

*Together with No. 40, *Abernathy et al. v. Sullivan,* also on certiorari to the same court, argued January 7, 1964.

NEW YORK TIMES CO. v. SULLIVAN.   255

(c) Factual error, content defamatory of official reputation, or both, are insufficient to warrant an award of damages for false statements unless "actual malice"—knowledge that statements are false or in reckless disregard of the truth—is alleged and proved. Pp. 279–283.

(d) State court judgment entered upon a general verdict which does not differentiate between punitive damages, as to which under state law actual malice must be proved, and general damages, as to which it is "presumed," precludes any determination as to the basis of the verdict and requires reversal, where presumption of malice is inconsistent with federal constitutional requirements. P. 284.

(e) The evidence was constitutionally insufficient to support the judgment for respondent, since it failed to support a funding that the statements were made with actual malice or that they related to respondent. Pp. 285–292.

273 Ala. 656, 144 So. 2d 25, reversed and remanded.

Herbert Wechsler argued the cause for petitioner in No. 39. With him on the brief were *Herbert Brownell, Thomas F. Daly, Louis M. Loeb, T. Eric Embry, Marvin E. Frankel, Ronald S. Diana* and *Doris Wechsler.*

William P. Rogers and *Samuel R. Pierce, Jr.* argued that cause for petitioners in No. 40. With *Mr. Pierce* on the brief were *I. H. Wachtel, Charles S. Conley, Benjamin Spiegel, Raymond S. Harris, Harry H. Wachtel, Joseph B. Russell, David N. Brainin, Stephen J. Jelin* and *Charles B. Markham.*

M. Roland Nachman, Jr. argued the cause for respondent in both cases. With him on the brief were *Sam Rice Baker* and *Calvin Whitesell.*

Briefs of *amici curiae*, urging reversal, were filed in No. 39 by *William P. Rogers, Gerald W. Siegel* and *Stanley Godofsy* for the Washington Post Company, and by *Howard Ellis, Keith Masters* and *Don H. Reuben* for the Tribune Company. Brief of *amici curine*, urging reversal, was filed in both cases by *Edward S. Greenbaum, Harriet F. Pilpel, Melvin L. Wulf, Nanette Dembitz* and *Nancy F. Wechsler* for the American Civil Liberties Union et. al.

MR. JUSTICE BRENNAN delivered the opinion of the Court.

We are required in this case to determine for the first time the extent to which the constitutional protections for speech and press limit a State's power to award damages in a libel action brought by a public official against critics of his official conduct.

Respondent L. B. Sullivan is one of the three elected Commissioners of the City of Montgomery, Alabama. He testified that he was "Commissioner of Public Affairs and the duties are supervision of the Police Department, Fire Department, Department of Cemetery and Department of Scales." He brought this civil libel action against the four individual petitioners, who are Negroes and Alabama clergymen, and against petitioner the New York Times Company, a New York corporation which publishes the New York Times, a daily newspaper. A jury in the Circuit Court of Montgomery County awarded him damages of $500,000, the full amount claimed, against all the petitioners, and the Supreme Court of Alabama affirmed. 273 Ala. 656, 144 So. 2d 25.

Respondent's complaint alleged that he had been libeled by statements in a full-page advertisement that was carried in the New York Times on March 29, 1960.[1] Entitled "Heed Their Rising Voices," the advertisement began by stating that "As the whole world knows by now, thousands of Southern Negro students are engaged in widespread non-violent demonstrations in positive affirmation of the right to live in human dignity as guaranteed by the U. S. Constitution and the Bill of Rights." It went on to charge that "in their efforts to uphold these guarantees, they are being met by an unprecedented wave of terror by those who would deny and negate that document which the whole world looks upon as setting the pattern for modern freedom. . . ." Succeeding

---

[1] A copy of the advertisement is printed in the Appendix.

NEW YORK TIMES CO. *v.* SULLIVAN.   257

paragraphs purported to illustrate the "wave of terror" by describing certain alleged events.   The text concluded with an appeal for funds for three purposes: support of the student movement, "the struggle for the right-to-vote," and the legal defense of Dr. Martin Luther King, Jr., leader of the movement, against a perjury indictment then pending in Montgomery.

The text appeared over the names of 64 persons, many widely known for their activities in public affairs, religion, trade unions, and the performing arts.   Below these names, and under a line reading "We in the south who are struggling daily for dignity and freedom warmly endorse this appeal," appeared the names of the four individual petitioners and of 16 other persons, all but two of whom were identified as clergymen in various Southern cities.   The advertisement was signed at the bottom of the page by the "Committee to Defend Martin Luther King and the Struggle for Freedom in the South," and the officers of the Committee were listed.

Of the 10 paragraphs of text in the advertisement, the third and a portion of the sixth were the basis of respondent's claim of libel.   They read as follows:

Third paragraph:

"In Montgomery, Alabama, after students sang 'My Country, 'Tis of Thee' on the State Capitol steps, their leaders were expelled from school, and truckloads of police armed with shotguns and tear-gas ringed the Alabama State College Campus.   When the entire student body protested to state authorities by refusing to re-register, their dining hall was padlocked in an attempt to starve them into submission."

Sixth paragraph:

"Again and again the Southern violators have answered Dr. King's peaceful protests with intimidation and violence.   They have bombed his home almost killing his wife and child.   They have assaulted his person.   They have arrested him seven times—for 'speeding,' 'loitering' and similar 'offenses.' And now they have charged him with 'perjury'—a *felony* under which they could imprison him for *ten years. . . .*"

Although neither of these statements mentions respondent by name, he contended that the word "police" in the third paragraph referred to him as the Montgomery Commissioner who supervised the Police Department, so that he was being accused of "ringing" the campus with police.   He further claimed that the paragraph would be read as imputing to the police, and hence to him, the padlocking of the dining hall in order to starve the students into submission.[2]   As to the sixth paragraph, he contended that since arrests are ordinarily made by the police, the statement "They have arrested [Dr. King] seven times" would be read as referring to him; he further contended that the "They" who did the arresting would be equated with the "They" who committed the other described acts and with the "Southern violators." Thus, he argued, the paragraph would be read as accusing the Montgomery police, and hence him, of answering Dr. King's protests with "intimidation and violence," bombing his home, assaulting his person, and charging him with perjury.   Respondent and six other Montgomery residents testified that they read some or all of the statements as referring to him in his capacity as Commissioner.

It is uncontroverted that some of the statements contained in the two paragraphs were not accurate descriptions of events which occurred in Montgomery.   Although Negro students staged a demonstration on the State Capitol steps, they sang the National Anthem and not "My

---

[2] Respondent did not consider the charge of expelling the students to be applicable to him, since "that responsibility rests with the State Department of Education."

NEW YORK TIMES CO. *v.* SULLIVAN.   259

Country, 'Tis of Thee." Although nine students were expelled by the State Board of Education, this was not for leading the demonstration at the Capitol, but for demanding service at a lunch counter in the Montgomery County Courthouse on another day. Not the entire student body, but most of it, had protested the expulsion, not by refusing to register, but by boycotting classes on a single day; virtually all the students did register for the ensuing semester. The campus dining hall was not padlocked on any occasion, and the only students who may have been barred from eating there were the few who had neither signed a preregistration application nor requested temporary meal tickets. Although the police were deployed near the campus in large numbers on three occasions, they did not at any time "ring" the campus, and they were not called to the campus in connection with the demonstration on the State Capitol steps, as the third paragraph implied. Dr. King had not been arrested seven times, but only four; and although he claimed to have been assaulted some years earlier in connection with his arrest for loitering outside a courtroom, one of the officers who made the arrest denied that there was such an assault.

On the premise that the charges in the sixth paragraph could be read as referring to him, respondent was allowed to prove that he had not participated in the events described. Although Dr. King's home had in fact been bombed twice when his wife and child were there, both of these occasions antedated respondent's tenure as Commissioner, and the police were not only not implicated in the bombings, but had made every effort to apprehend those who were. Three of Dr. King's four arrests took place before respondent became Commissioner. Although Dr. King had in fact been indicted (he was subsequently acquitted) on two counts of perjury, each of which carried a possible five-year sentence, respondent had nothing to do with procuring the indictment.

Respondent made no effort to prove that he suffered actual pecuniary loss as a result of the alleged libel.[3] One of his witnesses, a former employer, testified that if he had believed the statements, he doubted whether he "would want to be associated with anybody who would be a party to such things that are stated in that ad," and that he would not re-employ respondent if he believed "that he allowed the Police Department to do the things that the paper say he did." But neither this witness nor any of the others testified that he had actually believed that statements in their supposed reference to respondent.

The cost of the advertisement was approximately $4800, and it was published by the Times upon an order from a New York advertising agency action for the signatory Committee. The agency submitted the advertisement with a letter from A. Philip Randolph, Chairman of the Committee, certifying that the persons whose names appeared on the advertisement had given their permission. Mr. Randolph was known to the Times' Advertising Acceptabilty Department as a responsible person, and in accepting the letter as sufficient proof of authorization it followed its established practice. There was testimony that the copy of the advertisement which accompanied the letter listed only the 64 names appearing under the text, and that the statement; "We in the south...warmly endorse this appeal," and the list of names thereunder, which included those of the individual petitioners, were subsequently added when the first proof of the advertisement was received. Each of the individual petitioners testified that he had not authorized the use of his name, and that he had been unaware of its use until receipt of respondent's demand for a retraction. The manager of the Advertising Ac-

---

[3] Approximately 394 copies of the edition of the Times containing the advertisement were circulated in Alabama. Of these, about 35 copies were distributed in Montgomery County. The total circulation of the Times for that day was approximately 650,000 copies.

ceptability Department testified that he had approved the advertisement for publication because he knew nothing to cause him to believe that anything in it was false, and because it bore the endorsement of a "number of people who are well known and whose reputation" he "had no reason to question." Neither he nor anyone else at the Times made an effort to confirm the accuracy of the advertisement, either by checking it against recent Times news stories relating to some of the described events or by any other means.

Alabama law denies a public officer recovery of punitive damages in a libel action brought on account of a publication concerning his official conduct unless he first makes a written demand for a public retraction and the defendant fails or refuses to comply. Alabama Code, Tit. 7, § 914. Respondent served such a demand upon each of the petitioners. None of the individual petitioners responded to the demand, primarily because each took the position that he had not authorized the use of his name on the advertisement and therefore had not published the statements that respondent alleged had libeled him. The Times did not publish a retraction in response to the demand, but wrote respondent a letter stating, among other things, that "we...are somewhat puzzled as to how you think the statements in any way reflect on you," and "you might, if you desire, let us know in what respect you claim that the statements in any way reflect on you." Respondent filed this suit a few days later without answering the letter. The Times did, however, subsequently publish a retraction of the advertisement upon the demand of Governor John Patterson of Alabama, who asserted that the publication charged him with "grave misconduct and...improper actions and omissions as Governor of Alabama and Ex-Officio Chairman of the State Board of Education of Alabama." When asked to explain why there had been a retraction for the Governor but not for respondent, the

Secretary of the Times testified: "We did that because we didn't want anything that was published by The Times to be a reflection on the State of Alabama and the Governor was, as far as we could see, the embodiment of the State of Alabama and the proper representative of the State and, furthermore, we had by that time learned more of the actual facts which the ad purported to recite and, finally, the ad did refer to the action of the State authorities and the Board of Education presumably of which the Governor is the ex-officio chairman...." On the other hand, he testified that he did not think that "any of the language in there referred to Mr. Sullivan."

The trial judge submitted the case to the jury under instructions that the statements in the advertisement were "libelous per se" and were not privileged, so that petitioners might be held liable if the jury found that they had published the advertisement and that the statements were made "of and concerning" respondent. The jury was instructed that, because the statements were libelous *per se*, "the law...implies legal injury from the bare fact of publication itself," "falsity and malice are presumed," "general damages need not be alleged or proved but are presumed," and "punitive damages may be awarded by the jury even though the amount of actual damages is neither found nor shown." An award of punitive damages—as distinguished from "general" damages, which are compensatory in nature—apparently requires proof of actual malice under Alabama law, and the judge charged that "mere negligence or carelessness is not evidence of actual malice or malice in fact, and does not justify an award of exemplary or punitive damages." He refused to charge, however, that the jury must be "convinced" of malice, in the sense of "actual intent" to harm or "gross negligence and recklessness," to make such an award, and he also refused to require that a verdict for respondent differentiate between compensatory and punitive damages. The judge rejected petitioner's contention that his rulings abridged the freedoms of speech and of the press that are guaranteed by the First and Fourteenth Amendments.

In affirming the judgment, the Supreme Court of Alabama sustained the trial judge's rulings and instructions in all respects. 273 Ala. 656, 144 So. 2d 25. It held that "where the words published tend to injure a person libeled by them in his reputation, profession, trade or business, or charge him with an indictable offense, or tend to bring the individual into public contempt," they are "libelous per se"; that "the matter complained of is, under the above doctrine, libelous per se, if it was published of and concerning the plaintiff"; and that is was actionable without "proof of pecuniary injury..., such injury being implied." *Id.*, at 673, 676, 144 So. 2d, at 37, 41. It approved the trial court's ruling that the jury could find the statements to have been made "of and concerning" respondent, stating: "We think it common knowledge that the average person knows that municipal agents, such as police and firemen, and others, are under the control and direction of the city governing body, and more particularly under the direction and control of a single commissioner. In measuring the performance or deficiencies of such groups, praise or criticism is usually attached to the official in complete control of the body." *Id.*, at 674–675, 144 So. 2d, at 39. In sustaining the trial court's determination that the verdict was not excessive, the court said that malice could be inferred from the Times' "irresponsibility" in printing the advertisement while "the Times in its own files had articles already published which would have demonstrated the falsity of the allegations in the advertisement"; from the Times' failure to retract for respondent while retracting for the Governor, whereas the falsity of some of the allegations was then known to the Times and "the matter contained in the advertisement was equally false as to both parties"; and from the testimony of the Times' Secretary that, apart from the statement that the dining hall was padlocked, he thought the two paragraphs were "substantially correct." Id., at 686–687, 144 So. 2d, at 50–51. The court reaffirmed a statement in an earlier opinion that "There is no legal measure of damages in cases of this character." *Id.*, at 686, 144 So. 2d, at 50. It rejected petitioners' constitutional contentions with the brief statements that "The First Amendment of the U.S. Constitution does not protect libelous publications," and "The Fourteenth Amendment is directed against State action and not private action." *Id.*, at 676, 144 So. 2d, at 40.

Because of the importance of the constitutional issues involved, we granted the separate petitions for certiorari of the individual petitioners and of the Times. 371 U.S. 946. We reverse the judgment. We hold that the rule of law applied by the Alabama courts is constitutionally deficient for failure to provide the safeguards for freedom of speech and of the press that are required by the First and Fourteenth Amendments in a libel action brought by a public official against critics of his official conduct.[4] We

---

[4] Since we sustain the contentions of all the petitioners under the First Amendment's guarantees of freedom of speech and of the press as applied to the States by the Fourteenth Amendment, we do not decide the questions presented by other claims of violation of the Fourteenth Amendment. The individual petitioners contend the judgment against them offends the Due Process Clause because there was no evidence to show that they had published or authorized the publication of the alleged libel, and that the Due Process and Equal Protection Clauses were violated by racial segregation and racial basis in the courtroom. The Times contends that the assumption of jurisdiction over its corporate person by the Alabama courts overreaches the territorial limits of the Due Process Clause. The latter claim is foreclosed from our review by the ruling of the Alabama courts that the Times entered a general appearance in the action and thus waived its jurisdictional objection: we cannot say that the ruling said, "but as substantial support" in print Alabama does note. See *Thompson v. Wilson*, 221 Ma. 299, 140 S. 439 (1932); compare *N. A. A. C. P. v. Alabama*, 357 U. S. 449, 454–458.

further hold that under the proper safeguards the evidence presented in this case is constitutionally insufficient to support the judgment for respondent.

I.

We may dispose at the outset of two grounds asserted to insulate the judgment of the Alabama courts from constitutional scrutiny. The first is the proposition relied on by the State Supreme Court—that "The Fourteenth Amendment is directed against State action and not private action." That proposition has no application to this case. Although this is a civil lawsuit between private parties, the Alabama courts have applied a state rule of law which petitioners claim to impose invalid restrictions on their constitutional freedoms of speech and press. It matters not that that law has been applied in a civil action and that it is common law only, though supplemented by statue. See, *e.g.*, Alabama Code, Tit. 7, §§ 908–917. The test is not the form in which state power has been applied but, whatever the form, whether such power has in fact been exercised. See *Ex parte Virginia*, 100 P. S. 339, 346, 347; *American Federation of Labor v. Swing*, 312 U.S. 321.

The second contention is that the constitutional guarantees of freedom of speech and of the press are inapplicable here, at least so far as the Times is concerned, because the allegedly libelous statements were published as part of a paid, "commercial" advertisement. The argument relies on *Valentine v. Chrestensen*, 316 U.S. 52, where the Court held that a city ordinance forbidding street distribution of commercial and business advertising matter did not abridge the First Amendment freedoms, even as applied to a handbill having a commercial message on one side but a protest against certain official action on the other. The reliance is wholly misplaced. The Court in *Christense* reaffirmed the constitutional protection for "the freedom of communicating information and disseminating opinion"; its holding was based upon the factual conclusions that the handbill was "purely commercial advertising" and that the protest against official action had been added only to evade the ordinance.

The publication here was not a "commercial" advertisement in the sense in which the word was used to *Chrestensen.* It communicated information, expressed opinion, recited grievances, protested claimed abuses, and sought financial support on behalf of a movement whose existence and objectives are matters of the highest public interest and concern. See *N. A. A. C. P. v. Button,* 371 U. S. 415, 435. That the Times was paid for publishing the advertisement is an immaterial in this connection as is the fact the newspapers and books are sold. *Smith v. California,* 361 U. S. 147, 150; ef. *Bantam Books, Inc., v. Sullivan,* 372 U. S. 58, 64, n. 6. Any other conclusion would discourage newspapers from carrying "editorial advertisements" of this type, and so might shut off an important outlet for the promulgation of information and ideas by persons who do not themselves have access to publishing facilities—who wish to exercise their freedom of speech even though they are not members of the press. Cf. *Lovell v. Griffin,* 303 U. S. 444, 452; *Schneider v. State,* 308 U. S. 147, 164. The effect would be to shackle the First Amendment in its attempt to secure "the widest possible dissemination of information from diverse and antagonistic sources." *Associated Press v. United States,* 326 U. S., 1, 20. To avoid placing such a handicap upon the freedoms of expression, we hold that if the allegedly libelous statements would otherwise be constitutionally protected from the present judgment, they do not forfeit that protection because they were published in the form of a paid advertisement.[5]

---

[5] See American Law Institute, Restatement of Torts, § 593, Comment b (1938).

II.

Under Alabama law as applied in this case, a publication is "libelous per se" if the words "tend to injure a person...in his reputation" or to "bring [him] into public contempt"; the trial court stated that the standard was met if the words are such as to "injure him in his public office, or impute misconduct to him in his office, or want of official integrity, or want of fidelity to a public trust...." The jury must find that the words were published "of and concerning" the plaintiff, but where the plaintiff is a public official his place in the governmental hierarchy is sufficient evidence to support a finding that his reputation has been affected by statements that reflect upon the agency of which he is in charge. Once "libel per se" has been established, the defendant has no defense as to stated facts unless he can persuade the jury that they were true in all their particulars. *Alabama Ride Co. v. Vance*, 235 Ala. 263, 178 So. 438 (1938); *Johnson Publishing Co. v. Davis*, 271 Ala. 474, 494–495, 124 S. 2d 441, 457–458 (1960). His privilege of "fair comment" for expressions of opinion depends on the truth of the facts upon which the comment is based. *Parons v. Age-Herald Publishing Co.*, 181 Ala. 439, 450, 61 So. 345, 350 (1913). Unless he can discharge the burden of proving truth, general damages are presumed, and may be awarded without proof of pecuniary injury. A showing of actual malice is apparently a prerequisite to recovery of punitive damages, and the defendant may in any event forestall a punitive award by a retraction meeting the statutory requirements. Good motives and belief in truth do not negate an inference of malice, but are relevant only in mitigation of punitive damages if they jury chooses to accord them weight. *Johnson Publishing Co. v. Davis*, supra, 271 Ala., at 495, 124 So. 2d, at 458.

The question before us is whether this rule of liability, as applied to an action brought by a public official against critics of his official conduct, abridges the freedom of speech and of the press that is guaranteed by the First and Fourteenth Amendments.

Respondent relies heavily, as did the Alabama courts, on statements of this Court to the effect that the Constitution does not protect libelous publications.[6] Those statements do not foreclose our inquiry here. None of the cases sustained the use of libel laws to impose sanctions upon expression critical of the official conduct of public officials. The dictum in *Pennekamp v. Florida*, 328 U. S. 331, 348–349, that "when the statements amount to defamation, a judge has such remedy in damages for libel as do other public servants," implied no view as to what remedy might constitutionally be afforded to public officials. In *Beauharnais v. Illinois*, 343 U. S. 250, the Court sustained an Illinois criminal libel statute as applied to a publication held to be both defamatory of a racial group and "liable to cause violence and disorder." But the Court was careful to note that it "retains and exercises authority to nullify action which encroaches on freedom of utterance under the guise of punishing libel"; for "public men, are, as it were, public property," and "discussion cannot be denied and the right, as well as the duty, of criticism must not be stilled." *Id.*, at 263–264, and n. 18. In the only previous cases that did present the question of constitutional limitations upon the power to award damages for libel of a public official, the Court was equally divided and the question was not decided. *Schenectady Union Pub. Co. v. Sweeney*, 316 U.S. 642.

---

[6] *Konigsberg v. State Bar of California*, 366 U. S. 36, 49, and n. 10; *Times Film Corp. v. City of Chicago*, 365 U. S. 43, 48; *Roth v. United States*, 354 U. S. 476, 486–487; *Beauharnais v. Illinois*, 343 U. S. 250, 266; *Pennekamp v. Florida*, 328 U. S. 333, 348–349; *Chaplinsky v. New Hampshire*, 315 U. S. 568, 572; *Near v. Minnesota*, 283 U. S. 697, 715.

In deciding the question now, we are compelled by neither precedent nor policy to give any more weight to the epithet "libel" than we have to other "mere labels" of state law. *N. A. A. C. P. v. Button*, 371 U. S. 415, 429. Like insurrection,[7] contempt,[8] advocacy of unlawful acts,[9] breach of the press,[10] obscenity,[11] solicitation of legal business,[12] and the various other formulae for the respression of expression that have been challenged in this Court, libel can claim no talismanic immunity from constitutional limitations. It must be measured by standards that satisfy the First Amendment.

The general proposition that freedom of expression upon public questions is secured by the First Amendment has long been settled by our decisions. The constitutional safeguard, we have said, "was fashioned to assure unfettered interchange of ideas for the bringing about of political and social changes desired by the people." *Roth v. United States*, 354 U. S. 476, 484. "The maintenance of the opportunity for free political discussion to the end that government may be responsive to the will of the people and that changes may be obtained by lawful means, an opportunity essential to the security of the Republic, is a fundamental principle of our constitutional system." *Stromberg v. California*, 283 U. S. 359, 369. "[I]t is a prized American privilege to speak one's mind, although not always with perfect good taste, on all public institutions," *Bridges v. California*, 314 U. S. 252, 270, and this opportunity is to be afforded for "vigorous advocacy" no less than "abstract discussion." *N. A. A. C. P. v. Button*, 371 U. S. 415, 429.

---

[7] *Herndon v. Lawry*, 301 U. S. 242.

[8] *Bridges v. California*, 314 U. S. 252; *Pennekamp v. Florida*, 328 U. S. 331.

[9] *De Jonge v. Oregon*, 299 U. S. 353.

[10] *Edwards v. South Carolina*, 372 U. S. 229.

[11] *Ruth v. United States*, 354 U. S. 476.

[12] *N. A. A. C. P. v. Button*, 371 U. S. 415.

The First Amendment, said Judge Learned Hand, "presupposed that right conclusions are more likely to be gathered out of a multitude of tongues, than through any kind of authoritative selection. To many this is, and always will be, folly; but we have staked upon it our all." *United States v. Associated Press,* 52 F. Supp. 362, 372 (D. C. S. D. N. Y. 1943). Mr. Justice Brandeis, in his concurring opinion in *Whitney v. California,* 274 U.S. 357, 375–376, gave the principle its classic formulation:

> "Those who won our independence believed...that public discussion is a political duty; and that this should be a fundamental principle of the American government. They recognized the risks to which all human institutions are subject. But they know that order cannot be secured merely through fear of punishment for its infraction; that it is hazardous to discourage thought, hope and imagination; that fear breeds repression; that repression breeds hate; that hate menaces stable government; that the path of safety lies in the opportunity to discuss freely supposed grievances and proposed remedies; and that the fitting remedy for evil counsels is good ones. Believing in the power of reason as applied through public discussion, they eschewed silence coerced by law—the argument of force in its worst form. Recognizing the occasional tyrannies of governing majorities, they amended the Constitution so that free speech and assembly should be guaranteed."

Thus we consider this ease against the background of a profound national commitment to the principle that debate on public issues should be uninhibited, robust, and wide-open, and that it may well include vehement, caustic, and sometimes unpleasantly sharp attacks on government and public officials. See *Terminiello v. Chicago,* 337 U. S. 1.4; *De Jonge v. Oregon,* 299 U. S. 353,

365. The present advertisement, as an expression of grievance and protest on one of the major public issues of our time, would seem clearly to qualify for the constitutional protection. The question is whether it forfeits that protection by the falsity of some of its factual statements and by its alleged defamation of respondent.

Authoritative interpretations of the First Amendment guarantees have consistently refused to recognize an exception for any test of truth—whether administered by judges, juries, or administrative officials—and especially one that puts the burden of proving truth on the speaker. Cf. *Speiser v. Randall,* 357 U. S. 513, 525–526. The constitutional protection does not turn upon "the truth, popularity, or social utility of the ideas and beliefs which are offered," *N. A. A. C. P. v. Button,* 371 U. S. 415, 445. As Madison said, "Some degree of abuse is inseparable from the proper use of every thing; and in no instance is this more true than in that of the press." 4 Elliot's Debates on the Federal Constitution (1876), p. 571. In *Cantwell v. Connecticut,* 340 U. S. 296, 310, the Court declared:

> "In the realm of religious faith, and in that of political belief, sharp differences arise. In both fields the tenets of one man may seem the rankest error to his neighbor. To persuade others to his own point of view, the pleader, as we know, at times, resorts to exaggeration, to vilification of men who have been, or are, prominent in church or state, and even to false statement. But the people of this nation have ordained in that light of history, that, in spite of the probability of excesses and abuses, these liberties are, in the long view, essential to enlightened opinion and right conduct on the part of the citizens of a democracy."

That erroneous statement is inevitable in free debate, and that it must be protected if the freedoms of expression are to have the "breathing space" that they "need...to survive," *N. A. A. C. P. v. Button*, 371 U. S. 415, 433, was also recognized by the Court of Appeals for the District of Columbia Circuit in *Sweeney v. Patterson*, 76 U. S. App. D. C. 23, 24, 128 F. 2d 457, 458 (1942), cert. Denied, 317 U. S. 678. Judge Edgerton spoke for a unanimous court which affirmed that dismissal of a Congressmen's libel suit based upon a newspaper article charging him with anti-Semitism in opposing a judicial appointment. He said:

> "Cases which impose liability for erroneous reports of the political conduct of the officials reflect the obsolete doctrine that the governed must, not criticize their governors.... The interest of the public here outweighs the interest of the appellant or any other individual. The protection of the public requires not merely discussion, but information. Political conduct and views which some respectable people approve, and others condemn, are constantly imputed to Congressmen. Errors of fact, particularly in regard to a man's mental states and processes, are inevitable.... Whatever is added to the field of libel is taken from the field of free debate."[13]

Injury to official reputation affords no more warrant for repressing speech that would otherwise be free than does factual error. Where judicial officers are involved, this Court has held that concerns for the dignity and

---

[13] See also Mill, On Liberty (Oxford: Blackwell, 1947), at 47:
"...[T]o argue sophistically, to suppress facts or arguments, to misstate the elements of the case, or misrepresent the opposite opinion...all this, even to the most aggravated degree, is so continually done in perfect good faith, by persons who are not considered, and in many other respects may not deserve to be considered, ignorant or incompetent, that it is rarely possible, on adequate grounds, consciously to stamp the misrepresentation as morally culpable; and still less could law presume to interfere with this kind of controversial misconduct."

reputation of the courts does not justify the punishment as criminal contempt of criticism of the judge or his decision. *Bridges v. California* 314 U. S. 252. This is true even though the utterance contains "half-truths" and "misinformation." *Pennekamp v. Florida,* 328 U. S. 331, 342, 343, n. 5, 345. Such repression can be justified, if at all, only by a clear and present danger of the obstruction of justice. See also *Craig v. Harvey,* 331 U. S. 367; *Wood v. Georgia,* 370 U. S. 375. If judges are to be treated as "men of fortitude, able to thrive in a hardy climate," *Craig v. Harvey,* supra, 331 U. S., at 376, surely the same must be true of other government officials, such as elected city commissioners.14 Criticism of their official conduct does not lose its constitutional protection merely because it is effective criticism and hence diminishes their official reputations.

If neither factual error nor defamatory content suffices to remove the constitutional shield from criticism of official conduct, the combination of the two elements is no less inadequate. This is the lesson to be drawn from the great controversy over the Sedition Act of 1798, I Stat. 596, which first crystallized a national awareness of the central meaning of the First Amendment. See Levy, Legacy of Suppression (1960), at 258, *et. seg.*; Smith, Freedom's Fetters (1956), at 426, 431, and *passim.* That statute made it a crime, punishable by a $5,000 fine and five years in prison, "if any person shall write, print, utter or publish...any false, scandalous and malicious

---

14 The climate in which public officials operate, especially during a political campaign, has been described by one commentator in the following terms: "Charges of gross incompetence, disregard of the public interest, communist sympathies, and the like usually have filled the air; and hints of bribery, embezzlement, and other criminal conduct are not infrequent." Noel, Defamation of Public Officers and Candidates, 49 Col. L. Itev. 875 (1949).

For a similar description written 60 years earlier, see Chase, Criticism of Public Officers and Candidates for Office, 23 Am. L. Rev. 346 (1889).

writing or writings against the government of the United
States, or either house of the Congress..., or the President...,
with intent to defame...or to bring them, or either of them, or
either of any of them, the hatred of the good people of the
United States." The Act allowed the defendant the defense of
truth, and provided that the jury were to be judges both of the
law and the facts. Despite these qualifications, the Act was vigorously condemned as unconstitutional in an attack joined in
by Jefferson and Madison. In the famous Virginia Resolution
of 1798, the General Assembly of Virginia resolved that it

> "doth particularly protest against the palpable and
> alarming infractions of the Constitution, and in the two
> late cases of the 'Alien and Sedition Acts,' passed at the
> last session of Congress.... [The Sedition Act] exercis-
> es... a power not delegated by the Constitution, but, on
> the contrary, expressly and positively forbidden by one
> of the amendments thereto—a power which, more than
> any other, ought to produce universal alarm, because it
> is levelled against the right of freely examining public
> characters and measures, and of free communication
> among the people thereon, which has ever been justly
> deemed the only effectual guardian of every other
> right." 4 Elliot's Debates, *supra*, pp. 553–554.

Madison prepared the Report in support of the protest.
His premise was that the Constitution created a form of
government under which "The people, not the government, possess the absolute sovereignty." The structure
of the government dispersed power, and of power
itself at all levels. This form of government was "altogether different" from the British form, under which the
Crown was sovereign and the people were subjects. "Is

NEW YORK TIMES CO. v. SULLIVAN.   275

it not natural and necessary, under such different circumstances," he asked, "that a different degree of freedom in the use of the press should be contemplated?" *Id.*, pp. 569–570. Earlier, in a debate in the House of Representatives, Madison had said: "If we advert to the nature of the Republican Government, we shall find that the censorial power is in the people over the Government, and not in the Government over the people." 4 Annals of Congress, p. 934 (1794). Of the exercise of that power by the press, his Report said: "In every state, probably, in the Union, the press has exerted a freedom in canvassing the merits and measures of public men, of every description, which has not been confined to the strict limits of the common law. On this footing the freedom of the press has stood; on this foundation it yet stands...." 4 Elliot's Debates, *supra*, p. 570. The right of free public discussion of the stewardship of public officials was thus, in Madison's view, a fundamental principle of the American form of government.[15]

---

[15] The Report on the Virginia Resolutions further stated:

"[I]t is manifestly impossible to punish the intent to bring these who administer the government into disrepute or contempt, without striking at the right of freely discussing public characters and measures; ...which, again, is equivalent to a protection of those who administer the government, if they should at any time deserve the contempt or hatred of the people, against being exposed to it, by free animadversions on their characters and conduct. Nor can there be a doubt...that a government thus entrenched in penal statues against the just and natural effects of a culpable administration, will easily evade the responsibility which is essential to a faithful discharge of its duty.

"Let it be recollected, lastly, that the right of electing the members of the government constitutes more particularly the essence of a free and responsible government. The value and efficacy of this right depends on the knowledge of the comparative merits and demerits of the candidates for public trust, and on the equal freedom, consequently, of examining and discussing these merits and demerits of the candidates respectively." 4 Elliot's Debates, *supra*, p. 575.

Although the Sedition Act was never tested in this Court,16 the attack upon its validity has carried the day in the court of history. [16] Fines levied in its prosecution were repaid by Act of Congress on the ground that it was unconstitutional. See, *e.g.*, Act of July 4, 1840, c. 45, 6 Stat. 802, accompanied by H. R. Rep., No. 86, 26th Cong., 1st. Sess. (1840). Calhoun, reporting to the Senate on February 4, 1836, assumed that its invalidity was a matter "which no one now doubts." Report with Senate bill No. 122, 24th Cong., 1st Sess. P. 3. Jefferson, as President, pardoned those who had been convicted and sentenced under the Act and remitted their fines, stating: "I discharged every person under punishment or prosecution under the sedition law, because I considered, and now consider, that law to be a nullity, as absolute and as palpable as if Congress had ordered us to fall down and worship a golden image." Letter to Mrs. Adams, July 22, 1804, 4 Jefferson's Works (Washington ed.), pp. 555, 556. The invalidity of the Act has also been assumed by Justices of this Court. See Holmes, J., dissenting and joined by Brandeis, J., in *Abrams v. United States*, 250 U. S. 616, 630; Jackson, J., dissenting in *Beauharnais v. Illinois*, 343 U.S. 250, 288–289; Douglas, The Right of the People (1958), p. 47. See also Cooley, Constitutional Limitations (8th ed., Carrington, 1927), pp. 899–900; Chafee, Free Speech in the United States (1942), pp. 27–28. These views reflect a broad consensus that the Act, because of the restraint it imposed upon criticism of government and public officials, was inconsistent with the First Amendment.

There is no force in respondent's argument that the constitutional limitations implicit in the history of the Sedition Act apply only to Congress and not to the States. It is true that the First Amendment was originally addressed only to action by the Federal Government, and

---

[16] The Act expired by its terms in 1801.

NEW YORK TIMES CO. v. SULLIVAN.   277

that Jefferson, for one, while denying the power of Congress "to controul the freedom of the press," recognized such a power in the States. See the 1804 Letter to Abigail Adams quoted in *Dennis v. United States*, 341 U. S. 494, 522, n. 4 (concurring opinion). But this distinction was eliminated with the adoption of the Fourteenth Amendment and the application to the States of the First Amendment's restrictions. See, e. g., *Gitlow v. New York*, 268 U. S. 652, 666; *Schneider v. State*, 308 U. S. 147, 160; *Bridges v. California*, 314 U. S. 252, 268; *Edwards v. South Carolina*, 372 U. S. 229, 235.

What a State may not constitutionally bring about by means of a criminal statue is likewise beyond the reach of its civil law of libel.17 The fear of damage awards under a rule such as that invoked by the Alabama courts here may be markedly more inhibiting than the fear of prosecution under a criminal statute. See *City of Chicago v. Tribune Co.*, 307 Ill. 595, 607, 139 N. E. 86, 90 (1923). Alabama, for example, has a criminal libel law which subjects to prosecution "any person who speaks, writes, or prints of and concerning another any accusation falsely and maliciously importing the commission by such person of a felony, or any other indictable offense involving moral turpitude," and which allows as punishment upon conviction a fine not exceeding $500 and a prison sentence of six months. Alabama Code, Tit. § 14, (character) 350. Presumably a person charged with violation of this statute enjoys ordinary criminal-law safeguards such as the requirements of an indictment and of proof beyond a reasonable doubt. These safeguards are not available to the defendant in a civil action. The judgment awarded in this case—without the need for any proof of actual pecuniary loss—was one thousand times greater than the maximum fine provided by the Alabama criminal statute, and one hundred times greater than that provided by the Sedition Act.

---

[17] Cf. *Farmers Union v. WDAY*, 360 U. S. 525, 535.

And since there is no double-jeopardy limitation applicable to civil lawsuits, this is not the only judgment that may be awarded against petitioners for the same publication.[18] Whether or not a newspaper can survive a succession of such judgments, the pall of fear and timidity imposed upon those who would give voice to public criticism is an atmosphere in which the First Amendment freedoms cannot survive. Plainly the Alabama law of civil libel is "a form of regulation that creates hazards to protected freedoms markedly greater than those that attend reliance upon the criminal law." *Bantam Books, Inc.,* v. *Sullivan,* 372 U. S. 58, 70.

The state rule of law is not saved by its allowance of the defense of truth. A defense for erroneous statements honestly made is no less essential here than was the requirement of proof of guilty knowledge which, in *Smith* v. *California,* 361 U. S. 147, we held indispensable to a valid conviction of a bookseller for possessing obscene writings for sale. We said:

> "For if the bookseller is criminally liable without knowledge of the contents, . . . he will tend to restrict the books he sells to those he has inspected; and thus the State will have imposed a restriction upon the distribution of constitutionally protected as well as obscene literature. . . . And the bookseller's burden would become the public's burden, for by restricting him the public's access to reading matter would be restricted. . . . [H]is timidity in the face of his absolute criminal liability, thus would tend to restrict the public's access to forms of the printed word which the State could not constitu-

---

[18] The Times states that four other libel suits based on the advertisement have been filed against it by others who have served as Montgomery City Commissioners and by the Governor of Alabama; that another $500,000 verdict has been awarded in the only one of these cases that has yet gone to trial; and that the damages sought in the other three total $2,000,000.

NEW YORK TIMES CO. *v.* SULLIVAN.   279

tionally suppress directly.   The bookseller's self-censorship, compelled by the State, would be a censorship affecting the whole public, hardly less virulent for being privately administered.   Through it, the distribution of all books, both obscene and not obscene, would be impeded."   (361 U. S. 147, 153–154.) A rule compelling the critic of official conduct to guarantee the truth of all his factual assertions—and to do so on pain of libel judgments virtually unlimited in amount—leads to a comparable "self-censorship"   Allowance of the defense of truth, with the burden of proving it on the defendant, does not mean that only false speech will be deterred.[19]   Even courts accepting this defense as an adequate safeguard have recognized the difficulties of adducing legal proofs that the alleged libel was true in all its factual particulars.   See, *e. g., Post Publishing Co.* v. *Hallam*, 59 F. 530, 540 (C. A. 6th Cir. 1893); see also Noel, Defamation of Public Officers and Candidates, 49 Col. L. Rev. 875, 892 (1949).   Under such a rule, would-be critics of official conduct may be deterred from voicing their criticism, even though it is believed to be true and even though it is in fact true, because of doubt whether it can be proved in court or fear of the expense of having to do so.   They tend to make only statements which "steer far wider of the unlawful zone." *Speiser* v. *Randall, supra,* 357 U. S., at 526.   The rule thus dampens the vigor and limits the variety of public debate.   It is inconsistent with the First and Fourteenth Amendments.

The constitutional guarantees require, we think, a federal rule that prohibits a public official from recovering damages for a defamatory falsehood relating to his official conduct unless he proves that the statement was made

---

[19] Even a false statement may be deemed to make a valuable contribution to public debate, since it brings about "the clearer perception and livelier impression of truth, produced by its collision with error."   Mill, On Liberty (Oxford: Blackwell, 1947), at 15; see also Milton, Areopagitica, in Prose Works (Yale, 1959), Vol. II, at 561.

with "actual malice"—that is, with knowledge that it was false or with reckless disregard of whether it was false or not. An oft-cited statement of a like rule, which has been adopted by a number of state courts,[20] is found in the Kansas case of *Coleman* v. *MacLennan*, 78 Kan. 711, 98 P. 281 (1908). The State Attorney General, a candidate for re-election and a member of the commission charged with the management and control of the state school fund, sued a newspaper publisher for alleged libel in an article purporting to state facts relating to his official conduct in connection with a school-fund transaction. The defendant pleaded privilege and the trial judge, over the plaintiff's objection, instructed the jury that

> "where an article is published and circulated among voters for the sole purpose of giving what the de-

[20] *E. g., Ponder* v. *Cobb*, 257 N. C. 281, 299, 126 S. E. 2d 67, 80 (1962); *Lawrence* v. *Fox*, 357 Mich. 134, 146, 97 N. W. 2d 719, 725 (1959); *Stice* v. *Beacon Newspaper Corp.*, 185 Kan. 61, 65–67, 340 P. 2d 396, 400–401 (1959); *Bailey* v. *Charleston Mail Assn.*, 126 W. Va. 292, 307, 27 S. E. 2d 837, 844 (1943); *Salinger* v. *Cowles*, 195 Iowa 873, 889, 191 N. W. 167, 174 (1922); *Snively* v. *Record Publishing Co.*, 185 Cal. 565, 571–576, 198 P. 1 (1921); *McLean* v. *Merriman*, 42 S. D. 394, 175 N. W. 878 (1920). Applying the same rule to candidates for public office, see, *e. g., Phoenix Newspapers* v. *Choisser*, 82 Ariz. 271, 276–277, 312 P. 2d 150, 154 (1957); *Friedell* v. *Blakely Printing Co.*, 163 Minn. 226, 230, 203 N. W. 974, 975 (1925). And see *Chagnon* v. *Union-Leader Corp.*, 103 N. H. 426, 438, 174 A. 2d 825, 833 (1961), cert. denied, 369 U. S. 830.

The consensus of scholarly opinion apparently favors the rule that is here adopted. *E. g.,* 1 Harper and James, Torts, § 5.26, at 449–450 (1956); Noel, Defamation of Public Officers and Candidates, 49 Col. L. Rev. 875, 891–895, 897, 903 (1949); Hallen, Fair Comment, 8 Tex. L. Rev. 41, 61 (1929); Smith, Charges Against Candidates, 18 Mich. L. Rev. 1, 115 (1919); Chase, Criticism of Public Officers and Candidates for Office, 23 Am. L. Rev. 346, 367–371 (1889); Cooley, Constitutional Limitations (7th ed., Lane, 1903), at 604, 616–628. But see, *e. g.,* American Law Institute, Restatement of Torts, § 598, Comment a (1938) (reversing the position taken in Tentative Draft 13, § 1041 (2) (1936)); Veeder, Freedom of Public Discussion, 23 Harv. L. Rev. 413, 419 (1910).

NEW YORK TIMES CO. *v.* SULLIVAN.   281

fendant believes to be truthful information concerning a candidate for public office and for the purpose of enabling such voters to cast their ballot more intelligently, and the whole thing is done in good faith and without malice, the article is privileged, although the principal matters contained in the article may be untrue in fact and derogatory to the character of the plaintiff; and in such a case the burden is on the plaintiff to show actual malice in the publication of the article."

In answer to a special question, the jury found that the plaintiff had not proved actual malice, and a general verdict was returned for the defendant. On appeal the Supreme Court of Kansas, in an opinion by Justice Burch, reasoned as follows (78 Kan., at 724, 98 P., at 286):

"It is of the utmost consequence that the people should discuss the character and qualifications of candidates for their suffrages. The importance to the state and to society of such discussions is so vast, and the advantages derived are so great, that they more than counterbalance the inconvenience of private persons whose conduct may be involved, and occasional injury to the reputations of individuals must yield to the public welfare, although at times such injury may be great. The public benefit from publicity is so great, and the chance of injury to private character so small, that such discussion must be privileged."

The court thus sustained the trial court's instruction as a correct statement of the law, saying:

"In such a case the occasion gives rise to a privilege, qualified to this extent: any one claiming to be defamed by the communication must show actual malice or go remediless. This privilege extends to a great variety of subjects, and includes matters of

public concern, public men, and candidates for office."
78 Kan., at 723, 98 P., at 285.

Such a privilege for criticism of official conduct[21] is
appropriately analogous to the protection accorded a
public official when *he* is sued for libel by a private citizen.
In *Barr* v. *Matteo*, 360 U. S. 564, 575, this Court held the
utterance of a federal official to be absolutely privileged
if made "within the outer perimeter" of his duties. The
States accord the same immunity to statements of their
highest officers, although some differentiate their lesser
officials and qualify the privilege they enjoy.[22] But all
hold that all officials are protected unless actual malice
can be proved. The reason for the official privilege is said
to be that the threat of damage suits would otherwise
"inhibit the fearless, vigorous, and effective administration of policies of government" and "dampen the ardor
of all but the most resolute, or the most irresponsible, in
the unflinching discharge of their duties." *Barr* v.
Matteo, supra, 360 U. S., at 571. Analogous considerations support the privilege for the citizen-critic of government. It is as much his duty to criticize as it is the
official's duty to administer. See *Whitney* v. *California,*
274 U. S. 357, 375 (concurring opinion of Mr. Justice
Brandeis), quoted *supra,* p. 270. As Madison said, see
supra, p. 275, "the censorial power is in the people over the
Government, and not in the Government over the people." It would give public servants an unjustified preference over the public they serve, if critics of official conduct

---

[21] The privilege immunizing honest misstatements of fact is often
referred to as a "conditional" privilege to distinguish it from the
"absolute" privilege recognized in judicial, legislative, administrative
and executive proceedings. See, *e. g.,* Prosser, Torts (2d ed., 1955),
§ 95.

[22] See 1 Harper and James, Torts, § 5.23, at 429–430 (1956);
Prosser, Torts (2d ed., 1955), at 612–613; American Law Institute,
Restatement of Torts (1938), § 591.

NEW YORK TIMES CO. *v.* SULLIVAN.   283

did not have a fair equivalent of the immunity granted to the officials themselves.

We conclude that such a privilege is required by the First and Fourteenth Amendments.

III.

We hold today that the Constitution delimits a State's power to award damages for libel in actions brought by public officials against critics of their official conduct. Since this is such an action,[23] the rule requiring proof of actual malice is applicable.   While Alabama law apparently requires proof of actual malice for an award of punitive damages,[24] where general damages are concerned malice is "presumed."   Such a presumption is inconsistent

---

[23] We have no occasion here to determine how far down into the lower ranks of government employees the "public official" designation would extend for purposes of this rule, or otherwise to specify categories of persons who would or would not be included. Cf. *Barr v. Matteo,* 360 U. S. 564, 573–575. Nor need we here determine the boundaries of the "official conduct" concept. It is enough for the present case that respondent's position as an elected city commissioner clearly made him a public official, and that the allegations in the advertisement concerned what was allegedly his official conduct as Commissioner in charge of the Police Department. As to the statements alleging the assaulting of Dr. King and the bombing of his home, it is immaterial that they might not be considered to involve respondent's official conduct if he himself had been accused of perpetrating the assault and the bombing. Respondent does not claim that the statements charged him personally with these acts; his contention is that the advertisement connects him with them only in his official capacity as the Commissioner supervising the police, on the theory that the police might be equated with the "They" who did the bombing and assaulting. Thus, if these allegations can be read as referring to respondent at all, they must be read as describing his performance of his official duties.

[24] *Johnson Publishing Co.* v. *Davis,* 271 Ala. 474, 487, 124 So. 2d 441, 450 (1960). Thus, the trial judge here instructed the jury that "mere negligence or carelessness is not evidence of actual malice or malice in fact, and does not justify an award of exemplary or punitive damages in an action for libel." [*Footnote 24 continued on p. 284*]

with the federal rule. "The power to create presumptions is not
a means of escape from constitutional restrictions," *Bailey v. Alabama*, 219 U. S. 219, 230; "the showing of malice required for
the forfeiture of the privilege is not presumed but is a matter for
proof by the plaintiff...." *Lawrence v. Fox*, 357 Mich. 134, 146, 97
N. W. 2d 719, 725 (1959).[25] Since the trial judge did not instruct
the jury to differentiate between general and punitive damages,
it may be that the verdict was wholly an award of one or the
other. But it is impossible to know, in view of the general verdict
returned. Because of this uncertainty, the judgment must be reversed and the case remanded. *Stromberg v. California*, 283 U. S.
359, 367–368; *Williams v. North Carolina*, 317 U. S. 287, 291–292;
see *Yates v. United States*, 354 U. S. 298, 311–312; *Cramer v. United
States*, 325 U. S. 1, 36, n. 45.

Since respondent may seek a new trial, we deem that
considerations of effective judicial administration require
us to review the evidence in the present record to deter-

The court refused, however, to give the following instruction which
had been requested by the Times:

"I charge you...that punitive damages, as the name indicates are
designed to punish the defendant, the New York Times Company, a
corporation, and that other defendants in this case,...and I further
charge you that such punitive damages may be awarded only in the event
that you, the jury, are convinced by a fair preponderance of the evidence
that the defendant...was motivated by personal ill will, that is actual
intent to do the plaintiff harm, or that the defendant...was guilty of
gross negligence and recklessness and not of just ordinary negligence or
carelessness in publishing the matter complained of so as to indicate a
wanton disregard of plaintiff's rights." The trial court's error in failing
to require any finding of actual malice for an award of general damages
makes it unnecessary for as to consider the sufficiency under the federal
standard of the instructions regarding actual malice that were given as
to punitive damages.

[25] Accord, *Coleman v. MacLennon*, supra, 78 Kan., at 741, 98 P., at 292;
Gough v. Tribune-Journal Co., 75 Idaho 510, 285 P. 2d 664, 668 (1954).

mine whether it could constitutionally support a judgment for respondent. This Court's duty is not limited to the elaboration of constitutional principles; we must also in proper cases review the evidence to make certain that those principles have been constitutionally applied. This is such a case, particularly since the question is one of alleged trespass across "the line between speech unconditionally guaranteed and speech which may legitimately be regulated." *Speiser v. Randall,* 357 U. S. 513, 525. In cases where that line must be drawn, the rule is that we "examine for ourselves the statements in issue and the circumstances under which they were made to see...whether they are of a character which the principles of the First Amendment, as adopted by the Due Process Clause of the Fourteenth Amendment, protect." *Pennekamp v. Florida,* 328 P. S. 331; see also *One, Inc., v. Olesen,* 355 U. S. 371; *Sunshine Book Co. v. Summerfield,* 355 U. S. 372. We must "make an independent examination of the whole record," *Edwards v. South Carolina,* 372 U. S. 229, 235, so as to assure ourselves that the judgment does not constitute a forbidden intrusion on the field of free expression.26

Applying these standards, we consider that the proof presented to show actual malice lacks the convincing

---

[26] The Seventh Amendment does not, as respondent contends, preclude such an examination by this Court. That Amendment, providing that "no fact tried by a jury, shall be otherwise reexamined in any Court of the United States, than according to the rules of the common law," is applicable to state cases coming here. *Chicago, B. & Q. R. Co;. v Chicago,* 166 U. S. 226, 242–243. Ef. *The Justices v. Murray,* 9 Wall 274. But its ban on reexamination of facts does not preclude us from determining whether governing rules of federal law have been properly applied to the facts. "[T]this Court will review the finding of facts by a State court...where a conclusion of law as to a Federal right and a finding of fact are so intermingled as to analyze the facts." *Fiske v. Kansas,* 274 U. S. 380, 285–386. See also *Haynes v. Washington,* 373 U. S. 503, 515–516.

clarity which the constitutional standard demands, and hence that it would not constitutionally sustain the judgment for respondent under the proper rule of law. The case of the individual petitioners requires little discussion. Even assuming that they could constitutionally be found to have authored the use of their names on the advertisement, there was no evidence whatever that they were aware of any erroneous statements or were in any way reckless in that regard. The judgment against them is thus without constitutional support.

As to the Times, we similarly conclude that the facts do not support a finding of actual malice. The statement by the Times' Secretary that, apart from the padlocking allegation, he thought the advertisement was "substantially correct," affords no constitutional warrant for the Alabama Supreme Court's conclusion that it was a "cavalier ignoring of the falsity of the advertisement [from which] the jury could not have been impressed with the bad faith of the Times, and its maliciousness inferable therefrom." The statement does not indicate malice at the time of the publication; even if the advertisement was not "substantially correct"—although respondent's own proofs tend to show that it was—that opinion was at least a reasonable one, and there was no evidence to impeach the witness' good faith in holding it. The Times' failure to retract upon respondent's demand, although it later retracted upon the demand of Governor Patterson, is likewise not adequate evidence of malice for constitutional purposes. Whether or not a failure to retract may ever constitute such evidence, there are two reasons why it does not here. *First*, the letter written by the Times reflected a reasonable doubt on its part as to whether the advertisement could reasonably by taken to refer to respondent at all. *Second*, it was not a final refusal, since it asked for an explanation on this point— a request that respondent chose to ignore. Nor does the retraction upon the demand of the Governor supply the necessary proof. It may be doubted that a failure to retract which is not itself evidence of malice can retroactively become such by virtue of a retraction subsequently made to another party. But in any event that did not happen here, since the explanation given by the Times' Secretary for the distinction drawn between respondent and the Governor was a reasonable one, the good faith of which was not impeached.

Finally, there is evidence that the Times published the advertisement without checking its accuracy against the news stories in the Times' own files. The mere presence of the stories in the files does not, of course, establish that the Times "knew" the advertisement was false, since the state of mind required for actual malice would have to be brought home to the persons in the Times' organization having responsibility for the publication of the advertisement. With respect to the failure of those persons to make the check, the record shows that they relied upon their knowledge of the good reputation of many of those whose names were listed as sponsors of the advertisement, and upon the letter from A. Philip Randolph, known to them as a responsible individual, certifying that the use of the names was authorized. There was testimony that the persons handling the advertisement saw nothing in it that would render it unacceptable under the Times' policy of rejecting advertisements containing "attacks of a personal character":[27] their failure to reject it on *this ground* was not unreasonable. We think

---

[27] The Times has set forth in a booklet its "Advertising Acceptability Standards." Listed among the classes of advertising that the newspaper does not accept are advertisements that are "fraudulent or deceptive," that are "ambiguous in wording and...may mislead," and that contain "attacks of a personal character." In replying to respondent's interrogatories before the trial, the Secretary of the Times stated that "as the advertisement made no attacks of a personal character upon any individual and otherwise met the advertisement acceptability standards promulgated," it had been approved for publication.

the evidence against the Times supports at most a finding of negligence in failing to discover the misstatements, and is constitutionally insufficient to show the recklessness that is required for a finding of actual malice. Cf. *Charles Parker Co.* v. *Silver City Crystal Co.,* 142 Conn. 605, 618, 116 A. 2d 440, 446 (1955); *Phoenix Newspapers, Inc.,* v. *Choisser,* 82 Ariz. 271, 277-278, 312 P. 2d 150, 154-155 (1957).

We also think the evidence was constitutionally defective in another respect: it was incapable of supporting the jury's finding that the allegedly libelous statements were made "of and concerning" respondent. Respondent relies on the words of the advertisement and the testimony of six witnesses to establish a connection between it and himself. Thus, in his brief to this Court, he states:

> "The reference to respondent as police commissioner is clear from the ad. In addition, the jury heard the testimony of a newspaper editor . . . ; a real estate and insurance man . . . ; the sales manager of a men's clothing store . . . ; a food equipment man . . . ; a service station operator . . . ; and the operator of a truck line for whom respondent had formerly worked . . . . Each of these witnesses stated that he associated the statements with respondent . . . ." (Citations to record omitted.)

There was no reference to respondent in the advertisement, either by name or official position. A number of the allegedly libelous statements—the charges that the dining hall was padlocked and that Dr. King's home was bombed, his person assaulted, and a perjury prosecution instituted against him—did not even concern the police; despite the ingenuity of the arguments which would attach this significance to the word "They," it is plain that these statements could not reasonably be read as accusing respondent of personal involvement in the acts

NEW YORK TIMES CO. *v.* SULLIVAN.   289

in question. The statements upon which respondent principally relies as referring to him are the two allegations that did concern the, police or police functions: that "truckloads of police . . . ringed the Alabama State College Campus" after the demonstration on the State Capitol steps, and that Dr. King had been "arrested . . . seven times." These statements were false only in that the police had been "deployed near" the campus but had not actually "ringed" it and had not gone there in connection with the State Capitol demonstration, and in that Dr. King had been arrested only four times. The ruling that these discrepancies between what was true and what was asserted were sufficient to injure respondent's reputation may itself raise constitutional problems, but we need not consider them here. Although the statements may be taken as referring to the police, they did not on their face make even an oblique reference to respondent as an individual. Support for the asserted reference must, therefore, be sought in the testimony of respondent's witnesses. But none of them suggested any basis for the belief that respondent himself was attacked in the advertisement beyond the bare fact that he was in overall charge of the Police Department and thus bore official responsibility for police conduct; to the extent that some of the witnesses thought respondent to have been charged with ordering or approving the conduct or otherwise being personally involved in it, they based this notion not on any statements in the advertisement, and not on any evidence that he had in fact been so involved, but solely on the unsupported assumption that, because of his official position, he must have been.[26] This reliance on the bare

---

[26] Respondent's own testimony was that "as Commissioner of Public Affairs it is part of my duty to supervise the Police Department and I certainly feel like it [a statement] is associated with me when it describes police activities." He thought that "by virtue of being

fact of respondent's official position[29] was made explicit by the Supreme Court of Alabama. That court, in holding that the trial court "did not err in overruling the demurrer [of the Times] in the aspect that the libelous

---

Police Commissioner and Commissioner of Public Affairs," he was charged with "any activity on the part of the Police Department." "When it describes police action, certainly I feel it reflects on one as an individual." He added that "It is my feeling that it reflects not only on me but on the other Commissioners and the community."

Grover C. Hall testified that to him the third paragraph of the advertisement called to mind "the City government—the Commissioners," and that "now that you ask it I would naturally think a little more about the police Commissioner because his responsibility is exclusively with the constabulary." It was "the phrase about starvation" that led to the association:" the other didn't hit me with any particular force."

Arnold D. Blackwell testified that the third paragraph was associated in his mind with "the Police Commissioner and the police force. The people on the police force." It he had believed the statement about the padlocking of the dining hall, he would have thought "that the people on our police force or the heads of our police force were acting without their jurisdiction and would not be competent for the position." "I would assume that the Commissioner had ordered the police force to do that and therefore it would be his responsibility."

Harry W. Kaminsky associated the statement about "truckloads of police" with respondent "because he is the Police Commissioner." He thought that the reference to arrests in the sixth paragraph "implicates the Police Department, I think, or the authorities that would do that— arrest folks for speeding and loitering and such as that." Asked whether he would associate with respondent a newspaper report that the police had "beat somebody up or assaulted them on the streets of Montgomery," he replied: "I still say he is the Police Commissioner and those men are working directly under him and therefore I would think that he would have something to do with it." In general, he said, "I look at Mr. Sullivan when I see the Police Department."

H. M. Price, Sr., testified that he associated the first sentence of the third paragraph with respondent because: "I would just auto-matically consider that the Police Commissioner in Montgomery

[Footnote 29 is on p. 291]

matter was not of and concerning the [plaintiff,]" based its ruling on the proposition that:

> "We think it common knowledge that the average person
> knows that municipal agents, such as police and firemen,
> and others, are under the control and direction of the city
> governing body, and more particularly under the direc-
> tion and control of a single commissioner. In measuring
> the performance or deficiencies of such groups, praise or
> criticism is usually attached to the official in complete
> control of the body," 273 Ala., at 674–675, 144 So. 2d, at
> 39.

This proposition has disquieting implications for criticism of governmental conduct. For good reason, "no
court of last resort in this country has ever held, or even
suggested, that prosecutions for libel on government have
any place in the American system of jurisprudence."
City of Chicago v. Tribune Co., 307 Ill. 595, 601, 139 N. E.

---

would have to put his approval on those kind of things as an individual."

William M. Parker, Jr., testified that he associated the statements in
the two paragraphs with "the Commissioners of the City of
Montgomery," and since respondent "was the Police Commissioner," he
"thought of him first." He told the examining counsel: "I think if you
were the Police Commissioner I would have thought it was speaking of
you."

Horace W. White, respondent's former employer, testified that the
statement about "truck-loads of police" made him think of respondent
"as being the head of the Police Department." Asked whether he read
the statement as charging respondent himself with ringing the campus
or having shotguns and tear-gas, he replied: "Well, I thought of his
department being charged with it, yes sir. He is the head of the Police
Department as I understand it." He further said that the reason he
would have unwilling to re-employ respondent if he had believed the
advertisement was "the fact that he allowed the Police Department to do
the things that the paper say he did."

[29] Compare *Ponder v. Cubb,* 257 N. C. 284, 426 S. E. 2d 67 (1962).

Opinion of the Court.   376 U.S.

S6. S8 (1923). The present proposition would sidestep this obstacle by transmitting criticism of government, however impersonal it may seem on its face, into personal criticism, and hence potential libel, of the officials of whom the government is composed. There is no legal alchemy by which a State may thus crate the cause of action that would otherwise be denied for a publication which, as respondent himself said of the advertisement, "reflects not only one on me but on the other Commissioners and the community." Raising as it does the possibility that a good-faith critic of government will be penalized for his criticism, the proposition relied on by the Alabama courts strikes at the very center of the constitutionally protected area of free expression.[30] We hold that such as proposition may not constitutionally be utilized to establish that an otherwise impersonal attack on governmental operations was a libel of an official responsible for those operations. Since it was relied on exclusively here, and there was no other evidence to connect the statements with respondent, the evidence was constitutionally insufficient to support a finding that the statements referred to respondent.

The judgment of the Supreme Court of Alabama is reversed and the case is renamed to that court for further proceedings not inconsistent with this opinion.

Reversed and remanded.

[30] Insofar as the proposition means only that the statements about police conduct libeled respondent by implicitly criticizing his ability to run the Police Department, recovery is also precluded in this case by the doctrine of fair comment. See American Law Institute, Restatement of Torts (1938), § 607. Since the Fourteenth Amendment requires recognition of the conditional privilege for honest misstatements of fact, it follows that the dense of fair comment must be afforded for honest expression of opinion based upon privileged, as well as true, statements of fact. Both defenses are of course defensible if the public official proves actual malice, as was not done here.

MR. JUSTICE BLACK, with whom MR. JUSTICE DOUGLAS joins, concurring.

I concur in reversing this half-million-dollar judgment against the New York Times Company and the four individual defendants. In reversing the Court holds that "the Constitution delimits a State's power to award damages for libel in actions brought by public officials against critics of their official conduct." *Ante,* p. 283. I base my vote to reverse on the belief that the First and Fourteenth Amendments not merely "delimit: a State's power to award damages to "public officials against critics of their official conduct" but completely prohibit a State from exercising such a power. The Court goes on to hold that a State can subject such critics to damages if "actual malice" can be proved against them. "Malice," even as defined by the Court, is an elusive, abstract concept, hard malice be proved provides at best an evanescent protection for the right critically to discuss public affairs and certainly does not measure up to the sturdy safeguard embodied in the First Amendment. Unlike the Court, therefore, I vote to reverse exclusively on the ground that the Times and the individual defendants had an absolute, unconditional constitutional right to publish in the Times advertisement their criticisms of the Montgomery agencies and officials. I do not base my vote to reverse on any failure to prove that these individual defendants signed the advertisement or that their criticisms of the Police Department was aimed at the plaintiff Sullivan, who was then the Montgomery City Commissioner having supervision of the city's police; for present purposes I assume these things were proved. Nor is my reason for reversal the size of the half-million-dollar judgment, large as it is. If Alabama has constitutional power to use its civil libel law to impose damages on the press for criticizing the way public officials perform or fail

72. 509 O-65—23.

to perform their duties, I know of no provision in the Federal Constitution which either expressly or implicitly bars the State from fixing the amount of damages.

The half-million-dollar verdict does give dramatic proof; however, that state libel laws threaten the very existence of an American press virile enough to publish unpopular views on public affairs and bold enough to criticize the conduct of public officials. The factual background of this case emphasizes the imminence and enormity of that threat. One of the acute and highly emotional issues in this country arises out of efforts of many people, even including some public officials, to continue state-commanded segregation of races in the public schools and other public places, despite our several holdings that such a state practice is forbidden by the Fourteenth Amendment. Montgomery is one of the localities in which widespread hostility has sometimes extended itself to persons who favor desegregation, particularly to so-called "outside agitators," a term which can be made to fit papers like the Times, which is published in New York. The scarcity of testimony to show that Commissioner Sullivan suffered any actual damages at all suggests that these feelings of hostility had at least as much to do with rendition of this half-million-dollar verdict as did an appraisal of damages. Viewed realistically, this record lends support to an inference that instead of being damaged Commissioner Sullivan's political, social, and financial prestige has likely been enhanced by the Times' publication. Moreover, a second half-million-dollar libel verdict against the Times based on the same advertisement has already been awarded to another Commissioner. There a jury again gave the full amount claimed. There is no reason to believe that there are not more such huge verdicts lurking just around the corner for the Times or any other newspaper or broadcaster which might dare to criticize public officials. In fact, briefs before us show that in Alabama there are now pending eleven libel suits by local and state officials against the Times seeking $5,600,000, and five such suits against the Columbia Broadcasting System seeking $1,700,000. Moreover, this technique for harassing and punishing a free press—now that it has been shown to be possible—is by no means limited to cases with racial overtones; it can be used in other fields where public feelings may make local as well as out-of-state newspapers easy prey for libel verdict seekers.

In my opinion the Federal Constitution has dealt with this deadly danger to the press in the only way possible without leaving the free press open to destruction—by granting the press an absolute immunity for criticism of the way public officials do their public duty. Compare *Barr v. Matteo*, 360 U. S. 564. Stopgap measures like those the Court adopts are in my judgment not enough. This record certainly does not indicate that any different verdict would have been rendered here whatever the Court had charged the jury about "malice," "truth," "good motives," "justifiable ends," or any other legal formulas which in theory would protect the press. Nor does the record indicate that any of these legalistic words would have caused the courts below to set aside or to reduce the half-million-dollar verdict in any amount.

I agree with the Court that the Fourteenth Amendment made the First applicable to the States.1 This means to me that since the adoption of the Fourteenth Amendment a State has no more power than the Federal Government to use a civil libel law or any other law to impose damages for merely discussing public affairs and criticizing public officials. The power of the United

---

1 See cases collected in Speiser v. Randall, 357 U. S. 513, 530 (concurring opinion).

States to do that is, in my judgment, precisely nil. Such was the general view held when the First Amendment was adopted and ever since.[2] Congress never has sought to challenge this viewpoint by passing any civil libel law. It did pass the Sedition Act in 1798,[3] which made it a crime—"seditious libel"—to criticize federal officials or the Federal Government. As the Court's opinion correctly points out, however, *ante*, pp. 273–276, that Act came to an ignominious end and by common consent has generally been treated as having been a wholly unjustifiable and much to be regretted violation of the First Amendment. Since the First Amendment is now made applicable to the States by the Fourteenth, it no more permits the States to impose damages for libel than it does the Federal Government.

We would, I think, more faithfully interpret the First Amendment by holding that at the very least it leaves the people and the press free to criticize officials and discuss public affairs with impunity. This Nation of ours elects many of its important officials; so do the States, the municipalities, the counties, and even many precincts. These officials are responsible to the people for the way they perform their duties. While our Court has held that some kinds of speech and writings, such as "obscenity," *Roth v. United States*, 354 U. S. 476, and "fighting words," *Chaplinsky v. New Hampshire*, 315 U. S. 568, are not expression within the protection of the First Amendment,[4] freedom to discuss public affairs and public officials

---

[2] See, e.g., 1 Tucker, Blackstone's Commentaries (1803), 297, 299 (editor's appendix), St. George Tucker, a distinguished Virginia jurist, took part in the Annapolis Convention of 1780, sat on both state and federal courts, and was widely known for his writings on judicial and constitutional subjects.

[3] Act of July 14, 1798, 1 Stat. 596.

[4] But see *Smith v. California*, 361 U. S. 147, 155 (concurring opinion; *Roth v. United States*, 354 U. S. 476, 508 (dissenting opinion).

is unquestionably, as the Court today holds, the kind of speech the First Amendment was primarily designed to keep within the area of free discussion. To punish the exercise of this right to discuss public affairs or to penalize it through libel judgments is to abridge or shut off discussion of the very kind most needed. This Nation, I suspect, can live in peace without libel suits based on public discussions of public affairs and public officials. But I doubt that a country can live in freedom where its people can be made to suffer physically or financially for criticizing their government, its actions, or its officials. "For a representative democracy ceases to exist that moment that the public functionaries are by any means absolved from their responsibility to their constituents; and this happens whenever the constituent can be restrained in any manner from speaking, writing, or publishing his opinions upon any public measure, or upon the conduct of those who may advise or execute it."[5] An unconditional right to say what one pleases about public affairs is what I consider to be the minimum guarantee of the First Amendment.[6]

I regret that the Court has stopped short of this holding indispensable to preserve our free press from destruction.

Mr. Justice Goldberg, with whom Mr. Justice Douglas joins, concurring in the result.

The Court today announces a constitutional standard which prohibits "a public official from recovering damages for a defamatory falsehood relating to his official conduct unless he proves that the statement was made with

---

[5] 1 Tucker, Blackstone's Commentaries (1803), 297 (editor's appendix); ef. Brant, Seditious Libel: Myth and Reality, 39 N. Y. U. L. Rev. 1.

[6] Cf. Meiklejohn, Free Speech and Its Relation to Self-Government (1948).

'actua. malice'—that is, with knowledge that it was false or with reckless disregard of whether it was false or not." *Ante*, at 279–280. The Court thus rules that the Constitution gives citizens and newspapers a "conditional privilege" immunizing non-malicious misstatements of fact regarding the official conduct of a government officer. The impressive array of history[1] and precedent marshaled by the Court however, confirms my belief that the Constitution affords greater protection than that provided by the Court's standard to citizen and press in exercising the right of pubic criticism.

In my view, the First and Fourteenth Amendments to the Constitution afford to the citizen and to the press an absolute, unconditional privilege to criticize official conduct despite the harm which may flow from excesses and abuses. The prized American right "to speak one's mind," cf. *Bridges v. California*, 314 U. S. 252, 270, about public officials and affairs needs "breathing space to survive," *N. A. A. C. P. v. Button*, 371 U. S. 415, 433. The right should not depend upon a probing by the jury of the motivation[2] of the citizen or press. The theory

---

[1] I fully agree with the Court that the attack upon the validity of the Sedition Act of 1798, 1 Stat. 596, "has carried the day in the court of history," *ante*, at 276, and that the Act would today be declared unconstitutional. It should be pointed out, however, that the Sedition Act proscribed writings which were "false, scandalous *and malicious.*" (Emphasis added.) For prosecutions under the Sedition Act charging malice, see, e. g., Trial of Matthew Lyon (1798), in Wharton, State Trials of the United States (1849), p. 333; Trial of Thomas Cooper (1800) in id., at 659; Trial of Anthony Haswell (1800), in *id.*, at 684; Trial of James Thompson Calendar (1800), in *id.*, at 688.

[2] The requirement of proving actual malice or reckless disregard may, in the mind of the jury, add little to the requirement of proving falsity, a requirement which the Court recognizes not to be an adequate safeguard. The thought suggested by Mr. Justice Jackson in *United States v. Ballard*, 322 U. S. 78, 92–93, is relevant here; "[A]s a matter of either practice or philosophy I do not see how

254   Goldberg, J., concurring in result.

of our Constitution is that every citizen may speak his mind and every newspaper express its view on matters of public concern and may not be barred from speaking or publishing because those in control of government think that what is said or written is unwise, unfair, false, or malicious. In a democratic society, one who assumes to act for the citizens in an executive, legislative, or judicial capacity must expect that his official acts with be commented upon and criticized. Such criticism cannot, in my opinion, be muzzled or deterred by the courts at the instance of public officials under the label of libel.

It has been recognized that "prosecutions for libel on government have [no] place in the American system of jurisprudence." *City of Chicago v. Tribune Co.*, 307 Ill. 595, 601, 139 N. E. 86, 88. I fully agree. Government, however, is not an abstraction; it is made up of individuals—of governors responsible to the governed. In a democratic society where men are free by ballots to remove those in power, any statement critical of governmental action is necessarily "of and concerning" the governors and any statement critical of the governors' official conduct is necessarily "of and concerning" the government. If the rule that libel on government has no place in our Constitution is to have real meaning, then libel on the official conduct of the governors likewise can have no place in our Constitution.

We must recognize that we are willing upon a clean slate.[3] As the Court notes, although there have been

---

we can separate an issue as to what is believed from consideration as to what is believable. The most convincing proof that one believes his statements is to show that they have been true in his experience. Likewise, that one knowingly falsified is best proved by showing that what he said happened never did happen," See note 4, *infra.*

[3] It was not until *Gitlow v. New York*, 268 U. S. 652, decided in 1925, that it was intimated that the freedom of speech guaranteed by

"statements of this Court to the effect that the Constitution does not protect libelous publications . . . [n]one of the cases sustained the use of libel laws to impose sanctions upon expression critical of the official conduct of public officials." *Ante,* at 268. We should be particularly careful, therefore, adequately to protect the liberties which are embodied in the First and Fourteenth Amendments. It may be urged that deliberately and maliciously false statements have no conceivable value as free speech.   That argument, however, is not responsive to the real issue presented by this case, which is whether that freedom of speech which all agree is constitutionally protected can be effectively safeguarded by a rule allowing the imposition of liability upon a jury's evaluation of the speaker's state of mind.   If individual citizens may be held liable in damages for strong words, which a jury finds false and maliciously motivated, there can be little doubt that public debate and advocacy will be constrained.   And if newspapers, publishing advertisements dealing with public issues, thereby risk liability, there can also be little doubt that the ability of minority groups to secure publication of their views on public affairs and to seek support for their causes will be greatly diminished.   Cf. *Farmers Educational & Coop. Union* v. *WDAY, Inc.,* 360 U. S. 525, 530.   The opinion of the Court conclusively demonstrates the chilling effect of the Alabama libel laws on First Amendment freedoms

---

the First Amendment was applicable to the States by reason of the Fourteenth Amendment.   Other intimations followed.   See *Whitney* v. *California,* 274 U. S. 357; *Fiske* v. *Kansas,* 274 U. S. 380.   In 1931 Chief Justice Hughes speaking for the Court in *Stromberg* v. *California,* 283 U. S. 359, 368, declared: "It has been determined that the conception of liberty under the due process clause of the Fourteenth Amendment embraces the right of free speech."   Thus we deal with a constitutional principle enunciated less than four decades ago, and consider for the first time the application of that principle to issues arising in libel cases brought by state officials.

NEW YORK TIMES CO. *v.* SULLIVAN.   301

in the area of race relations.   The American Colonists
were not willing, nor should we be, to take the risk that
"[m]en who injure and oppress the people under their
administration [and] provoke them to cry out and complain" will also be empowered to "make that very complaint the foundation for new oppressions and prosecutions."   *The Trial of John Peter Zenger*, 17 Howell's St.
Tr. 675, 721–722 (1735) (argument of counsel to the
jury).   To impose liability for critical, albeit erroneous
or even malicious, comments on official conduct would
effectively resurrect "the obsolete doctrine that the governed must not criticize their governors."   Cf. *Sweeney*
v. *Patterson*, 76 U. S. App. D. C. 23, 24, 128 F. 2d 457, 458.

Our national experience teaches that repressions breed
hate and "that hate menaces stable government."   *Whitney* v. *California*, 274 U. S. 357, 375 (Brandeis, J., concurring).   We should be ever mindful of the wise counsel
of Chief Justice Hughes:

> "[I]mperative is the need to preserve inviolate the
> constitutional rights of free speech, free press and
> free assembly in order to maintain the opportunity
> for free political discussion, to the end that govern-
> ment may be responsive to the will of the people and
> that changes, if desired, may be obtained by peace-
> ful means.   Therein lies the security of the Republic,
> the very foundation of constitutional government."
> *De Jonge* v. *Oregon*, 299 U. S. 353, 365.

This is not to say that the Constitution protects defamatory statements directed against the private conduct of
a public official or private citizen.   Freedom of press and
of speech insures that government will respond to the will
of the people and that changes may be obtained by peaceful means.   Purely private defamation has little to do
with the political ends of a self-governing society.   The
imposition of liability for private defamation does not

abridge the freedom of public speech or any other freedom protected by the First Amendment.4 This, of course, cannot be said "where public officials are concerned or where public matters are involved.... [O]ne main function of the First Amendment is to ensure ample opportunity for the people to determine and resolve public issues. Where public matters are involved, the doubts should be resolved in favor of freedom of expression rather than against it." Douglas, The Right of the People (1958), p. 41.

In many jurisdictions, legislators, judges and executive officers are clothed with absolute immunity against liability for defamatory words uttered in the discharge of their public duties. See, *e. g., Barr v. Matteo,* 360 U. S. 564; *City of Chicago v. Tribune Co.,* 307 Ill., at 610, 139 N. E., at 91. Judge Learned Hand ably summarized the policies underlying the rule:

> "It does indeed go without saying that an official, who is in fact guilty of using his powers to vent his spleen upon others, or for any other personal motive not connected with the public good, should not escape liability for the injuries he may so cause; and if it were possible in practice to confine such complaints to the guilty, it would be monstrous to deny recovery. The justification for doing so is that it is impossible to know whether the claim is well founded until the

---

[4] In most cases, as in the case at bar, there will be little difficulty in distinguishing defamatory speech relating to private conduct from that relating to official conduct. I recognize, of course, that there will be a gray area. The difficulties of applying a public-private standard are, however, certainly of a different genre from those attending the differentiation between a malicious and nonmalicious state of mind. If the constitutional standard is to be shaped by a concept of malice, the speaker takes the risk not only that the jury will inaccurately determine his state of mind but also that the jury will fail properly to apply the constitutional standard set by the elusive concept of malice. See note 2, supra.

case has been tried, and that to submit all officials, the innocent as well as the guilty, to the burden of a trial and to the inevitable danger of its outcome, would dampen the ardor of all but the most resolute, or the most irresponsible, in the unflinching discharge of their duties. Again and again the public interest calls for action which may turn out to be founded on a mistake, in the face of which an official may later find himself hard put to it to satisfy a jury of his good faith. There must indeed be means of punishment public officers who have been truant to their duties; but that is quite another matter from exposing such as have been honestly mistaken to suit by anyone who has suffered from their errors. As is so often the case, the answer must be found in a balance between the evils inevitable in either alternative. In this instance it has been thought in the end better to leave unredressed the wrongs done by dishonest officers than to subject those who try to do their duty to the constant dread of retaliation....

"The decisions have, indeed, always imposed as a limitation upon the immunity that the official's act must have been within the scope of his powers; and it can be argued that official powers, since they exist only for the public good, never cover occasions where the public good is not their aim, and hence that to exercise a power dishonestly is necessarily to overstep its bounds. A moment's reflection shows, however, that the cannot be the meaning of the limitation without defeating the whole doctrine. What is meant by saying that the officer must be setting within his power cannot be move than that the occasion must be such as would have justified the act, if he had been using his power for any of the purposes on whose account it was vested in him...." *Gregoire v. Biddle*, 177 F. 2d 579, 581.

If the government official should be immune from libel actions so that his ardor to serve the public will not be dampened and "fearless, vigorous, and effective administration of policies of government" not be inhibited, *Barr v. Matteo, supra,* at 571, then the citizen and the press should likewise be immune from libel actions for their criticism of official conduct. Their ardor as citizens will thus not be dampened and they will be free "to applaud or to criticize the way public employees do their jobs, from the least to the most important." [5] If liability can attach to political criticism because it damages the reputation of a public official as a public official, then no critical citizen can safely utter anything but faint praise about the government or its officials. The vigorous criticism by press and citizen of the conduct of the government of the day by the officials of the day will soon yield to silence if officials in control of government agencies, instead of answering criticisms, can resort to friendly juries to forestall criticism of their official conduct. [6]

The conclusion that the Constitution affords the citizen and the press an absolute privilege for criticism of official conduct does not leave the public official without defenses against unsubstantiated opinions or deliberate misstatements. "Under our system of government, counterargument and education are the weapons available to expose these matters, not abridgment . . . of free speech . . . ." *Wood* v. *Georgia,* 370 U. S. 375, 389. The public

---

[5] MR. JUSTICE BLACK concurring in *Barr* v. *Matteo,* 360 U. S. 564, 577, observed that: "The effective functioning of a free government like ours depends largely on the force of an informed public opinion. This calls for the widest possible understanding of the quality of government service rendered by all elective or appointed public officials or employees. Such an informed understanding depends, of course, on the freedom people have to applaud or to criticize the way public employees do their jobs, from the least to the most important."

[6] See notes 2, 4, *supra.*

NEW YORK TIMES CO. *v.* SULLIVAN.   305

official certainly has equal if not greater access than most private citizens to media of communication. In any event, despite the possibility that some excesses and abuses may go unremedied, we must recognize that "the people of this nation have ordained in the light of history, that, in spite of the probability of excesses and abuses, [certain] liberties are, in the long view, essential to enlightened opinion and right conduct on the part of the citizens of a democracy." *Cantwell* v. *Connecticut*, 310 U. S. 296, 310. As Mr. Justice Brandeis correctly observed, "sunlight is the most powerful of all disinfectants." [7]

For these reasons, I strongly believe that the Constitution accords citizens and press an unconditional freedom to criticize official conduct. It necessarily follows that in a case such as this, where all agree that the allegedly defamatory statements related to official conduct, the judgments for libel cannot constitutionally be sustained.

---

[7] See Freund, The Supreme Court of the United States (1949), p. 61.

Appendix: U.S. Constitution

Preamble

We the People of the United States, in Order to form a more perfect Union, establish Justice, insure domestic Tranquility, provide for the common defence, promote the general Welfare, and secure the Blessings of Liberty to ourselves and our Posterity, do ordain and establish this Constitution for the United States of America.

Article I.

Section 1

All legislative Powers herein granted shall be vested in a Congress of the United States, which shall consist of a Senate and House of Representatives.

Section 2

The House of Representatives shall be composed of Members chosen every second Year by the People of the several States, and the Electors in each State shall have the Qualifications requisite for Electors of the most numerous Branch of the State Legislature.

No Person shall be a Representative who shall not have attained to the Age of twenty five Years, and been seven Years a Citizen of the United States, and who shall not, when elected, be an Inhabitant of that State in which he shall be chosen.

Representatives and direct Taxes shall be apportioned among the several States which may be included within this Union, according to their respective Numbers, which shall be determined by adding to the whole Number of free

Persons, including those bound to Service for a Term of Years, and excluding Indians not taxed, three fifths of all other Persons.

The actual Enumeration shall be made within three Years after the first Meeting of the Congress of the United States, and within every subsequent Term of ten Years, in such Manner as they shall by Law direct. The Number of Representatives shall not exceed one for every thirty Thousand, but each State shall have at Least one Representative; and until such enumeration shall be made, the State of New Hampshire shall be entitled to chuse three, Massachusetts eight, Rhode Island and Providence Plantations one, Connecticut five, New York six, New Jersey four, Pennsylvania eight, Delaware one, Maryland six, Virginia ten, North Carolina five, South Carolina five and Georgia three.

When vacancies happen in the Representation from any State, the Executive Authority thereof shall issue Writs of Election to fill such Vacancies.

The House of Representatives shall chuse their Speaker and other Officers; and shall have the sole Power of Impeachment.

Section 3

The Senate of the United States shall be composed of two Senators from each State, chosen by the Legislature thereof, for six Years; and each Senator shall have one Vote.

Immediately after they shall be assembled in Consequence of the first Election, they shall be divided as equally as may be into three Classes. The Seats of the Senators of the first Class shall be vacated at the Expiration of the second Year, of the second Class at the Expiration of the fourth Year, and of the third Class at the Expiration of the sixth Year, so that one third may be chosen every second Year; and if Vacancies happen by Resignation, or otherwise, during the Recess of the Legislature of any State, the Executive thereof may make temporary Appointments until the next Meeting of the Legislature, which shall then fill such Vacancies.

No person shall be a Senator who shall not have attained to the Age of thirty Years, and been nine Years a Citizen of the United States, and who shall not, when elected, be an Inhabitant of that State for which he shall be chosen.

The Vice President of the United States shall be President of the Senate, but shall have no Vote, unless they be equally divided.

The Senate shall chuse their other Officers, and also a President pro tempore, in the absence of the Vice President, or when he shall exercise the Office of President of the United States.

The Senate shall have the sole Power to try all Impeachments. When sitting for that Purpose, they shall be on Oath or Affirmation. When the President of the United States is tried, the Chief Justice shall preside: And no Person shall be convicted without the Concurrence of two thirds of the Members present.

Judgment in Cases of Impeachment shall not extend further than to removal from Office, and disqualification to hold and enjoy any Office of honor, Trust or

Profit under the United States: but the Party convicted shall nevertheless be liable and subject to Indictment, Trial, Judgment and Punishment, according to Law.

Section 4

The Times, Places and Manner of holding Elections for Senators and Representatives, shall be prescribed in each State by the Legislature thereof; but the Congress may at any time by Law make or alter such Regulations, except as to the Place of Chusing Senators.

The Congress shall assemble at least once in every Year, and such Meeting shall be on the first Monday in December, unless they shall by Law appoint a different Day.

Section 5

Each House shall be the Judge of the Elections, Returns and Qualifications of its own Members, and a Majority of each shall constitute a Quorum to do Business; but a smaller number may adjourn from day to day, and may be authorized to compel the Attendance of absent Members, in such Manner, and under such Penalties as each House may provide.

Each House may determine the Rules of its Proceedings, punish its Members for disorderly Behavior, and, with the Concurrence of two-thirds, expel a Member.

Each House shall keep a Journal of its Proceedings, and from time to time publish the same, excepting such Parts as may in their Judgment require Secrecy; and the Yeas and Nays of the Members of either House on any question shall, at the Desire of one fifth of those Present, be entered on the Journal.

Neither House, during the Session of Congress, shall, without the Consent of the other, adjourn for more than three days, nor to any other Place than that in which the two Houses shall be sitting.

Section 6

The Senators and Representatives shall receive a Compensation for their Services, to be ascertained by Law, and paid out of the Treasury of the United States. They shall in all Cases, except Treason, Felony and Breach of the Peace, be privileged from Arrest during their Attendance at the Session of their respective Houses, and in going to and returning from the same; and for any Speech or Debate in either House, they shall not be questioned in any other Place.

No Senator or Representative shall, during the Time for which he was elected, be appointed to any civil Office under the Authority of the United States which shall have been created, or the Emoluments whereof shall have been increased during such time; and no Person holding any Office under the United States, shall be a Member of either House during his Continuance in Office.

Section 7

All bills for raising Revenue shall originate in the House of Representatives; but the Senate may propose or concur with Amendments as on other Bills.

Every Bill which shall have passed the House of Representatives and the Senate, shall, before it become a Law, be presented to the President of the United States; If he approve he shall sign it, but if not he shall return it, with his Objections to that House in which it shall have originated, who shall enter the Objections at large on their Journal, and proceed to reconsider it. If after such Reconsideration two thirds of that House shall agree to pass the Bill, it shall be sent, together with the Objections, to the other House, by which it shall likewise be reconsidered, and if approved by two thirds of that House, it shall become a Law. But in all such Cases the Votes of both Houses shall be determined by Yeas and Nays, and the Names of the Persons voting for and against the Bill shall be entered on the Journal of each House respectively. If any Bill shall not be returned by the President within ten Days (Sundays excepted) after it shall have been presented to him, the Same shall be a Law, in like Manner as if he had signed it, unless the Congress by their Adjournment prevent its Return, in which Case it shall not be a Law.

Every Order, Resolution, or Vote to which the Concurrence of the Senate and House of Representatives may be necessary (except on a question of Adjournment) shall be presented to the President of the United States; and before the Same shall take Effect, shall be approved by him, or being disapproved by him, shall be repassed by two thirds of the Senate and House of Representatives, according to the Rules and Limitations prescribed in the Case of a Bill.

Section 8

The Congress shall have Power To lay and collect Taxes, Duties, Imposts and Excises, to pay the Debts and provide for the common Defence and general Welfare of the United States; but all Duties, Imposts and Excises shall be uniform throughout the United States;

To borrow money on the credit of the United States;

To regulate Commerce with foreign Nations, and among the several States, and with the Indian Tribes;

To establish an uniform Rule of Naturalization, and uniform Laws on the subject of Bankruptcies throughout the United States;

To coin Money, regulate the Value thereof, and of foreign Coin, and fix the Standard of Weights and Measures;

To provide for the Punishment of counterfeiting the Securities and current Coin of the United States;

To establish Post Offices and Post Roads;

To promote the Progress of Science and useful Arts, by securing for limited Times to Authors and Inventors the exclusive Right to their respective Writings and Discoveries;

To constitute Tribunals inferior to the supreme Court;

To define and punish Piracies and Felonies committed on the high Seas, and Offenses against the Law of Nations;

To declare War, grant Letters of Marque and Reprisal, and make Rules concerning Captures on Land and Water;

To raise and support Armies, but no Appropriation of Money to that Use shall be for a longer Term than two Years;

To provide and maintain a Navy;

To make Rules for the Government and Regulation of the land and naval Forces;

To provide for calling forth the Militia to execute the Laws of the Union, suppress Insurrections and repel Invasions;

To provide for organizing, arming, and disciplining the Militia, and for governing such Part of them as may be employed in the Service of the United States, reserving to the States respectively, the Appointment of the Officers, and the Authority of training the Militia according to the discipline prescribed by Congress;

To exercise exclusive Legislation in all Cases whatsoever, over such District (not exceeding ten Miles square) as may, by Cession of particular States, and the acceptance of Congress, become the Seat of the Government of the United States, and to exercise like Authority over all Places purchased by the Consent of the Legislature of the State in which the Same shall be, for the Erection of Forts, Magazines, Arsenals, dock-Yards, and other needful Buildings; And

To make all Laws which shall be necessary and proper for carrying into Execution the foregoing Powers, and all other Powers vested by this Constitution in the Government of the United States, or in any Department or Officer thereof.

Section 9

The Migration or Importation of such Persons as any of the States now existing shall think proper to admit, shall not be prohibited by the Congress prior to the Year one thousand eight hundred and eight, but a tax or duty may be imposed on such Importation, not exceeding ten dollars for each Person.

The privilege of the Writ of Habeas Corpus shall not be suspended, unless when in Cases of Rebellion or Invasion the public Safety may require it.

No Bill of Attainder or ex post facto Law shall be passed. No capitation, or other direct, Tax shall be laid, unless in Proportion to the Census or Enumeration herein before directed to be taken.

No Tax or Duty shall be laid on Articles exported from any State.

No Preference shall be given by any Regulation of Commerce or Revenue to the Ports of one State over those of another: nor shall Vessels bound to, or from, one State, be obliged to enter, clear, or pay Duties in another.

No Money shall be drawn from the Treasury, but in Consequence of Appropriations made by Law; and a regular Statement and Account of the Receipts and Expenditures of all public Money shall be published from time to time.

No Title of Nobility shall be granted by the United States: And no Person holding any Office of Profit or Trust under them, shall, without the Consent of the Congress, accept of any present, Emolument, Office, or Title, of any kind whatever, from any King, Prince or foreign State.

Section 10

No State shall enter into any Treaty, Alliance, or Confederation; grant Letters of Marque and Reprisal; coin Money; emit Bills of Credit; make any Thing but gold and silver Coin a Tender in Payment of Debts; pass any Bill of Attainder, ex post facto Law, or Law impairing the Obligation of Contracts, or grant any Title of Nobility.

No State shall, without the Consent of the Congress, lay any Imposts or Duties on Imports or Exports, except what may be absolutely necessary for executing it's inspection Laws: and the net Produce of all Duties and Imposts, laid by any State on Imports or Exports, shall be for the Use of the Treasury of the United States; and all such Laws shall be subject to the Revision and Controul of the Congress.

No State shall, without the Consent of Congress, lay any duty of Tonnage, keep Troops, or Ships of War in time of Peace, enter into any Agreement or Compact with another State, or with a foreign Power, or engage in War, unless actually invaded, or in such imminent Danger as will not admit of delay.

Article II.

Section 1

The executive Power shall be vested in a President of the United States of America. He shall hold his Office during the Term of four Years, and, together with the Vice-President chosen for the same Term, be elected, as follows:

Each State shall appoint, in such Manner as the Legislature thereof may direct, a Number of Electors, equal to the whole Number of Senators and Representatives to which the State may be entitled in the Congress: but no Senator or Representative, or Person holding an Office of Trust or Profit under the United States, shall be appointed an Elector.

The Electors shall meet in their respective States, and vote by Ballot for two persons, of whom one at least shall not lie an Inhabitant of the same State with themselves. And they shall make a List of all the Persons voted for, and of the Number of Votes for each; which List they shall sign and certify, and transmit sealed to the Seat of the Government of the United States, directed to the President of the Senate. The President of the Senate shall, in the Presence of the Senate and House of Representatives, open all the Certificates, and the Votes shall then be counted. The Person having the greatest Number of Votes shall be the President, if such Number be a Majority of the whole Number of Electors appointed; and if there be more than one who have such Majority, and have an equal Number of Votes, then the House of Representatives shall immediately chuse by Ballot one of them for President; and if no Person have a Majority, then from the five highest on the List the said House shall in like Manner chuse the President. But in chusing the President, the Votes shall be taken by States, the Representation from each State having one Vote; a quorum for this Purpose shall consist of a Member or Members from two-thirds of the States, and a Majority of all the States shall be necessary to a Choice. In every Case, after the Choice of the President, the Person having the greatest Number of Votes of the Electors shall be the Vice President. But if there should remain two or more who have equal Votes, the Senate shall chuse from them by Ballot the Vice-President.

The Congress may determine the Time of chusing the Electors, and the Day on which they shall give their Votes; which Day shall be the same throughout the United States.

No person except a natural born Citizen, or a Citizen of the United States, at the time of the Adoption of this Constitution, shall be eligible to the Office of President; neither shall any Person be eligible to that Office who shall not have attained to the Age of thirty-five Years, and been fourteen Years a Resident within the United States.

In Case of the Removal of the President from Office, or of his Death, Resignation, or Inability to discharge the Powers and Duties of the said Office, the same shall devolve on the Vice President, and the Congress may by Law provide for the Case of Removal, Death, Resignation or Inability, both of the President and Vice President, declaring what Officer shall then act as President, and such Officer shall act accordingly, until the Disability be removed, or a President shall be elected.

The President shall, at stated Times, receive for his Services, a Compensation, which shall neither be increased nor diminished during the Period for which he shall have been elected, and he shall not receive within that Period any other Emolument from the United States, or any of them.

Before he enter on the Execution of his Office, he shall take the following Oath or Affirmation:

"I do solemnly swear (or affirm) that I will faithfully execute the Office of President of the United States, and will to the best of my Ability, preserve, protect and defend the Constitution of the United States."

Section 2

The President shall be Commander in Chief of the Army and Navy of the United States, and of the Militia of the several States, when called into the actual Service of the United States; he may require the Opinion, in writing, of the principal Officer in each of the executive Departments, upon any subject relating to the Duties of their respective Offices, and he shall have Power to Grant

Reprieves and Pardons for Offenses against the United States, except in Cases of Impeachment.

He shall have Power, by and with the Advice and Consent of the Senate, to make Treaties, provided two thirds of the Senators present concur; and he shall nominate, and by and with the Advice and Consent of the Senate, shall appoint Ambassadors, other public Ministers and Consuls, Judges of the Supreme Court, and all other Officers of the United States, whose Appointments are not herein otherwise provided for, and which shall be established by Law: but the Congress may by Law vest the Appointment of such inferior Officers, as they think proper, in the President alone, in the Courts of Law, or in the Heads of Departments.

The President shall have Power to fill up all Vacancies that may happen during the Recess of the Senate, by granting Commissions which shall expire at the End of their next Session.

Section 3

He shall from time to time give to the Congress Information of the State of the Union, and recommend to their Consideration such Measures as he shall judge necessary and expedient; he may, on extraordinary Occasions, convene both Houses, or either of them, and in Case of Disagreement between them, with Respect to the Time of Adjournment, he may adjourn them to such Time as he shall think proper; he shall receive Ambassadors and other public Ministers; he shall take Care that the Laws be faithfully executed, and shall Commission all the Officers of the United States.

Section 4

The President, Vice President and all civil Officers of the United States, shall be removed from Office on Impeachment for, and Conviction of, Treason, Bribery, or other high Crimes and Misdemeanors.

Article III.

Section 1

The judicial Power of the United States, shall be vested in one Supreme Court, and in such inferior Courts as the Congress may from time to time ordain and establish. The Judges, both of the supreme and inferior Courts, shall hold their Offices during good Behavior, and shall, at stated Times, receive for their Services a Compensation which shall not be diminished during their Continuance in Office.

Section 2

The judicial Power shall extend to all Cases, in Law and Equity, arising under this Constitution, the Laws of the United States, and Treaties made, or which shall be made, under their Authority; to all Cases affecting Ambassadors, other public Ministers and Consuls; to all Cases of admiralty and maritime Jurisdiction; to Controversies to which the United States shall be a Party; to Controversies between two or more States; between a State and Citizens of another State; between Citizens of different States; between Citizens of the same State claiming Lands under Grants of different States, and between a State, or the Citizens thereof, and foreign States, Citizens or Subjects.

In all Cases affecting Ambassadors, other public Ministers and Consuls, and those in which a State shall be Party, the Supreme Court shall have original Jurisdiction. In all the other Cases before mentioned, the Supreme Court shall have appellate Jurisdiction, both as to Law and Fact, with such Exceptions, and under such Regulations as the Congress shall make.

Trial of all Crimes, except in Cases of Impeachment, shall be by Jury; and such Trial shall be held in the State where the said Crimes shall have been committed; but when not committed within any State, the Trial shall be at such Place or Places as the Congress may by Law have directed.

Section 3

Treason against the United States, shall consist only in levying War against them, or in adhering to their Enemies, giving them Aid and Comfort. No Person shall be convicted of Treason unless on the Testimony of two Witnesses to the same overt Act, or on Confession in open Court.

The Congress shall have power to declare the Punishment of Treason, but no Attainder of Treason shall work Corruption of Blood, or Forfeiture except during the Life of the Person attainted.

Article IV.

Section 1

Full Faith and Credit shall be given in each State to the public Acts, Records, and judicial Proceedings of every other State. And the Congress may by general Laws prescribe the Manner in which such Acts, Records and Proceedings shall be proved, and the Effect thereof.

Section 2

The Citizens of each State shall be entitled to all Privileges and Immunities of Citizens in the several States.

A Person charged in any State with Treason, Felony, or other Crime, who shall flee from Justice, and be found in another State, shall on demand of the executive Authority of the State from which he fled, be delivered up, to be removed to the State having Jurisdiction of the Crime.

No Person held to Service or Labour in one State, under the Laws thereof, escaping into another, shall, in Consequence of any Law or Regulation therein, be discharged from such Service or Labour, But shall be delivered up on Claim of the Party to whom such Service or Labour may be due.

Section 3

New States may be admitted by the Congress into this Union; but no new States shall be formed or erected within the Jurisdiction of any other State; nor any State be formed by the Junction of two or more States, or parts of States, without the Consent of the Legislatures of the States concerned as well as of the Congress.

The Congress shall have Power to dispose of and make all needful Rules and Regulations respecting the Territory or other Property belonging to the United States; and nothing in this Constitution shall be so construed as to Prejudice any Claims of the United States, or of any particular State.

Section 4

The United States shall guarantee to every State in this Union a Republican Form of Government, and shall protect each of them against Invasion; and on Application of the Legislature, or of the Executive (when the Legislature cannot be convened) against domestic Violence.

Article V.

The Congress, whenever two thirds of both Houses shall deem it necessary, shall propose Amendments to this Constitution, or, on the Application of the Legislatures of two thirds of the several States, shall call a Convention for proposing Amendments, which, in either Case, shall be valid to all Intents and Purposes, as part of this Constitution, when ratified by the Legislatures of three fourths of the several States, or by Conventions in three fourths thereof, as the one or the other Mode of Ratification may be proposed by the Congress; Provided that no Amendment which may be made prior to the Year One thousand eight hundred and eight shall in any Manner affect the first and fourth Clauses in the Ninth Section of the first Article; and that no State, without its Consent, shall be deprived of its equal Suffrage in the Senate.

Article VI.

All Debts contracted and Engagements entered into, before the Adoption of this Constitution, shall be as valid against the United States under this Constitution, as under the Confederation.

This Constitution, and the Laws of the United States which shall be made in Pursuance thereof; and all Treaties made, or which shall be made, under the Authority of the United States, shall be the supreme Law of the Land; and the Judges in every State shall be bound thereby, any Thing in the Constitution or Laws of any State to the Contrary notwithstanding.

The Senators and Representatives before mentioned, and the Members of the several State Legislatures, and all executive and judicial Officers, both of the United States and of the several States, shall be bound by Oath or Affirmation, to support this Constitution; but no religious Test shall ever be required as a Qualification to any Office or public Trust under the United States.

Article VII.

The Ratification of the Conventions of nine States, shall be sufficient for the Establishment of this Constitution between the States so ratifying the Same.

Done in Convention by the Unanimous Consent of the States present the Seventeenth Day of September in the Year of our Lord one thousand seven hundred and Eighty seven and of the Independence of the United States of America the Twelfth. In Witness whereof We have hereunto subscribed our Names.

Go Washington—President and deputy from Virginia

New Hampshire—John Langdon, Nicholas Gilman

Massachusetts—Nathaniel Gorham, Rufus King

Connecticut—Wm Saml Johnson, Roger Sherman

New York—Alexander Hamilton

New Jersey—Wil Livingston, David Brearley, Wm Paterson, Jona. Dayton

Pensylvania—B Franklin, Thomas Mifflin, Robt Morris, Geo. Clymer, Thos FitzSimons, Jared Ingersoll, James Wilson, Gouv Morris

Delaware—Geo. Read, Gunning Bedford jun, John Dickinson, Richard Bassett, Jaco. Broom

Maryland—James McHenry, Dan of St Tho Jenifer, Danl Carroll

Virginia—John Blair, James Madison Jr.

North Carolina—Wm Blount, Richd Dobbs Spaight, Hu Williamson

South Carolina—J. Rutledge, Charles Cotesworth Pinckney, Charles Pinckney, Pierce Butler

Georgia—William Few, Abr Baldwin

Attest: William Jackson, Secretary

AMENDMENT I

Congress shall make no law respecting an establishment of religion, or prohibiting the free exercise thereof; or abridging the freedom of speech, or of the press; or the right of the people peaceably to assemble, and to petition the Government for a redress of grievances.

AMENDMENT II

A well regulated Militia, being necessary to the security of a free State, the right of the people to keep and bear Arms, shall not be infringed.

AMENDMENT III

No Soldier shall, in time of peace be quartered in any house, without the consent of the Owner, nor in time of war, but in a manner to be prescribed by law.

AMENDMENT IV

The right of the people to be secure in their persons, houses, papers, and effects, against unreasonable searches and seizures, shall not be violated, and no Warrants shall issue, but upon probable cause, supported by Oath or affirmation, and particularly describing the place to be searched, and the persons or things to be seized.

AMENDMENT V

No person shall be held to answer for a capital, or otherwise infamous crime, unless on a presentment or indictment of a Grand Jury, except in cases arising in the land or naval forces, or in the Militia, when in actual service in time of War or public danger; nor shall any person be subject for the same offense to be twice put in jeopardy of life or limb; nor shall be compelled in any criminal case to be a witness against himself, nor be deprived of life, liberty, or property, without due process of law; nor shall private property be taken for public use, without just compensation.

AMENDMENT VI

In all criminal prosecutions, the accused shall enjoy the right to a speedy and public trial, by an impartial jury of the State and district wherein the crime shall have been committed, which district shall have been previously ascertained by law, and to be informed of the nature and cause of the accusation; to be confronted with the witnesses against him; to have compulsory process for obtaining witnesses in his favor, and to have the Assistance of Counsel for his defence.

AMENDMENT VII

In suits at common law, where the value in controversy shall exceed twenty dollars, the right of trial by jury shall be preserved, and no fact tried by a jury, shall be otherwise re-examined in any Court of the United States, than according to the rules of the common law.

AMENDMENT VIII

Excessive bail shall not lie required, nor excessive fines imposed, nor cruel and unusual punishments inflicted.

AMENDMENT IX

The enumeration in the Constitution, of certain rights, shall not be construed to deny or disparage others retained by the people.

AMENDMENT X

The powers not delegated to the United States by the Constitution, nor prohibited by it to the States, are reserved to the States respectively, or to the people.

AMENDMENT XI

The Judicial power of the United States shall not be construed to extend to any suit in law or equity, commenced or prosecuted against one of the United States by Citizens of another State, or by Citizens or subjects of any foreign State.

AMENDMENT XII

The Electors shall meet in their respective States, and vote by ballot for President and Vice-President, one of whom, at least, shall not be an inhabitant of the same State with themselves; they shall name in their ballots the person voted for as President, and in distinct ballots the person voted for as Vice-President, and they shall make distinct lists of all persons voted for as President, and of all persons voted for as Vice-President and of the number of votes for each, which lists they shall sign and certify, and transmit sealed to the seat of the Government of the United States, directed to the President of the Senate;

The President of the Senate shall, in the presence of the Senate and House of Representatives, open all the certificates and the votes shall then be counted;

The person having the greatest number of votes for President, shall be the President, if such number be a majority of the whole number of Electors appointed; and if no person have such majority, then from the persons having the highest numbers not exceeding three on the list of those voted for as President, the House of Representatives shall choose immediately, by ballot, the President.

But in choosing the President, the votes shall be taken by States, the representation from each State having one vote; a quorum for this purpose shall consist of a member or members from two-thirds of the States, and a majority of all the States shall be necessary to a choice. And if the House of Representatives shall not choose a President whenever the right of choice shall devolve upon them, before the fourth day of March next following, then the Vice-President shall act as President, as in the case of the death or other constitutional disability of the President.

The person having the greatest number of votes as Vice-President, shall be the Vice-President, if such number be a majority of the whole number of Electors appointed, and if no person have a majority, then from the two highest numbers on the list, the Senate shall choose the Vice-President; a quorum for the purpose shall consist of two-thirds of the whole number of Senators, and a majority of the whole number shall be necessary to a choice. But no person constitutionally ineligible to the office of President shall be eligible to that of Vice-President of the United States.

AMENDMENT XIII

1. Neither slavery nor involuntary servitude, except as a punishment for crime whereof the party shall have been duly convicted, shall exist within the United States, or any place subject to their jurisdiction.

2. Congress shall have power to enforce this article by appropriate legislation.

AMENDMENT XIV

1. All persons born or naturalized in the United States, and subject to the jurisdiction thereof, are citizens of the United States and of the State wherein they reside. No State shall make or enforce any law which shall abridge the privileges or immunities of citizens of the United States; nor shall any State deprive any person of life, liberty, or property, without due process of law; nor deny to any person within its jurisdiction the equal protection of the laws.

2. Representatives shall be apportioned among the several States according to their respective numbers, counting the whole number of persons in each State, excluding Indians not taxed. But when the right to vote at any election for the choice of Electors for President and Vice-President of the United States, Representatives in Congress, the executive and judicial officers of a State, or the members of the Legislature thereof, is denied to any of the male inhabitants of such State, being twenty-one years of age, and citizens of the United States, or in any way abridged, except for participation in rebellion, or other crime, the basis of representation therein shall be reduced in the proportion which the

number of such male citizens shall bear to the whole number of male citizens twenty-one years of age in such State.

3. No person shall be a Senator or Representative in Congress, or elector of President and Vice-President, or hold any office, civil or military, under the United States, or under any State, who, having previously taken an oath, as a member of Congress, or as an officer of the United States, or as a member of any State legislature, or as an executive or judicial officer of any State, to support the Constitution of the United States, shall have engaged in insurrection or rebellion against the same, or given aid or comfort to the enemies thereof. But Congress may by a vote of two-thirds of each House, remove such disability.

4. The validity of the public debt of the United States, authorized by law, including debts incurred for payment of pensions and bounties for services in suppressing insurrection or rebellion, shall not be questioned. But neither the United States nor any State shall assume or pay any debt or obligation incurred in aid of insurrection or rebellion against the United States, or any claim for the loss or emancipation of any slave; but all such debts, obligations and claims shall be held illegal and void.

5. The Congress shall have power to enforce, by appropriate legislation, the provisions of this article.

Amendment XV

1. The right of citizens of the United States to vote shall not be denied or abridged by the United States or by any State on account of race, color, or previous condition of servitude.

2. The Congress shall have power to enforce this article by appropriate legislation.

Amendment XVI

The Congress shall have power to lay and collect taxes on incomes, from whatever source derived, without apportionment among the several States and without regard to any census or enumeration.

Amendment XVII

The Senate of the United States shall be composed of two senators from each State, elected by the people thereof, for six years; and each Senator shall have one vote. The electors in each State shall have the qualifications requisite for electors of the most numerous branch of the State legislature.

When vacancies happen in the representation of any State in the Senate, the executive authority of such State shall issue writs of election to fill such vacancies: Provided, That the legislature of any State may empower the executive thereof to make temporary appointments until the people fill the vacancies by election as the legislature may direct.

This amendment shall not be so construed as to affect the election or term of any senator chosen before it becomes valid as part of the Constitution.

Amendment XVIII

1. After one year from the ratification of this article, the manufacture, sale, or transportation of intoxicating liquors within, the importation thereof into, or the exportation thereof from the United States and all territory subject to the jurisdiction thereof for beverage purposes is hereby prohibited.

2. The Congress and the several States shall have concurrent power to enforce this article by appropriate legislation.

3. This article shall be inoperative unless it shall have been ratified as an amendment to the Constitution by the legislatures of the several States, as provided in the Constitution, within seven years from the date of the submission hereof to the States by Congress.

Amendment XIX

The right of citizens of the United States to vote shall not be denied or abridged by the United States or by any States on account of sex.

The Congress shall have power by appropriate legislation to enforce the provisions of this article.

Amendment XX

1. The terms of the President and Vice-President shall end at noon on the 20th day of January, and the terms of Senators and Representatives at noon on the 3d day of January, of the years in which such terms would have ended if this article had not been ratified; and the terms of their successors shall then begin.

2. The Congress shall assemble at least once in every year, and such meeting shall begin at noon on the 3d day of January, unless they shall by law appoint a different day.

3. If, at the time fixed for the beginning of the term of the President, the President-elect shall have died, the Vice-President-elect shall become President. If a President shall not have been chosen before the time fixed for the beginning of his term, or if the President-elect shall have failed to qualify, then the Vice-President-elect shall act as President until a President shall have qualified; and the

Congress may by law provide for the case wherein neither a President-elect nor a Vice-President-elect shall have qualified, declaring who shall then act as President, or the manner in which one who is to act shall be selected, and such person shall act accordingly until a President or Vice-President shall have qualified.

4. The Congress may by law provide for the case of the death of any of the persons from whom the House of Representatives may choose a President whenever the right of choice shall have devolved upon them, and for the case of the death of any of the persons from whom the Senate may choose a Vice-President whenever the right of choice shall have devolved upon them.

5. Sections 1 and 2 shall take effect on the 15th day of October following the ratification of this article.

6. This article shall be inoperative unless it shall have been ratified as an amendment to the Constitution by the legislatures of three-fourths of the several States within seven years from the date of its submission.

AMENDMENT XXI

1. The eighteenth article of amendment to the Constitution of the United States is hereby repealed.

2. The transportation or importation into any State, Territory, or possession of the United States for delivery or use therein of intoxicating liquors, in violation of the laws thereof, is hereby prohibited.

3. The article shall be inoperative unless it shall have been ratified as an amendment to the Constitution by conventions in the several States, as provided in the Constitution, within seven years from the date of the submission hereof to the States by the Congress.

AMENDMENT XXII

1. No person shall be elected to the office of the President more than twice, and no person who has held the office of President, or acted as President for more than two years of a term to which some other person was elected President shall be elected to the office of the President more than once. But this Article shall not apply to any person holding the office of President when this Article was proposed by the Congress, and shall not prevent any person who May be holding the office of President, or acting as President, during the term within which this Article becomes operative from holding the office of President or acting as President during the remainder of such term.

2. This article shall be inoperative unless it shall have been ratified as an amendment to the Constitution by the legislatures of three-fourths of the several States within seven years from the date of its submission to the States by the Congress.

Amendment XXIII

1. The District constituting the seat of government of the United States shall appoint in such manner as the Congress may direct: A number of electors of President and Vice-President equal to the whole number of Senators and Representatives in Congress to which the District would be entitled if it were a State, but in no event more than the least populous State; they shall be in addition to those appointed by the States, but they shall be considered, for the purposes of the election of President and Vice-President, to be electors appointed by a State; and they shall meet in the district and perform such duties as provided by the twelfth article of amendment.

2. The Congress shall have power to enforce this article by appropriate legislation.

Amendment XXIV

1. The right of citizens of the United States to vote in any primary or other election for President or Vice-President, for electors for President or Vice-President, or for Senator or Representative in Congress, shall not be denied or abridged by the United States or any State by reason of failure to pay any poll tax or other tax.

2. The Congress shall have power to enforce this article by appropriate legislation.

Amendment XXV

1. In case of the removal of the President from office or of his death or resignation, the Vice-President shall become President.

2. Whenever there is a vacancy in the office of the Vice-President, the President shall nominate a Vice-President who shall take office upon confirmation by a majority vote of both Houses of Congress.

3. Whenever the President transmits to the President pro tempore of the Senate and the Speaker of the House of Representatives his written declaration that he is unable to discharge the powers and duties of his office, and until he transmits to them a written declaration to the contrary, such powers and duties shall be discharged by the Vice-President as Acting President.

4. Whenever the Vice-President and a majority of either the principal officers of the executive departments or of such other body as Congress may by law provide, transmit to the President pro tempore of the Senate and the Speaker of the House of Representatives their written declaration that the President is unable to discharge the powers and duties of his office, the Vice-President shall immediately assume the powers and duties of the office as Acting President.

Thereafter, when the President transmits to the President pro tempore of the Senate and the Speaker of the House of Representatives his written declaration that no inability exists, he shall resume the powers and duties of his office unless the Vice-President and a majority of either the principal officers of the executive department or of such other body as Congress may by law provide, transmit within four days to the President pro tempore of the Senate and the Speaker of the House of Representatives their written declaration that the President is unable to discharge the powers and duties of his office. Thereupon Congress shall decide the issue, assembling within forty-eight hours for that purpose if not in session. If the Congress, within twenty-one days after receipt of the latter written declaration, or, if Congress is not in session, within twenty-one days after Congress is required to assemble, determines by two-thirds vote of both Houses that the President is unable to discharge the powers and duties of his office, the Vice-President shall continue to discharge the same as Acting President; otherwise, the President shall resume the powers and duties of his office.

AMENDMENT XXVI

1. The right of citizens of the United States, who are eighteen years of age or older, to vote shall not be denied or abridged by the United States or by any State on account of age.

2. The Congress shall have power to enforce this article by appropriate legislation.

AMENDMENT XXVII

No law, varying the compensation for the services of the Senators and Representatives, shall take effect, until an election of Representatives shall have intervened.

Index